Words Their Way™ with English Learners

Word Study for Phonics, Vocabulary, and Spelling Instruction

Donald R. Bear
University of Nevada, Reno

Lori Helman
University of Minnesota, Twin Cities

Shane Templeton
University of Nevada, Reno

Marcia Invernizzi
University of Virginia

Francine Johnston
University of North Carolina at Greensboro

PEARSON

Merrill
Prentice Hall

Upper Saddle River, New Jersey
Columbus, Ohio

This book is dedicated to the students and teachers who learn from and teach each other in multilingual classrooms. We learn from you in the process.

Library of Congress Cataloging-in-Publication Data

Words their way with English learners : word study for phonics, vocabulary, and spelling instruction/Donald R. Bear . . . [et al.].
  p. cm.
  Includes bibliographical references and index.
  ISBN 0-13-191567-3
  1. English language--Study and teaching--Foreign speakers.   2. English language--Orthography and spelling--Study and teaching (Elementary)   3. Vocabulary--Study and teaching (Elementary)   4. Word recognition.   5. Reading--Phonetic method. I. Bear, Donald R. II. Title.

  PE1128.A2W667 2007
  372. 652' 1044--dc22   2006021813

Vice President and Executive Publisher: Jeffery W. Johnston
Senior Editor: Linda Ashe Bishop
Senior Development Editor: Hope Madden
Senior Production Editor: Mary M. Irvin
Senior Editorial Assistant: Laura Weaver
Design Coordinator: Diane C. Lorenzo

Cover Designer: Ali Mohrman
Cover Image: SuperStock
Production Manager: Pamela D. Bennett
Director of Marketing: David Gesell
Marketing Manager: Darcy Betts Prybella
Marketing Coordinator: Brian Mounts

This book was set in Palatino by Carlisle Communications, Ltd. It was printed and bound by Banta Book Group. The cover was printed by Phoenix Color Corp.

Chapters and figures in this book have been adapted for use in this book from materials that originally appeared in *Words Their Way: Word Study for Phonics, Vocabulary, and Spelling Instruction*, First, Second, and Third Editions, by Donald R. Bear, Marcia Invernizzi, Shane Templeton, and Francine Johnston, copyright © 1996, 2000, 2004 by Pearson Education, Inc.

Pearson Education Ltd.
Pearson Education Singapore Pte. Ltd.
Pearson Education Canada, Ltd.
Pearson Education—Japan

Pearson Education Australia Pty. Limited
Pearson Education North Asia Ltd.
Pearson Educación de Mexico, S.A. de C.V.
Pearson Education Malaysia Pte. Ltd.

10 9 8 7 6 5 4 3 2 1
ISBN: 0-13-191567-3

Preface

WHAT IS WORD STUDY?

Word study is an integrated way to teach phonics, vocabulary, and spelling to improve literacy skills, and it can be a powerful instructional method for teachers and their English-learning students. In this book you'll find word study activities rooted in the developmental and instructional frameworks presented in *Words Their Way: Word Study for Phonics, Vocabulary, and Spelling Instruction* (Bear, Invernizzi, Templeton, & Johnston, 2004). This practical way to study words with students is based on research on developmental spelling and word knowledge. *Words Their Way with English Learners* builds on the same proven framework of assessments and instruction, this time in light of the needs and strengths of students with oral and perhaps written skills in a language other than English. By learning what they bring with them to their study of English, and providing targeted, hands-on practice with their new language, you can help students master English. The activities in this text explore specific linguistic features and present memorable and meaningful ways to teach your students written English.

WHERE DOES WORD STUDY BEGIN WITH ENGLISH LEARNERS?

Through the *Words Their Way* method of word study, you begin by evaluating your students' language needs. With this information you can empower your students to grasp their new language at the word level, developing skills to understand how English differs from their home language, and providing students with the skills to predict word meaning through spelling. *Words Their Way with English Learners* will help you build vocabulary, spelling, and word recognition skills in English learners, thus providing them the foundation to master a new language.

Words Their Way with English Learners will help you determine the background knowledge and ways of understanding print that your students bring with them from their home languages; it will show you where their instruction in English orthography should begin, and how best to guide students as they develop literacy in English.

HOW TO USE THIS BOOK: AN OVERVIEW

Chapters 1 through 3 introduce you to the stages of spelling and reading development, the assessments to use to determine where your students fall along this developmental continuum, and the best ways to organize your classroom for word study.

- Chapter 1 presents an overview of the research behind the developmental and instructional models for word study. It describes the way students' knowledge of other oral and written languages folds into their learning of English language and literacy.

- Chapter 2 is the assessment chapter, explaining guidelines for observation and assessment and showing you how to interpret English learning students' spelling in light of the influence of the other oral and written languages they know. As we observe in detail in Chapter 2, like monolingual English spellers, nearly all misspellings by English learners are "interestingly correct." This book provides interpretations of students' spelling to show what features to consider when teaching phonics, vocabulary, and spelling to English learners.
- Chapter 3 presents routines for classroom management and organization. The schedules introduce students to word sorting, and the routines provide the directed instruction that English learners need to study phonics, vocabulary, and spelling.

Once you've assessed your students' development based on the tools provided in Chapter 2, and have used Chapter 3 to form leveled groups and develop routines for word study, the information and materials in Chapters 4 through 7 as well as the Appendix will guide your specific instruction. Each of these chapters focuses on a specific stage of spelling, outlining the most appropriate and effective word study instruction for each respective developmental level from the emergent learner through readers and writers in the derivational relations stage. Each of these chapters closes with a rich bank of word study activities that promise to engage your students, motivate them, and improve their oral and written abilities in English.

- Chapters 4 through 7 present word study activities including concept sorts, word sorts, literature ideas, and games for each developmental level, using what students know about other languages to develop methods to teach phonics, vocabulary, and spelling. Each chapter begins with a research-based description of the stage and some principles of instruction germane to the particular stage of spelling development, followed by word study activities to clarify aspects of English. The activities sections are tabbed for your convenience, creating a user-friendly classroom resource.
- The Appendix at the back of the book contains all of the assessment tools; word lists in English, Spanish, Chinese, Korean, Vietnamese, and Arabic; picture and word sorts; sound boards; and game templates you'll need to get your word study instruction underway. Here you will find all of the reproducible materials in one place. It begins with the assessment materials discussed in Chapter 2. These pages are perforated for your convenience.

COMPANION VOLUMES

We believe you'll find that the hands-on, word sorting approach to word study is an invaluable literacy tool for both your English learners and your students whose primary language is English. Broaden your word study understanding and instruction with the variety of additional materials available. Purchase any of the following invaluable professional resources at **http://www.allynbaconmerrill.com:**

Words Their Way: Word Study for Phonics, Vocabulary, and Spelling Instruction, Third Edition, by Donald R. Bear, Marcia Invernizzi, Shane Templeton, and Francine Johnston

Words Their Way: Letter and Picture Sorts for Emergent Spellers, by Donald R. Bear, Marcia Invernizzi, and Francine Johnston

Words Their Way: Word Sorts for Letter Name–Alphabetic Spellers, by Francine Johnston, Donald R. Bear, and Marcia Invernizzi

Words Their Way: Word Sorts for Within-Word Pattern Spellers, by Marcia Invernizzi, Francine Johnston, and Donald R. Bear

Words Their Way: Word Sorts for Syllables and Affixes Spellers, by Francine Johnston, Marcia Invernizzi, and Donald R. Bear

Words Their Way: Word Sorts for Derivational Relations Spellers, by Francine Johnston,
   Donald R. Bear, and Marcia Invernizzi
Words Their Way Video, by Donald R. Bear, Marcia Invernizzi, Shane Templeton, and
   Francine Johnston

ACKNOWLEDGMENTS

There are many educators who have guided our way and assisted us in writing this first edition. We thank doctoral students Regina Smith and Karen Carpenter for their activities and sorts. Helen Shen at the University of Iowa and Minwha Yang at DePaul University are two students who have been kind enough to share here the spelling inventories and scoring guides that they have created. We are indebted to the people who translated the picture words for us: Iman Chahine, University of Minnesota (Arabic); Thuy Ho, University of Virginia (Vietnamese); Qiang Li, University of Iowa (Chinese); Mathew Xiong, University of Minnesota (Hmong); and Minwha Yang, DePaul University (Korean). Tamara Baren, Keonghee Tao Han, Carol Caserta-Henry, and Shari Nielsen have been a reservoir of information and experience. Thanks to Linda Woessner and Kristen Polanski for sharing their classrooms with us. We also thank our colleagues at our respective universities: University of Nevada, Reno; University of Minnesota, Twin Cities; University of Virginia; and University of North Carolina at Greensboro.

We would also like to thank the reviewers of our manuscript for their insights and comments: Kristi McNeal, California State University, Fresno; Maria J. Meyerson, National University Nevada; and Patricia P. Kelly, Virginia Tech.

Brief Contents

Contents

Contents ix

Note: Every effort has been made to provide accurate and current Internet information in this book. However, the Internet and information posted on it are constantly changing, so it is inevitable that some of the Internet addresses listed in this textbook will change.

About the Authors

Donald Bear
Donald Bear is Director of the E. L. Cord Foundation Center for Learning and Literacy in the Department of Educational Specialties, College of Education at the University of Nevada, Reno where he and his students teach and assess students who experience difficulties learning to read and write. A former preschool and elementary teacher, Donald currently researches literacy development with a special interest in students who speak different languages and he partners with schools and districts to think about how to assess and conduct literacy instruction.

Lori Helman
Lori Helman is Assistant Professor in the Department of Curriculum and Instruction at the University of Minnesota, Twin Cities. Her research focuses on the reading and spelling development of students learning English as a new language. Lori was a bilingual teacher, a district literacy coordinator, and a new teacher leader in her region before coming to higher education. She teaches classes in reading development for diverse students, effective instruction for students with reading difficulties, and leadership skills for reading specialists.

Shane Templeton
Shane Templeton is Foundation Professor of Literacy Studies in the Department of Educational Specialties at the University of Nevada, Reno. A former classroom teacher at the primary and secondary levels, he has focused his research on the development of orthographic and vocabulary knowledge. He has written several books on the teaching and learning of reading and language arts and is a member of the Usage Panel of the American Heritage Dictionary.

Marcia Invernizzi
Marcia Invernizzi is Director of the McGuffey Reading Center in the Curry School of Education at the University of Virginia. She and her multilingual doctoral students enjoy exploring developmental universals in non-English orthographies. A former English and reading teacher, Marcia extends her experience working with children who experience difficulties learning to read and write in numerous intervention programs, such as Virginia's Early Intervention Reading Initiative and Book Buddies.

Francine Johnston
Francine Johnston is Associate Professor in the School of Education at the University of North Carolina at Greensboro, where she teaches courses in reading, language arts, and children's literature. Francine is a former first-grade teacher and reading specialist, and she continues to work with schools as a consultant and researcher. Her research interests include current spelling practices and materials as well as the relationship between spelling and reading achievement.

Word Study with English Learners and the Development of Orthographic Knowledge

1

UNDERSTANDING WORD STUDY WITH ENGLISH LEARNERS

Ralph Emerson compared language to a city, and in the building of this city, every human being brings a stone (Emerson, 1895). Similarly, in organizing classroom instruction, educators build on the language and literacy students bring with them.

Phonics, vocabulary, and spelling activities for English learners of all ages and literacy levels should be guided by a developmental perspective, always valuing the knowledge that students bring with them from their background languages and experiences. Young, emergent-level English learners study sounds and letters, rhymes, and beginning sounds. At the other end of the developmental continuum, English learners who are advanced, mature readers use their literacy in one language to make meaningful connections with English roots, affixes, and cognates. (Cognates are words in different languages that share similar meanings and similar spellings.)

The word study activities in this book expand and deepen students' word knowledge and vocabularies. Many of the examples are from Spanish speakers, who comprise the largest group of English learners in U.S. schools, but examples are also drawn from a variety of other language groups learning English. When possible, commonalities and contrasts among the different languages are presented. For example, the final /d/ and /t/ sounds are omitted among English learners from several languages, including Spanish and Thai, as well as many dialects of English. Knowing about these commonalities makes it possible to focus on the same skill with students from different language backgrounds.

The word study activities in this book support oral and written language development, particularly in the area of vocabulary learning. For example, the pictures in the concept sorts are a vehicle for discussions that involve students in using new vocabulary. When students read a series of words aloud to check their sorting, they hear and experience ways to pronounce the letters. And during instruction for pronunciation, teachers use the sorts to read aloud for practice. Reading a set of prefixes in English, such as words with *re-* and *in-*, and looking for meaning connections, give support to words students are learning to pronounce and understand. At the upper levels of word study, students learn a more technical, content-oriented vocabulary as they compare Greek–Latin connections in English and their home language.

Who Are the Students We Teach?

The percentage of students from diverse language backgrounds is growing dramatically in U.S. schools. You may be one of the many teachers working to adjust your literacy teaching methods to build on the strengths and meet the needs of English learners in your classroom. This text is written for you.

Instruction in Multilingual and Multiliterate Contexts

Bilingual Programs
Bilingual programs encourage literacy development in students' home languages and in English.

Students who are English learners grow up in multilingual and multiliterate contexts and experience different learning scenarios in American schools. Some English learners are able to participate in **bilingual programs** that allow them to develop their literacy skills in their home language while learning to speak, read, and write in English. Other programs involve specially tailored instruction to support students as they tackle content in all-English settings. In some schools, "newcomer" programs provide an initial setting for helping English learners transition into the new cultural and academic content of their schools. Recent research findings have pointed out that English learners who do not receive language support in school show much less progress in reading and math achievement when compared to similar students who participate in language support programs such as bilingual education or **sheltered English** (August & Shanahan, 2006; Genesse, Lindholm-Leary, Saunders & Christian, 2005; Slavin & Cheung, 2003; Thomas & Collier, 2002).

Sheltered English
Sheltered English is an approach to instruction that provides additional support for students learning English by simplifying language, defining vocabulary, and providing time for students to discuss content-area studies.

Perhaps in your classroom you have just a few English learners who need support with academic language. Perhaps your classroom consists predominantly of students who do not speak English as a first language. Maybe your English-learning students all come from one language background, such as Spanish. Or possibly your school works with students from dozens of primary languages. All of these scenarios commonly exist in elementary and secondary classrooms in the United States. Students may be the children of immigrants, or they may have themselves just arrived from another country. Some English learners may have a strong language and literacy background in their home language, and they may have studied English before arriving. Some students come to the U.S. classroom with few or no print-related experiences because they have not attended school before, or they may come from a culture that is primarily oral in its use of language.

What Do Students Bring to Learning to Read in English?

Teachers need to know what students bring to their learning. Over the school year, when you meet with your English learners, you will want to discuss their English learning. At other times, you will ask students to write about their learning and then discuss one of their key points during a conversation. This will allow you to capture your students' thinking.

Spelling Inventory
A carefully designed spelling assessment used to determine what students know about words and their structures.

Research has helped to capture students' thinking about how they are learning to read and write in English (Jiménez, Garcia & Pearson, 1996; Kenner, Kress, Al-Khatib, Kam, & Tsai, 2004). Students said things that you will probably hear from your students. One teacher recently shared insights from her work. Students were asked to write and then talk about what was hard about learning to read and write. Dang, who speaks Hmong and was born in the United States, wrote I THINK THAT HOW TO SPEU LONGER WORDS ARE HARDER. (How to spell longer words are harder.) Dang may have been saying that he was proficient with single-syllable and easy two-syllable words, and his writing reveals this. His **spelling inventory** (see Chapter 2) indicated that he was in the latter part of the within word pattern stage of spelling. In his misspelling of *spell* as *SPEU*, the lack of the final *ll* may be attributed to the difficulty he may have in pronouncing the /l/ sound.

Mark, who also speaks Hmong and was born in the United States, wrote PANOSS WORDS OUT. (Pronounce words out.) Mark was slightly less proficient than Dang in reading and spelling, but near enough in development for he and Dang to be in the same group. Mark did not spell the /r/ sound, which typifies the difficulty he may experience in grade-level reading and writing. In small groups the study of the /r/ and /l/ sounds will help both students' understanding of the words, their vocabularies, and the way they pronounce the words.

Four Steps to Plan Word Study Instruction with English Learners

Four steps can be followed to plan word study instruction (see Figure 1-1). These steps are based on what students bring to the teaching situation. Throughout this book, we will help you learn how to put these steps into action.

1. *Compare oral languages.* What languages do students speak? What are the basic characteristics of those languages? What sounds and linguistic structures exist in their home languages, but not in English? English can be compared to other languages in several ways: through phonology, the sounds of the language; phonetics, how the sounds are produced with air passing through the throat and mouth; morphology, how words are structured; semantics, meanings of words and vocabularies; and syntax, how words are ordered into sentences. In the instructional chapters of this book, word study activities compare sounds and words in ways that provide some of the language contrasts students need in order to learn new words and concepts in English.

Students' languages may be compared with English to find the syntactic differences and similarities. For example, certain English grammatical structures may be so different that it helps to have students practice the new constructions. In the area of phonology, the sound system, there are sounds in English that do not exist in students' primary languages. If a sound in English does not exist in a student's primary language, look for what she or he substitutes. In most cases, English learners make substitutions based on a close match. For example, Arabic does not have a /p/ sound and many Arabic speakers substitute a /b/ for /p/ in English. The use of specific phonics and phonemic awareness activities that highlight these comparisons at the appropriate time is worthwhile.

2. *Compare written languages.* What is the structure of the home writing system? Consider the directionality of the writing: Does the writing run left to right, right to left, top to bottom? Notice how the sounds are spelled: Is the writing system an alphabet, characters (as in Chinese), or a Romanization of pronunciation (as in Vietnamese)? It is helpful for you as a teacher to learn what consonant and vowel sounds exist and know what letters are used to spell different vowel sounds. If it is a character writing system, what are the properties of the characters or the different parts of characters? Do they represent sound or meaning? Have conversations with students about their home languages and literacies, and as they become comfortable in your classroom ask them to share their writing, favorite books, and stories from their home languages. Students who can read characters can pronounce them and describe their meanings. Welcome parents and elders to show classmates the written languages of students.

Once you have a sense of what sounds and letters exist in the students' primary oral and written languages, compare them with English. How do the letter– or character–sound correspondences in the student's written language compare to the letter–sounds in written English? For example, the letter *a* in Spanish sounds like the short *o* in English and students sometimes spell the short *o* sounds with *a* based on their knowledge of Spanish spelling.

---

1. Compare oral languages.
2. Compare written languages.
3. Know what language and literacy experiences students have had.
4. Plan word study to help students achieve.

FIGURE 1-1 Four Steps to Plan Word Study Instruction with English Learners

3. *Know what language and literacy experiences students have had.* Like three quarters of the world's population, students in classrooms learning English are in varying stages of using two or more languages (Crystal, 2006). Many English learners were born in this country, but live in parallel cultures for language and literacy. Often, students live in settings where there is little literacy-based interaction, and this lack of experience has an impact on learning.

Of the nearly 3 million English-learning Spanish speakers in K–12 classrooms in the United States, half were born in the United States and 30% were born in Mexico. These students have a wide range of experiences with English. In a large demographic study of children with limited English proficiency (LEP), 46% had been born in the United States. Of the students born outside the U.S., 15% had lived in this country for 5 or more years, 22% had been in the United States for 1 to 4 years, and close to 20% of the English learners had lived in the United States for less than a year (Zehler, Fleischman, Hopstock, Stephenson, Pendzick, & Sapru, 2003). Thus, students come to school with a range of language experiences.

Children's success in learning one language is highly related to their learning of another. For example, children with numerous language and literacy experiences have extensive vocabularies when they enter school. In a groundbreaking longitudinal study, some children, by the age of 3, had heard 3 million more words than other children (Hart & Risley, 1995). English learners who already have a strong vocabulary in one language have more to draw on when they learn English. Literacy learning in school builds on the language and literacy experience children have in the home, the number of books in the home, the number of opportunities children have to see parents engaged in literate activities, and the amount of conversation they hear and are involved in (Bear & Helman, 2004).

The level of family literacy predicts the achievement of the children, regardless of the country in which the parents or grandparents were educated (Reese, Garnier, Gallimore, & Goldenberg, 2000). The more years of schooling among adult family members, the greater children's literacy achievement. What students know in one language or literacy is used to learn oral and written English. Rather than complicate learning, literacy in another language facilitates learning to read and write in English. Informally get to know the level of education among family members, even grandparents.

4. *Plan word study to help students achieve.* Select activities and strategies for successful learning experiences, develop expectations for learning, and plan the *intensity* and *duration* of instruction for each student. Because of the differences in language and literacy experiences among students, this book includes activities at different levels of oral and written English development. In setting goals, consider where a student should be developmentally at the end of the school year. What progress will be observed if, for example, a student is involved in small-group instruction an extra hour three times a week at a particular developmental level for 20 weeks?

English learners with little literacy in their home language are often older when they enter particular stages of development. When students are older, modifications are needed. The instructional match with development is still there, but given the age of the students, word study and some of the games must be designed to interest older learners.

Like all readers, older learners require interesting, relevant, and instructional-level reading materials; the problem is that there are not many materials written at students' instructional and intellectual levels. To supplement reading materials, beginning reading activities are adapted for students in the intermediate grades. For example, through the Personal Readers discussed in Chapter 5, students expand their vocabularies when they listen to and summarize grade-level content materials at the same time as they create materials for repeated reading. Through activities for older students and more advanced readers, students learn vocabulary and find greater meaning in their reading.

Verbal Planning and Proficiency

How do students plan their language and reading? Verbal planning can be described as students' ability to plan what to say or write, and to organize what is heard and read. Verbal fluency in speech and reading makes verbal planning possible. Proficiency in verbal planning is possible when students are familiar and at ease with a language; when the mechanics of language come easily, leaving plenty of room for thinking at a higher cognitive level. Without the ability to plan verbally, comprehension does not flourish. You will notice that many English learners can read many words they do not comprehend. If all of our energies are consumed in figuring out *how* to express ourselves, then there is little time to spend on comprehension and understanding. The guiding question is this: *How easily do students plan their verbal activities in their primary and second languages?*

Assessments of fluency indicate proficiencies in word knowledge, and assessments of expression are a way to understand students' comprehension. Fluent and expressive oral reading is a measure of proficiency.

Competence in oral and written language requires verbal planning that is at least at a phrasal level. English learners are more effective speakers when they express themselves in phrases. To speak in phrases requires a good knowledge of the syntax or grammar of the language and also a sufficiently rich vocabulary to quickly organize speech into phrases.

Verbal planning in literacy needs to take place at several levels: with words, in letter–sound relationships, and in phrases. Readers must make the match between the words they say and the words printed on the page, easily and quickly. This ability is apparent during the emergent stage when students accurately fingerpoint-read a few lines of memorized text. At the same time they begin to plan reading at a phrasal level, they learn letter–sound relationships at the word level.

Literacy proficiency requires rapid recognition of words so that the words, like words in speech, can be organized into phrases. To begin to plan reading at a phrasal level, a sight vocabulary of approximately 250 words in English is required. Students in the transitional stage of reading have this sight vocabulary and *begin* to read with some fluency and with increasing expression. Oral reading expression at this level shows us what students comprehend.

"Brain energy to think," a quote by the American author Jack London, enhances our thinking about verbal planning. To paraphrase, London advised writers to write clearly for their readers, leaving plenty of "brain energy to think," comprehend, and understand (London, 1917). Think about the verbal planning English learners have at their fingertips when they read and write. Observe English learners in their reading and writing and verbal expression to see if they have enough brain energy left, after analyzing and planning their language, to think.

Four Examples of Literacy Proficiency Among English Learners

What are students' proficiencies in their primary oral and written languages and English? Consider four examples of ways in which students' languages and literacies blend:

1. Some English learners come to school proficient in their home oral and written language. Instructional planning will follow a path that directs comparisons between home language and English literacies. Home literacies support oral and literacy development in English.
2. Learning a second language enriches students' first languages (Guion, Flege, Liu & Yeni-Komshian, 2000; Lieberman, 1991; Ransdell, Arecco, & Levy, 2001; Schmitt & McCarthy, 1997). Bilingual English learners have oral language competencies in English and another language, and achieve where they would be expected given their age and experiences. Achievement in the two languages will not be equal (Grosjean,

2000), but should be within a grade level of current placement. Bilingual learners negotiate between languages and literacies (August & Shanahan, 2006; Tolchinsky & Teberosky, 1998). Students' first languages will impact the strategies they employ. Students' literacies enhance rather than detract from their learning, though it is clear that the more closely two orthographies are aligned, the easier the second writing system is to learn (Bialystok, & McBride-Chang, 2005)

3. Learners who are proficient speakers but nonliterate in their first language must learn to speak and read English at the same time. This is true for Hmong students, because Hmong has traditionally been a primarily oral form of communication. Most Hmong students did not learn to read or write their language before coming to the United States.

4. Some students may not have adequate language development in their first language. These students have much to achieve and this can only be accomplished through intensive and extended experiences in language and literacy. As is true in all communities, there are often significant educational, social, and economic differences among English learners.

What Do Students Achieve in Word Study?

The word study activities in *Words Their Way with English Learners* clarify the teaching of phonics, vocabulary, and spelling for English learners. If, for example, you are teaching English learners who are studying short vowels in the letter name–alphabetic stage, you would refer to the letter name–alphabetic chapter in this book for activities that clarify consonants and vowels that are often confused in English. In addition, with students who are learning English, much attention must be paid to the meaning of the words to develop vocabulary along with phonics and spelling.

Vocabulary Improves with Word Study

Vocabulary instruction should be a part of each word study lesson. Teachers clarify the meaning of the words in the sorts during the lesson even when a sound contrast is the focus, and students should be asked to use the words to enhance their meanings.

Some word study activities focus exclusively on vocabulary instruction. The **concept sorts** are semantic sorts that grow vocabularies as students sort words and pictures by how they are related in meaning. **Picture sorts** are particularly effective with older students who do not know much English: They can complete the sort using the pictures and then listen to others use the English terms as they explain how they sorted.

Vocabulary is taught in **content sorts** in which students categorize key vocabulary words from content areas. Teachers model how the concepts are related, and students add these sorts to the content sections of their **word study notebooks.** Students' word study notebooks connect reading and word study. Students hunt for related words in their reading and add them to these word study notebook lists over the course of a content area unit of study. These notebooks are a resource that English learners use to review new vocabulary they have recorded in them.

Word Study Is Integrated for Greater Learning

Integrated instruction combines areas of instruction as instructional goals interact. This integration means that curricular areas flow into each other. When phonics, vocabulary, and spelling are integrated with reading and writing, more instructional time is available to teach in cohesive, small groups for differentiated instruction. Some of the ease of learning oral language that is so evident during the critical period of language development

---

Some English learners have oral proficiency in their home languages but lack basic literacy proficiency in those same languages.

Concept Sort
A concept and vocabulary development activity in which pictures, objects, or words are grouped by shared attributes or meanings.

Picture Sort
Pictures are sorted into categories based on similarities and differences. Pictures may be sorted by sound or by meaning.

Content Sorts
Students sort words or pictures from content areas in science and social studies to organize the ideas relationally. These sorts serve as springboards to discuss the concepts that underlie key content vocabulary.

Word Study Notebooks
Notebooks in which students write word sorts that follow particular spelling patterns, and keep other notes related to word study activities.

in young learners is less evident each year. With less ease and experience, older English learners at basic levels benefit from explicit language instruction, and guided practice studying words that are matched to students' developmental and linguistic needs. Integrating the language and literacy curricula gives students sufficient exposure to the words and word patterns they are asked to learn.

The *essential literacy components* of phonemic awareness, phonics, fluency, vocabulary, and comprehension that are integral to so many literacy initiatives are addressed in five *essential literacy activities* summarized as RRWWT: *Read to, Read with, Write with, Word Study,* and *Talk with* activities (Bear & Barone, 1998; Bear, Johnston, & Invernizzi, 2006). Every effective literacy program involves these five types of activities. These activities are organized to match students' development and build in time for vocabulary instruction and verbal interaction.

Foreign English-Language Learners Examine the Layers of English Spelling in Their Word Study

English is an international language, and around the world, people of all ages are learning English. Foreign language teachers use word sorts and activities to teach secondary and adult students who do not live in English language settings. These English as a foreign language (EFL) learners are like secondary and postsecondary students in the United States enrolled in Spanish and French language courses. These learners are at the other end of the experiential continuum from the English learners enrolled in English-based classrooms.

English as a foreign language learners who are highly literate in their primary language progress through the stages of orthographic development in English in a similar fashion if there is a sufficient amount of English in their current instructional setting. If the learners' primary languages are closely related to English, then the foreign English learners may progress through the stages at a faster pace. After a spelling assessment, teachers guide EFL learners to the word study activities that are at their developmental levels. Throughout the instructional chapters there are word study activities that may be used with EFL students. EFL teachers can use the lists of words created in sorting to highlight some points about English pronunciation; for example, a common question would be *"Do you hear that all of these words have the same vowel sound in the middle?"*

Many benefits are derived from examining words carefully and relationally. Teaching at students' instructional level is essential and is tied to their development.

FOUNDATIONS OF ORTHOGRAPHIC KNOWLEDGE

Why is it important to know about students' orthographic knowledge, the knowledge students have of how words are spelled? The short answer is that orthographic knowledge and development in the areas of phonics, vocabulary, and spelling are essential to reading and writing development.

There is a reciprocal relationship between reading and writing development. Reading informs writing, and writing makes for better readers and spellers. Autobiographies and biographies of many great authors reveal that they are usually voracious readers, particularly in their genres. They learn how to write by reading and imitating others as they develop their own styles. (Bear & Templeton, 2000)

There are also powerful and significant relationships between reading and spelling. Spelling is a conservative measure of what students know about words, for if students know how to spell a word, they nearly always know how to read the word. Students' spelling is interesting in that it demonstrates their orthographic knowledge and thus the type of instruction that would be useful.

The groundbreaking research of Edmund Henderson (1990) provides a good sense of the relationship between reading and spelling development. For purposes of

```
┌─────────────────────────────────────────────────────────┐
│  Alphabet/Sound ─────────► Pattern ─────────► Meaning      │
└─────────────────────────────────────────────────────────┘
```

FIGURE 1-2   Three Layers of Orthographies

organization and instruction, five stages of spelling and reading have been proposed. As is discussed in depth in *Words Their Way* (Bear, Invernizzi, Templeton, & Johnston, 2004), our research aligns with similar models proposed by Chall (1983), Ehri (1997), and Perfetti (2003).

Layers of English Orthography

All writing systems have three layers: sound, pattern, and meaning (see Figure 1-2). The sound layer reflects the sound–symbol relationships, and in alphabetic orthographies, the sound layer is labeled the alphabet layer. The stages of spelling development follow from these three layers. Every language has its unique blend of these layers. It will be beneficial to begin with a description of the three layers in English.

The *sound* or *alphabet layer* is described as the layer where letter–sound correspondences are made; for example, the letter *b* makes the /b/ sound. This layer is the most basic layer and is relatively complex in English with long vowels and short vowels, and vowels that are influenced by neighboring letter-sounds (for example, see the influences of *r, l*, and *w; car, call, cow*) for a total of 44 sounds.

The second layer of English writing is the *pattern layer*. Letters in English are arranged into patterns beginning with patterns for single syllable words. Consonant–vowel–consonant (CVC) is the basic pattern and describes the common closed syllable, a syllable that ends with a consonant sound. There are a number of long-vowel patterns in English that include the CVVC (rain), CVCe (time), and the CVV (pie) patterns. Two-syllable word patterns are related to how syllables combine; as seen in the contrasts between the sound and patterns in *legal*, an open VCV pattern, and *napkin* and *dinner*, both VCCV pattern words.

The *meaning layer* reflects the *morphology* of the language. Morphology is of two types: inflectional and derivational. *Inflectional* morphology involves the addition of suffixes such as *-ed, -ing*, and *-s* to base words to indicate tense and number, such as when *walk* becomes *walked*, or *boy* changes to *boys*. *Derivational* morphology involves the addition of prefixes and suffixes to base words or Greek and Latin word roots to indicate a change in a part of speech and differences in meaning that are sometimes quite subtle, at other times quite significant. For example, *pre- + approve = preapprove, dis- + approve = disapprove; derive* (a verb) *+ -ation = derivation* (a noun). Instruction begins with easy morphological features such as prefixes and suffixes *(un-, re-, -ly, -tion)* and inflectional endings *(-es, -ing, -ed)* added to base words. It extends to Greek and Latin word roots, such as *spec* in *spectacle, spectator, speculate* and *therm* in *thermometer, thermal, thermos*. These roots serve as the bases of technical and specialized vocabularies.

As many linguists have observed, spelling carries the history of English. Some people think that spelling is a jumbled mess, but in fact, the three layers work together to make reading and writing something that can be done efficiently and quickly enough to have time to comprehend and think about what was read. Thomas Jefferson was asked to approve a spelling reform that would make English spelling match the way words are pronounced. Jefferson did not endorse the simplified spelling proposal because he did not want to strip English of its roots and history (Bear, 1992).

The Balance of the Three Layers in English

English seems to have good balance and interaction among these three layers. Before the printing press, spelling varied among writers and slowed down reading. In Jefferson's day, spelling was settling down, and today, with modern dictionaries and electric forms, spelling is quite stable. In fact, in English, if the alphabet layer was represented more directly, too many words would be spelled the same and meaning could be confused. Try reading the widely distributed poem "Candidate for a pullet surprise" quickly:

I have a spelling checker/It came with my P.C.

It plane lee marks four my revue/Miss steaks aye can knot sea.

Eye ran this poem threw it,/Your sure reel glad two no.

Its vary polished in it's weigh./My checker tolled me sew. (Zar, 2000)

The many combinations of letters for long and short vowels are part of the history and complexities of even single-syllable words in English, with some long vowel words coming directly from the French. In each of the following word pairs, the first word is older than the more recent addition of French origin: *cow/beef; pig/pork; white/beige.* And as you may know, many military, religious, and legal words came directly from the French vocabulary when the Normans became the rulers of the English-speaking world in the 11th and 12th centuries.

> In upper-level word study, the meaning layer is crucial to vocabulary development.

English is well suited to accommodate new terms and to grow its vocabulary. There are probably 300,000 word forms, and nearly a million words including all word forms *(crash, crashed, crashing).* There are nearly 600,000 words in dictionaries and another 400,000 words that are mostly scientific and uncataloged. Speakers do not use anywhere close to the million available English words. In a week, mature readers read 2,000 different words of the 55,000 words they have learned. Specialized vocabulary is acquired at work or in professional studies.

Stages of Literacy Development in English

Readers and writers orchestrate these three layers through "progressively more complex reciprocal interactions" (Bronfenbrenner & Evans, 2000, p. 117) that are presented as stages or phases of development (Invernizzi & Hayes, 2004). The five stages of development follow from the layers of English orthography as can be seen in Figure 1-3. These stages overlap because learning is gradual and learners do not abruptly move from one stage to the next, and because there is an interaction among the layers; students who have progressed to the meaning level realize that changes in the meaning layer produce changes in the sound of the word. For example, notice the sound and meaning changes by adding a suffix to *compose* to form *composition.* At a particular moment in students' development, a specific phase or stage dominates their thinking about words (Rieben, Saada-Robert, & Moro, 1997).

The Synchrony of Literacy Development

In Figure 1-3, the stages of reading are related to stages of spelling development. This is described as the *synchrony of development.* This figure includes reading behaviors and spelling errors characteristic of each stage. Specific reading behaviors come into place, in synchrony, with specific spelling behaviors. There is such a close relationship in the development between reading and spelling that the spelling assessments discussed in Chapter 2 can be used to think about grouping for instruction.

Figure 1-3 shows us that the first two stages of spelling are the emergent and letter name–alphabetic stages. The layers at the top of the figure illustrate how these stages flow from the alphabet layer as students learn the basic sound–symbol correspondences and collect a beginning sight vocabulary. Follow the progression of spelling errors at the bottom of the figure and compare the spelling to the reading. For example, students in the middle of the letter name–alphabetic stage often spell *float* as FLOT. Moving up the figure to reading stages, notice how students in the beginning stage characteristically read in a word-by-word fashion, fingerpoint-read, and read unexpressively. By the end

ALPHABET/SOUND

PATTERN

MEANING

Reading and Writing Stages/Phases:

Emergent *Early Middle Late*	**Beginning** *Early Middle Late*	**Transitional** *Early Middle Late*	**Intermediate** *Early Middle Late*	**Advanced** *Early Middle Late*
Pretend read	Read aloud, word-by-word, fingerpoint reading	Approaching fluency, phrasal, some expression in oral reading	Reads fluently, with expression. Develops a variety of reading styles. Vocabulary grows with reading.	
Pretend write	Word-by-word writing, writing starts with a few words to paragraph in length	Approaching fluency, more organization, several paragraphs	Writes fluently, builds expression and voice, experiences different writing styles and genre. Writing shows personal problem solving and personal reflection.	

Spelling Stages/Phases:

Emergent →	**Letter Name-Alphabetic →**	**Within-Word Pattern →**	**Syllables and Affixes →**	**Derivational Relations →**

Examples of misspellings:

	Emergent	Letter Name-Alphabetic	Within-Word Pattern	Syllables and Affixes	Derivational Relations
bed	b bd	bad	*bed*		
ship	s sp	sep shep	*ship*		
float	f ft	fot flot flott	flowt floaut flote *float*		
train	t trn	jran tan chran tran	teran traen trane *train*		
cattle	c kd	catl cadol	catel catol	cattel *cattle*	
cellar	s slr	salr celr	saler celer	seler celler seller *cellar*	
pleasure	p pjr	plasr plager	plejer pleser plesher	pleser plesher plesour plesure *pleasure*	
confident				confedent confiednet	confident confedent confident *confident*
opposition				opasishan oppasishion	oposisian opposition oposisian *opposition*

FIGURE 1-3 Synchrony of Literacy Development in English

of the letter name–alphabetic stage of spelling, students learn spelling patterns, in particular the short vowel CVC pattern, or closed syllable.

The name of the next stage of spelling, the within-word pattern stage, illustrates how important the idea of patterns is at this time. Students recognize the long-vowel patterns (CVCe, CVVC, CVV, CV), and they learn to spell the complex vowel patterns (for example, *-ought, -edge, -earn*). Single-syllable words are mastered in spelling, and in reading, students have enough power in word recognition to verbally plan the reading for fluency and expression.

Upper-level word knowledge is made up of two stages: the syllables and affixes stage and the derivational relations stage. The syllables and affixes stage begins with the study of patterns and how syllables combine. Students are ready to examine open and closed syllables, and they develop the skill of knowing where to look at words to begin to divide them into syllables. This pattern work is a fulcrum. On one end is the alphabet level when students draw on their knowledge of sound differences associated with *e*-drop and consonant doubling (for example, *taping* and *tapping*). By the end of this stage there is a tottering back and forth between the alphabet and the meaning layer. As part of the meaning layer, students learn simple prefixes and suffixes.

The derivational relations stage is a time when students examine the function and spelling of meaning-bearing parts of words. Students see that word endings have meaning grammatically (for example, *-ic* is an adjectival form, and *-ion* turns a verb into a noun), and semantically they study more difficult prefixes and suffixes. As the name of the stage indicates, learners examine and come to understand how different words can be *derived* from a single base word or word root: From the base word *relate* we can derive the words *relative, relationship, relativity, correlate, correlation, correlative*, and so forth. Notably, students come to understand the *spelling–meaning connection* (Templeton, 1983, 2004): Words that are related in meaning are often related in spelling as well, despite changes in sound. For example, notice how the spelling *deriv* remains constant despite the change in pronunciation when different suffixes are added: *deriv*e–*deriv*ative–*deriv*ation.

The corresponding reading stages in these upper levels are the intermediate and advanced reading stages. Silent reading is the dominant mode of reading by students, and they find ways to adjust their reading styles to suit different purposes. Intermediate readers acquire these styles and increase their reading rates gradually. Advanced readers are accomplished readers who can read rapidly, and they learn new reading skills as they enter new genres and fields of study. They learn new vocabulary words as they learn new concepts. They can already adjust their reading rates to skim and scan, and they can adjust their rate according to the relative difficulty of the materials.

The Slant of Development

As you think of the synchrony of development you may wonder about the relationship between reading and spelling, since there are words that are read easily but that are difficult to spell. The idea of a *slant of development* illustrates the relationship between the two: Reading achievement will always look slightly ahead of spelling. Students who spell *float* as FLOT read *float* correctly when the word is a part of a text or presented in a list. Reading and spelling draw on the same orthographic knowledge base. As a recognition task, reading is a little easier to do correctly, compared to a productive task like spelling. This slant is a relationship that makes it possible to use students' spelling to think about their word knowledge and reading development.

In parent meetings, teachers share Figure 1-3 to show this relationship between reading and spelling. Sometimes, parents know more about how their children spell than they do about their reading. Showing parents the relationship among reading, spelling, and writing places students' literacy behaviors in perspective.

Layers in Other Orthographies

In each written language, the three orthography layers are blended uniquely. If this blend is understood for students' languages, then it is clearer to the teacher what students will bring from their primary languages and literacies as they learn to speak and read English. The sound/alphabet, pattern, and meaning layers are evident in all writing systems. Where there is not an alphabet, the first layer is examined for other sound–symbol correspondences.

Along the developmental continuum, look for *when* the three layers overlap compared to English. You will see that different writing systems, or orthographies, not only blend the layers in different ways but their layers are of varying complexities. *When* the layers overlap depends on the structure and history of the writing system. For example, in a comparison of English and Spanish orthographies, one of the first things to observe is how faithful Spanish is to pronunciation and how in English, long vowels and many short vowel words are spelled with abstract patterns in which letters combine to make a sound. The long vowel patterns in English (for example, CVCe: *tale*, CVVC: *tail*; CVV: *tie*) are unnecessary in Spanish writing. This difference often means that students from Spanish language backgrounds rely more on the alphabetic layer than on the pattern layer.

Sounds of Language and Language Families

In the alphabet or sound layer, sound–symbol correspondences are examined. What sounds exist in a language, and how does the writing system represent those sounds? One thousand sounds have been cataloged, but most languages have two or three dozen. Most languages have between five and seven vowels. Some writing systems include vowels, and other orthographies (like Hebrew) do not, so that the reader uses context to a greater extent to understand the words. See Comrie, Matthew, and Polinsky (1996) for a wonderful collection of information about languages and writing systems.

Figure 1-4 presents an abbreviated list of language "families" that are organized geographically (Comrie et al., 1996). Languages in a particular family share similarities

> Look for *when* the alphabet, pattern, and meaning layers overlap.

Indo-European		Altaic	Sino-Tibetan	Afro-Asiatic	Austro-Asiatic
Germanic	*Slavic*	Turkish	Mandarin	Arabic	Vietnamese
English	Polish	Kazakh	Wu	Saudi	Khmer
Dutch	Czech	Turkmenan	Cantonese	Iraqi	
German	Russian	Mongolian	Xiang	Egyptian	
Danish	Bulgarian	Manchu	Gan	Algerian	
Swedish	Serbian/	Korean	Hakka	Hebrew	
	Croatian	Japanese			
Romance	*Indo-Iranian*				
French	Hindi/Urdu				
Italian	Nepali				
Spanish	Bengali				
Portuguese	Punjabi				
Romanian	Persian				
	Kurdish				
	Tajik				
	Pashto				

FIGURE 1-4   Select Language Families

in sound and often in written forms. English is an Indo-European, Germanic language. The languages in Figure 1-4 represent only a few of the 5,000 languages that have more than a million speakers. Beginning with these groups, some commonalities and differences can be noted. For example, the Germanic languages are similar in their basic vocabularies, and Old English sounds very much like German. The Romance languages also sound alike and look alike. For example, drawing from Latin, the writing systems in most Romance languages are quite similar in that in each of these orthographies, the letter–sound relationships are very consistent, and all letters are sounded out.

English learners will be unfamiliar with particular sounds that do not exist in their primary languages (Helman, 2004). For them, acquiring new sounds requires instruction and practice, like walking students through the comparisons in picture sorts for rhyming and beginning sounds, as covered in Chapter 4.

Shallow and Deep Orthographies

Writing systems that are easy to pronounce are highly regular in their sound–symbol correspondences. These writing systems are described as *shallow, transparent,* or *translucent* orthographies. Spanish and Italian spelling are highly regular; written words are easy to decode because there are fewer sounds and there are highly consistent, one-to-one correspondences between sounds and letters. Spanish is classified as a shallow or transparent orthography because students do not need to reach deeply in Spanish to spell its 24 sounds. Orthographies may be described as more or less shallow, or *semi-translucent* or *semi-transparent.* German is an example of a semi-transparent orthography because it is a combination of transparent and deep features.

French and English are *deep* or *opaque* orthographies; the correspondences between letters and sounds are often much less direct. In English spelling, for example, upper-level learners reach deeply into the pattern and meaning of words and word parts to spell proficiently. The pattern layer begins with the CVC pattern for short vowels, a relatively transparent pattern, because each letter forms a predictable and discernible sound. When students study long-vowel patterns they begin to examine a relatively opaque feature of English. Short-vowel word study is mostly transparent in that each letter stands for a unique sound, whereas in the spelling of long vowels, students deepen their view of the orthography to include the more abstract long-vowel *patterns* in English, that is, the silent *e* in *tame* or the vowel digraph in *meat* contrasted to the short vowel in *met.*

There are also interesting histories and etymologies of English words that include Greek and Latin roots, like the common meaning found among words that share the Latin root *plico/plicatum* (fold) as in *duplicate* (twofold), *multiplication* (manifold), and even *implicate* (to be folded in) and *complication* (a folded situation) (Lundquist, 1989). The relationships in meaning among words with shared roots are important to vocabulary development. English learners unlock the meaning of polysyllabic words when they look for related words and shared roots.

In Figure 1-5, three written languages are compared across their sound, pattern, and meaning layers, layers that are common to all writing systems (cf. Perfetti, 2003). The shaded areas in this figure signify overlap among layers. The involvement of each layer in English, Spanish, and Chinese is illustrated in this figure. Growth in students' understanding of these layers is gradual, and in English, the overlap noted in the boxed areas in Figure 1-5 between the alphabet and pattern layers occurs when students examine the sounds of short-vowel sounds and patterns, the consonant–vowel–consonant (CVC) pattern, a pattern that is

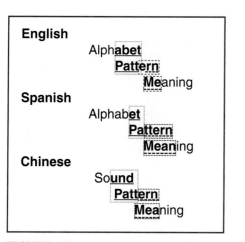

FIGURE 1-5 Overlap in Layers of English, Spanish, and Chinese Orthographies

prevalent in English. For example, both *cap* and *stick* are CVC patterns and short-vowel sounds, and a combination of pattern and sound in word study is necessary.

Spanish, a Shallow or Transparent Orthography

Compared to English, the alphabet layer in Spanish accounts for a greater part of the foundation of a strong reading vocabulary that makes reading fluency possible. Readers and spellers rely on the transparency of Spanish and the power of the alphabetic principle to read and spell polysyllabic words through the beginning and transitional stages of literacy development. As illustrated in Figure 1-5, Spanish readers and writers rely on the alphabetic principle much longer than readers and writers of deep orthographies.

As students learn more sight words in Spanish, they are able to look at words more abstractly, beyond strict letter–sound correspondences. This ability to work with abstractness in spelling is fundamental to the pattern layer. In English, the pattern layer can take a long time to master because there are so many long-vowel patterns for each vowel sound. In Spanish, there are only a few cases where there are ambiguities, as when students learn that there is not just one sound for *g*, but a hard *g* and a soft *g* sound.

Compared to English, the pattern and meaning layers of Spanish orthography are examined almost simultaneously. One of the first times Spanish readers and writers move beyond the letter–sound regularities is when they include accents to spell easy words. As they learn accentuation, students make links between spelling and meaning, and they analyze Spanish spelling at a slightly more abstract level. They learn that the accent can signal changes in word meaning. There are several levels of difficulty when considering the use of accents. Let's look at a few examples of how pattern and meaning layers overlap:

- Accent marks sometimes determine meaning in Spanish. The *e* is accented in *té* (tea), but not in *te (you)*. The *i* is accented in *sí*, meaning *yes*, but not in *si* meaning *if*. A similar example would be the spelling of *sólo*; with an accent on the first *o*, the word means *only, by itself*, and without an accent, *solo* means *alone*.
- Accent marks can sometimes change the part of speech. For several Spanish words, the accent is optional and is used to avoid confusion readers may have about how the word is being used. For example, in a sentence like *Esta casa es bonita (This house is pretty)*, an accent on the *e* in *Esta* is not needed because the noun *(casa)* is present. However, when *ésta* is a pronoun an accent is needed; that is, *Ésta es más bonita (This one is prettier)*.
- Adding suffixes to words can require an accent. For example, in adding *-ación*, a suffix like *-ation* in English, an accent mark is added to adjust for the change in stress that is created. In this way the word for *classify (clasificar)* becomes *classification (clasificación)*. The correct use of accents at the intermediate stage in Spanish is a sign of upper-level literacy. At about the same time, students study simple prefixes such as *in-* as in *inoperable (inoperable)* and *des-* as in *descubrir (discover)* and *describir (describe)*. Whenever possible, hunt for cognates between English and students' first languages for further meaning connections.

In comparison, given the opaqueness of English, about the same time that English learners study the long-vowel patterns, Spanish spellers examine the basic Spanish prefixes, an orthographic pattern that English-speaking students study in the next stage of spelling, the syllables and affixes stage.

Chinese, a Deep Orthography

Chinese writing is a character-based deep or opaque orthography, and what might be called words are composites of between one and several characters. Nouns are two or three characters in length. Characters are always single syllables with phonetic and meaning components (Spinks, Liu, Perfetti, & Tan, 2000).

To teach Mandarin pronunciation to non-Mandarin Chinese speakers, beginning in kindergarten and first grade, children are introduced to pinyin, an alphabetic system. During the first and second grades, students learn characters and stop using pinyin, and so the use of an alphabetic system is brief. Chinese is a character-based orthography, and is sometimes called a logographic writing system. In daily writing, 3,000 of the 40,000 characters are used.

In elementary schools, children in China learn 2,500 to 3,000 characters. The exact number of characters to be learned at each grade level is determined at a provincial level. Shen and Bear (2000) describe the distribution across the elementary grades in Zhejiang Province: first grade, 430 characters; second grade, 680; third grade, 580; fourth grade, 450; fifth grade, 200; and sixth grade, 160.

As illustrated in Figure 1-5, the meaning layer enters into students' examination of the orthography relatively early in their examination of characters, for each character is composed of a meaning element called a *radical*. Students learn about the pattern layer of Chinese around second grade as they add nearly 700 more of the 3,000 high-frequency characters to the approximately 400 characters they learned in first grade. Within characters, students learn about the 214 meaning units, the radicals, in modern Chinese. The meaning layer in Chinese is qualitatively different than the meaning layer in English. In English, the meaning layer is found in prefixes, suffixes, and roots. In Chinese, the meaning layer is found in characters. In upper-level word study in English, students study the history of words by their roots, and in Chinese, students study the history of words by examining the background of the characters. An example is the word *amber*, which comes from a dictionary of Chinese symbols with the subtitle *Hidden Symbols in Chinese Life and Thought*. *Amber* is written in Chinese as 琥珀 and pronounced *hu-po* in Mandarin. The entry notes that "Amber was imported from what is now Burma, and from parts of Central Asia. It symbolized 'courage,' and its Chinese name *hu-po* means 'tiger soul,' the tiger being known as a courageous animal. In early times, it was believed that at death the tiger's spirit entered the earth and became amber" (Eberhard, 1986, p. 18).

Chinese writing is different from alphabetic systems even though the same layers of the orthography are present. Some of the differences between English and Chinese can be seen in the beginning of a letter excerpted from Chang (2001) in Figure 1-6. A word-for-word transliteration of the letter illustrates the different grammatical structures. In trying to match the written form of the first sentence with the transliteration, notice how each syllable is spelled with a single character. As you can see, Chinese writing takes up less space than English. Chinese readers may be slowed by word recognition in English and since the script is spread out, the word recognition takes more time than expected (Chang, 2001).

Knowing about Chinese helps us to know about other languages spoken and written by hundreds of millions of people. Chinese writing began about 1500 B.C.E. and has served as the basis for many other writing systems derived in Asiatic and Indic writing systems. This was true for Korean until the 15th century when King Sejong commissioned the creation of a 28-letter phonetic alphabet that consisted of 40 characters. As a result, this Korean alphabet is one of the most phonetically transparent orthographies in the world.

The differences in the complexity of orthographies are apparent in the relative difficulties students have in learning to read in different languages. A more regular orthography presents fewer problems for learners. A recent study compared Italian and English word reading, and found that there were more reading difficulties among English readers than Italian, a more regular writing system (Paulesu et al., 2001). Word reading difficulties are apparent earlier for students learning a writing system such as English, a deep orthography. In contrast, in a shallow, phonetically based writing system such as Spanish, Italian, or Romanian, students may have fewer difficulties learning to read words because there are fewer vowel sounds, fewer vowel changes, and more regular sound–symbol correspondences. Difficulties in reading and spelling may not appear until later, when polysyllabic word patterns are encountered.

FIGURE 1-6A   First Sentence of a Letter Written in Chinese
Source: (From Chang, 2001, p. 322).

```
lirong:
        lai      xin      shou dao le, xiexie ni de wen hou.  meiyou zaoxie
        come    letter   receive,      thank your regard.      not     earlier
hui    xin,    qing      youanliang!
return letter, please   forgive!
        ni    jinli      shenti zenmeyang? xuexi shunli  ma?
        you recently body   how?          study smooth [interrogative]?
yiding    xiang wangchyang yiyang guo de hen  yukai  be?
certainly, as     usual          same          very happy [particle inviting confirmation]?
```

FIGURE 1-6B   Transliteration of the First Six Sentences of the Letter
Source: (From Figure 1-6A).

```
Dear Lirong:
        Thank you for your letter, and thanks for the regards. I'm sorry that I didn't
write earlier. Please forgive me!
        How have you been recently? Is everything going well with your studies? Are
you enjoying life as usual?
```

FIGURE 1-6C   Idiomatic Translation of the Sentences
Source: (From Figure 1-6B).

Stages of Literacy Development in Other Languages

The stages of literacy development are based on the three layers of orthographic development, and they are linked to specific strategies students use to spell, strategies that have been studied in several languages. Through the activities in this book, English learners at each developmental level learn how to examine the structure of words, and this makes reading more fluent (Henderson, 1992; Perfetti, 1985).

Spelling stages and orthographic development have been studied in many languages including English, Finnish, French, German, Greek, Portuguese, Spanish, Chinese, and Korean. The following studies serve as some of our research base and provide additional information about particular languages: English (Ellis, 1997; Templeton & Morris, 2000), Finnish (Korkeamäki & Dreher, 2000), French (Gill, 1980; Rieben et al., 1997), German (Wimmer & Hummer, 1990), Greek (Porpodas, 1989), Hebrew (Geva, Wade-Woodley, & Shany, 1993), Portuguese (Pinheiro, 1995), Spanish (Bear, Templeton, Helman, & Baren, 2003; Cuetos, 1993; Fashola, Drum, Mayer, & Kang, 1996; Ferroli & Krajenta, 1990; Valle-Arroyo, 1990; Zutell & Allen, 1988), and even character-based orthographies such as Chinese (Perfetti & Zhang, 1991; Shen & Bear, 2000; Shu & Anderson, 1999) and Korean (Yang, 2005).

Stages of literacy development of English like those described by Chall (1983) and Henderson (1990) are adapted to describe how students learn other written languages. Stages can be compared across languages because students in a particular stage apply specific principles, principles that underlie that stage of development. For example, when attempting to spell a word, students in all writing systems who are in the late emergent and beginning stages of spelling (in English, the letter name–alphabetic stage) rely on how a word is articulated, or feels in the mouth as they say it to spell. This is a principle that is discussed in detail in Chapter 5, the letter name–alphabetic stage.

Another example of the characteristic of stages in other languages is the transitional reading stage when reading fluency just begins. In English, students begin to read in phrases, and this accompanies the within-word pattern stage of spelling. In shallow orthographies, such as Spanish, reading fluency is acquired more rapidly because the words are easier to read, and this means that students learning to read shallow orthographies can begin to read with a beginning phrasal fluency when they are in an alphabetic stage of spelling.

The synchrony of reading, spelling, and writing development is found in other languages. In Figure 1-7, the model of Spanish literacy development illustrates the synchrony of learning. This developmental model shows when to expect particular reading and spelling behaviors. Notice how the stages of reading are beneath the alphabet, pattern, and meaning layers of Spanish orthography. The three layers of orthographies, alphabet–pattern–meaning, govern development. Languages offer their own mix of the onset and overlap of the three layers, however, and the actual features that comprise each layer.

Alphabet ⟶ Pattern ⟶ Meaning

Emergente (Emergent)
Sonido prominente (Salient sound): *S or U* for *suma*
Emergente (Emergent)

Nombre de letra/alfabética (Letter name/alphabetic)
Representación completa de sonidos (Complete sound representation): *PAN* for *pan*
Principiante (Beginning)

Patrones entre palabras (within word pattern)
Letras mudas y sonidos contrastes (Silent letters or ambiguous sounds): *quisiera*
De transición (Transitional)

Acentos y afijos (syllables and affixes)
Sílabas y el uso de afijos (Syllables and use of affixes): *geometría*
Intermedio (Intermediate)

Derivaciones y sus relaciones (Derivational relations)
Raices de palabras (Word roots): *herbívoro*
Avanzado (Advanced)

FIGURE 1-7 Spelling Stages, Focus of Spelling, and Reading Stages in Spanish

After the letter name stage in Spanish, when the alphabetic principle is learned, students examine the ambiguities of Spanish spelling. This stage is similar to the within-word pattern stage of English spelling. During this stage of reading in Spanish, learners examine the pattern and meaning layers in Spanish writing.

Stages of development can be described for Chinese, which is a character-based orthography. In a study of 1,200 children's writing and spelling samples, a developmental sequence that follows the three layers was observed. By the end of first grade, students learn approximately 430 characters, and by this time students are toward the end of the beginning stage of reading (Shen & Bear, 2000). Ninety-six percent of the first graders' spelling errors were classified as phonological errors, and by sixth grade these sound–symbol confusions were down to 53%. As sound–symbol type errors decreased, pattern errors increased from 4% in first grade to 33% in sixth. Meaning-based substitutions of characters in writing and spelling gradually increased to 11% by sixth grade (Shen & Bear, 2000).

Stages of development in different languages are influenced by the character of the orthography and the balance among the three layers. Many English learners begin their literacy development when they enter school, which may also be the first time that they are in a predominantly English-speaking setting. For instance, consider Alma. Alma is currently a third grader who speaks Spanish at home. She began to learn to read and write when she entered kindergarten in an English immersion school setting. There have been few books available to Alma in Spanish, and she is currently more literate in English than in Spanish. Alma reads about a year behind in grade-level measures, and is just beginning to tackle long-vowel patterns in spelling. Word study instruction with Alma must strive for a balance among phonics, vocabulary, and spelling instruction

INTEGRATED WORD STUDY INSTRUCTION

Word study instruction is an integral part of the daily activities of the classroom.

Word study is integrated in daily activities. Vocabulary instruction is contextualized when word study is related and drawn from students' reading and content studies. Look across literacy instruction to find ways to integrate word study instruction. The essential literacy activities described earlier as RRWWT *(Read to, Read with, Write with, Word Study, and Talk with)* can provide a format for integrated instruction to frame the ways in which word study addresses the language and literacy learning needs of English learners.

The essential RRWWT literacy activities provide a context for each of the word study activities that follows. Figure 1-8 lists the types of activities that fit the RRWWT framework. The far-right-hand column of this figure posts the suggested amount of time to devote to this activity during the literacy block. In addition to these times for small-group, explicit instruction, additional time is included for independent reading and writing.

These activities belong in every literacy program, and to make progress in reading, students benefit from word study instruction or practice each day, along with additional time dedicated to reading independently. The next chapter guides you to identify the most relevant word study activities for your students, and to connect reading materials and children's literature to students' instructional reading levels.

Essential Literacy and Related Curricula	Procedures and Activities	Minutes Daily Instruction
Read To Motivation Comprehension Narrative structures Vocabulary Social interaction	*Read To* students from literature that offers rich oral language and that involves students in discussions as in directed listening–thinking activities. *Read To* students from informational texts that support content learning. Vocabulary instruction has meaning when supported by what we read to students.	15–30
Read With Comprehension Fluency Concept of word in print Word recognition Vocabulary	*Read With* activities vary by developmental level. Directed reading–thinking activities are a standard activity. Discussions to comprehend are as essential in these lessons as they are in the *Read To* activities. Support in repeated reading is helpful to many students for fluency and word recognition.	10–30
Write With Writing process Narrative structure Verbal expression Concept and language development Motivation Writing correctness and mechanics	*Write With* instruction presents writing strategies that students use when they write independently. Writing with students creates a community of writers who can learn from each other as they explore a common topic, theme, or editing skill. Writing activities for emergent and beginning writers encourage students to analyze the speech stream.	10–30
Word Study Phonics Vocabulary Spelling Concept development Morphological knowledge	*Word Study* activities include picture sorts for sounds, concept sorts, word sorts, word study games, word hunts, word study notebooks, written reflections, charting, exploring interesting words, word study games, and becoming familiar with reference materials.	10–20
Talk With Language expression Vocabulary Motivation and social interaction Concept development	*Talk With* students for their oral language to grow. Creative dramatics, storytelling, and discussion groups about meaningful topics make it possible for vocabulary, language structures, and thinking to mature. *Talk With* activities support the vocabulary and conceptual learning from the *Read With* activities.	15–20

FIGURE 1-8 The RRWWT Essential Literacy Activities

2

Assessment

This chapter presents the process and materials required to assess the spelling, word knowledge, and vocabulary of English learners. Along with the supporting materials in the Appendix, this chapter guides teachers in understanding the developmental approach laid out in the instructional chapters that follow. Students' spelling in English can be classified by the stages of spelling and the types of errors that are common among English learners. Understanding these errors can help teachers choose which types of word sorts to pursue with their students. *Why do English learners make particular spelling errors?* Consider how spelling in Mrs. Holmes' second-grade class leads her to study students' oral and written languages.

Mrs. Holmes Asks, "Why Does Roberta Spell *Bed* as *Ber*?"

Mrs. Holmes observed that Roberta and a few other students spelled the word *bed* as BER; she had seen it enough to sense that this was not a random error. She noticed this pattern because the word *bed* is the first word of the Elementary Spelling Inventory (see Appendix, page 217). One student spelled *bed* BEDR, to be safe. This was an unusual spelling error and Mrs. Holmes did not at that time know enough about Spanish to interpret the error herself. What is it about Spanish that would lead a Spanish speaker to substitute an *R* for the /d/ sound? She waited to ask the reading specialist or a colleague who knew more about Spanish.

In the meantime, Mrs. Holmes thought about the students who made this spelling error. Mrs. Holmes saw that they were in the letter name–alphabetic stage of spelling; they knew how to spell most beginning and ending consonants and were learning to spell short-vowel words. They also read like beginning readers—in a word-by-word manner—just the behavior that one would expect for letter name–alphabetic stage spellers. For this particular case, Mrs. Holmes turns to Chapter 5, the instructional chapter for letter name–alphabetic spellers, and finds that the R/D substitution is discussed and that sorts are provided that help students contrast these final sounds.

Assessment is a time to take a close look at students' literacy and language. The word *assessment* is derived from the Latin word *assidere*, meaning "to sit beside," and that is what teachers do when they assess students' spelling and language.

The first section of this chapter, Assessing Spelling Developmentally, walks through the spelling assessment process, beginning with the choice of assessment, its administration, its interpretation, and the subsequent planning for instruction. The model of spelling development presented in Chapter 1 is the foundation of this assessment process. A spelling assessment indicates what stages of spelling students are in and, consequently, what chapters to turn to for activities to teach students phonics, spelling, and vocabulary. Specific spelling inventories are provided and discussed, along with student spelling examples. This section also includes scoring guides and checklists that are used to identify which phonics, spelling instruction, and written vocabulary activities to pursue from the instructional chapters, Chapter 4 through 7.

In the second part of Chapter 2, the spelling errors characteristic of learners of different writing systems are examined. Spelling inventories from three languages are presented to administer to students from these three language backgrounds: Hangul (the name for Korean writing), Chinese, and Spanish. While this text limits the discussion to three specific inventories, these inventories illustrate the process of developing spelling assessments in other languages. They will help you make sense of students' writing and reading in any language.

In the third section of this chapter, Oral Language and Vocabulary Learning, the assessment of oral language development of English learners is presented. To plan literacy instruction, teachers must understand students' oral and written language experiences and interests. These assessments of oral language highlight the types of *Talk With* and *Read to* experiences that can be built into word study activities.

ASSESSING SPELLING DEVELOPMENTALLY

Students' spelling can be analyzed to assess students' word knowledge and to plan word study and reading instruction (Invernizzi, Landrum, Howell, & Warley, 2005). Three steps are used to assess students' spelling:

1. Begin by collecting samples of students' spellings. Inventories provide an easy way to do this and directions are included in the Appendix.
2. Next, score and analyze spelling to determine a spelling stage. Make a copy of the feature guide in the Appendix to score each student's spelling.
3. Form differentiated instructional groups and partnerships for word study based on students' development. Use the assessment results to choose which features to study, and select word sorts and other activities from the scope and sequence, and from the collections of activities in the instructional chapters, Chapters 4 through 7.

Use one of the spelling inventories and feature guides to form word study groups. You will find two templates in the Appendix that can be used to organize groups. Most teachers administer a spelling inventory at the beginning, middle, and end of the year to monitor progress and to pass on information to next year's teachers. Some school districts and statewide literacy initiatives use the inventories to assess and monitor students' development.

1. Collect developmental spellings.
2. Score and analyze spelling with a feature guide.
3. Choose features and activities for word study.

Developmental spelling inventories include words to assess salient features that are related to particular stages of spelling (Schlagal, 1992). In these inventories, words on the lists are ordered, in part, by difficulty. Not only do students' spelling errors indicate their stage of spelling, the spelling assessments also reveal what students know about the structure of words, knowledge that they use when they read as well as spell (Bear & Templeton, 2000). Word study instruction in phonics, vocabulary, and spelling is based in large part on what is learned in these inventories.

Collect Developmental Spellings

How do you know which spelling inventory to administer? The summary of the assessment materials in this chapter and in the Appendix indicate which inventory is most appropriate. Administer the inventories to students as you would any spelling test, but do not let students study the words in advance. The spelling errors students make during first-draft, uncorrected writing can also be used to analyze students' spelling development and should be used to confirm what is observed in the spelling inventories.

Begin with the inventory best suited to most students, where students will miss at least five words. Many teachers of English learners often begin with the Primary Spelling Inventory (page 214) to see if students know how to spell single-syllable words. Review the Primary Spelling Inventory, and if you think students can spell 15 or more of the 26 words correctly, then administer the Elementary Spelling Inventory (page 217) which surveys spelling development over all five stages.

- *Primary Spelling Inventory and Feature Guide.* This 26-word list is used with students in grades K–3, from emergent spelling to early syllables and affixes spelling. The easiest word is *fan* and the most difficult word is *riding*.
- *Elementary Spelling Inventory and Feature Guide.* This inventory covers a wider range in 25 words, from K–6 and from emergent spelling to derivational relations. The easiest word is *bed* and the most difficult word is *opposition*.
- *Picture Spelling Inventory and Feature Guide.* Use the picture inventory in the Appendix with students who have only a basic understanding of English. The pictures provide extra support and clarity for students. This 20-word list is designed for grades K–3 and ranges from emergent spelling to early syllables and affixes spelling. The easiest word is *lip* and the most difficult word is *whistle*.
- *Qualitative Spelling Checklist.* This one-page questionnaire provides a way to analyze the spelling of students' first-draft writing and a general assessment of spelling stages. Examples are given of the types of spelling errors students make across all five stages of spelling. Make a copy of the checklist found in the Appendix for each student (see page 223). The key step is to collect enough misspellings to determine a stage. This may mean that two or three first-draft writing samples will need to be collected.

This collection of spelling inventories satisfies most spelling and word knowledge assessment needs with English learners.

Guidelines to Administer Spelling Inventories to English Learners. Follow the directions provided in the inventories in the Appendix. Note the following points to prepare students to spell the words on an inventory:

- *Ease tensions about spelling words students do not already know how to spell.* While it is important to value correctness, on the spelling inventories and in first-draft writing, students should spell words the best they can. Some English learners have attended schools where mistakes in writing were strongly discouraged. Model for students how to spell difficult words: "What letter would I write to spell the first sound that I hear when I say the word _____?"
- *Read words in the sentences provided and provide additional support as needed.* Make up an additional sentence, use the word in a phrase, locate pictures, use a movement to clarify meaning (for example, blow a *whistle*), and provide a synonym.
- *Have students say the words as they spell.* Saying the words can remind students of sound similarities between English and their primary language. Articulatory information from saying the word is supportive to students.
- *An optional step is to ask students to place a question mark or star beside words when they are not sure of the meaning of a word.* What students flag with a question mark provides insight into the students' vocabulary development. This is particularly effective with students at the third-grade level and beyond. You may ask students to spell the starred words a second time to observe what other strategies they have.

Score and Analyze Spelling with a Feature Guide

For each student, make a copy of the feature guide that accompanies the spelling inventory. Check the features that students spell correctly and write in the features that students substitute for the correct spelling. Total the errors for each column. *The first column in which the student missed two or more features is the place to begin word study instruction.*

As can be seen in the feature guide in Table 2-1 and in the feature guides in the Appendix, the top two rows show the relationship between spelling stages and the features that students study. Look to the top of the column for the stage of spelling development for the student being assessed. The stage of spelling indicates the appropriate instructional chapter in this book to refer to for word study activities.

Look to see if there are patterns in the substitutions your students make. Many of the patterns we have observed in the spelling of English learners are highlighted and discussed in the instructional chapters. Table 2-1 presents in italics some of the substitutions that have been observed. For example, students from at least seven languages often find the /b/ and /p/ sounds confusing in the final position. These contrasts in final sounds are examined early in the letter name–alphabetic stage in word sorts with English learners.

Instructional Level: What Students Use but Confuse in Their Spelling

An active assessment of spelling reveals three aspects of learning:

1. What students know, or their independent level
2. What they use but confuse, their instructional level
3. What they are not attending to or what they leave absent, their frustration level. (Invernizzi, Abouzeid, & Gill, 1994)

These three aspects of students' learning are critical goals for assessment, and they can be determined for spelling by using one of the feature guides to score a student's spelling.

TABLE 2-1	Errors Often Made by English Learners on the Elementary Spelling Inventory Feature Guide for the First Eight Words

SPELLING STAGES→	EMERGENT LATE			EARLY	LETTER NAME–ALPHABETIC MIDDLE		LATE	WITHIN-WORD PATTERN EARLY		MIDDLE
Features→	Consonants Beginning		Final		Short Vowels		Digraphs and Blends		Long-Vowel Patterns	
Late EMERGENT to LETTER NAME–ALPHABETIC										
1. bed	b	*p*	d	*– t r*	e	*i a*				
2. ship			p	*– b*	i	*i e*	sh	*ch*		
3. when			n	*– m*	e	*i a*	wh	*w*		
4. lump	l	*r*			u	*a o*	mp	*p m n*		
WITHIN-WORD PATTERN										
5. float							fl	*f fal vol*	oa	*ou*
6. train			n	*– m*			tr	*ter t*	ai	*ei*
7. place									a-e	*ei*
8. drive			v	*f*			dr	*v tr ch jr*	i-e	*ai*

*The letters in italics are errors that English language learners make. A dash (–) means that the feature is omitted.

TABLE 2-2	**Finding Students' Instructional Spelling Levels**	
Assessment Guidelines Learning Level Spelling Performance	**Mitra Early Letter Name– Alphabetic Speller**	**Daniel Middle Letter Name– Alphabetic Speller**
Spelling errors →	BD for bed SP for ship YN for when LP for lump JRF for drive LIN for line WS for whistle	BAD for bed ship - correct WEN for when LOP for lump JRIV for drive LIN for line WISTL for whistle
Independent level • What students know • What students spell correctly • No formal instruction is needed.	*Spells some* beginning and final consonants.	Spells beginning and ending consonants, some blends and digraphs, many short-vowel word families.
Instructional level • **What students use but confuse** • **Features misspelled, substitutions** • ***The place to focus word study* instruction:** Demonstrate, Practice, Reflect, Extend	**Spells most beginning and final consonants, and an occasional vowel. Uses letter name strategy (Y for w) and articulation (JRF for drive) Continue to study beginning and ending sounds and easy short-vowel families.**	**Includes a vowel in each stressed syllable. Vowel and consonant substitutions based on articulation and letter name strategy. Study short vowels.**
Frustration level • What students leave absent • Deletions, features omitted • Instruction at this level is introductory and brief.	Omits vowels and most blends and digraphs. Brief discussion of short vowels	Deletes long-vowel patterns, and some blends and digraphs.

Table 2-2 summarizes these three levels with two student examples. The two examples outline what students use but confuse, or their instructional levels. Mitra and Daniel are at slightly different levels of development. The implications for instruction need to be reflected in assignments and small-group activities: Mitra begins by studying beginning and ending sounds and Daniel needs to start with short vowels.

Five Types of Spelling Errors: A Framework to Analyze Spelling by English Learners

Five types of spelling errors are common among English learners. These error types are noted in the feature guides for the spelling inventories that follow. These are features that contrast English with students' primary languages and literacies.

Voiced
A voiced sound is one in which the vocal cords vibrate.

1. *Misspellings reflect minimal contrasts between the primary language and English.* Often, two sounds are entirely alike except in one way. These sounds are called *minimal pairs*; for example, in English, /s/ and /z/ make a minimal pair—they are articulated in the same way, except that the /z/ is **voiced.**

Languages have different sets of sounds. For example, not all languages have a /z/ sound. If a sound in English does not exist in the primary language, then students are likely to substitute a letter-sound from the first language that is similar. For example, Chinese speakers may spell /z/ with an *s*. Spanish speakers often substitute *s* for *z* as well. This is an important aspect of literacy development at the letter name–alphabetic stage. A full feature list for consonants and vowels that are likely to be confusing is presented in Chapter 5.

2. *English learners often substitute whole words.* English-language learners and especially older learners may substitute a known word for an unknown word because the words share sounds and sometimes functions. These substitutions occur more frequently with English-language learners than with native English speakers. Some students have a relatively small set of known words in English and they may not recognize the sounds at the ends of words or syllables. For example students might spell WHILE for *when* or BORDER for *broadcast*. Students who are familiar with writing systems that are quite different from English may be less skillful at making sound discriminations, and may substitute whole words more often than do students who have learned more transparent orthographies like that of Spanish.

3. *English learners often do more sounding out.* English learners use their knowledge of consonants and vowels in their primary language to spell and analyze words. This is evident in the reading and spelling of students who are accustomed to (1) a transparent writing system such as Spanish, in which the letters make the same sound in all words; or (2) a language with an open syllable structure in which many or most of the syllables end with vowel sounds; for example, consonant–vowel (CV) as in *papa* and *suma*. In Spanish and in many other languages, such as Hmong or Chinese, the syllables are frequently open. As we discussed in Chapter 1, English writing is not transparent; it is opaque because letters combine to make a variety of sounds. In a transparent orthography such as Spanish, *name* would represent a word pronounced "nah-may." Spanish-speaking students expect that each letter will be sounded, so they look for greater consistency in the sound–symbol correspondences, and they do more sounding out than English-speaking students do.

English includes many words with a closed syllable structure, for example, consonant–vowel–consonant (CVC), *sit*. Conversely, Spanish speakers expect fewer syllables to end with a consonant sound, and they leave off ending consonants more often than students who are accustomed to a CVC syllable structure.

Contrasted with English, Spanish speakers also do not expect there to be ending syllables, such as the inflectional endings so common in English; for example, words that end in *-ing, -ed*. On the other hand, students may add sounds when they try to slowly pronounce as they spell; for example, DIMENED for *dimmed*. This insertion of sounds is also seen among students whose primary languages do not have consonant blends similar to those found in English. For example, students trying to make sense of consonant clusters may add a vowel between consonants (FEREND for *friend*) or delete a final sound as in spelling *nest* as NES.

Chinese speakers may insert a slight vowel sound or something that sounds like a breath between *s*- consonant blends; *smoke* may be spelled SIMOK. Here again, students add vowels between the consonant blends.

All vowels are sounded out in Hangul, the Korean script, and because all syllables are accented in Korean, unaccented syllables and the schwa/uh/ sound are not perceived clearly by Korean-speaking students in the upper levels of spelling in English (Yang, 2005). At the end of final syllables, Korean-speaking students often add a sound; for example, Korean-speaking students may spell *church* as CHURCHI, and *English* as INGLISHI (Keonghee Tao Han, 2005, personal communication).

4. *Greater variability is seen in the spelling of English learners.* English learners may appear inconsistent in their spelling. For example, a student may spell *happy* and *ocean* correctly, but spell *kite* KIT and *bed* BEAD. Many English-language learners memorize the spelling of words that are beyond their basic orthographic knowledge. This may occur because they are older English learners with greater conscious analysis and memorization skills than younger learners.

5. *Students may omit ending and middle syllables.* Students' knowledge of the easy inflectional endings will have an impact on their spelling. For the less proficient English learner, contextual knowledge does not guide spelling the way it does for students with a complete grasp of the structure and vocabulary of English. For example, when English speakers hear "*We camped down by the river last weekend,*" the past tense indicates that the spelling is *camp + ed* even if, for dialectical reasons, the *-ed* is unarticulated. Someone who does not (1) hear the /t/ sound in *camped* and (2) does not automatically know that the sentence is written in the past tense will have less information to support spelling.

Spelling some polysyllabic words may overload students. The words can be hard to say and spell (words such as *repetition, constitution, separately*). As a result, while students concentrate on spelling the beginning and ending sounds, the middle syllables can escape attention and are omitted. If internal syllables are omitted often, then the student is probably studying words at a frustration level. For instruction, take a step backward and choose easier words to convey the concepts that the students are ready to understand. Later, with reading experience and word study, learners will also study morphology, and this study will help them attend to and understand parts of words they had been omitting. Their study of **morphology** will help them understand how words with the same endings are related in spelling and meaning, for example words that end in *-er, -ily, -ies, -ion*. These words provide an opportunity to not only study the meaning of words, but also their grammatical functions. Through continued study of these word structures, students have a stronger foundation to articulate some of the less obvious, unaccented, ending syllables.

Morphology
The study of word structure, and the meaningful components of words.

Choose Features and Activities

At this point in the assessment process, it is possible to go directly to the classroom composite on page 224 in the Appendix to develop word study groups. With these groups in mind, turn to the instructional activities to choose word study activities in later chapters. The first place on the feature guide where a student misses two or more is the place to begin instruction; you will group students by the features that they are studying. Write students' names under the stage of development on the classroom composite on page 224 of the Appendix. Then, divide the class into relatively even groups for word study. Turn to the instructional chapter based on the developmental stage of each group, and follow the sequence of instruction for that stage.

ASSESSMENT AT EACH SPELLING STAGE

There are special considerations to keep in mind at each stage of development when assessing English learners. The assumptions that students make about sounds and spelling in their primary language will contrast with how English spelling is organized. The following discussions of each stage include at least one sample of student spelling that brings to life the contrasts English learners experience.

Assessments with English Learners in the Emergent Stage

During the emergent stage, students grow from scribbling in their writing to the ability to spell the key sounds in words. The progression of writing development can be seen

FIGURE 2-1 Progression of Emergent Spelling (Used by permission from Bear & Barone, 1998.)

in Figure 2-1, viewing clockwise. Students begin with scribbling that mimics cursive writing. The circles and lines of the next sample are a closer approximation to individual letters. The last two examples include letters, and the shape that looks like a 2 may be an attempt at a letter, like *s*.

Students will contrast and substitute sounds in English with similar sounds in their primary language.

Related Early Literacy Assessments

Several related assessments inform the teacher's knowledge of emergent spelling: alphabet knowledge, concept of word in print, and writing. If students do not write in a conventional manner, then it is useful to learn what alphabet knowledge students have.

Alphabet Knowledge

A number of inventories are available for assessing alphabet knowledge. At the beginning of kindergarten, most students know the names of between 10 and 18 letters. At the end of kindergarten, students on average know the names of 20 uppercase letters. When children know more than 9 letters, they can begin to study letter sounds. Look for accuracy and speed in naming the letters.

See what letters, strokes, words, and characters students know in their primary languages. Students enjoy sharing alphabets, and looking at similarities between their alphabet and the English alphabet. Alphabets are a fascinating topic to students, especially as they speculate about the similarities across languages. Chapter 4 has several alphabet activities.

Concept of Word in Print

The ability to point accurately to text is a crucial part of learning phonics and spelling in the emergent stage (Morris, Bloodgood, Lomax & Perney 2003). Students develop a concept of word in print through lots of experiences with print, including (1) learning letter names, (2) the students' own attempts at writing, (3) the teacher modeling how print works through shared reading/big book experiences and shared writing, and (4) the teacher helping students become aware of and working with beginning consonant sounds. Concept of word in print is important because learners who do not point accurately to a line or two of memorized or familiar text will not be able to demonstrate an ability to segment all of the consonant and vowel phonemes in words, nor will they make sound–symbol correspondences in reading and spelling. Concept of word is assessed with easy rhymes or stories and through observing specific reading behaviors. Concept of word in English takes slightly longer to acquire than in other languages. In Chinese, each character represents a syllable, and therefore the match between the figure and the recitation is one to one (Lee, 1990). In contrast, English has one-syllable as well as polysyllabic words. Students who fingerpoint accurately to *Humpty Dumpty* and recognize most of the words in the rhyme in isolation demonstrate that they have developed a concept of word in print.

In a primary language, students acquire concept of word in print toward the end of the emergent stage. However, during the early grades it may be difficult to find familiar text in English for a child who does not know much English. Therefore, there may be a delay in the acquisition of concept of word among English learners in the emergent stage. This means that without extended literacy experiences during kindergarten, English-language learners may not come to first grade with a stable concept of word in print. The activities in Chapter 4 help students to acquire concept of word in print.

Writing

It is always useful to observe how students spell in their unedited free writing of words that have not been copied. Encourage students to write without fear of making spelling errors. Show emergent writers that drawing and writing can perform the same function, and that they can talk and write or draw at the same time.

Character-based writing systems involve different ways of looking at writing that include sound and meaning associations in the pattern of the characters. Mandarin Chinese educators begin to teach students how to pronounce Mandarin with an alphabetic system, called pinyin. Then in first grade, students study characters. Left-to-right directionality in English does not take much time to learn for most students, but students who are used to writing letters from a different direction and with different forms may write slowly at first. For older learners unfamiliar with the alphabet, learning to make the letters is a tedious process. Many activities to learn the alphabet are presented in Chapter 4.

Assessments with English Learners in the Letter Name–Alphabetic Stage

English learners acquire three strategies during this stage:

1. *Students use the letter names of the alphabet to spell.* For most letters, the letter name is a significant clue to spelling. The /b/ sound is part of the letter name, "bee." The letter name strategy is evident when a child spells *when* as YN. What letter name makes the /w/ sound? Not the letter name *w* (*w* comes from the idea of a "double-u"), but rather for this speller, the letter name *y*, "wye," makes the /w/ sound, and thus *when* is spelled YN.

2. *Letter name spellers use how and where sounds are made or articulated in their mouths to analyze and spell words.* For example, in spelling the /dr/ sound, students who do not know the blend *dr* as in *drum* may spell *drum* with a *j*, JRUM, because the /jr/ feels like /dr/ (actually, the /jr/ is a little easier to pronounce than the /dr/).

The same strategy of using articulation and a letter name strategy is seen in the way students spell vowels. The letter name works well for the long vowels, as in PAL for *pail*. The way students spell short vowels is perhaps the most sophisticated use of the letter name strategy. Students say the word aloud as they spell, and then they use the letter name of the long vowel that *feels closest in the mouth* to the short vowel. The substitutions are systematic and predictable, and as is addressed in Chapter 5, the short **e** is spelled with the letter name *a* (*bed* is spelled BAD), and the short **i** is spelled with the letter name *e* (*ship* is spelled SHEP). There are a few more factors to consider with English learners who bring their home language and sound system to reading and writing. Most often, the English learner is familiar with a different system of vowels, and they need to clarify how English vowels are spelled and pronounced.

3. *The alphabetic principle is foundational during this stage.* Students use what they know about letter names to learn letter–sound correspondences, beginning with high-frequency letters in words (*b, m, r, s* as opposed to *j, k, q, v, w, x*). Students in the letter name–alphabetic stage collect sight words and establish letter–sound correspondences. There is a reciprocal relationship between the growth of phonics knowledge and the number of sight words students acquire.

As can be seen in Mitra's spelling in Table 2-2, students attend first to beginning and then ending consonants to spell and read words. Then, like Daniel, they turn their attention to sounds in the middle. English learners follow a similar path: They learn beginning sounds, focus on final sounds, and then on medial sounds. Many languages have a greater number of open syllables, syllables that end in a vowel sound. In those languages, more final vowels are represented in students' spelling, and fewer final consonant sounds.

During the letter name–alphabetic stage, students learn about consonant blends and digraphs and short vowels. In the next stage, they will turn their attention to long vowels and continue to study consonant blends and digraphs, but this stage is all about phonological awareness (Ehri, 2006).

The Primary Spelling Inventory (page 214) is probably the best inventory to use with letter name spellers because it has seven single-syllable, short-vowel words. The Elementary Spelling Inventory (page 217) is used by primary teachers, and the way students spell the first 10 words is a clear indication of their knowledge of the alphabetic principle and long-vowel patterns. The Picture Spelling Inventory (page 220) contains 10 short vowels to assess letter name stage spelling.

Examples of Students' Spelling During the Letter Name–Alphabetic Stage

The first example for this stage (see Figure 2-2) is by a Korean-speaking kindergartener, Hyun, who is an early letter name–alphabetic speller. The first word *top* is spelled TO. While the omission of sounds is common among students at this stage, the final /p/ sound is problematic for many Korean-speaking students because no final /p/ sound exists in Korean.

Hyun spelled the first and last sounds of *lid* (LD) and *bet* (BET). The spelling of *wag* as WC is unusual for English speakers. As will be seen in greater detail in Chapter 5, /g/ and /k/ are different only by voicing: The voiced /g/ sound may be substituted by the /k/ because Korean speakers do not make this distinction between voiced (/g/) and unvoiced (/k/) sounds. Thus, C represents the /k/ substitution for /g/. Even though it may be unclear why students spell the way they do, the crucial part of the assessment is to determine what students do correctly, and with which orthographic features they are experimenting. Once this is determined instruction begins with easy contrasts like final /k/ with final /t/. As students are ready, the finer contrasts (/k/ to /g/) are introduced. As an early letter name speller, Hyun continued with beginning sound word study and discrimination of final sounds in phonemic awareness activities. Phonemic awareness in older learners can be easier if they have extensive sight vocabularies.

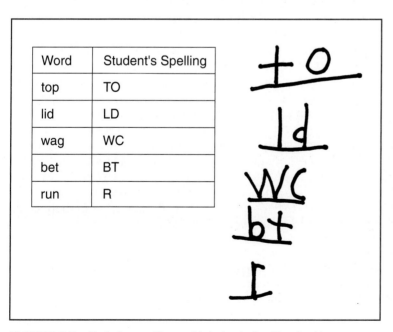

Word	Student's Spelling
top	TO
lid	LD
wag	WC
bet	BT
run	R

FIGURE 2-2 Early Letter Name–Alphabetic Spelling by Hyun, a Korean Speaker

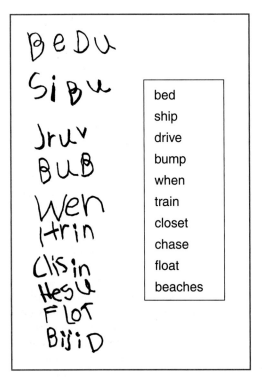

bed

ship

drive

bump

when

train

closet

chase

float

beaches

FIGURE 2-3 Middle Letter
Name–Alphabetic Spelling by Reyna,
a Spanish Speaker

The next spelling sample (Figure 2-3) is from Reyna, a
6-year-old Spanish speaker in the middle letter name–alphabetic
stage. The most prominent error is that she has inserted a final
vowel at the end of the first two words, which are short vowels
and closed syllables, as well as at the end of *chase*, spelled HESU.

The B for *p* substitution for *ship* is a common misspelling
among English learners. The letter name strategy is evident in
the spelling of digraphs and blends. The *dr* blend is often spelled
as JR. Other blends and digraphs are omitted, which is common
among letter name–alphabetic spellers.

Reyna makes reasonable substitutions for the vowels. The
long vowel substitution of E for *a-e* in *chase* is common given
how close the **e** sound in Spanish is to the long **a** in English.

Reyna's instructional level is at the letter name stage. Many
of the error types discussed for this stage are evident in her
spelling. Reyna's spelling of *train* as HRIN is related to the similarity in sound between /tr/ and /ch/. When pronouncing the
tr in *truck* slowly, the /ch/ sound can be felt in the mouth just
before the /r/. In addition, the letter name for *h* in Spanish is
"ah-cheh," and she may use the letter name for *h* to spell /ch/.
In spelling *closest*, Reyna has represented the unstressed final
syllable but has not included the final /t/ sound. This ending
matches syllabically but not phonologically in the last word, BI-
JID for *beaches*. Note also how Reyna has spelled the /ch/ sound
with a J, a sound that is close in articulation to the /ch/.

The next spelling sample makes the bridge between the letter name and the next spelling stage. This sample demonstrates
how students sound out unfamiliar vowels at the same time as they learn more sight
words and something about long vowels.

Benjamín's sample (Figure 2-4) is from the primary inventory. He knows beginning
consonants, blends, and digraphs: *ch-, dr-, sh-, bl-, fr-, ch-, -ck*. He spells just one short
vowel correctly though, the misspellings are common for middle letter name spellers:
DREM for *dream*, DEG for *dig*, GOM for *gum*. It is also interesting to see that Benjamín
has learned to spell two common long-vowel words: *hope, wait*. He will, however, benefit from a careful study of short vowels before he goes on to study long vowels.

At first, some spelling errors by English learners look like within-word pattern
spelling errors in which students are using but confusing long-vowel patterns, for example, (VCVe/NALE for *name*, VCCV/CAIK for *cake*, or CVV/SAI for *say*). Benjamín
has several spelling errors that involve two vowels: SHAIN for *shine*, BLEAD for *blade*,
COUCH for *coach*, and FRAIT for *fright*. As noted earlier, English learners do more
sounding out and may represent more sounds as they elongate unfamiliar vowels. In this
case the two vowel sounds in the diphthongized vowels of long **i** and long **a** are spelled
out: Long **i** is made up of /ah/ and /ee/, and long **a** is made up of /eh/ and /ee/.

It is a positive development to see final sounds represented correctly in all of the
single-syllable words. When it comes to two-syllable words, Benjamín has perhaps combined an *-ed* and *-ing* with -INT spelling *chewing* as CHOINT.

Assessments with English Learners
in the Within-Word Pattern Stage

Learning during this stage calls for a balance in studying long-vowel *patterns* and
continuing to learn about the vowel *sounds*. For many English learners the distinctions
between long and short vowels do not exist in their primary languages. In Spanish, for
example, there are strong and weak vowels, and in tonal languages, vowels are tuned or

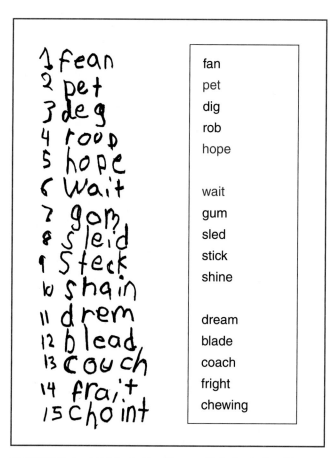

```
1 fean          fan
2 pet           pet
3 deg           dig
4 roob          rob
5 hope          hope
6 Wait          wait
7 gom           gum
8 sleid         sled
9 Steck         stick
10 shain        shine
11 drem         dream
12 blead        blade
13 Couch        coach
14 frait        fright
15 Choint       chewing
```

FIGURE 2-4   Middle Letter Name–Alphabetic Spelling, by Benjamín, a Spanish Speaker

differentiated by changes in pitch (high, mid, low, rise, fall, rise-fall, etc.). In Cantonese, only the **a** makes the distinction between short and long vowels. Students will experience confusion among vowels that are close in articulation; that is, long **e** and short **i** (*sheep/ship, eat/it, bean/bin*).

This is a good time to ask students to make additional attempts at spelling words they think they have misspelled. Ask students not to cross through previous attempts: "Write your new tries to the side. Make a few guesses if you like." These attempts are interesting diagnostically, and show you the depth of a student's knowledge.

Example of Spelling During the Within-Word Pattern Stage

Soo is a Korean-speaking student whose spelling reflects the development of English learners (see Figure 2-5). Soo spelled 10 out of 26 words correctly (39%). She is beginning to mark some long-vowel spelling patterns as in DREME for *dream*, and FRITE for *fright*. She is also omitting long-vowel markings for other words, for example, BLAD for *blade*, COCH for *coach*. Soo is inconsistent in spelling the /sh/ sound, doing it correctly in *shine* but representing it with an S in WISES for *wishes*.

These difficulties are apparent in the scoring of Soo's feature guide in Figure 2-6. The feature guide for Soo's spelling indicates that she should study specific consonant digraphs and their related contrasts in her primary language. She has learned to spell short vowels and, as can be seen in the sudden dropoff in scores, Soo should examine long-vowel patterns.

Soo's spelling reflects contrasts between Korean and English. For Korean-speaking students, the /r/ and /l/ sounds may be indistinguishable. Notice also that *spoil* does not have an ending *l* and the *r* in *growl* is omitted. Throughout, the *r*'s and *l*'s were difficult for her to represent. Soo's speech reflected these confusions between /r/ and /l/. She spelled only two of the inflectional endings (*riding* and WISES for *wishes* compared to SHOUT for *shouted* and CAMPTE for *camped*). Again, Soo did not enunciate these sounds in speaking. Her study of morphology in later stages will reveal some of the grammatical relations to consider in spelling and reading.

Assessments with English Learners in the Syllables and Affixes and Derivational Relations Stages

The upper level is composed of two spelling stages, the syllables and affixes stage and the derivational relations stage. These stages are combined in this book for English learners: By the time students are in the later part of the syllables and affixes stage, they participate in the word study without much accommodation. You will see that the emphasis for word study from that point on makes links between the derivations and word parts that are shared across languages.

Assessment of syllables and affixes spelling begins with a look at how students combine syllables and how they spell unaccented syllables in two-syllable words. They study what is called **inflectional morphology**, which includes the principle of consonant

Inflectional Morphology
The process of adding suffixes that change the structure of words grammatically (*stop/stopped/stopping*).

Word	Student's Spelling
fan	fean
pet	pet
dig	dig
rob	rob
hope	hope
wait	wate
gum	gum
sled	sled
stick	stick
shine	shine
dream	dreme
blade	blad
coach	coch
fright	frite
chewing	chuin
crawl	cran
wishes	wises
thorn	drn
shouted	shout
spoil	spoy
growl	joun
third	serd
camped	campte
tries	chride
clapping	clapn
riding	riding

FIGURE 2-5 Within-Word Pattern Spelling by Soo, a Korean Speaker

doubling (*hop/hopping* compared to *hope/hoping*). Easy prefixes and suffixes are learned during this stage, and students study how to spell different endings, such as -*ed*, -*es*, -*ies*, -*ment*. Many English learners are also learning how these suffixes function grammatically. Their knowledge of English grammar and syntax will begin to support their spelling efforts during this stage. Therefore, in Chapter 7 you will find a variety of word study activities that combine grammar and spelling instruction.

The syllables and affixes stage is a time to study pronunciation of one- and two-syllable words, vowel sounds in two-syllable words, and endings; for example, the three sounds of -*ed*: /t/, /d/, /ed/. Therefore, in the assessments, teachers listen for how students pronounce these final sounds (for example *locked* /t/, *waved* /d/, *painted* /ed/).

The spelling of two-syllable words illustrates how word study incorporates English grammar and inflectional morphology. In the syllables and affixes stage, spelling is closely linked to the study of past tense, verb forms, and gerunds (words that end in -*ing*). Students study some of the spelling patterns of two-syllable words, like consonant doubling, at the same time as they study gerunds. Students study words that end with -*s* and -*es* at the same time as they study plurals, and the pronunciation of the /s/ compared to the sound of /z/.

To assess derivational relations stage spelling, students' knowledge of more complex prefixes (*con-*, *a-*, *ad-*) and suffixes (-*ance*, -*ent*, -*ious*) is assessed, as is their knowledge of words (*credible*, *spectacles*, *tendon*) derived from their roots (*cred*, *spect*, *ten*). In word study activities, English learners in this final stage make comparisons of roots across languages. Their knowledge of their home language enriches the study of word families and histories.

An assessment of orthographic knowledge indicates what vocabulary needs to be taught. Students in the derivational relations stage learn the specialized vocabulary of the content areas through reading and through content lessons. Students benefit from direct instruction of vocabulary that they have not acquired informally through reading. Students who are in the secondary grades and who have just reached the syllables and affixes stage will benefit from a vocabulary program that encompasses the academic, procedural, and content vocabulary that students need for success in school. This means that students need to learn the meaning of words that stretch across the content areas, words like *thesis*, *procedure*, and *attribute*, along with specialized content vocabulary (*respiratory*, *autocracy*, *sonnet*). The elementary inventory is used to assess English learners in these last two spelling stages.

In a number of studies at the upper level, students' feature scores correlated highly with other literacy measures, including standardized measures of reading, vocabulary,

Feature Guide for Primary Spelling Inventory

Directions: Check the features that are present in each student's spelling. In the bottom row, total the features spelled correctly. Note the first column of features in which the student missed more than one feature. Check the spelling stage that summarizes the student's development. Begin instruction on the features needed.

Student's Name: Soo   Teacher: Riznak   Grade: 3   Date: October 10

SPELLING STAGES →	EMERGENT (LATE)	LETTER NAME–ALPHABETIC (EARLY / MIDDLE / LATE)				WITHIN WORD PATTERN (EARLY / MIDDLE / LATE)		SYLLABLES & AFFIXES		
Features →	Beginning Consonants	Final Consonants	Short Vowels	Consonant Digraphs	Consonant Blends	Long-Vowel Patterns	Other Vowel Patterns	Inflected Endings	Feature Points	Words Spelled Correctly
1. fan	f ✓	n ✓	a *ea*						2	0
2. pet	p ✓	t ✓	e ✓						3	1
3. dig	d ✓	g ✓	i ✓						3	1
4. rob	r ✓	b ✓	o ✓						3	1
5. hope	h ✓	p ✓				o-e ✓			3	1
6. wait	w ✓	t ✓				ai *a-e*			2	0
7. gum	g ✓	m ✓	u ✓						3	1
8. sled			e ✓		sl ✓				2	1
9. stick			i ✓		st ✓				2	1
10. shine				sh ✓		i-e ✓			2	1
11. dream					dr ✓	ea *e-e*			1	0
12. blade					bl ✓	a-e *a*			1	0
13. coach				ch ✓		oa *o*			1	0
14. fright					fr ✓	igh *i-e*			1	0
15. chewing				ch ✓			ew *ui*	ing *nt*	1	0
16. crawl					cr ✓		aw *a*		1	0
17. wishes				sh ✓				es ✓	1	0
18. thorn				th *dr*			or -		0	0
19. shouted				sh ✓			ou ✓	ed -	2	0
20. spoil					sp ✓		oi *oy*		1	0
21. growl							ow *ou*		0	0
22. third				th *s*			ir *er*		0	0
23. camped								ed *te*	0	0
24. tries								ies *ide*	0	0
25. clapping								pping *pn*	0	0
26. riding								ding ✓	1	1
Circle cells with more than 1 error	7 (7)	7 (7)	6 (7)	4 (7)	7 (7)	2 (7)	1 (7)	2 (7)	36 (56)	10 26

SPELLING STAGES:

☑ EARLY ☐ MIDDLE ☐ LATE
☐ LETTER NAME–ALPHABETIC
☑ WITHIN-WORD PATTERN
☐ SYLLABLES & AFFIXES
☐ DERIVATIONAL RELATIONS

Words Spelled Correctly: 10 /26
Feature Points: 36 /56
Total 46 /82

FIGURE 2-6   Soo's Feature Guide for Primary Spelling Inventory

1 bed
2 ship
3 when
4 lump
5 float
6 train
7 place
8 drive
9 bright
10 throat
11 spoylled
12 serving
13 chood
14 cary's
15 march't
16 shawr
17 bottel
18 faver
19 riben
20 seller
plasher
Ptorchenet
cofedent
sevliz
capa sesheh

Elementary List

bed
ship
when
lump
float
train
place
drive
bright
throat
spoil
serving
chewed
carries
marched
shower
bottle
favor
ripen
cellar
pleasure
fortunate
confident
civilize
opposition

FIGURE 2-7 Syllables and Affixes Spelling by Gustavo, a Spanish Speaker

and comprehension (Bear, Templeton, & Warner, 1991; Edwards, 2003). Derivational spellers are also advanced readers. They use reading academically, and they know how to be flexible in their reading rates depending on the materials and purpose for reading. Derivational spellers learn new vocabulary primarily from reading.

Examples of Students' Spelling During the Syllables and Affixes and Derivational Relations Stages

Gustavo, whose primary language is Spanish, began school in the United States in kindergarten, and as an end-of-year fourth grader, he is in the early part of the syllables and affixes stages of spelling (Figure 2-7). Gustavo has learned to spell long- and short-vowel patterns as well as consonant blends and digraphs.

The first word Gustavo misspells is *spoil*, spelled SPOYLLED. That Gustavo included an -ed means that he is listening for this ending. He is still learning some of the complex vowel patterns as seen in his spelling of *chewed* and *shower*. When spelling *ripen*, the B in RIBEN makes sense as a substitution of /b/ for /p/. What are most noticeable about his spellings are the ending syllables. He is experimenting with the apostrophe to spell inflectional endings as in CARY'S for *carries*, and MARCH'T for *marched*. He will benefit from instruction focusing on simple affixes, and how spellings change when they are added.

With polysyllabic words Gustavo omits meaningful units in the base words such as *please* in *pleasure* or his use of SHEN instead of *tion* in *opposition*. Systematic study of inflectional suffixes, beginning with the easiest ones, will be important for this student to understand grammatical relations. As a fourth grader, vocabulary study will be important to support his learning in the content areas. There will be many polysyllabic words that he cannot spell and which he may not be able to read or understand. When he studies his science or social studies it will be useful to scaffold his understanding of content words. This is addressed in Chapter 7.

The final sample, Figure 2-8, is from Julia, a student born in the United States who speaks Vietnamese along with her family and friends. Julia is in the derivational relations stage, and she demonstrates a thorough knowledge of the principles that students learn in the syllables and affixes stage of spelling: most inflectional suffixes, consonant doubling, and patterns for unaccented syllables (*bottle, ripen*). She does confuse CARRIED for *carries*. Her spelling of the last five words is telling. She has learned inflectional suffixes like -ate in *fortunate* (PHORTENNATE), the -ent in *confident* (CONPHONDENT), the -ize in *civilize* (SIVELIZE), and the -tion in *opposition* (OPPISITION). The PH for the /f/ sound comes from the use of the PH in her spelling in Vietnamese. Julia is a perfect candidate to study roots and related words (*confide/confident, oppose/opposition*). Instead of drawing on cognates, Julia studies the meaning connection among words as she explores dictionaries and the etymological references presented in Chapter 7.

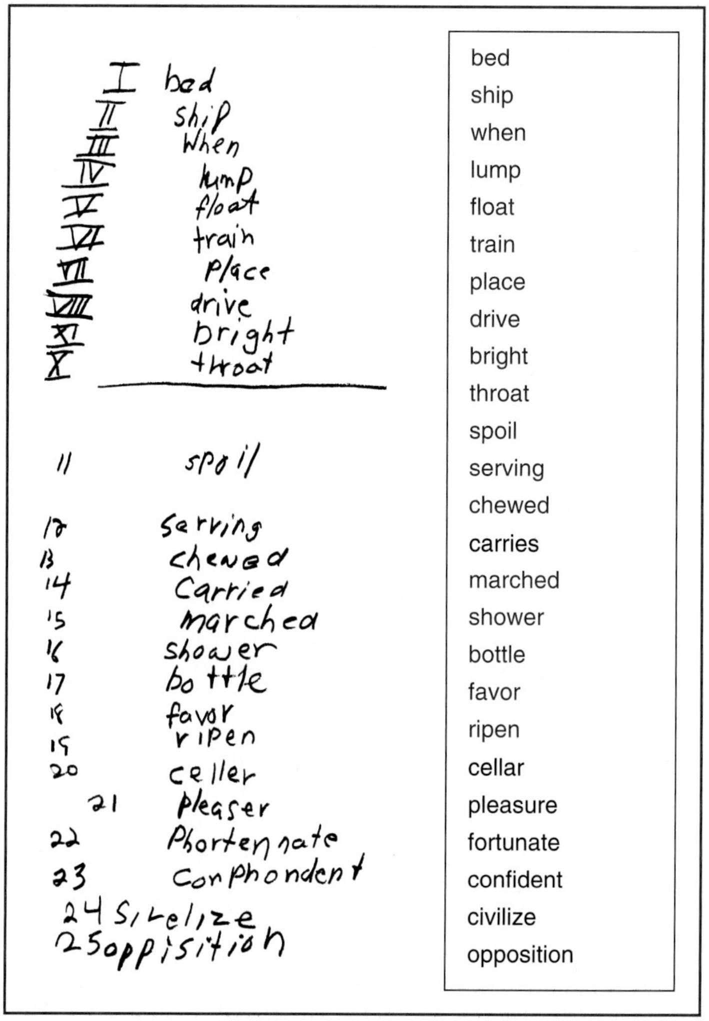

Dialects, Creoles, and Learning to Read and Spell

There is a continuum of language variations that range from minor differences in regional accents and the pronunciation of a few vowels, to extensive differences in pronunciation, vocabulary, and sentence structure or grammar. Students who speak a **dialect** or **creole** of English benefit from word study that clarifies the sound contrasts between standard English and their speech. They do not speak another language, but a version of English that is highly influenced by other languages. Listen for the variations of English you hear among students. In your area, you may meet students who, along with their families and friends, speak in a dialect created out of the interactions among languages, cultures, and speakers of different ages.

Here are four questions to consider as you listen for English-based dialects and Creoles:

- Do you know of a specific language that influences the student's speech in English? Is there a Spanish, African, or Asian language influence? For example, Tagalog is influenced by Spanish.
- How do the ways in which students pronounce words vary from what you expect to hear?

FIGURE 2-8 Early Derivational Relations Stage Spelling by Julia, a Vietnamese Speaker

Dialect
A variation of a language used by a group of people, usually in a certain region.

Creole
A language that originated from a combination of two or more languages.

- What do you notice grammatically? Is there a particular part of speech that is omitted or said in a different order? Are verbs or pronouns omitted or in a different order?
- What phrasing illustrates what you hear in the student's speech or writing? Consider the student's use of these language forms and standard English in the classroom. Are there times when students use one form of English and not another?

English-language learners will speak with a dialect that combines the regional English where they live with the influence of their primary language. If you teach children in specific geographic areas, there is an opportunity to learn the dialect's vocabulary, pronunciation, and grammar, such as Gullah in South Carolina and Georgia, Jamaican Creole, and Hawaii in Creole English.

Students who speak English-based dialects do not need to change their pronunciation to learn to read and spell. Just like English-language learners, speakers of dialects benefit from word study that shows them how their speech is related to the alphabetic, pattern, and meaning layers of English spelling.

Assessment of Spelling in Students' Primary Languages

To learn about students' orthographic knowledge in their primary languages, administer spelling inventories in their first languages, and analyze the spelling of their first-draft writing. In the following section, spelling inventories to assess students' orthographic knowledge in Spanish, Chinese, and Korean are presented. The examples highlight the order of features in the spelling development in other languages. For educators who want to develop inventories in other languages, these examples are presented as models.

Assessments function best when a fluent reader administers the inventory to the student. English language teachers often speak other languages and can administer, analyze, and interpret the students' spelling. Parents and other teachers may be able to administer the inventory or provide some interpretation. A tape-recorded version is quite useful when there is no opportunity to bring in a native speaker. In most communities there will be someone who is literate and can interpret the confusions at the base of the misspellings. The analyses of students' spelling in their home languages illustrate what is learned about students' word knowledge and influences planning word study in English.

Foreign Language Learning and Spelling Assessments

Foreign language spelling assessments and word study activities have broad applicability. Foreign language teachers use spelling inventories to assess students' word and orthographic knowledge. In other countries, the assessments are used by English foreign language teachers to understand the word knowledge of students learning English as a foreign language. Teachers develop word and character sorts as active ways to teach students about the three layers of the writing system that their students are learning as a foreign language.

Inventories and Spelling Development in Spanish, Chinese, and Korean

Three inventories are presented here with analyses of students' spelling in Spanish, Chinese, and Korean. These inventories are based on the developmental stages of those languages and describe a hierarchy in the acquisition of features. These inventories, which are provided in the Appendix (pp. 230–237), have been administered to many students: several thousand in Spanish, 1,200 in Chinese, and 409 in Korean. (Helman, 2004; Shen & Bear, 2000; Yang, 2005)

Spanish Inventory

The Spanish Spelling Inventory (in the Appendix pp. 226–229) assesses features across the developmental continuum in a similar way to that of the English inventories. The names of the stages are different, and in some cases represent slightly different features. For example, in Spanish, as in English, an emergent speller is likely to hear and encode a highly prominent sound in the word; however, in Spanish this sound is as likely to be a vowel sound as a consonant sound. This is because Spanish has fewer CVC words; its most common word structure is CVCV, so the vowels are more prominent.

Because Spanish is a much more transparent orthography than English, the within-word pattern or *patrones* stage is less complex. At the early phase, it involves the use of silent letters such as *h*, the use of *u* to create the hard sound of *g* as is *guisante*, or with the *qu*, and contrasting letters that have the same sound such as *v-b*, *s-c-z*, *y-ll*, or *g-j*. Later in the patrones stage more complex vowel patterns are assessed.

el	el
suma	suma
pan	pan
red	red
campos	campos
plancha	plancha
brincar	brincar
fresa	fresa
aprieto	aprieto
guisante	guisante
Quiciera	quisiera
guigante	gigante
actristes	actrices
voy	voy
LLiero	hierro
bilingue	bilingüe
Lapizes	lápices
estraño	extrano
altobus	autobús
halla	haya
Jeolmativa	geometría
caimal	caimán
intalgime	intangible
elviboro	herbívoro
cicologo	psicólogo

FIGURE 2-9 Julisa's Spanish Spelling Sample

At the syllables and affixes level, the Spanish spelling inventory focuses on accents and affixes, assessed in words that require the use of accent marks. Finally, the derivational relations stage looks at the correct encoding of Latin or Greek elements in words based on meaning, when phonetic options are ambiguous' such as the inclusion of p in *psicólogo*.

The sample shown in Figure 2-9 is from Julisa, a third grader, in October of the school year. Julisa is in the middle within-word pattern, or *patrones*, level of spelling development—as can be seen in her spelling in Figure 2-9 and in the feature guide scoring in Figure 2-10. She has mastered all of the features in this inventory at the emergent and alphabetic levels involving the representation of sounds in words, including digraphs, blends, and pre-consonantal nasals. She begins to use but confuses letters that can represent the same sound, such as using a C for s in QUICIERA, and *ll* for the beginning sound in *hierro*. She also overgeneralizes the GUI as she attempts to spell *gigante*. The place to begin word study with Julisa is in the area of silent letters and those with interchangeable sounds (contrastes). She scored 4 out of 7 features at the early within-word pattern level, and 3 out of 5 features at the late within-word pattern level. Although she did write one accent mark on her spelling words, this generally seems to be a feature she is not regularly using yet, so the **acentos y afijos** level of study is currently above her instructional level.

Given the transparency of the Spanish orthographic system, Julisa will likely be able to decode just about any text at this point in her literacy development. Her need to consider pronunciation of unfamiliar, multisyllabic, accented words may break up the fluency and expressiveness of her reading in some cases. Most likely, the limits of her academic word knowledge and background experiences would be the greatest constraint on her reading level at this point.

Chinese Spelling Inventory

The Chinese Spelling Inventory in the Appendix (page 230) and feature guide (page 232) assess three types of spelling errors and two stages of orthographic development among elementary Chinese students from first through sixth grades. The spelling errors in this inventory assess students' orthographic knowledge in the first two stages. The first stage is referred to as the *phonological correspondence* stage (Shen & Bear, 2000). Chinese is a deep orthography that provides no obvious sound–script correspondences. Despite this lack of sound–script correspondence, first and second graders rely heavily on phonological strategies to write Chinese characters.

During the early part of this beginning phonological correspondence stage, students substitute based on pinyin, a phonetic alphabet designed to teach Mandarin. Their attempts in spelling are based on articulation, how the target and substitution are made in the mouth. In addition, students in this phonological correspondence stage substitute characters that sound alike, that is, homophonic characters. These characters sound alike but are not related in shape or meaning.

The second stage is the *parallel growth of graphic patterns and semantic components stage*. During this stage students gradually shift from predominantly phonologically-based strategies to graphemic and semantic strategies. At this stage, the children make graphic substitutions and use their knowledge of the configurations of characters to borrow elements, particularly radicals. In other words, they focus on the graphic patterns within characters by using radicals and characters that look alike. For the semantic strategies, they also make substitutions based on similarities in meaning that the characters denote. Their creation of characters that are phonetic-semantic compounds and

Feature Guide to the Spanish Spelling Inventory

Directions: Check the features that are present in each student's spelling. Check the spelling stage that summarizes the student's development. In the bottom row, total the features used correctly. Check the spelling stage that summarizes the student's development. Begin instruction at that stage with a focus on the types of features where the student missed two or more features in a column.

Student's Name: Julisa   Teacher: Brisley   Grade: 3   Date: October 15

ETAPAS DE LA ESCRITURA →	EMERGENTE TARDÍA		ALFABÉTICA TEMPRANA	ALFABÉTICA MEDIA	ALFABÉTICA TARDÍA	PATRONES TEMPRANA	PATRONES TARDÍA	ACENTOS Y AFIJOS	DERIVACIONES Y SUS RELACIONES		
Características →	Vocal Prominente	Consonante Prominente	Vocales/ Consonantes	Representación de Sonidos	Dígrafos, Sílabas Cerradas	Contrastes, Letras Mudas	Diptongos Homófonos	Tildes, Plurales, Afijos	Raíces	Puntos	Palabra
1. el	e √	l √								2	1
2. suma	u √	s √								2	1
3. pan	a √	p √								2	1
4. red			re √	d √						2	1
5. campos				os √	mp √					2	1
6. plancha				pl √	ch √					2	1
7. brincar			c (k) √	ar √	n √					2	1
8. fresa			sa √	fr √						2	1
9. aprieto		o √	o √	ie √						2	
10. guisante				ante √		gui √				2	
11. quisiera				iera √		qui √				2	
12. gigante			ga √		nt √	gi gu(i)				2	
13. actrices				tr √	ac √			ces tes		2	
14. voy						v √	oy √			2	1
15. hierro						h ll	ie √			1	
16. bilingüe						b √	üe ue			1	
17. lápices						c z		á a			
18. extraño				ñ √				ex es		1	
19. autobús								ú u	auto alto	1	
20. haya							h-y ll				
21. geometría								ía iva	metr mati		
22. caimán							ai √	án al		1	
23. intangible								ible ime	tang tal		
24. herbívoro								í i	herb elv		
25. psicólogo								có co	psi ci		
Totales	3 (3)	3 (3)	5 (5)	10 (10)	5 (5)	4 (7)	3 (5)	0 (9)	0 (5)	33 (52)	9 (25)

SPELLING STAGES:

□ TEMPRANA ☑ MEDIA □ TARDÍA

□ TEMPRANA
□ EMERGENTE
☑ ALFABÉTICA
□ PATRONES
□ ACENTOS Y AFIJOS
□ DERIVACIONES Y SUS RELACIONES

Words Spelled Correctly: 9/25
Feature Points: 32/52
Total   41/77

FIGURE 2-10   Feature Guide to the Spanish Spelling Inventory for Julisa's Spelling

their creation of other morphological, knowledge-based, but nonstandard characters indicate that as they learn the graphic components of characters, they understand the meaning of radicals and their derivatives.

Unlike English-speaking children who have more distinct experiences with the three layers of orthographies (sound, pattern, and meaning), after the initial phonological correspondence stage, Chinese-speaking children demonstrate parallel development of both graphemic and semantic knowledge throughout the rest of their elementary school years. This difference is due primarily to the logographic nature of the Chinese language in which the physical structure of the characters is much more complicated than in alphabetic writing.

The writing sample in Figure 2-11 is from a third grader who is in the transition period from the phonological correspondence stage to the parallel growth of graphic patterns and semantic components stage. In his writing, there is only one *pinyin* spelling (*lian* substitute for 连). We still see, however, quite a number of homophonic substitutions. Two substitutions in the writing sample are 那 (nà) substituted for 拿 (ná), and the other is a substitution of a homophonic character 因 (yin) and 洋 (yang) substituting for the word 营养 (yingyang). In this example, 那, 因, and 洋 have no graphic or meaning connections with 拿 and 营养; they are related only in pronunciation.

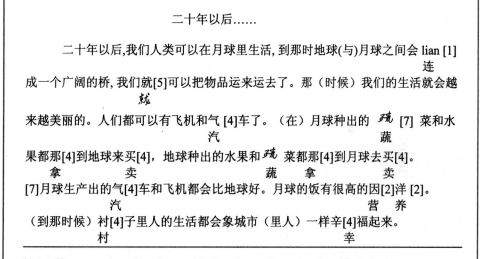

Note: The correct spelling is provided underneath each misspelled character. Characters in parentheses are interpolations to render the essay intelligible.
[1] = Pinyin substitution; [2] = homophonic character substitution; [4] = substitution of a sound- and shape-similar character; [5] = addition or deletion of a stroke; [7] = change in configuration.

English translation:

Twenty Years Later

Twenty years later, mankind can live on the moon. By that time, there will be a wide bridge connecting the earth with the moon. Thus we can move goods back and forth. At that time our lives will get more and more beautiful. Everyone will have an airplane and a car. Fruits and vegetables which are grown on the earth will be shipped to the moon for sale. The airplane and cars produced on the moon will be better than those on earth. The food on the moon will be highly nutritious.

At that time the life of village people will be as happy as the life of city people.

FIGURE 2-11 Chinese Writing Sample to a Prompt with Translation

In addition to these two types of phonological strategies, we also see the use of three types of graphemic strategies. One is the addition (or deletion) of a stroke, such as writing 㧊 for 就; the other is the change in configuration for the target character as when 蔬 is written as 疏. The third strategy is the substitution of a character that is similar in both sound and shape to the target character. In this writing, there were no semantic substitutions such as in the substitution of 气 (air) for 汽 (gas), 买 (buy) for 卖 (sold), and 辛 (hardship) for 幸 (lucky).

The Chinese Spelling Inventory presented in the Appendix on page 230, is used with native Chinese speakers learning to read Mandarin Chinese. This list is composed of 36 characters. Each of them is presented in a word and also a sentence context. The substitutions students make in spelling on this spelling inventory and in their writing provide powerful insights into their orthographic knowledge and their literacy development. Nine categories of spelling are scored.

A feature guide to score students' spelling of these 36 characters according to these nine error types is also presented in the Appendix (page 232). The errors are recorded underneath the type of error. In addition, the distribution of errors across grades 1 through 6 from a sample of 1,200 children provides an indication of how a student's errors may relate to the errors of children at these grade levels.

Korean Inventory

The Korean Developmental Spelling Inventory in the Appendix (page 233) assesses four stages of Korean spelling development. The Korean developmental continuum is similar to English spelling growth: children learn alphabetic features first, then pattern features, and meaning features later. In the first stage, *alphabetic*, Korean children learn beginning

Syllable Block System
How syllables are organized in Korean.

and ending consonants and short vowels. Because of the **syllable block system,** which helps children recognize syllable boundaries with ease, Korean children learn to spell alphabetic features in single and multisyllabic words in the alphabetic stage.

In the second stage, *alphabetic-meaning*, children begin spelling meaning features that are alphabetically consistent. Korean has a highly transparent spelling system, so that even some meaning features are alphabetic. For example, a child can spell derivational endings using letter-sound knowledge without fully understanding their grammatical functions.

In the *pattern* stage, children learn to spell long-vowel patterns, sound reduction patterns (for example, consonants ㅅ/s/, ㅆ/s'/, ㅈ/c/, ㅊ/c^h/, ㄷ/t/, ㅌ/t^h/ are pronounced as /t/ at the final position), and **coarticulation** patterns that occur in the syllable junctures (for example, in 웃기는/ut-k'i-nùn/, ㄱ/k/ changes its phoneme to ㄲ/k'/ because of the influence of ㅅ/t/). Also, children learn to alternate the endings of base words. Finally, children learn to spell compound consonant clusters that are not pronounced in modern Korean speech.

Coarticulation
The influence of one speech sound by a neighboring sound, for instance how the sound of t changes in the word *truck.*

The example in Figure 2-12 is by Hanna, a third grader, during the second half of the school year. Hanna is in the pattern stage of Korean spelling development. She has mastered all alphabetic and alphabetic-meaning stage features, beginning and ending consonants, short vowels, derivational endings, and the past-tense morpheme -*ed.* Her spellings showed that she is using but confusing long-vowel patterns, especially the vowels that do not represent their own syllable.

Hanna has not yet mastered the seven final consonant patterns she needs to understand sound reduction pattern of consonants at the final position. Out of five opportunities to spell each feature, Hanna correctly spelled the glide vowel pattern twice (2/5) and the seven final consonant patterns three times (3/5).

Hanna presented only limited knowledge in spelling features in the meaning stage. Although she occasionally spells some words correctly, she does not fully understand how to manipulate base words or derived words, or represent correct compound consonant clusters. Based on the spelling test, a teacher needs to work with Hanna on pattern features that she is currently using but confusing, the seven final consonant patterns and glide vowel patterns.

소홀히	(correct)
목청껏	(correct)
섞여	(correct)
곤란해	(correct)
어른거린다	(correct)
발돗움하고	발돋움하고
떼가	(correct)
틀었더니	(correct)
값비싼	(correct)
웃기는	(correct)
늠름하다	(correct)
덮쳤다	(correct)
엇저녁에	엊저녁에
놋숟가락을	(correct)
지새우며	(correct)
세베돈을	세뱃돈을
꾀매야	꿰매야
목내	목례
예깃거리가	얘깃거리가
왠만큼	웬만큼
쇠었다	(correct)
높다라게	높다랗게
갈라났다	(correct)
낳았다	나았다
빨갓더라	빨갛더라
하애지지	하얘지지
글히고	긁히고
억매여	얽매여
배앓이를	(correct)
읖조려	읊조려

FIGURE 2-12 Hanna's Korean Spelling Sample

Because the Korean spelling system is highly transparent, Hanna will be able to decode any Korean words that she is asked to read. She may occasionally pause or decode slowly when she encounters unfamiliar multisyllabic words, or unfamiliar compound consonant clusters. It is likely that Hanna needs to expand her vocabulary as well as background knowledge to thrive in reading comprehension in academic texts.

Assessments of Orthographic Knowledge in Primary Languages

Only three languages have been discussed, while there may be a dozen or more languages represented in your school. Guidelines to assess development at each spelling stage are presented here. Remarkably, certain reading and writing behaviors are characteristic of the different stages regardless of language. For example, disfluent, unexpressive oral reading and using a letter name strategy to spell are two characteristics of all beginning readers and letter name–alphabetic stage spellers. A broad statement such as this one holds true across languages, even as the specifics of literacy development in any given language will vary based on its characteristics. Each language has its own structure, which influences the range of when students' reading and spelling development is observed. For example, in Spanish, a highly phonetic language, reading rates of beginning readers are faster.

To assess orthographic knowledge, misspellings are classified as confusions at one of the three layers of word knowledge: sound/alphabet, pattern, or meaning. As observed in the developmental sequence in Figure 1-3 (page 10), the spelling stages follow these three layers. Key aspects of assessment at each stage are outlined to focus on the levels of development of your students in their primary languages.

Emergent

A continuum of development can be considered for this stage from scribbles to directionality, and an increasing use of letter-like forms and known letters that represent a message.

Assessments in the key areas of phonemic awareness, concept of word in print, alphabet knowledge, and phonological knowledge are essential to understand students' emergent literacy (Bear, Johnston, & Invernizzi, 2006). In assessments of letter and character recognition, listen for familiarity in students' accuracy and fluency.

Phonemic awareness in Spanish can be assessed using the pictures in the Appendix of this book. Here are four sets of Spanish words to contrast beginning sound discrimination: *I am going to say two words. Do they sound alike at the beginning? Pair words and ask if they sound alike: araña/sol?*

araña–spider	avión–airplane	árbol–tree
sol–sun	silla–chair	sopa–soup
bebé–baby	ballena–whale	barco–boat
escoba–broom	escritorio–desk	escuela–school

In addition, these pictures are used as cues for the words that students segment with tiles or chips. Students are shown how to push tiles forward for each sound that they hear in a word: *sol* (sun) has three sounds, and three chips from the pile are moved forward. *Pez* is another word that has three sounds and can be used to demonstrate sounds using chips. The Appendix provides a list of words in five languages for the pictures in this book that can be used to assess phonemic awareness (pp. 323–340).

Letter Name–Alphabetic

Assessment in this stage across languages focuses on phonological awareness, and misspellings are analyzed as they are based on articulation. For this reason, a phonetic feature guide for a language predicts the confusions students will make in other languages. There are many similarities in the sounds across languages and, therefore, there are similar confusions, particularly for consonant contrasts: *f/v, b/v* (Swan & Smith, 2001) In addition, **consonant blends** and **consonant digraphs** are often confused. For example, in Chinese the /z/ sound may be confused with the /zh/ sound in the same way that children in English at this stage spell the /sh/ sound with an S.

Another point of interest is the way vowels are articulated in other languages. A map of where the vowels are made in the mouth predicts the contrasts and substitutions students will make; vowels close to each other in position are those that are confused in spelling. A vowel chart for Spanish is presented in Chapter 5, and in the activities in Chapter 5 teachers see how students discriminate among vowel sounds as they match pictures of objects that share vowel sounds.

Look for letter name–alphabetic spellers to be beginning readers who are rather disfluent and unexpressive in their reading. They are acquiring a basic sight vocabulary. Reading rates will vary, but expect reading rates below 100 words per minute, and more like 40 to 80 words per minute in materials, depending on where the student is in this stage (early, middle, late) and the difficulty of the materials. (The rates in Chinese and similar nonalphabetic languages use other measures including syllables-per-second, which applies across all languages, and characters per minute.)

Within-Word Pattern

This is the time when abstract and complex patterns are studied. In some languages these complexities in pattern for single-syllable words are not extensive given the consistency of the letter–sound correspondences. Therefore, the within-word pattern stage is not a lengthy one for students in many languages, particularly the highly transparent writing systems. Often the features in focus are the accents in the language and the vowels connected to the letters *r, rr, l, ll*.

Students in this transitional reading stage sound fluent in their oral reading. They read with phrasing and expression in easy materials and they read polysyllabic words with fair ease. Reading rates are in the 100 to 120 words per minute range. Writing fluency is much improved, and in a 20-minute period students will write a paragraph or two with good punctuation.

Syllables and Affixes and Derivational Relations

In most cultures, these upper-level spelling stages are entered beginning in the intermediate grades. These stages are all about the meaning layers and the patterns that are created when syllables are added or deleted from words. The words in spelling inventories relate to syllable patterns and meaning connections. Shifts in sound occur when syllables are added to words without changes in spelling (*compete/competition*) and the parts that are added are prefixes and suffixes. If a language has unaccented syllables, then assess if they are spelled correctly even though the unaccented syllable can be ambiguous or hard to predict by sound. The role of grammar and syntax in spelling is seen in how students spell words with inflected morphemes. Often these inflected, final syllables are unaccented, and unaccented syllables are often misspelled in the syllables and affixes stage. For example,

---

Consonant Blends
Two- or three-letter consonant sequences such as *bl* or *str* that still retain the individual sounds.

Consonant Digraphs
Consonant digraphs are two consonants that represent one sound, such as *ch* or *th*.

in English, the sound of *-ed* varies, and the correct spelling will depend on the students' making the meaning connection between *-ed* and past tense endings.

ORAL LANGUAGE AND VOCABULARY LEARNING

Why do teachers need to know about students' oral language and vocabulary learning? Students who have well-developed oral languages and vocabularies in a home language have a strong base to build on when learning to read and write in English. In the area of word study, consider three reasons why the study of students' languages is important for effective word study:

1. We value what we learn about languages for what we learn about our students. Languages are fascinating! Languages are complex, they are ever changing, and they interact. Each language tells a story about its users (McCabe & Bliss, 2003).
2. There are similarities among languages. Languages share roots and sounds, and this can be seen in their common histories. These similarities can be heard among students.
3. There are differences among languages. Languages have different sounds, words, and ways of saying things. These differences are examined and clarified in word study activities.

Studying students' home languages is a way to travel and learn about other people in other cultures and countries. To get to know the English-language development of students, listen for their language use in their home languages.

Critical Questions About Students' Languages and Learning

To survey students' language use, and to plan *Talk With* language activities, consider the following questions and areas of inquiry. Key concepts in these questions are highlighted for emphasis. These questions open discussions among teachers serving the children in your class, and can be phrased in ways that will open discussions among students (Bear, 2005).

1. What *language* or languages other than English does the student *speak*?
2. *How often* does the student use the primary language? What *percentage* of the time is this primary language spoken?
3. How common is the language in *this school*?
4. What is the student's preferred language in which to view *television*?
5. *How long* has the student been *learning English*?
6. How would you describe the student's willingness to *start a conversation*? (Dickinson, McCabe, & Sprague, 2003, p. 558)
7. Is he or she *understandable* when speaking in English? (Dickinson, McCabe, & Sprague–2003, p. 558)
8. How often does the student use *varied vocabulary* or try out new words (words heard in stories or from teacher)? (Dickinson, McCabe, & Sprague, 2003, p. 558)
9. Does the student speak in *connected phrases*?
10. Is the student *expressive* in his or her speech?
11. Are there sounds in English that you notice are difficult for the student to *pronounce*?
12. How many years did the student receive *formal education* in the home language?
13. What is the level of *literacy development* of the student in the home language?
14. Does the student *read text* in the *home language* with accuracy, fluency, and expression?
15. Does the student use the *home language* for *writing* in classroom activities?
16. In writing, does the student *blend* the home language with English?

These questions explore students' language experiences in their home language. Go over these questions with the students' other teachers and parents.

A few of these 16 questions survey students' educational experiences. The students who have had educational experiences in any language bring academic vocabularies, knowledge of school processes, and information to the literacy table about how and why people read and study words.

Levels of Proficiency and Formal Tests of Oral Language

In most school districts, students' language development is assessed. For example, using the levels of oral proficiency described in Table 2-3, students in the first two levels would receive support services. (Zehler, Fleischman, Hopstock, Stephenson, Pendzick, & Sapru, 2003, p. 40).

Several formal and standardized tests of oral language are available in English and Spanish, and most districts have a common assessment they use with English learners. Some of these tests are scored to give an indication of how a student's performance compares with a national sample. Additional tests are presented in students' primary languages, although few have been standardized. This is a growing area of study and development, and new tests should become available each year.

A number of professional resources review these tests including the *Handbook of English Language Proficiency Tests* (EAC West, 1995), *Handbook of Spanish Language Proficiency Tests* (EAC West, 1996), *Resources About Assessment and Accountability for ELLs* (NCELA, and 2006), and *State Assessment Policy and Practice for English Language Learners* (Rivera & Collum, 2006).

Most language tests involve a combination of subtests that examine the speaking and listening domains: *listening comprehension, vocabulary, sentence repetition, story retelling,* and *verbal analogies*. Tape recordings are played for the oral language measures. Several of these language assessments include reading and writing in subtests that include *letter identification, word recognition, reading comprehension, writing through dictation for mechanics, spelling, usage, grammar,* and *handwriting*.

TABLE 2-3	Levels of Oral Proficiency
Levels of Oral Proficiency in English	**Description**
Emergent/early receptive language	Very little or no understanding of oral English; may try to communicate in primary language or with body language and one- to two-word phrases
Beginning	Beginning proficiency, limited understanding of oral and English language, amount of receptive and expressive verb tense; phrasal talking
Early intermediate	Advanced beginning, limited proficiency, repertoire, and vocabulary; conversationally fluent phrasally and moderately expressive; limited academic knowledge means less verbal or written fluency
Intermediate	Intermediate proficiency, large receptive vocabulary, most verb tenses used correctly, basic vocabulary for conversation in place; most fundamental academic terms are known and used; academic and specialized vocabulary is limited and oral and written expression lack complex sentence structures
Advanced	High level of proficiency, academic, content knowledge, and syntax close to proficiency of monolingual English speakers
Comments	

Source: Adapted from Zehler, Fleischman, Hopstock, Stephenson, Pendzick, & Sapru, September 2003, page 40.

Talking with Families

Getting to know students' families is the best way to understand their literacy background. In whole-class meetings with parents, teachers can provide an overview of development and families can view books and word study materials arranged by developmental levels. During this meeting, students can take their families on a room tour and follow a checklist of areas to visit. This meeting can often lay a foundation for individual meetings.

English-language development specialists help schedule individual meetings with families of entering children to find out about the child's language learning and talk about translation services. If possible, the person who will translate contacts the parents prior to the meeting to let them know that she or he will be there, that they may bring any information about the child's learning and development, and to ask if the parents have any questions. In the meeting, parents are asked to discuss their child's educational experiences and share any samples they may have brought. This is a good time to ask parents a few questions about language and literacy at home. Along with introducing the curriculum and school materials, students' instructional levels are discussed. Using the developmental chart from Chapter 1, children are identified along the continuum. Materials used in whole-class and small-group activities at each developmental level are on display. The students' writing samples, current reading materials, and other work are exhibited so that parents see what their children are learning.

An important step is to ask parents what their goals are for their children's learning. Teachers should take careful notes, and repeat back what they hear the parents say. At the end of the meeting, teachers have information about students' experiences and interests. Teachers can introduce and give parents samples of their children's writing, a book to read, and a word study game to play at home. They can also explain that when children come home with materials they have usually done the activity at school and are now practicing it. Show parents how to be involved in listening, talking about favorite pictures, or playing or timing the word study game.

3

Word Study Organization with English Learners

Sheltered Instructional Approaches
Ways to present lessons so they are more easily understood by students learning English, such as using pictures and objects, clarifying language, and frequently checking for understanding.

Rachel teaches a second-grade class that is alive with students from a variety of language backgrounds. Her students receive their instruction in English, and she uses **sheltered instructional approaches** to support their learning. Rachel has found that traditional spelling activities do not seem to help her English learners understand the patterns and organization of the English writing system. Her students memorize individual words, but do not generalize what they learn to their reading and writing. Their reading of early second-grade materials is for the most part accurate, but they do not read with adequate comprehension. Their oral reading generally meets the district standard for fluency, but is not particularly expressive, even in easy reading materials.

After learning about word study and implementing the Elementary Spelling Inventory (see Chapter 2), Rachel gained insights into her students' understanding of how words work in English. She began to see that the strategies her students use in their writing reflect their developmental level, and that students from language backgrounds other than English also use what they know from their home languages to represent words they are learning.

From her student Marco's spelling inventory, Rachel discovered that he was in the mid- to late-letter name–alphabetic stage of development. He spelled *ship* as SHEP, *when* as WEN, and *lump* as LUBP. When it came to words with long-vowel patterns, Marco spelled *train* as TRANE, *place* as PLEAS, and *float* as FLEUTE. Marco's guessing behaviors were probably related to being "in over his head"; he knew that some sounds required two vowels, but didn't have the specific knowledge to represent all of them yet.

As a teacher who has worked with English learners, Rachel was pleased to find out that word study involves a set of active and collaborative learning opportunities for students. She knows that such activities support students as they learn challenging material in a new language. Based on the developmental spelling assessment, Rachel assigned Marco to a word study group with four other students at a similar level. In the teacher-guided portion of one recent lesson, Rachel introduced a sort that compared "ump" and "amp" word families. Rachel began with a small-group discussion, in which she modeled the sort and took time to talk about some of the vocabulary that was new to her students—in this case the words *champ, clamp, pump,* and *plump.* She asked if anyone knew the meanings, supplied her own definitions, and used the words in sentences. Students then divided into pairs to sort their word cards together. They were encouraged to share what they knew about the words and to question and converse as they sorted. They were also asked to use some of the words in sentences to demonstrate their understanding of word meanings.

TYPES OF SORTING FOR ENGLISH LEARNERS

In the developmental chapters to follow, you will find specific sorts of each of the following kinds, all with detailed directions to use with your students. English-language learners benefit from the same kinds of sorts that monolingual English speakers do in the classroom:

- Sound sorts
- Pattern sorts
- Concept or meaning sorts
- Variations on these.

Sound Sorts

Sound sorts require students to compare commonalities and differences in what they hear in a word. For example, a simple sound sort may ask students to sort pictures by their beginning sounds. At a more advanced level, they can focus on the number and stress of syllables (for example, the reduced vowel sound in the middle of *composition* when a suffix is added to *compose*). Sound sorts provide an excellent way to build on the commonalities of sounds between a student's home language and English. Later, sound sorts focus on the specific sounds in English that may not be present in a student's home language, such as an sh/ch sort for Spanish speakers. Many examples of sound sorts that build on or highlight differences among various primary languages and English are presented throughout the next four chapters of this book.

Pattern Sorts

Students at various developmental levels look to the visual representation of letter groups to understand patterns in the writing system. Pattern sorts are introduced with short and long vowels, and later include the ways syllables combine to form closed and open syllables (*hop/hopping, hope/hoping*). In these sorts, students begin with the sound and then explore the visual patterns in their sorts. English learners may find the visual sorting of words easier than hearing differences in the speech sounds. It is important to systematically introduce English learners to the common spelling patterns of English; students who speak and read highly alphabetic first languages may need extra support in transitioning to the deep and complex nature of English orthography.

Concept or Meaning Sorts

Meaning sorts may involve clustering words or pictures based on concepts, or sorting words that have a meaning–spelling relationship. For example, pictures can be sorted into mammals, birds, and reptiles using any language. Concept sorts using pictures or objects are wonderful formats for English learners to gain vocabulary, especially when students are paired with English speakers who can supply English labels. Spelling–meaning sorts allow students at the advanced levels from a variety of primary languages to look for common roots between their home language and English (see Chapter 7 for more examples).

Variations of Sorts

There are a variety of ways to conduct sound, pattern, and concept sorts, including these:

- Teacher-directed word sorts
- Student-centered sorts
- Guess my category sorts

- Partner sorts
- Writing sorts
- Word hunts
- Picture hunts
- Brainstorming
- Repeated individual sorts
- Speed sorts
- Draw and label/cut and paste sorts.

What special considerations will be important as you plan variations of sorts for English learners? A few suggestions follow.

Teacher-Directed Word Sorts

These sorts are essential in introductory word study lessons for students with limited English skills. Teachers set up categories with key words, explicitly stating why each picture or word belongs in each category. English learners rely on the guidance and visual model that a demonstration provides. In seeing you sort, they learn more about the key words and their properties. It is critical that English learners know the names and pronunciation of the key words or pictures used in the sorts. This is the place for teachers to go over unfamiliar words meanings.

Student-Centered Sorts

In a student-centered or open-ended sort, students are given pictures or words and asked to create their own categories. Teachers can use these sorts to assess what students are learning about how words work. English learners can show what they know. They control the pace of the demonstration, and they have props in the form of the words or pictures as they explain why they sorted the way they did. Even if English learners do not yet have the specific English vocabulary to clearly articulate their thinking, you must find ways for students to explain their sorts—perhaps through peer translators or by writing down the titles of their categories in their home language.

Guess My Category Sorts

In this activity, the teacher demonstrates a sort without labeling the categories. Because pictures are a good bridge for conceptual understanding for English learners, it is important to start with picture sorts and check with your students frequently to see that they are following the guessing game. Can they identify which category a new picture should go into? Can they express verbally, draw, or act out what makes each category unique? Checking for understanding with English learners will guide your pacing, and will also allow you to know when guess my category word sorts may be appropriate.

Partner Sorts

Partner sorts are particularly important for students learning English because of the language support they can provide. Students are paired with a partner who provides the English label or who can explain the meaning of words. Partners can work together to sort pictures or words for additional practice.

Writing Sorts

These sorts require students to write the focus words in columns. No-peeking sorts require students to write the focus words without the visual support of word cards.

One partner calls out the words while the other writes them into categories. Save no-peeking writing sorts for features that are well known to English learners, and use these writing sorts as opportunities for informal assessment in a low-pressure environment. Always model the correct spelling visually after each word so that students can self-correct.

Word Hunts and Picture Hunts

These variations of sorts are excellent ways for students to look through books, magazines, and environmental print for the features they are studying. For English learners, it is important to be clear whether they are searching for a visual pattern or a sound. For example, a group of students in a second-grade classroom recently went on a word hunt for words that made the long **e** sound, such as those they had been sorting in *ee/ea/e_e* patterns. In addition to words like *tree, meat,* and *Pete,* José's list included *bread* and *dead.* José was searching for the visual pattern but did not have enough familiarity with the spoken versions of the words to differentiate the vowel sounds in these words. *Bread* and *dead* then become good oddballs to talk about.

Working with partners and asking students to say words aloud are ways to support English learners in word hunts. The printed materials that are available should have many familiar words for students to hunt through. Sometimes students search for words that are too difficult for them; they want to memorize words and are competent in memorizing unrelated materials. Arrange for students to hunt for pictures and words by sounds and patterns that are at their developmental levels.

Brainstorming

Brainstorming involves thinking up as many examples as possible. This may be one of the most difficult tasks for English learners to do because it requires a broad familiarity with oral and written words. Create small groups that include students from different levels of English proficiency, including, if possible, students who can translate for the most limited speakers. Write down brainstormed lists on charts that students can refer to in the future. Encourage English learners to copy or word process brainstormed lists into a personal word study notebook for future reference.

Repeated Individual Sorts and Speed Sorts

Provide many opportunities for students to repeat sorts until they can do them fluidly. This builds confidence and an expectation of mastery for student and teacher alike. These activities help students gain fluency and automaticity in their word work. It is as critical that English-language learners be expected to achieve at this level of individual performance as it is for monolingual students. Take a step back when sorts are too laborious for students—what is the highest level at which they were fluent and automatic?

Draw and Label/Cut and Paste Sorts

These sorts are great ways to help English learners develop vocabulary as they learn a spelling or phonics concept. When students draw a picture, they demonstrate whether they understand the principle being studied, and also show teachers their range of vocabulary. Cut and paste sorts give students a picture that will anchor a new vocabulary word. Encourage students to label pictures from these sorts with their names, and then create their own picture dictionaries for future use. This picture–word reference is a comforting fallback as new words are learned.

How to Select Words for Sorting with English Learners

The ideas just listed bring up several important questions: Are picture sorts better than word sorts for English learners, and when should each be used? How much language do students need before they are ready for sorting? Here are some beginning suggestions to help you think about these questions.

Picture sorts provide a visual, meaning-based support to students, and offer a bridge to vocabulary learning. A student involved in a concept sort with pictures, such as sorting different kinds of animals, will be able to be successful without knowing the names of words in English. Recently in Mrs. Johnson's first-grade classroom, English learner Awa sorted her animal picture cards into groups. She had a group of sea animals, a group of furry animals, and a group of birds. She put animals that did not fit into these groups into a "leftover" category. Awa was able to explain the categories to her teacher using her limited English; however, she could not name all of the animal pictures. Mrs. Johnson encouraged her to say the names of the animals she knew, if not in English, then using her home language. Before completing the conversation, Mrs. Johnson practiced saying the names of three animals that Awa didn't know from her picture cards—shark, bear, and rabbit. She did not want to overload her with too many words at once, but wanted to use the teachable moment to reinforce Awa's developing vocabulary with some key words. This example shows the useful bridge that concept sorts with pictures can play to help English learners become familiar with sorting procedures, use thinking skills, and learn new words in English in the process.

Sound sorts using pictures provide similar visual support for English learners. Because a student needs to know the name of the picture in order to sort it correctly, however, the task is more language driven. For example, kindergartener Alfredo is sorting picture cards by beginning sounds *b, m, r,* and *s.* When he gets to a picture of a *seal,* he doesn't know where it goes, because he doesn't know its name. He has several options: He can set the picture card aside for the time being, he can ask a schoolmate or teacher what the name is, or he can sort it based on his home language. The Spanish name for *seal,* "foca," does not help Alfredo sort the picture into the given letter-sound categories, so in this case he sets the picture aside. If too many pictures are unknown to Alfredo, he will not get the practice he needs sorting sounds, and the task may become frustrating for him. In that case, it would be more effective for him to be part of a structured lesson where the vocabulary is introduced at the same time.

Teachers may also consider adding pictures that have the same beginning sounds as in a student's home language, and allowing students to sort these pictures in the given categories. For example, if Alfredo had pictures of *sandía* (watermelon), *mesa* (table), or *ballena* (whale), he could add those to the beginning sound picture sort he was doing in English without the same vocabulary challenge. As Alfredo's vocabulary grows in English, he will rely less and less on the labels for words in Spanish to complete his sorts.

Word sorts reinforce visual spelling patterns, but do not necessarily teach vocabulary on their own. It is important that English learners say the sorting words aloud as they go; this ensures that students connect spelling patterns to what they hear in spoken words. Guided sorting with teachers and sorting with a partner or in heterogeneous language groups allow students to explore word meanings. Encourage English learners to ask questions all the time!

To address our previous questions, at the early stages of language learning, picture sorts are more appropriate for English learners. They create a meaning bridge to conceptual learning in a new language. As more vocabulary-dependent sorting is introduced, take care to support students' vocabulary knowledge by using common pictures and teaching vocabulary within the lesson. When moving on to word sorts, ensure that students are making the oral–written language connection by saying words out loud. This should happen throughout the sort, and will be reinforced when students "read" their sort out loud to a teacher after they have finished. When they do not know the

Three Steps to consider with English learners when sorting on their own:
1. Set unknown pictures and words aside, and return to them with assistance.
2. Ask a schoolmate.
3. Use words from the student's home language to sort.

meaning of a word, students refer to picture dictionaries or people for reference. Students will find it helpful to know that it is expected and valued for them to ask about words they do not understand or are having trouble pronouncing.

How much English do students need to be successful in sorting? Concept sorts with pictures or objects are the least demanding in terms of English language skills, and can be good vocabulary learning activities. Picture sorts for sounds require students to know the names of enough of the pictures to demonstrate the sound relationship being sorted. Sound–picture sorts can also be conducted in the student's home language as a bridge to English literacy. Use the list of picture words in other languages found in the Appendix (page 323) to create sound sorts that you would like the student to eventually do in English. Start simply with several words in a student's home language (for example, in Spanish, S: *sol, seis, suéter, silla*; M: *mano, muñeca, mapa, mitón*). After modeling the sort, introduce some English words that would fit in, such as *soap, saw,* and *moon*. Certain Spanish words can even be translated as cognates, related in spelling and sound across languages, such as *suéter/sweater, seis/six, mapa/map,* and *mitón/mitten*. This may help students remember the English words they are learning.

To be effective, word sorts require students to know how to read, say, and attach meaning to words being sorted. When students are learning vocabulary at the same time as they are learning spelling patterns in sorts, it is crucial to provide them with built-in vocabulary instruction for the words they are working with, as well as access to resource people who will respond to their pronunciation and meaning questions. This allows word study to become a process of integrated learning for spelling, phonics, and vocabulary.

WORD STUDY INSTRUCTION IN MULTILINGUAL CLASSROOM SETTINGS

All students in your classroom will profit from participating in word study. Whether you teach in an English immersion classroom or another type of program, you will want to arrange a management system for your literacy instruction that allows you to meet with small groups of students in word study on a regular basis. Consider a student's developmental level in forming these groups, but also take into account whether or not a student is an English learner who needs additional language support. At certain times it will be important to have heterogeneous language groups so that you have a range of oral proficiency in your small groups; at other times you will want to group students who need the most help in their oral English skills together to give them focused support.

Students benefit from learning the procedures you expect them to use in word study activities. These include how students get access to materials; when they work in a teacher-guided group and when they work independently; how they collaborate with peers; and common procedures for sorts, games, and other literacy activities. These processes can be described and practiced until the routines are well established. In the next section, a variety of support strategies are outlined that apply to many multilingual classroom situations.

Supportive Strategies for Literacy Instruction

Many challenges exist for students learning to read and write in a new language. For this reason, language learners need effective teachers and well-thought-out instruction in literacy. Sheltered classroom techniques include making the content as understandable as possible through language modification and the use of **realia,** frequent clarification, appropriate questioning strategies, and formative assessment of student errors (Diaz-Rico & Weed, 2002). Research in the field of diverse learners has found that a core

Realia
Real objects and hands-on materials.

set of teaching practices helps create successful learning for all students, including language-minority students (Center for Research on Education, Diversity and Excellence, 2004). Other studies describe the benefits of bilingual instruction and the use of specific instructional strategies for English learners (cf. August & Shanahan, 2006; Bialystok, Luk, & Kwan, 2005; Cummins, Chow, & Schecter, 2006; deJong & Harper, 2005; Genesee, Lindholm-Leary, Saunders, & Christian, 2005; Gersten & Jímenez, 1998; Slavin & Cheung, 2005).

When the research is taken as a whole, findings can be organized around several general principles. Instruction for English-language learners is most effective

- When it is explicit and systematic
- When it allows students to interact with others in their learning community
- When it helps students make connections to what they already know
- When students actively construct knowledge.

After reading the following overview of support strategies for English learners, note that Table 3-1 describes specific examples of how these ideas relate to word study instruction.

Explicit and Systematic Instruction

Explicit and systematic instruction makes it easier for English learners to understand the material and teachers' expectations for reading and writing tasks. Hearing something once orally likely will not be sufficient for learners of a new language to "get it." Think back to a time when you may have been immersed in a language that you did not understand well, perhaps on a trip or in a language class. What did you do to help yourself get a handle on the information coming your way? Did you look for picture clues? Ask someone to tell you again slowly? Look for a map or other graphic to orient you? English learners in our classrooms grasp for the same kinds of support. Here are some ways that teachers provide clear and explicit instruction:

- *Modeling* involves doing an example while students watch. Whatever you are making or doing in class can be physically demonstrated to provide multisensory input for students.
- *Contextualization* involves clarifying instruction with real-life objects, "being there" experiences, expressive body language, role playing, puppets, visual depictions, and so on. When teachers contextualize lessons, students have a better chance to connect an activity to "real life."
- *Metacognition* occurs when people become conscious of, and articulate, the in-the-head processes they are using during a literacy event. It can be seen as "thinking out loud."
- *Instructional level teaching* involves matching the classroom tasks and materials to the background knowledge and developmental level of individual students. Instruction should not be above students' heads, not too easy, but rather, "just right"—challenging but doable.
- *Modifying language* is what teachers do when they make their instructional language more comprehensible to English learners, who are often overwhelmed by the fast and complex stream of words coming their way. Teachers can help alleviate this overload by doing several simple but important things: Monitor the speed of their talk, clearly articulate words, face the listener, emphasize key words, and avoid idioms such as "chewed her out," which can be very confusing to new language learners.
- *Simple to complex support* involves breaking down tasks into sequential steps, or trying a scaled-down example first. The goal is to help students move from an easy format to progressively more complex versions.

- *Clustering* is the strategy of putting together pieces of information that go together. It may also involve chunking activities into sections so that students can work through them piece by piece.
- *Guided practice* happens when the teacher leads students in applying a skill or concept that has already been introduced. The teacher oversees, gives feedback, and reinforces the students in their application of the new skill.

Engaging in a Learning Community

It is not enough for students to receive clear and understandable instruction. Students also need to use what they are learning with others, and feel confident that they are valued members of their learning community. If students get the feeling they are not expected to learn, or that the new knowledge is not useful with others, they are less likely to be successful. The following support strategies build on the foundation that students are social beings who strive to have successful personal interactions:

- *Low-anxiety environment* means enabling interactions and learning activities that are not stressful, but rather, allow for students to make mistakes or discuss things they are not sure about. This leads to an atmosphere where deeper thinking flourishes and students do not need to have the "right answer" in order to speak up.
- *Student-to-student interactions* help build a positive learning community as students use oral and written language with peers in partnerships, cooperative learning teams, and other small-group activities.
- *Holding positive expectations for students* is a belief that teachers have about their students' learning potential. It is communicated by what teachers say, and what they do. Phrases that begin with "They don't have . . . ," "They didn't get . . . ," and "They can't . . ." communicate a teacher's lack of faith in students' abilities and possibilities. On the other hand, teachers who view students as being on a developmental continuum assess students to find out what their current knowledge base is and then plan appropriate next steps for instruction.
- *Student-to-teacher connections* are another bond in the learning community. Teachers who build strong personal connections with students, and work persistently with students who do not learn the first time through, help them to succeed.

Highlighting Connections

When students see how new knowledge fits into their current understanding of the world, learning takes root most effectively. English learners bring a home language, experiences with literacy activities, and personal, academic, and cultural experiences with them to the classroom. Instruction that connects with students' knowledge base and shows students the "big picture" of how academic information interrelates is described next:

- *Whole to part to whole* instruction involves giving students the big picture first, such as using a whole piece of text (book, poem, song, and so on). Next, a component or skill is pulled out for a mini-lesson or practice. Afterwards, the skill is applied in context again.
- *Oral and written language connections* are important to highlight for students. Use any occasion you can to help students see the correspondence between what they say or hear and how it is written in English. The alphabetic nature of written language will become more apparent to students the more they engage with it.
- *Schema building* helps students see where new information fits into their "mental file cabinet." Teachers encourage this when they point out relationships between things, instead of studying isolated bits that do not seem connected.
- *Graphic organizers* are visual tools to help organize our thinking with symbols or designs. They support students in seeing conceptual relations, and their use by students in the classroom also lets teachers know if they understand the big picture.

- *Connections to personal experience* help students relate a concept, idea, or skill to something that happened in their lives or in the classroom community. This emotional link aids learning.
- *Connect to background knowledge* by finding something a student knows that relates to the new information being learned. This may involve building on academic knowledge in a student's home language, or making a connection to information that has been previously learned.

Active Construction of Knowledge

English learners who are engaged in and contributing to the learning process will remember more, be able to apply their learning, and show teachers if and where confusions exist. The following support strategies help teachers provide active learning opportunities for their students:

- *Modified questioning strategies* involve using a range of questions in the classroom that allow all students, even those with very limited English language skills, to respond. Questions can be adapted so that a student response is pointing, a yes or no response, a one- to two-word response, a sentence response, or an open-ended, hypothetical response.
- *Hands-on activities* involve manipulating learning materials, creating things, going on field trips, and doing experiments or simulations. Hands-on activities provide nonverbal support for students to learn and demonstrate their growing understanding.
- *Purposeful activities* are those that students can apply immediately in their lives to solve a problem or accomplish a task.
- *Total physical response* is when students learn by moving, touching, pointing, and role playing. It allows the body to reinforce new learning.
- *Using music* helps students remember a skill or concept by putting a tune or rhythmic pattern to it. Students actively participate by chanting, singing, clapping, or keeping the beat.
- *Involve multiple intelligences* by helping students learn concepts and practice them through a variety of activities such as writing, sharing, singing, listening, counting, graphing, moving, doing, speaking, drawing, constructing, and so on.
- *Time for children to talk* allows for participation that goes beyond simply listening to information or reading about it. It helps students actively engage with a topic and share their understandings with others, linking the content to the individual and group's personal experiences.

Table 3-1 lays out the four key strands of English-learner support, and provides sample word study applications for each strategy.

ORGANIZATION OF WORD STUDY INSTRUCTION

How does word study work in a multilingual classroom? What kinds of material and resources are needed? What might the daily and weekly schedule look like? This section addresses these issues for classrooms with English learners.

Materials

Word study involves the use of many hands-on materials for sorts, games, and other activities. In classrooms with students from diverse languages and background literacy experiences, the range of developmental levels may be quite wide. For instance,

TABLE 3-1 — Strategies to Support English Learners

1. Explicit and Systematic Instruction

Strategy	Example Word Study Applications
Modeling	Teachers model developmental writing so that students feel comfortable writing in the best way they know how. New sorts may be modeled to highlight a pattern that will be prominent in upcoming studies.
Contextualization	Real objects are used often in a concept sort. A common stimulus or experience is used as the basis for a group experience story.
Metacognition	"Think out loud" with students about writing conventions and spelling as chart-sized messages are created in a group setting.
Instructional level teaching	A developmental spelling inventory is used to assess students' word knowledge, and to place them in word study activities at the appropriate developmental level.
Modified language	Vocabulary development is explicitly integrated into word study activities for English learners. In addition, students are encouraged to select out known from unknown words in the sorts they are doing.
Simple to complex	Students build on their growing orthographic knowledge through the developmental levels, from the simplest level of sound, through pattern, and then the complex meaning layer.
Clustering	Word study activities involve consistent procedures and regular activities that can be clustered and taught to students for their ongoing use. Procedures might be shared for how to do a word sort or word hunt, what to write up in a word study notebook, sorting with a partner, and so on.
Guided practice	Many word study sorts and lessons, especially those that involve a new concept or pattern, involve teacher guidance and informal assessment. Students are asked to explain their thinking for decisions made in the sorting process and this provides an opportunity for teachers to talk through misconceptions with them.

2. Engaging in a Learning Community

Strategy	Example Word Study Applications
Low-anxiety environment	Games, songs, and chants are integrated into word study activities. Students are encouraged to share ideas.
Student-to-student interactions	Word study provides numerous opportunities for student interactions such as sorting with a partner, playing games in a small group, going on a word hunt together, and brainstorming word derivations with others.
Positive expectations	Effective word study teachers provide rigorous instruction and hold high expectations for student accomplishment at their developmental levels. All students, including English learners, are expected to become accurate, fluent, and automatic in their sorting.
Student-to-teacher connections	Opportunities for student-to-teacher interactions in word study include individualized writing conferences, using student dictations for rereading, and structuring extra time for dialogue to communicate students' understanding of spelling patterns.

3. Highlighting Connections

Strategy	Example Word Study Applications
Whole to part to whole	Start with a whole piece of connected text to demonstrate a spelling pattern. Next pull out the pattern of focus for word work. Finally, look for the pattern in real-life contexts through word hunts, etc.
Oral and written language	Connect oral and written language in word study activities through no-peeking sorts, story dictations, and vocabulary notebooks.

(continued)

TABLE 3-1	(continued)

3. Highlighting Connections

Strategy	Example Word Study Applications
Schema building	Word study helps students build schema by seeing how word families, patterns, and morphemes unite words into categories.
Graphic organizers	Organizing like words in columns in word study notebooks and sorts, classifying words into Venn diagrams, and analyzing words by semantic features are some examples of how graphic organizers are used in word study.
Personal experiences	Investigate words of personal interest and meaning, use the names of children in class for letter and sound learning, and create personal readers of dictated stories to help students build on their personal experience in word study activities.
Background knowledge	Word study builds on background knowledge when words and pictures for sorts are familiar to students, and are connected to vocabulary in their home language. Look for cognates between students' home languages and English, and compare word roots and affixes to those in students' home languages.

4. Active Construction of Knowledge

Strategy	Example Word Study Applications
Modified questioning strategies	Begin with concept sorts that do not require the names of specific words. Move to simple sorts that compare "words that do" with "words that don't." Allow students to explain their word study decisions in their home language.
Hands-on activities	Sorts, games of all types, word hunts, and language experience activities make word study full of hands-on activities.
Purposeful activities	Write letters, cards, and lists for families, friends, and the community. Connect word study to lots of reading and writing practice.
Total physical response	Word study may be expanded to involve physical actions such as people sorting, acting out spelling patterns with movements, or demonstrating word relationships through physical lineups.
Using music	Songs, chants, rhymes, and rhythms are integrated throughout word study to help understand and remember patterns.
Multiple intelligences	Word study activities encourage students to learn and practice concepts through writing, sharing, singing, listening, counting, graphing, moving, doing, speaking, drawing, and displaying.
Time to talk	Sorts and games may be played with partners and groups. Students discuss words and reflect on decisions they made while sorting.

fourth-grade teachers may have readers from the emergent through the advanced levels. In addition, teachers may have students who speak little to no English, those who are extremely knowledgeable in English, and many who fit somewhere in between on that continuum. Each of these groups will require a modification of instructional materials. What can you do to be prepared for these multiple needs? Here are some tips:

1. Make use of word study material that is already available. This book has many reproducible sorts, games, and activities for you to copy and put right to use, and you can find valuable reproducible resources in other *Words Their Way* products at **http://www.prenhall.com/bear.** In addition, your school's adopted reading or spelling program may include sorts that fit into this developmental model.

2. Gather nonconsumable materials for concept sorts that can be used for multiple purposes. Many educational publishers have picture dictionaries, picture card sets, and small collections of manipulatives that can be used in sorts. These materials are very versatile, and are quite helpful for extending English learners' vocabularies. Students can also go on "hunts" in magazines and newspapers to find pictures for sorts. Use these language-building resources over and over again for many sorts and games in your classroom.

3. Enlist parents, aides, older students, and other volunteers to put together the games and sorts from this book and the other word study resources. Games and sorts can be colored, cut out, glued onto file folders, and laminated for long-term use.

4. Have students learn how to make their own sorts as part of their word study lesson. If students are mature enough to quickly write the sorting words, they can create the cards to use in their lessons prior to the sorting session. This activity may even come to take the place of more traditional (and isolated) handwriting lessons.

Sound Board
A page with pictures and letters illustrating the sounds in English.

5. Make extensive use of the word study notebook as an ongoing reference book for students. Students' word study notebooks might include a **sound board** for the vowels and consonants in English, perhaps with space for notes about how the letters compare to the sounds in the students' home languages. Word study notebooks with English learners contain personal dictionaries of words students are learning in English, with translations of key vocabulary words. They are also a place for students to record the written version of sorts they have completed, and the lists of words they have found on word hunts. A well-developed word study notebook is a valuable resource for English learners to come back to over and over as they are cementing their familiarity with English words.

6. Maintain consistent procedures for where and how word study materials are stored, and teach students to oversee their care. File folder games are easily stored in a plastic tub that can be labeled or color coded so that students return materials to their proper place. A rotating leadership job in the class might be to straighten up word study materials at the end of the day or week. The more that students can take over these responsibilities, the easier the word study system will be to manage.

7. Begin collecting materials from the primary languages of students in your class. Books, flash cards, newspapers, and other print-related materials exist in a variety of languages—see the reference list in the Appendix (page 347) for some examples of where to find them. Having these materials available allows teachers and students to compare and contrast languages. If possible, create sorts for other languages using the picture vocabulary cards in this book (pages 243–276). Store these sorts in color-coded tubs for students to use to gain experience with word study activities.

Scheduling

Your schedule for word study activities will depend on many factors, including your grade level, the overarching structure of the school day, and how supplemental services for students are delivered. Most teachers, however, are able to set aside a literacy block of at least 90 minutes at the elementary grades to focus on literacy-related activities. On a daily basis, your schedule may look something like this:

- Welcome/school business: 5–10 minutes
- Transitional independent activity: 10 minutes
- Preview of literacy block activities: 5–10 minutes
- Literacy block (teacher-guided and independent small-group activities): 90 minutes.

Set aside time for listening to and reading a variety of literature and expository texts throughout the day according to your specific schedule.

Word study activities fit well into the literacy block either as a portion of the time or integrated into your group rotations. A sample rotation chart (Table 3-2) and procedures for working with small groups are discussed later in this chapter. In the basic progression of word study lessons over the course of a week, you and your students will:

- Introduce the sort
- Practice the sort and write it
- Work with partners on no-peeking and writing sorts
- Hunt for words (or pictures)
- Assess and play games.

To prepare English learners to be successful in the weekly progression of activities, arrange 5 to 10 minutes for a small-group preview of the vocabulary involved in the week's sorts on Monday. This could happen during the *transitional independent activity* time. Teachers will also need to provide ongoing support for English learners by checking in as frequently as possible throughout the week and providing language models to serve as resource people within lessons. The next section outlines some of the ways in which peers, volunteers, and school staff can be a part of the weekly word study schedule.

Structuring Interactions

In previous discussions in this book, we have noted the importance of socially mediated learning for English learners. Many aspects of learning a new language involve using language with others, and being able to practice and ask questions. Quiet seatwork is not often an effective technique for English learners' optimal growth! So, how do teachers structure productive word study interactions in the classroom? First let's consider possibilities for student-to-teacher or tutor interactions, then peer interactions within the classroom.

Student-to-Teacher (or Tutor) Interactions

Many elementary school teachers set up their language arts schedule around a concentrated block of instructional time of at least 90 minutes. In that typical arrangement, it is possible to structure three rotations of 30 minutes each. Once procedures for these rotations are well established, a teacher can meet with each group for 30 minutes every day, and in this way have a chance to interact with all students in the class. These groups are developmental, and while the teacher's main objective during this small-group time is to focus on instructional level reading with students, there should also be time for word study.

A variety of word study activities take place during the three literacy-block rotations, and the amount of word study that is included in the teacher-guided versus follow-up or center rotations may vary throughout the week (Table 3-2). For instance, on Monday, when the new sort of the week is introduced, teachers may spend 15 minutes of the 30-minute small-group time on a teacher-guided word sort. On Tuesday, when the word study sort is practiced, most of the time spent on word study will not be in the teacher-guided small group, but rather in the follow-up period for independent activities. On Friday, the weekly assessment can take place during the teacher-guided group, but games will likely occur during the center rotation.

In the model shown in Table 3-2, Group A requires the most teacher direction, and starts the week out with a teacher-guided lesson. While all of the groups meet with the teacher every day, Group C meets first with the teacher only on Wednesdays, so it is the group that should be most self-directed.

After a group has spent time with the teacher, the group moves on to an independent, seat activity. On some days this may mean writing out words for a sort, doing a word sort

TABLE 3-2	Possible Rotation Schedule for Three Groups A, B, and C														
Day of Week	Monday			Tuesday			Wednesday			Thursday			Friday		
Rotation #	1	2	3	1	2	3	1	2	3	1	2	3	1	2	3
Teacher-led group (circle)	A	B	C	B	C	A	C	A	B	A	B	C	B	C	A
Follow-up independent activities (seat)	B	C	A	C	A	B	A	B	C	B	C	A	C	A	B
Learning centers or workshops (center)	C	A	B	A	B	C	B	C	A	C	A	B	A	B	C

with a partner, reading or writing independently, and so on. During center times, students participate in learning activities that have been previewed ahead of time in the whole group, or they work on continuing projects. Examples of center activities are word study games, reading projects, listening to prerecorded stories, writing or creating books, and so on. Center activities will vary depending on the age and independence level of your students; it is helpful to set up consistent centers that students can come to do automatically.

While a literacy-block rotation schedule will ensure daily contact between the teacher and his or her students, it does require a lot of energy from a teacher who is managing it alone. Here are some thoughts on how to involve others to support your students during the literacy block:

1. Coordinate your literacy time with the support teachers at your school, and encourage these teachers to follow a "push-in" model of support services. Support staff can also pull English learners from center and seatwork activities to provide more directed language instruction.
2. Recruit volunteers from the parents in your class, your school's parent organization, or local community organizations. They can support students in their independent work or do one-on-one tutoring. These adults can run a center, and make the learning time even more productive. Adults with limited background in teaching will appreciate the consistency of becoming an expert at a specific center and running it each week.
3. Build a relationship with local colleges and universities that will send practicum students to your classroom.
4. Find a classroom of older students that can send cross-age tutors to your classroom on a regular basis during your literacy-block time. These could be upper-grade elementary, middle school, or high school students. Depending on the age level of your volunteers, they can run center projects, support students in their independent work, or do one-on-one literacy tutoring.

Peer Interactions

There are many ways to encourage students to share with and learn from each other during literacy time and other periods of the school day. This cooperation begins with an atmosphere of respect and helpfulness that is established and modeled by the teacher and other adults. The time a teacher spends in reinforcing positive interpersonal relations in the classroom will be repaid many times over by the productive learning atmosphere that is created. Consider the following collaborative structures for your students.

Flexible grouping. You will be working with small groups of students at similar developmental levels throughout the literacy-block time, so plan ways for flexible grouping when students are not at the teacher-guided group. As often as possible, make working groups heterogeneous by ability and language proficiency level so that students get to know each other and practice their English skills. Numerous opportunities for heterogeneous groupings are available in science, social studies, and thematic investigations; art, music, and other creative arts; physical education and life skills; and in language arts, in writer's workshops, in literature response groups, and during comprehension strategy instruction.

Proximal partners.   Create partnerships so that students have a "buddy" to practice with. These proximal partners can read to each other and work on interdisciplinary projects together. It is especially helpful for English learners if their buddy can provide a role model as a proficient English speaker. If you do not have enough language models to go around in your partnerships, it is often helpful to pair a more outgoing, but less proficient English speaker with a shyer, more proficient student. They will both learn from this balance of skills. Set procedures for how you expect partners to work. Demonstrate how they can be supportive without doing things for their partner; how they can ask questions instead of telling answers; how they can state things positively and not negatively when working together.

Integrating Word Study into the Language Arts Curriculum

Word study is an integral part of the essential literacy activities that are a part of each day in the classroom: *Read To, Read With, Write With, Word Study,* and *Talk With* (RRWWT). The literacy-block rotation schedule outlined in the preceding section includes word study activities as an integrated part of the language arts curriculum in both the teacher-guided and independent group activities. Word study and spelling activities should not be seen as isolated skills to be practiced independently; rather, they are in synchrony with reading and help inform a teacher's understanding of each student's literacy development. It is critical for English learners that the *Talk With* component of the essential literacy activities be consciously implemented in a word study program. Learning will gel and confusions will come to light when students have time to talk with teachers and peers.

How will teachers decide which skills to focus on in word study? The assessment process described in Chapter 2 will guide you as you begin. Once your developmental groups have been established, you will use regular, informal assessments, such as reviewing students' writing samples, and watching how students do in their sorting tasks to monitor their progress. Some teachers conduct weekly spelling assessments; if you do this, these lists should be individualized for the developmental levels of your small groups. It is very natural for the developmental groups you work with at the teacher table to need periodic readjustment, because students will vary in the pace of their learning. Once you know the word study features you will focus on in each group, remember to teach and reinforce unknown vocabulary for English learners. For example, a group that is examining long **a** patterns will need to know the meanings of *tale* and *tail, mane* and *main, made* and *maid,* and so on. Without the background vocabulary, this exercise will be confusing and esoteric to students.

What standards of accuracy should students be held accountable for in their writing, and what expectations should teachers have for how much editing to do with English-learning students? As with all students, English learners will need to be held accountable for those skills that they have mastered at their developmental level. For instance, students who are comfortable with putting beginning and ending sounds in the words they are writing should be expected to do that in their daily work. It would be inappropriate to hold these same students to accuracy in representing the vowel sounds. At times, however, English learners may have specific difficulty with English letter and sound representations that contrast with their home language. For example, a Spanish-speaking student, on occasion, may use the *r* to represent the sound of *d* in English. When students know a good number of sound–symbol correspondences, it is important to fine-tune and begin to hold expectations for accuracy even in areas of interlanguage confusions. Focused, supplemental instruction for students from specific language groups may be necessary to support this expectation.

At any developmental level, work that is to be published or presented in a public way should proceed through an editing process. The amount of time students invest in this process will depend on their skills and maturity level. Ask students to review and self-correct those items that they are generally able to manage at an independent level. Items that students are "using but confusing," or items at the students' **zone of proximal development (ZPD)** can be edited with teacher direction during a small-group lesson or writing conference. Writing errors that are beyond a student's developmental level can be corrected as needed by a teacher, but should not yet be the focus of lesson instruction.

Zone of Proximal Development
Students' instructional level: what they can do with some assistance.

Teaching Vocabulary

As has been noted throughout this chapter, vocabulary support and instruction are crucial challenges in the multilingual classroom. Without knowing the meaning of words, word study and other literacy tasks become abstract and confusing. Instead of helping students clarify how the orthography works, word study that is separated from comprehensible input creates disengagement and cements ill-founded understandings. Yet there are so many words to learn; how can enough vocabulary be taught to make word study meaningful? In each of the instructional chapters of this book, vocabulary instruction is integrated into the word study activities. Vocabulary instruction may look different at each developmental level, and for students of varying language proficiencies within a developmental level. For example, vocabulary instruction for an emergent reader who is 5 years old may look quite different than that for an emergent reader who is 15 years old and recently arrived in the United States. The following are some important ideas that extend throughout the stages.

- It takes multiple experiences with a word to learn it. An English-learning classroom needs to be print rich and full of formal and informal activities to practice language throughout the day.
- Some amount of preteaching of vocabulary will be necessary in word study lessons for English learners, and more will be needed for students with very limited proficiency. It is not efficient to wait for students' oral language to develop naturally before beginning literacy instruction—they will lose too much ground in the curriculum.
- It is important to focus on useful words, as opposed to those that students will rarely encounter or use. When an uncommon word is encountered in a text or word study lesson, it will probably be better to set it aside and focus instructional time on high-frequency words that students are likely to need on a regular basis.
- English learners need practice in saying words orally, matching them to their written versions, and using them in the context of conversations and writing.
- In word study, if a word is not known, students should learn to put the word to the side for the time being. This is an informal assessment that will help teachers set the vocabulary-learning agenda. It also communicates to the student that meaning is an integral part of the word study process.

Involving English-Learning Parents in Word Study

Most parents are interested in doing whatever they can to support their children's literacy learning in English. To encourage parents who do not speak English well, or who do not have literacy skills in English to participate in the classroom or to help with homework, teachers must scaffold this participation. Often it is necessary to send notes home in the students' home languages. It is also helpful to train students in class to show them what they can be practicing with their family at home.

Do not ask parents to teach new content to students. That can be confusing for all involved. Homework assignments should be practice, not instruction. Some do's for family involvement might include:

- *Do* encourage students to talk with families about what they are learning in school. They do not need to use English—more than likely, using English will severely limit the conversation—so they should be encouraged to use the home language.
- *Do* have students read their word study words to family members, demonstrate their sorts, and explain their reasoning.
- *Do* have students share the meanings of words in English, and ask their families to teach them how to say these words in their home language. For English learners, learning the translation of a word makes it easier to remember the meaning of a word.

TEN PRINCIPLES OF WORD STUDY INSTRUCTION WITH ENGLISH LEARNERS

Words Their Way (Bear, Invernizzi, Templeton, & Johnston, 2004) outlines 10 guiding principles for word study instruction (see Figure 3-1). In the following paragraphs, we have expanded on these principle to highlight issues of particular importance to English learners.

1. *Look for what students use but confuse.* As noted in the assessment procedures in Chapter 2, students' spellings give us information about their developmental understanding of the English writing system. For English learners, writing and spelling samples may also show how they are applying principles from the sound system, grammar, vocabulary, or orthography of their native language to their learning in English. For example, a Somali student who spells the long **i** in English by writing two **i**'s may be applying his or her knowledge of how this sound is written using Somali guidelines.

2. *A step backward is a step forward.* Sometimes students learning English are pushed too quickly in the curriculum without a firm understanding of the word study concept they are working with. At times, some students seem to suddenly forget the letter–sound correspondences of the short vowels as they move into studying the long vowels in English. Older students may attempt to memorize individual words without perceiving the principle or pattern these words represent. In both cases, it is important to take a step back to assess what the student truly has internalized about the English writing system. This understanding will be the solid ground on which to build more complex concepts. The lack of a firm foundation will lead to confusion and indecision at the higher levels of word study and reading.

1. Look for what students use but confuse.
2. A step backward is a step forward.
3. Use words students can read.
4. Compare words "that do" with words "that don't."
5. Sort by sound and sight.
6. Begin with obvious contrasts.
7. Don't hide exceptions.
8. Avoid rules.
9. Work for automaticity.
10. Return to meaningful texts.

FIGURE 3-1 Principles of Word Study

3. *Use words students can read.* It is important for word study to help students connect oral language to written language, and written words to match the concepts they represent. In this way, word study reinforces the language learning process. Because too many unknown words will turn the word study activity into an esoteric visual game, have students say words aloud as they sort. Encourage them to ask a partner if they do not know what a word means. Perhaps a few of these words can be incorporated into a vocabulary-learning lesson. English learners should be encouraged to set aside words they do not understand or cannot read.

Do not overstress pronunciation. If students consistently pronounce a sound in a nonstandard way, for example, pronouncing the **i** in *sit* as "seat," informal practice and refinement over time will be more effective than attempting to require students to hear a sound difference that does not exist in their dialect or language. Students will come to differentiate these sounds better as they encounter and discuss these features in words they hear and see in print and make the connection between oral writing. Wide reading will facilitate instruction in pronunciation as students begin to match spelling patterns with the slight sound differences they hear in oral language.

4. *Compare words "that do" with words "that don't."* As stressed earlier in this chapter, it is important for English learners to receive clear instruction and have many opportunities to test out their new learning. Comparing words "that do" with words "that don't" provides a simple contrast that supports students in seeing the "big idea" of an orthographic concept. When a teacher is not sure if students understand a certain word study pattern or the way words are contrasted in the two or three columns of a sort, it is a good idea to return to this most basic contrast and build on it.

5. *Sort by sound and sight.* Connecting written words to their spoken counterparts is critical for students learning a new language. For this reason, plenty of occasions to use sound sorts with pictures should be provided. Even as English learners progress to word sorts based on spelling patterns, help them to say the words and reflect on pronunciation issues. Remember, English learners do not have to say words exactly as the teacher does. Their version of the pronunciation will attach to the spelling patterns, and that is a good start.

6. *Begin with obvious contrasts.* In the spirit of moving from simple to complex, it is always good to introduce a new concept by comparing it to something that is very different. This is one reason kindergarten teachers may introduce three letters like *m, s,* and *l* at the beginning of alphabet study. These letters look very different in print, and the sounds they represent are very distinctive. This makes common sense.

Complications arise for teachers who work with students learning English as a new language. What if a student's home language does not have the same distinctions that English does? What if *l* and *r* sound the same in that language? What if there is no distinction between *sh* and *ch*? For this reason, it is important for teachers to know something about the phonology of their students' home languages. The obvious contrasts that are selected for classroom study should be distinctive in all students' home languages. As such, they will be a good place for everyone to start. After students have gained a beginning base in English sounds or patterns, focus on contrasts in English that may be confusing for English learners because of the sounds, grammar, or orthography of their home language. You will find contrast-type sorts throughout this book for English learners from different primary languages. For example, on page 284 there is a th/t sound sort that will be especially helpful for Spanish speakers who have difficulty with this contrast. Not all sorts will be appropriate for students from all language backgrounds, and these "fine-tuning" sorts should always come after the obvious contrasts have been established.

7. *Don't hide exceptions.* English has a deep orthography, and many of its patterns require looking below the surface. Sometimes the reason for a spelling pattern may need to be unearthed through a book on etymology. You do not need to pretend that English is a simple and straightforward system, but as a teacher you do need to communicate a confidence to students that you will guide them to understand it in a systematic way. When you discover words that do not follow the pattern you are studying, feel free to talk about them, and note their uniqueness. Think out loud with students about the consistencies in the language, and also the occasions in which it challenges us. Encourage students to develop a thoughtful and inquisitive attitude about words and spelling, and see where it leads you.

8. *Avoid rules.* Novices tend to want a "how to" formula, and those learning a new language are no exception to this. Unfortunately, sharing spelling "rules" may lead to a mechanistic attitude in students, and make it more difficult for English learners to gain the flexibility required to adapt to the ever-more-complex layers of the orthography. "Just teach me the rule" is what students want, but what happens when the rule does not apply in all situations? They may lose faith that the system works. Often, the rules they memorize are beyond what they can use in their own writing.

A more helpful teaching approach is to build on students' current developmental understandings, and help them see patterns in the written language. A word study notebook in which students have recorded related words can support English learners' exposure to common spelling patterns. These lists can be reviewed, reread, and referred to over time. In this way, students are encouraged to actively notice relationships among words, and question words that do not follow the pattern.

9. *Work for automaticity.* English learners need a firm foundation on which to build their English literacy learning. Accuracy and speed are the two important signs that students have mastered a sort. Teachers must expect the same high level of mastery for all students, including English learners. It is no favor to expect less than mastery, despite the many challenges to learning to read while learning to speak English. If English learners are pushed into harder and harder material without attaining automaticity, in the long run the foundation for their literacy learning may crumble under the weight of more complex material.

10. *Return to meaningful texts.* This principle is essential for English learners as they struggle to make meaning of literacy activities in the classroom, despite their limited oral language. What vocabulary words and language patterns do students understand? Are they experiencing these in their reading materials? How can teachers connect students with texts that are purposeful and understandable? If necessary, students may need to write the material themselves, and use their personal narratives as meaningful texts. When commercial texts are at a level that is difficult for English learners, either because of their unfamiliar content, vocabulary, or language structures, teachers can support comprehensibility with visuals and hands-on experiences, and by giving students time to reflect and discuss the material in groups. This contextualization will give students the experience of reading as a meaning-making activity.

Throughout this chapter we have described the power of word study as part of an effective literacy instruction program for English learners. Word study is based on the assessment of students' orthographic understanding of English words, and invites teachers to meet students at their developmental level and build on it in a systematic and explicit way. Word study helps English learners interact with others in their learning community as they investigate words in partnerships and groups through sorts, games, and other learning activities. In word study, English learners make connections between oral and written versions of English, and between their home languages and English. In addition, at all levels word study is an active process of pattern identification that involves many hands-on materials and procedures.

Word study activities for English learners build on the same child-centered principles as for those students from monolingual English backgrounds. Organization of word study instruction, and the corresponding scheduling, structuring of interactions, and integration of content into the language arts curriculum, however, are even more complex for teachers working with multilingual classrooms. In the next four chapters we offer materials and activities to take these foundational support strategies for working with English learners and put them into practice in a word study program for all students in your classroom.

4

Word Study with English Learners in the Emergent Stage

The emergent stage of literacy development is characterized by a budding awareness of how print works and how oral language connects to written language. The emergent learner knows that speech can be written down and that words on a page can be read, but does not yet understand the code through which this happens. The emergent stage is a time of great discovery and excitement in literacy learning!

English learners at the emergent stage do more than connect print to language; they do it in a new language. While some students have been learning the vocabulary, syntax, and sounds of English from birth, English learners enter the realm of the written code in this new language with limited oral resources. These students critically need a language-rich classroom that provides multiple daily opportunities to talk, chant, sing, listen to comprehensible language, and connect English to what they know in their first language. Before we share more details about the emergent stage and the components of a rich early literacy program, let's take a peek into one language-rich classroom for English learners.

Ms. Rosa's kindergarten classroom is cheerful and active. She has a library with many picture books and nonfiction reference materials. Her science center has a display of different kinds of rocks and hands-on materials such as rock pieces, magnifying glasses, magnets, bowls, and spoons for students to use in their manipulations.

An easily accessible writing center contains paper products of all sorts and pens, pencils, markers, and crayons. Ms. Rosa has arranged the room with a floor space where the group can gather to meet, listen to stories, present work, sing, move, and share. She also has four large tables where students work on literacy and other projects. Her room is decorated with student writing and student-created artifacts, interesting posters relating to the current theme, and sign-up lists where students will put their name cards. She has labeled some of the major objects and areas in the class such as "library," "scissors," and "writing center."

The students in Ms. Rosa's class come from a variety of linguistic backgrounds including Spanish, Hmong, Somali, and Vietnamese. Most are learning English as a new language. At the moment, Ms. Rosa is guiding her students in a writing project. Each student has a picture of someone or something connected to the school—the custodian, the principal, special teachers, the play structure, the cafeteria, and so on. Students are writing about their pictures and will share them as a group in a few minutes. Some students are drawing the words to tell their stories; others have used squiggly lines; and still others, random strings of letters. One student is sounding out her words and putting the letters she believes fit the sounds she hears. Her paper says *K D S* ("clean the school"). Ms. Rosa moves from student to student, modeling language and asking questions: "Yes, that is Mr. Yang, the assistant principal. What did you say about Mr. Yang? Do you know what he does?"

Following the writing activity, Ms. Rosa calls the students to the rug area, where they share their pictures and stories with each other. When students are unable to find the words to communicate in English, Ms. Rosa asks simple questions or encourages them to speak in their first language. Sometimes peers will help with a translation. With each sharing, Ms. Rosa clearly states the name of the person or object in each picture and has students try to say it along with her. On another day, she will use these pictures to play a guessing game. She will come back to these photos over and over throughout the year to reinforce meaningful vocabulary. This is also the way she helps students learn the names of the schoolmates and helpers in their classroom community.

Ms. Rosa understands that students beginning to learn about reading and writing in English need many opportunities to hear language, connect language to their experiences, practice language in supportive environments, and see the relationship between oral language and print. She has structured her literacy learning environment to provide maximum support and practice for her students.

FROM SPEECH TO PRINT WITH ENGLISH LEARNERS

All students bring many oral language resources with them to school. Most students know how to communicate their basic needs to the people who take care of them. They have vocabulary words for many of the people and objects in their lives, can distinguish and articulate the sounds that are used in their home language, and understand the patterns of the rhymes and stories that are told in their families. These strengths provide a foundation for connecting speech to print in the early literacy classroom. But how is the experience of learning about print in English different for those students who come to reading and writing without an oral language foundation in English?

English learners entering U.S. schools for the first time are likely to have less depth in their knowledge of English vocabulary and syntax than do their peers from English-speaking households. This limited experience with English words can influence other literacy skills for students. For example, they may perceive the sounds of English as though filtered through the framework of their home language. Consonant and vowel sounds may be "heard" as resembling sounds in the students' home languages. For example, students from some Asian languages may hear /l/ and /r/ sounds as being the same. Phonological awareness skills such as **sound isolation** and **phonemic segmentation** are supported by students' knowledge of a number of spoken words. For instance, students who know many words that start with /s/—*sun, sandwich, soap, school, store*—will find it easier to recognize and distinguish the /s/ sound in early literacy activities. Students who do not have a significant oral language base in English will need to have many opportunities to experience the rhythms and rhymes of language through poems, songs, and movement activities. These activities should introduce English sounds and rhythms and build on the home language experiences that students bring to the classroom.

What is key to literacy development for English learners in the emergent stage is that they use language with teachers and peers and see oral language they understand captured in print. English learners need structured opportunities to learn many new words to add to their repertoire so that these words can become the material of their literacy learning. Limited and informal experiences using oral English, like those associated with mainstream programs, will simply not be enough to support the kind of language development needed for English learners' literacy development. Literacy teaching for English learners demands the dual task of teaching vocabulary and language patterns

Sound Isolation
The ability to orally separate a specific sound from a spoken word, such as identifying that the beginning sound in *lake, lion,* and *leaf* is /l/, or that the ending sound in *kite, pet,* and *hat* is /t/.

Phonemic Segmentation
The process of dividing a spoken word into the smallest units of sound within that word. The word *sun* can be divided or segmented into three phonemes: /s/ /uh/ /n/.

along with any specific reading or writing skill. Every day in the classroom and in each literacy lesson taught, vocabulary learning and language practice must be a key focus.

As we discussed in Chapter 2, students bring specific language and literacy resources with them to the classroom. Emergent English learners may be students at the same age and grade level as their monolingual English peers, who have been to school in English instructional programs but have not yet developed full fluency. At all grade levels, teachers may encounter students who come to their classroom with an equivalent grade level of reading and writing proficiency in a home language but limited literacy experiences in English. Although these students are emergent in English reading and writing skills, they are more literate in their home language and are likely to move quickly beyond the emergent stage as they transfer reading and writing skills from their first language into English. Teachers at many grade levels may also find emergent-level students who come to their grade-level classroom with limited literacy experiences in their home language and limited literacy experiences in English. Throughout this chapter we describe activities for a range of emergent English learners, including older learners.

CHARACTERISTICS OF THE EMERGENT STAGE OF READING AND SPELLING

Emergent readers "try out" reading and writing behaviors as their awareness of print and knowledge of writing conventions grow. At the early emergent level, students "pretend read" a story, mimicking the tone and content of what has been modeled to them in book-sharing experiences. Later, students reread texts that they have memorized—often without missing a word! Eventually, emergent readers notice the speech–print connection in the texts they are reading and they begin to fingerpoint as they reread memorized texts. This one-to-one correspondence, or *concept of word*, is highly connected to students' developing phonemic awareness skills and facilitates both their learning of sight words and letter–sound correspondences.

English learners moving through the emergent stage profit from formal as well as informal opportunities to experience books and conversation. Remember, English learners have not had the same number of years of being immersed in book sharing and conversations in English as monolingual English as speakers. It will be difficult for English learners to invent their own stories based on the pictures in a book when their verbal planning is limited by their English vocabularies and knowledge of syntax. Allow students to "read" books using their home language. Teach students key vocabulary words as you introduce a new book; encourage them to tell stories using this vocabulary. For instance, Ms. Mason recently introduced her class to the book *Mary Wore Her Red Dress and Henry Wore His Green Sneakers* (Peek, 1998). She knew that after several readings, this book would become a favorite for students to reread to themselves and others. To support her English learners' ability to do this, she spent some time with them introducing key vocabulary words: *dress, red, green, yellow, blue, brown, purple, orange,* and *pink*. In future lessons, she will practice some of the clothing words such as *sneakers, sweater, jeans, pants, shirt,* and *hat*. These important words will give her students immediate help in retelling the new book.

Emergent writers begin with random marks or scribbles, progress to representational drawing, and later move to linear and letter-like forms. Eventually, students begin to write with the letters of the English alphabet, and by the end of the emergent stage they incorporate letters that correspond to the salient sounds of words they are trying to spell. An early emergent writer may write a shopping list to "buy milk and eggs" as some scribble marks on a page. Later in development, perhaps the same list looks like three curly-cue lines. With more experience, the attempts take on letter-like shapes. When emergent writers begin to use real letters, their spellings are often random strings such as *AX, LTV, AAM* for the shopping list just mentioned. A major accomplishment has occurred when students bsegin to perceive that the sounds in the words they are attempting to spell are related to the letters they choose to represent them. The late emergent speller may represent our previous shopping list as *B MK N Z* ("buy milk and eggs")—representing the most obvious sounds heard.

English learners will exhibit the same kinds of emergent writing, but are likely to bring their background experiences with print to the developmental writing process. Students who come to school with limited exposure to print, no matter what age they are, may demonstrate writing that is less letter-like. Students whose home language script is very different in form from English (Arabic, Chinese, and others) will need time and experience to start writing "like English." Depending on their home languages, immigrant students may also need added support to learn the left-to-right directionality of writing in English.

When students come to English schooling with some literacy skills in their home language, they may temporarily look like emergent learners, but they will quickly move into the beginning reader/letter name–alphabetic spelling stage. These students already have many of the skills that emergent learners are only developing—a knowledge of the connection between letters and the sounds they represent (the alphabetic principle), conventions of print such as directionality and spacing between words, and awareness of sounds in words (phonemic awareness). Their stay in the emergent level is only a temporary stopover to learn the shapes and names of English letters. This group will quickly be on its way to identifying and comparing the sound systems of the two languages in the beginning reader/letter name–alphabetic spelling stage described in the next chapter.

COMPONENTS OF EARLY LITERACY LEARNING

Personal Reader
An individual collection of familiar poems, dictated stories, or other pieces of text that students have memorized and can read with good accuracy. These reading materials are copied or typed and placed in a booklet for students to read again and again.

Group Experience Story
A chart story is created after students have shared an interesting experience together, such as a field trip, hands-on activity, or exciting read-aloud story. The teacher guides a small group of children, each in turn, to dictate a comment about the experience; their words are transcribed onto a piece of chart paper, and the story is reread for reading practice.

Several building blocks of literacy learning are addressed in the emergent stage. These include growing language and vocabulary skills, developing phonemic awareness, and learning the alphabet. These skills are enhanced as students learn to track print and develop a beginning sight-word vocabulary. Students at the emergent stage also refine their abilities to sort and categorize conceptually, and they attach language to their conceptual understandings. Our instruction for emergent learners thus involves many activities to develop vocabulary and concepts, to experience the rhythms and sounds of oral language and connect it to written texts, and to learn the letters of the alphabet.

In previous chapters we have outlined essential literacy activities for the classroom: *Read To, Read With, Write With, Word Study*, and *Talk With*—or *RRWWT*. These activities take place throughout the day, as described in Ms. Rosa's kindergarten, during whole-group, small-group, and individual lessons with students. They happen for students in formats that vary from listening to interesting stories, to rereading familiar rhymes in a **Personal Reader** notebook, to constructing a **group experience story** that is reread and discussed over and over again. The essential literacy activities are evident when students sort objects, pictures, letters, and words into categories and reflect aloud on their learning. The essential literacy activities can become a routine part of your classroom's literacy block; they can also be a part of integrated classroom themes that facilitate students' content area and vocabulary learning. In the next section we offer some suggestions for implementing *RRWWT* with emergent learners.

Read To

Reading aloud to students is a critical component in the emergent literacy classroom and of special importance to English learners. While reading to students, teachers introduce and reinforce new vocabulary and oral language structures, share interesting and motivating texts that are beyond a student's reading level, model fluent reading, and engage in discussions of content that encourage higher-order thinking. To make the most of the listening experience, English learners will need material that is engaging but not too difficult for them to understand.

Read to your students at the start of the day, at the end of the day, and during other transitional times throughout the school day. Read to your students whenever you can find a moment. Have a book of simple poems always at hand, and read one when you have 30 seconds to spare. Find a range of narrative and nonfiction texts to share aloud. Read notes, lists, and school announcements. Pay attention to the complexity of the message. Do your English learners understand the text? How do you know? Look for body cues such as eye contact and attentiveness. Do students respond to the humor? Can they make predictions about what is coming next? Check for understanding of key vocabulary words and important events in the material by engaging in discussion and review. Or have students "show you they know" with a drawing or demonstration. If you find that the material is above students' heads, search out texts that deal with the same ideas using simpler language and more visual support. Patterned texts such as *Mary Wore Her Red Dress* (Peek, 1998) offer repetitive language and simple sentence structures that listeners can understand and echo along with the teacher during read-alouds.

In the pre-K or kindergarten classroom, your read-aloud sessions will be short in duration (5 to 15 minutes) and will often involve student participation such as helping to make sound effect noises or role-playing the story. Preview literature so that you can scaffold unknown vocabulary or complex language structures with students. Books with expressive illustrations or photos and easy-to-understand text will be critical. Consider taking a "book walk"—talking through the storyline—with English learners, or having them preview the material with someone who speaks their home language before they listen to a story in English with the whole class. Characterization in creative dramatics provides movement to your descriptions; for example, *walking with a cane, stirring soup with a large spoon,* and *walking slowly like a proud lion* are all characterizations that young children of all language levels can enjoy.

In the primary-grades classroom, the best read-aloud materials will be picture books and expository texts that have interesting themes and information expressed in uncomplicated language. Books with not more than three sentences of text per illustration are ideal. Read-aloud materials aimed at the whole class may be too difficult for English learners to understand without additional support. Plan to introduce your read-aloud text to English learners in a small-group guided lesson so that students will have the background and vocabulary needed to contextualize the material when it is read aloud. Look for bilingual editions of books, books on tape in other languages, and support personnel to read stories in the home language first. Students will understand much more of the text in English when they have already heard it in their home language.

Older emergent learners who are in upper-grade classrooms will find most of the content of read-aloud materials presented in class to be over their heads. Provide opportunities for students with limited English proficiency to discuss the material with bilingual students or aides who can translate for them before and after a read-aloud session. Provide English learners with simpler texts that focus on the same content. Use additional visuals for reference. Help students focus on three to five key vocabulary words in each read-aloud session, or let them listen to simpler books on tape while you are reading aloud a harder text. Do not expect English learners to sit for extended periods of time listening to material in English that is beyond their listening comprehension levels.

Read With

Spending time with the teacher in *Read With* activities is a key part of the literacy block time in an elementary classroom. Emergent readers need time to practice their blossoming skills with the support of a more experienced guide. This practice will reinforce one-to-one matching of oral language to print, support directionality, and teach beginning sight words. *Read With* activities are most effective when a teacher can work with a group of students who are at similar developmental levels so that activities are appropriate to their instructional level. Teachers are encouraged to implement a center rotation system

Provide older emergent learners with simpler texts, visual and other vocabulary support, and opportunities to interact with bilingual peers.

so they can work with small groups of students with similar needs over the course of the literacy block time, while other students participate in more independent activities.

Reading With students happens through a number of ongoing literacy experiences in the early education classroom. Pre-K and kindergarten teachers help students read along with big books and chart stories as they model tracking. By using enlarged text and having multiple opportunities to reread these stories, students will memorize the text and point to words as they follow along. Little leveled books with predictable text help students "try out" reading in highly supportive situations. Look for predictable texts with common language patterns and sentence frames such as "I can see a _____" or "There's a _____ at the zoo," and so forth. In this way, students not only get to practice the agency of reading, but they also learn vocabulary that is supported by illustrations and practice natural language patterns (Johnston, Invernizzi, & Juel, 1998).

Create a book box of familiar reading materials for each of your students. These book boxes should house little books that students have memorized and can read on their own. Include a Personal Reader in each student's book box. The Personal Reader is a notebook or folder that contains typed-up copies of familiar poems, stories, and **dictated accounts** that students have memorized. Each time students reread a page of the Personal Reader, they can put a tally mark on it to document their efforts. Word banks can be created as students select familiar words to write on cards and add to a baggie of known words.

Write With

Writing With emergent students is a time to share how spoken words get translated into print. Typical examples of how this is done include taking **Language Experience** dictations from individual students, creating group experience stories, and working with a Morning Message or shared writing. These formats are explained in depth in the emergent activities section that follows. As teachers model how to put words and sentences onto paper, they describe what they are doing, giving students insight into the encoding process. Teachers should focus on skills that are at the developmental level of their emergent learners, such as left-to-right sweep, spacing between words, and choosing the beginning letters of words.

Providing time for emergent learners to practice their own developmental spelling as we saw in Ms. Rosa's kindergarten is also an excellent *Write With* activity. Developmental spelling challenges students to produce their best approximation of what English writing looks like. It also provides an informal assessment of students' letter knowledge and phonemic awareness abilities. Look to see if students are writing with letters or other symbols. Notice if they are selecting words from the environment, their personal lives, or using any letter–sound associations. Students may do their own unassisted writing through journal activities or in free-writing assignments that include drawing a picture and writing about it. Have students reread their writing to you, and when you want to remember their message, write down their dictated words below their personal efforts. Your writing will serve as a model for students' later approximations.

Scaffold your students' writing to a greater or lesser degree. In the examples mentioned, dictated stories involve a high degree of teacher support. The student is required to tell the story, but the teacher or a tutor records it. Journal writing involves a high level of student responsibility and less teacher involvement. Always consider the task and the student as you implement *Write With* activities. There are times when your English learners will need a highly structured lesson, such as a piece of writing built on frame sentences, in order to learn a language pattern or to reduce the complexity of a task. For instance, instead of asking students who are just learning English to come up with their own stories from scratch, you can provide them a framework in which to include their ideas: "I like _____. I like _____. I like _____. But I don't like _____." ("I like to run. I like to jump. I like to eat. But I don't like to go to bed.") (Koch, 2000)

Dictated Accounts
Retellings, personal sharings, or other oral language samples you have written down from students.

Language Experience
After experiencing a real-world activity, student language is elicited and recorded in print.

At other times, a more interactive approach is called for. Teachers often find that co-constructing a message with a student on paper or group of students on a chart is a useful way to support students' beginning writing skills. To create an interactive message on chart paper, work with students to generate a meaningful one-sentence message. Discuss how many words are in the sentence, and "think out loud" about the spelling and punctuation of it. Share the pen with students who feel they can write a certain letter or word on the chart paper. When your message is written, review the text for specific letters and other concepts of print. Have students highlight or circle the letters or words you are discussing.

Write With activities are most effective when they take place within the teacher-directed, small-group reading lesson. When done in the context of small groups, mini-lessons can be directed at the needs and developmental levels of the individuals involved. Certain *Write With* activities such as journaling may also be appropriate to independent centers or seatwork stations. Even when writing is used as an independent activity, students will profit from "reading" their story to a teacher at the end of the work time.

Emergent students at the kindergarten and pre-K level may have an attention span of only 5 minutes for *Write With* activities each day. Short lessons integrated regularly into small-group work will have a powerful impact in the long run. Emergent students in the primary grades will have longer attention spans and can draw and write on their own for 15 to 20 minutes. You may find that with increased fine motor skills, these students copy more words from books and environmental print in the classroom. Older emergent learners are likely to know the mechanics of handwriting and may copy or memorize a small set of essential words. Asking older emergent learners to use developmental spelling will help you understand what they have internalized about the English orthographic system.

Word Study

The focus of word study at the emergent level is to support students' learning of sounds, letters, and words in English. At the sound level, word study activities involve *phonological awareness* experiences such as working with rhymes in songs, books, and games; alliteration activities that encourage students to hear beginning sounds; and the blending and segmenting of sounds in words. Through these kinds of activities, students develop the phonemic awareness skills that will allow them to hear individual sounds in words and eventually attach related letters to represent those sounds.

Many word study activities at the emergent level are designed to encourage knowledge of the *alphabet* and *letter sounds*, often through the use of books, songs, games, and sorting and matching tasks. Because English learners have not grown up experiencing the English alphabet song and may have only limited exposure to print in English, they will require additional and more extensive opportunities to experience English letters in a variety of ways. The activity section that follows presents numerous ideas for sharing letters with students who have limited experiences in English.

Vocabulary and *concept development* are also crucial aspects of the word study component of the essential literacy activities. Concept sorts with pictures and objects extend English learners' higher-order thinking skills as they reinforce word learning. These sorts also help students practice the sorting procedure; students who are not yet reading, and those who are just learning the English vocabulary for the pictures, will still be able to profit from sorting by concepts (see Figure 4-1).

Word study activities are an integral part of the teacher-guided, small-group lesson during your literacy block time. If you have 20 minutes to work with each small group, plan to spend 6 to 8 minutes on the word study component. On a typical day you may use this 6 to 8 minutes to introduce a new concept sort or letter matching game and listen for words in a story that sound alike at the beginning. Your word study lesson can also be integrated into other components of the lesson such as your *Write With* activities. For instance, you can have students write a page for a

Materials: Picture cards for sorts

Procedure:

1. Select up to 10 pictures from the sort for the vocabulary study.

2. Preview these pictures with students. Name the picture and have students repeat the name.

3. Talk about the pictures. Have students generate examples. Teacher paraphrases and provides a simple definition. For example, in a transportation-related sort, Edgar may say, "I see a **jeep** on TV." Paraphrase the student response, for example, "Edgar saw a **jeep** on TV." Provide a simple definition of the word, for example, "A **jeep** is like a square car that can go off the road."

4. If students do not have enough English words to say something about a picture, the teacher should move into a more directive role. For example, "This is a tractor. A tractor helps a farmer plant." Body language and translating the definition into a student's home language is recommended to support this new language learning.

5. When all of the cards have been discussed, chant each word as a group one last time.

FIGURE 4-1 Previewing Vocabulary with English Learners Before Sorting

Photograph Library
A collection of photographs illustrating common words and everyday activities, usually organized by topics such as household items, colors, actions, tools, food, and so forth. These photograph collections are available from commercial publishers and provide a useful tool for teachers to clarify their instruction and develop new vocabulary with students.

personal alphabet book featuring a letter you worked with in word study or write a traveling story on a day you did a transportation concept sort.

The content of your concept sorts and vocabulary development may look different for various age groups of emergent learners. Young students will likely be working with simple concepts and vocabulary involving items such as living things, colors and shapes, or toys. Primary-age students are ready for more complex topics such as items around town, weather and related objects, or occupations. Older emergent learners should be exposed to concept sorts appropriate to their grade level such as technology, biology, and geography. Older emergent learners will need pictures and other visual support materials that do not look like they came from a preschool classroom. **Photograph libraries** and ESL picture dictionaries for older learners provide useful references for the English learning classroom. See the list of language development resources at the end of this book for sources of these materials.

Talk With

A crucial component of an effective literacy program is having time for students to put their language learning into practice through *Talk With* activities, and this is even more crucial for English learners. Remember, it is hard to connect literacy to language in the classroom if there is no talking going on! Integrate conversation and dialogue many times throughout your school day. Structure regular routines at the beginning and end of the day and during small-group lessons. You do not need to have a separate time of the day for *Talking With*. Here are some examples: Structure community circle discussions on a regular basis. If procedures are well known and input can be framed with a starter sentence, English learners are likely to feel comfortable about contributing. For example, Ms. Sanders' kindergarten students have learned that every day in their class they will go around the circle and contribute one idea to a class discussion. At first, many of the English learners were shy about speaking up, so they "passed" on their turn. With a predictable routine and a simple starter sentence such as "This weekend, I will . . ." or "My favorite animal is . . . ," the students have begun to contribute regularly.

Build in partner sharing as you share literature and nonfiction texts in class. Encourage students to read their writing in an Author's Chair format, and let peers give feedback. Ask open-ended questions and leave wait time for students to think and respond. Call on all students over the course of the day. Find ways to limit teacher talk, and open the floor to more student voices. For example, instead of always asking students to respond to the teacher (when only one child can talk at a time), ask the students to turn and talk to the person beside them to answer a question, offer a personal response, or ask a question. This increases the amount of talk time dramatically and gives less-verbal children a chance to talk in a low-risk setting. English language learners can be paired with peers who speak their home language or with monolingual-English speakers. Also provide opportunities for students to sing, chant, and tell stories. Set the context of your classroom to be accepting of *all* students' voices and to show respect even when students do not know the "right" answer or the right word.

Older emergent learners in particular need opportunities to dialogue with fellow students about the content of what they are learning. Let talk be a bridge to the content they cannot yet read on their own. Encourage bilingual peers to translate what is being learned for students with less proficiency in English.

The rest of this chapter outlines numerous specific teaching activities for structuring a variety of language-rich experiences for your students. These activities can be used for informal assessment of language development, and will help students to hear rhymes, syllables, and sounds in words; develop new vocabulary; share stories; and see their words written down in English.

Activities for English Learners in the Emergent Stage

Forty-two activities are provided for this stage that complement the fundamental activities presented as *RRWWT*. The activities are numbered and organized under basic headings: Concept Books and Sorts, Talk With and Read With Activities, and Alphabet Knowledge.

CONCEPT BOOKS AND SORTS

Concept Book Walks 4–1

Materials.   Gather a collection of simple concept books to share with a small group of English-learning students. The best books to choose have photographs or clear pictures so that vocabulary is easily understood. Often these concept books will be in the toddler or "board book" sections of bookstores, but it is important to choose books that are not too babyish. Some examples of engaging concept books include the following:

> *My First Animal Board Book* (Zarick, 2004)
> *Panda Big, Panda Small* (Cobrera, 1999)
> *Horn to Toes and in Between* (Boynton, 2000)
> *The Eye Book* (LeSieg, 2001)
> *Berenstain Bears, Bears on Wheels* (Berenstain, 1969)
> *Going Places* (Parr, 2002)
> *From Head to Toe* (Carle, 1997).

Procedures.   In your small-group lesson, lead students through the book, making the words come alive with dramatic effects or body language. Encourage students to act out or share experiences about the words or concepts being introduced. For example, while reading Eric Carle's *From Head to Toe,* invite students to move along with the actions of animals in the story. Read the story, point out the names and pictures of individual animals, have students touch the part of their own body represented on the page, and encourage students to chant the lines as they act them out. Make the most of these simple concept books. Keep them easily accessible around the classroom so that students can come back to review them whenever they have a chance.

Bilingual Concept Books 4-2

Materials.   Concept books that are written in two languages can teach you about your students' home languages while your students are learning English. Bilingual concept books also support students in making connections between their primary language and English, and this will help cement important vocabulary and conceptual learning. Some example bilingual concept books to use in this lesson include these:

My Opposites/Mis Opuestos (and others in the series) (Emberley, 2000)
Taking a Walk/Caminando (and others in the series) (Emberley, 1994)
My Family and I/Mi Familia y Yo (and others in the English/Spanish Foundations Series) (Rosa-Mendoza, 2001)
Food/La comida (and others in the Bilingual First Books series) (Beaton, 2003)
Where's the Kitten?/Kote Ti Chat La Ye?: English/ Haitian Creole Bilingual (and others in the Photoflap Board Books series) (Christian, 2005)
America: A Book of Opposites/Un Libro de Contrarios (Nikola-Lisa, 2001)
Brian Wildsmith's Farm Animals (Available in seven languages including Tagalog, Korean, Vietnamese, Spanish, and Chinese) (Wildsmith, 2001).

(Additional examples of bilingual books and bookstores that sell them are included in the resource section at the end of this book.)

Procedures.   Share the bilingual concept books with your students, and encourage them to read the words in their home language. Have them chant and act out the words in English. Ask students if the translation in the book is one that they would use in their home, or if they have a different way to say it. Keep a small reference section of bilingual concept books for students to use when they are struggling with a word. Use the bilingual books to compare letters and sounds in the two languages. Encourage monolingual English-speaking students to learn words in other languages by referring to the bilingual concept books, too!

Variations.   Have your students make bilingual concept books that expand on the words in the commercial books, and add them to the classroom collection or donate them to a partner class.

Using Illustrated Word Books 4-3

Materials.   Another important source of vocabulary activities for English learners is illustrated books of words or simple picture dictionaries. These texts can be used as student reference materials or as the source material and content for word-learning games. Some examples of these books include the following:

DK Children's Illustrated Dictionary (McIlwain, 1994)
My Big Word Book: Over 1000 Essential First Words and Pictures (and others in the Smart Kids series) (Priddy, 2002)

My Big Animal Book (and others in the Big Ideas for Little People series) (Priddy, 2002)
Richard Scarry's Best Word Book Ever (Scarry, 1999).

And for older emergent students:

Word by Word (Molinsky, 2005).

(Additional examples are included in the Bibliography at the end of this book.)

Procedures.   Introduce these resource books by pointing out the word–picture match, and any thematic or alphabetical organization to the text. Encourage students to use the books to look up and copy words. Students can use picture dictionaries to help them create their own desktop word walls or personal picture dictionaries. Use the photos or drawings in the books to create concept sorts.

Variations.   Play "I Spy" on individual pages of word books for students to guess what you are thinking of. For instance, on the "around town" page of a picture word book, tell students you are thinking of something that travels on the road. It has tires and carries people going to work. People ring the bell when they want it to stop. Provide clues until students can identify "bus."

Concept Sorts with Pictures 4-4 Through 4-12

Materials.   Table 4-1 lists the picture sorts that are included in the Appendix of this book. The final column offers suggestions for ways these cards can be sorted. Make copies of these sorts, cut them apart, and place them in envelopes or small plastic bags. To help keep multiple sets organized, consider using various colors of paper, or putting a small colored dot on each card so that it can easily be reorganized if students' cards get mixed up.

Procedures.   Demonstrate with students how to sort pictures into categories. For example, a concept sort related to transportation, such as Activity 4-11, features pictures of cars, vans, motorcycles, buses, skateboards, boats, planes, and so forth. In an initial closed sort, the teacher guides students to sort the pictures by water, air, and land travel. Later, students may be encouraged to sort the items by whether or not they have personally experienced this form of transportation. At other times the students may do an open sort, where they create the categories. One student sorted by whether the vehicle held one person or a whole family. Another student sorted by how many wheels the item had. A list of possible ways to sort the picture cards is listed in column 3 of Table 4-1. You and your students are invited to think of all kinds of variations of these sorts, too!

Variations.   Explicit vocabulary instruction fits very well with concept sort activities. Share the names of picture cards being used in sorts. Have students echo these names for you. Let them "quiz" others to see if they remember the names of each picture. Have students sort the picture cards into a group for which they do remember the English name and a group for which they don't. Encourage them to see if they can make the "don't know" group smaller each time. Have students use their home language to describe the pictures, while you help them to learn the English labels.

Other Considerations.   In addition to using the resources in this book, you can also find pictures for concept sorts in old magazines, calendars, or commercially produced picture or photo libraries or by searching for images through a search engine online. Creating a picture collection is a task in which students, family members, and community volunteers can often help. This is also one way that your collection of pictures can begin to represent the variety and focus of your school community and the themes that you teach in class.

TABLE 4-1	Overview of Concept Sorts in This Book	
Sort	Cards Provided (See Appendix)	Ideas
Furniture and Household Items 4–4	Broom, kitchen table, dining room chair, armchair, couch, lamp, door, house, kitchen, mop, rug, roof, tub, towel, vacuum, window, bed, closet, light switch, refrigerator, stairs, television, stereo, stove	In your house/not, plugged in/not, heavy/light
Living Things 4–5	Cat, dog, fish, pig, oak tree, snail, bird, cow, duck, fox, man, woman, boy, girl, plant, spider, flower, grass, vine, fruit tree, pine tree, whale, baby, horse	Animals/plants, legs/no legs, live in a house/live outdoors
Occupations 4–6	Doctor, police officer, firefighter, teacher, sales clerk, postal worker, bus driver, mother, father, artist, construction worker, custodian, soldier, librarian, farmer, cook, astronaut, gardener, banker, actor, painter, veterinarian, truck driver	You'd like to do/not, someone you know/not, work outdoors/work indoors
Personal Care 4–7	Comb, brush, toothpaste, towel, washcloth, tissue, hairbrush, glasses, soap, sink, toilet, person sleeping, bowl of fruit, hair dryer, shaving cream, razor, vitamins, scarf, mittens, lotion, shampoo, floss, fingernail clippers, bandage	In bathroom/not, cleans you/helps you in other ways
School and Office Items 4–8	Key, chair, desk, pen, pencil, stapler, lined paper, drawing paper, clock, scissors, envelope, paper clip, glue, school, table, tape, book, map, waste basket, markers, crayons, computer, cupboard, shelves	School/office, big/small, use to draw/no
Technology and Numbers 4–9	Computer, keyboard, digital alarm clock, wall clock, thermometer, calendar, watch, checkbook, plug, remote control, video recorder/player, camera, video camera, telephone, printer, microwave, date (March 12, 2007), $2+1=3$, $7-6=1$, dice, ruler, measuring tape, price tag, receipt	Has numbers/no, plugs in/no, used at school/no
Toys 4–10	Block, drum, board game, kite, toy car, doll, jacks, ball, teddy bear, scooter, train set, Etch-a-sketch, peg game, toy boat, dinosaur figure, Legos, sand bucket and shovel, paint set, model plane, toy house, comic book, baby book, rattle, puzzle	Outside/inside, by yourself/with others, noisy/quiet
Transpor-tation 4–11	Car, van, motorcycle, bus, train, bicycle, skateboard, subway train, school bus, boat, airplane, horse with rider, ship, sled, skates, truck, jet, sailboat, unicycle, taxi, horse and cart, jeep, tractor, helicopter	Water/air/land, one person/lots of people, have you done it/no
Weather and Related Objects 4–12	Sun, clouds, rain, snow, wind, sunglasses, scarf, mittens, gloves, umbrella, galoshes, sunscreen, jacket, bathing suit, sandals, sunrise, night (moon), fall, tree, rake, snowman, raincoat, thermometer, beach umbrella, fan	Seasons, nature/man-made, for cold/hot weather

GAMES USING CONCEPT PICTURE SORTS

The picture cards you use in concept sorts can be transformed into vocabulary-building games without much difficulty. Here are some sample ideas:

Memory or Concentration Games 4–13

Materials. Make two copies of one of the picture sorts provided in the Appendix of this book, such as the *School and Office Item* pictures. Cut the pictures apart.

FIGURE 4-2   Students Can Play Matching Games with Concept
Picture Cards

Procedures. Shuffle the cards and lay them face down on the table or floor. Students turn two pictures over to try to make matches such as two pencils, two desks, or two staplers (see Figure 4-2). If students cannot remember the name of items when they make a match, they may not keep it as a pair. However, someone (a teacher, assistant, volunteer, or peer) should be ready to supply the English word.

Musical Cards 4–14

Materials. Make a copy of one of the picture sorts provided in the Appendix of this book, such as the *Furniture and Household Items* cards. Cut the pictures apart.

Procedures. Spread individual picture cards around a rug area or on desktops in your classroom. As you play a bit of music, have students move from picture to picture seeing how many names they can identify. When the music stops, each student must find one and only one card to pick up. The teacher may ask students to say the name of their picture to the whole group. For instance, students reply with "broom," "table," "vacuum," and so forth. If students can't remember the name of their item, they can ask a peer for help.

Variations. The teacher can also have students do physical sorts with the item they are holding. "If what you have belongs in the kitchen, come stand over here." Or, "If you need to get plugged in to work, make a group over here." Students can also think of ways that the household items could be described and sorted. There are so many possibilities! Another variation of *Musical Cards* is for the teacher to ask questions about the items students are holding: "Who has something that helps us cook?" "Who has something that helps us clean?" "Who has something that makes sound?" Specific sentence patterns such as "I have a _____" can be practiced in this way. After each round, the music starts again and students find a new card to work with.

I Spy 4–15

Materials. Make a copy of one of the picture sorts provided in the Appendix of this book, such as the *Occupations* cards. Cut the pictures apart.

Procedures. In a small group of students, take four or five cards from the concept picture sort. For example, you might take the doctor, police officer, firefighter, teacher, and sales clerk cards from the *Occupations* sort. The teacher gives clues about a focus picture: "I'm thinking of someone who comes when there is a fire. This person rides in a big truck that has hoses for spraying water." Students guess which person the teacher is thinking of. As students' language proficiency increases, they can take turns being the "teacher" and being the leader of the *I Spy* game. Students may also be encouraged to add statements about the picture card once it has been identified ("There was a firefighter on TV last night.")

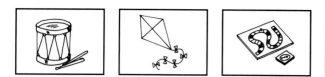

FIGURE 4-3   Concept Picture Cards Can Be Used to Learn and Practice Language

Build a Story 4–16

Materials. Make a copy of one of the picture sorts provided in the Appendix of this book, such as the *Toys* cards. Cut the pictures apart.

Procedures. Use the set of concept picture cards to help students create oral or written stories. For example, give four to six pictures from the *Toys* set to each student in a small group (see Figure 4-3). Have students create their own stories about the pictures they have. "I went to the store with my mom and we saw some toys. I asked her to buy me a drum, but she said 'no.' Then I saw a kite and a board game, but she still said 'no.' Finally, when we were leaving the store she said I could have one thing because I was good. I got a bucket and shovel." Students can tell their stories to each other, or try to make one long group story.

Variations. The teacher may choose to write a line from each student's story on chart paper for the group to reread.

Charades 4–17

Materials. Make a copy of one of the picture sorts provided in the Appendix of this book, such as the *Personal Care* cards. Cut the pictures apart.

Procedures. Review the set of pictures with a group of students. Have students take turns secretly picking a card and acting it out for others in the group to guess. Action words such as *sleeping, combing,* and *washing* will be especially good for this game, but nouns such as *toothpaste, fingernail clippers,* and *hair dryer* will also be fun to try!

Concept Board Games 4–18

The picture cards for concept sorts can also be incorporated into board games that students play independently with their peers.

Materials. Make a copy of the *Weather and Related Objects* picture sort cards included in the Appendix of this book. Use one of the blank board game models from the Appendix to create your own weather board game by drawing or pasting some weather-related graphics on the game board.

Procedures. To play, the student rolls a die, then turns over a picture card—let's say *raincoat.* If the student can say the name of the picture, she can move the number of spaces on the die. If not, she must stay where she is. To make this game more challenging for advanced speakers, students may be asked to put the word in a sentence before moving ahead ("I have a yellow raincoat."), or be asked to share as many describing words about the item as the number on the die ("It is slippery. It is shiny. It feels wet." Three moves.)

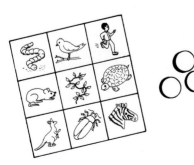

FIGURE 4-4   An Example Bingo Card

Bingo 4–19

Materials. Make multiple copies of one of the picture sorts provided in the Appendix of this book, such as the *Living Things* cards (see Figure 4-4). Cut the pictures apart. Teachers can use the cut-apart picture cards to create Bingo cards for students to play with. For example, the cards from the *Living Things* set can be mixed up so that every student's Bingo card has nine pictures from the collection, laid out in a grid format. No two Bingo boards should have exactly the same pictures in the same order.

Procedures.   A teacher or student leader can call out the picture names as they are picked, and students use tokens to cover the items on their board. When a "Bingo" or "Blackout" is achieved, that student wins. Encourage students to repeat the names of all of the pictures on their boards when the game is over.

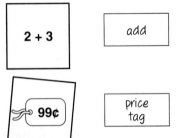
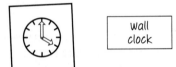

FIGURE 4-5 Students Can Create Labels and Match Them to Pictures

Concept Picture Sorts for Older Emergent Students 4-20

Materials.   Make a copy of one or more of the picture sorts provided in the Appendix of this book. Cut the pictures apart. Cut blank cards for students to write the name of each item on its own card.

Procedures.   Have older, emergent students write the names of objects onto word cards, such as the *Technology and Numbers* cards, and then match the pictures with the labels (see Figure 4-5). These labels may be done bilingually if students are literate in their home language.

Variations.   Older emergent learners may also appreciate having copies of the concept picture pages to keep in a word study notebook for reference. They can write the label for each picture on the page. Students can also use these reference pages to support themselves when completing simple writing projects.

TALK WITH AND READ WITH ACTIVITIES

Rhythm, Rhyme, and Phonological Awareness
Rain, Rain, Go Away 4-21

Materials.   Start with a simple rhyme or poem that uses natural language patterns. Many excellent rhymes and chants are available in books of poetry, children's songbooks, and collections of jump-rope jingles. Look for a rhyme that is fairly simple, and is presented in a relatively natural oral language pattern (e.g., "Rain, rain, go away, come again another day"). Rhythm and rhyme will help students memorize the verses.

Although it is valuable to share the cultural heritage passed along through classic nursery rhymes in English, it is also important to remember that many of these rhymes may appear to be total nonsense to English learners. "Hey diddle diddle, the cat and the fiddle, the cow jumped over the moon. The little dog laughed to see such sport, and the dish ran away with the spoon" is one example. This rhyme has many nonsensical phrases and ideas that may be difficult for an English learner to understand. What is a fiddle? What does "such sport" mean? How could a dish run away with a spoon? Memorizing such a rhyme will be especially difficult for an English learner when there are too many unknown words and the student does not have many clues as to the meaning of the text. In addition, spending a lot of time learning nonessential words is not the best use of teaching time at the early stages of English language development.

Procedure. Read the poem to your students several times, and encourage them to join in. Use expressive language, body motions, and rhythmic clapping so that students can participate more fully. Write the poem on a piece of chart paper or sentence strips in a pocket chart and point to the words as you reread the poem. Add pictures to aid understanding. In later readings, cut apart the chart or sentence strips and help students put the poem back together in the correct order. Make a notebook-sized copy of the poems you have learned and have students put them in their Personal Readers (folders of familiar materials for students to reread). Students will "try out" reading as they come back to these rhymes over and over, and their tracking, sight-word reading, and phonological awareness skills will get much needed reinforcement.

Variations. Letter and counting songs like "Five Little Ducks Went Out One Day" help students internalize the alphabet, numbers, and the days of the week in English.

Rhymes in Other Languages 4-22

A concept of rhyme will set a foundation for students' later development of more discrete phonological awareness skills. To scaffold this process, consider bringing rhymes from other languages into your classroom program.

Materials. Find rhymes from other languages by researching your local public library or the resource books and vendors listed at the end of this book. Your classroom parents and neighborhood community members are especially good resources for sharing the oral language traditions of your students. Many immigrant languages are primarily based on oral traditions, and sharing children's rhymes is a powerful way to bring parents into the classroom learning community!

A fun online resource for poems from around the world is Mama Lisa's World: Kid Songs from Around the World (**http://www.mamalisa.com/world/atoz.html**).

Here is an example of a rhyme about frogs and toads in Spanish that all students will enjoy learning:

Los Sapitos
La ranita soy yo
Glo, glo, glo.
El sapito eres tú
Glu, glu, glu.
Cantemos así
Gli, gli, gli.
Que la lluvia se fue
Gle, gle, gle.
Y la ronda se va
Gla, gla, gla.
(Traditional)

Procedures. Follow the same procedures listed in Activity 4-21 to help your students memorize this poem. Encourage native speakers to help others get the rhythm and pronunciation right. Act out the poem or clap to its beat. Have students point to the words as they reread it over numerous occasions.

Ask your students if they have ever heard the rhyme you have selected. Encourage them to help you pronounce it correctly, and ask them to tell you what the words mean. After helping your students memorize the rhyme, show them how to fingerpoint to the text you have written on paper.

Rhymes to Assess Concept of Word in English and Spanish 4–23

Here we give sample rhymes in both English and Spanish that illustrate an opportunity to informally assess *concept of word*.

English Rhymes to Assess Concept of Word in Text

Materials.   Select one of the following rhymes and copy it onto a piece of chart paper or sentence strips for the pocket chart.

Mix a pancake,
Stir a pancake,
Pop it in the pan;
Fry the pancake,
Toss the pancake,
Catch it if you can.
$\qquad\qquad\qquad\qquad$ Christina G. Rosetti

Rain on the green grass,
Rain on the tree,
Rain on the rooftop,
But not on me!

Procedures.   Teach your students one of the rhymes orally before doing this activity with the printed version. Practice the rhyme many times, using any support cues you can think of, such as body movements, voice intonation, or pictures reflecting the text. When your students have memorized the rhyme, introduce the written version on a chart or printed page. Model how you point to the words as you read and then have the children read along with you. Ask a student to read the rhyme to you and point to each word along the way. Notice the student's fingerpointing accuracy: Does she correctly match the word she is saying to the word she is pointing to? Do multiple-syllable words such as *pancake* or *rooftop* throw her off? What happens when she gets to the end of a printed sentence but hasn't yet finished saying the line? These observations will let you know whether or not your student has developed concept of word. After you have finished your assessment, model how to fingerpoint read by touching each word as you recite the rhyme. Do this a second time and ask your students to say the rhyme with you chorally. In a subsequent *Read With* session, take turns echo reading line by line. Have the student echo read and fingerpoint to each word in a line after you model.

Spanish Rhymes to Assess Concept of Word in Text

Materials.   The Spanish language has far fewer one-syllable words than does English, so students attempting to fingerpoint words in a rhyme are immediately thrust into the multiple-syllable word challenge. Here are two relatively simple rhymes that you can use to informally assess your Spanish-speaking students' concept of word in Spanish. Select one of the following rhymes and copy it onto a piece of chart paper or sentence strips for the pocket chart. The first rhyme is about the sun, the second about a snail.

El Sol

El sol que yo pinto
de lindo color
nos brinda su luz,
también su calor.

Traditional

El Caracol

Aquel caracol,
que va por el sol,
en cada ramita,
lleva una flor.

Traditional

Procedures. As you would in English, help your students to memorize the rhyme by repeated practice and by adding physical and visual clues. When students know the rhyme by heart, ask them to fingerpoint the words as they read from a chart or paper version. Notice if your students are able to correctly touch the words they are reading. When and how do they get off track? Do they attempt to recover their rhythm by starting the line again or noticing beginning letters? The answers to these questions will give you many insights into your students' developing concept of word. Now go back and show your students how to fingerpoint read as outlined earlier in this activity.

TALK WITH ACTIVITIES

Sharing Stories 4–24

One way to learn more about students' oral language proficiencies in English (and their home languages) is to elicit personal narratives about exciting real-life events. In this way, teachers have an opportunity to see students using language in a group setting with peers, where maximum fluency is likely to exist.

Materials. Come prepared to share an interesting, real-life story with your students, one that you hope will spark stories of their own. If your story is thematic, bring support materials such as simple word books or concept sort cards such as those in the Appendix of this book.

Procedures. In Chapter 2 of this book we described using *Tell a Story to Get a Story* (Mc Cabe & Bliss, 2003) as an informal oral language assessment. This technique may be used on a regular basis informally in your small-group lessons as well. Sharing stories is a good way to open a lesson, find out about students' background experiences, and "prime the pump" for the upcoming activities. Share your story with enthusiasm. Try to make it as dramatic as possible. When you are finished, ask an open-ended question to get students to tell their own stories. As they share, ask follow-up questions as necessary. Bring out your picture resources to help in case students have difficulty with specific vocabulary words. Figure 4-6, Mr. Chang's Lesson, illustrates how one teacher implemented this lesson.

Variations. If time permits, build on *Sharing Stories* by having students do a Language Experience or group experience story (see Activity 4-26). This provides an

Mr. Chang is a kindergarten teacher who combines a sharing-stories activity with a concept sort and a brief phonemic awareness lesson. Mr. Chang is working with a group of six English learners in his kindergarten class. Today he will focus on building the vocabulary of animal names, and he will do some phonemic awareness tasks to discriminate the beginning sounds in words. He knows that students need some meaningful words to work with in order to participate in phonemic awareness activities. He has decided to use *Tell a Story to Get a Story* as a way to get students talking. Mr. Chang begins, "I saw something very exciting this morning before I came to school—something I had never seen before. I looked out of my window at home, and in a little grassy area I saw a wild rabbit. It was sitting still, and every once in a while it would hop down the way. It did not see me, so it wasn't scared. I have never seen a rabbit by my house before. I didn't even know that rabbits live there! I wonder where it sleeps. Have you ever seen an animal that you can tell us about?"

Mr. Chang calls on students to share their experiences, and asks clarifying or open-ended questions as needed to support their narratives. If students cannot name the animal they have seen, he pulls out the animal sort picture cards to see if they can point to the animal they are discussing. He also has simple picture dictionaries or a photo library set at hand to help them point out their animals as needed.

Once students have had an opportunity to share their stories, Mr. Chang moves to a picture sort of animal cards. He starts by sorting the cards into "Animals we told stories about" and "Animals we didn't." Next he moves into a sort of wild animals and animals that live with people. In each round of sorts, students work with the teacher to remember and repeat the animal names and sort them into categories. Finally, Mr. Chang uses this new vocabulary to discuss beginning sounds. He works with students to find animal names that sound alike at the beginning such as *cat–cow, fox–fish, dog–duck*, and *bee–bug*. After all the correct matches have been made, the teacher picks three pairs and mixes them up. He hands individual cards to students and asks them to find the person whose animal starts with the same sound. Students must say the name of each animal out loud to find this sound match.

FIGURE 4-6   Mr. Chang's Lesson

opportunity to connect oral language to written words, and the stories will be available in future lessons to examine conventions of print and letter–sound correspondences. It will also provide comprehensible text for students to use in repeated readings of familiar materials.

Language Experience Dictations 4–25

Use students' background experiences and knowledge of English to create texts that you know they will understand. The Language Experience Approach (Stauffer, 1980) shows students the connection between oral language and print, validates students' experiences, and helps teachers understand their students' oral language development.

Materials.   It is usually helpful to have a warm-up conversation or a hands-on experience to lead into the language experience dictation. For instance, the *Sharing Stories* activity (Activity 4-24) prepares students for drawing and dictating a story about an animal they have seen. A field trip or an in-class activity such as making play dough, constructing a house with blocks, or observing a pet hamster are also examples of experiences that can lead to a dictation. Thus, materials will vary depending on the activity you choose. Have drawing and writing materials available for the students to illustrate their experience.

Procedures.   Provide an interesting activity such as making pancakes as you model the use of vocabulary such as *batter, sugar,* or *spoon.* Encourage the students to talk about what they see and do for the "language experience." Then invite individual students to offer sentences that you write down on a paper. Help each student to shape a sequential coherent account that is not too long. Repeat the sentences, pointing to the words, and have the student read along with you. Finally, ask the student to reread the dictation to you while pointing to each word. Make a copy of the dictation for the child to reread and illustrate. Keep the dictation in the student's Personal Reader folder to reread on an on-going basis and for harvesting words for word banks. This can be used as another informal assessment of the child's concept of word.

Considerations. Language experience dictations are designed to bridge the natural language of students to the printed word. Students who are learning English as a new language or who speak dialectical variations of academic English may use nonstandard forms in their oral speech. For example, one student recently dictated the phrase "He goed to the store to get a cake." A teacher may be torn about whether to write this language verbatim for the student, or whether to correct the sentence to "He went to the store to get a cake." On the one hand, the student will probably reread the text as spoken, and when he gets to the verb, he will say "goed." If the word has been written as "went," she will misread the text. On the other hand, many teachers feel uncomfortable having students reread text that may reinforce incorrect patterns. You will need to make a decision in context about which approach is most appropriate for the situation. If the primary goal is to show the oral language to written language connection, and this story is not aimed at a wider audience, write exactly what the child has said. If you can rephrase the sentence for the child and she repeats it correctly (e.g., "He *went* to the store."), and if the story will be shared with others, use the occasion as a teachable moment to correct and practice the standard language form.

Group Experience Stories 4–26

Group experience dictations provide a way for students to see their spoken words take form in much the same way that individual language experience activities do, this time in a small-group context.

Materials. Provide a memorable activity for students—a field trip, a hands-on science or art experience, a construction project—anything that involves the senses and sparks interest. Materials will vary depending on the specific activity. You will also need chart paper and colored markers to write students' sentences.

Procedures. Pull aside a group small enough so that you can see each person's eyes as you reread the text. Usually groups of four to eight students work well, and this ensures that everyone in the group has a chance to create a sentence. Elicit a comment about the experience from each student in turn, and write these statements on a large chart of paper. For example: "Mohamed said, 'My airplane went in the tree.' Marika said, 'I made a paper airplane that went up and down.' " Some teachers find it helpful to change the color of the text to differentiate each student's comment.

When all of the students' sentences have been written, reread the chart as you fingerpoint to each word. Discuss and clarify specific words and conventions of print. Students will love reconnecting to the meaningful text of the shared group experience, and will eagerly point out what each of their peers said!

Variations. Students can also be invited to dictate sentences that fit a predetermined pattern selected by the teacher that introduces targeted vocabulary or reinforces language from a familiar book. If the focus is on color words and clothing (after reading *Mary Wore Her Red Dress*) the account might read like this: "María said, 'I wore my yellow shirt.' Kia said, 'I wore my pink shorts.' Bao said, 'I wore my blue sneakers.' " Or an account about pets might read "Ramón has a dog for a pet. Leeza has a cat for a pet."

ALPHABET KNOWLEDGE

My Name, Your Name 4–27

Students' names are a great source of meaningful print for learning words and letters!

Materials.   You will need pieces of cardstock approximately 3 × 7 inches. Write the name of each student in your class clearly on its own piece.

Procedures.   At transitional times in the school day, use these cards as flash cards to help students begin to memorize each other's names. Use the name cards to select class helpers or a "student of the day." Play games with the name cards: Have students pick a name at random and deliver it to the correct person; use physical actions such as "hop" to Yasmin's name, "skip" to Miguel's name; use the name cards for students to "sign into class" in the morning or express their opinion on a topic of the day.

As students become more familiar with each other's names, use the cards to do group sorts. Lead the group to sort by how many letters each name has, or by whether it contains a certain letter, such as *o*. Eventually, have students sort the names by beginning letters. Work with names in each letter group to see if they sound the same at the beginning. Compare these groups to alphabet books that feature names such as *A My Name Is Alice* (Bayer, 1992) or *What's Your Name? From Ariel to Zoe* (Sanders, 1995).

Variations.   The name cards may also be used to stimulate oral language in a variety of ways. In a small group, choose a student's name card and encourage other students in the group to make sentences about the featured person. "Miguel has a green shirt." "Miguel runs fast." "Miguel rides the bus." The teacher may choose to write some of the sentences down on chart paper for a group experience story. Another way to elicit discussion is for students to pick two name cards and discuss how the spellings are the same or different. "Yasmin and Miguel's names both have the letter *i*." "They both have *m*s, but Miguel's *M* is big." "They both have six letters." "There are many letters that are in one of the names, but not the other, like *y, a, s, n, g*, and *u*."

A Community Alphabet 4–28

The names of students in your class, as well as familiar people, places, and objects in the school and neighborhood, can be used to create a relevant and meaningful way for students to connect letters to the real world—a community alphabet.

Materials.   Using photographs or drawings, illustrate each letter of the alphabet on a bulletin board area or pocket chart stand. Each of the uppercase and lowercase letters can feature someone or something from your school community. To help everyone feel a part of the community, all students' names should be included in the alphabet, even if it means you have five illustrations for *A*! If you are lacking someone for a particular letter, consider giving a classroom pet a name that starts with the unused letter (Zorba the guinea pig? Quentin the goldfish?). Find a book of baby names (or find lists on websites) and read through them with your students. They will hear the sound repeated many times and you can write down choices on the chalkboard for voting purposes.

Procedures.   Use the community alphabet to practice singing the ABC song or to play guessing games. If it is possible to duplicate the alphabet at an 8 1/2 × 11 inch size, make copies for students to keep and refer to at their tables.

Personal Alphabet Books 4–29

Materials.   Provide each student with a folder with enough pages for each letter of the alphabet. Old magazines can be cut up to provide pictures, or use pictures from concept sorts, photographs, and drawing materials to illustrate the personal alphabet book.

Procedures.   Create an Alphabet Scrapbook of pictures and important words to go with each letter of the alphabet. English learners will find this an especially helpful reference as they learn the letters and build their vocabularies in English. Encourage students to write the names of family members, friends, and school personnel in their personal alphabet books. They can illustrate the words with pictures and drawings. Important words that students use in their free writing (*like, I, have,* color words, etc.) should also be included, whenever possible, with a key picture. If students are literate in another language, they may want to write a translation of these words in their alphabet book. Students are encouraged to refer to these books throughout the day as needed. See *Words Their Way* (Bear et al., 2004) for additional ideas.

Playing with Letters 4–30

Materials.   Manipulatives, such as plastic or wooden letter tiles, magnetic letters, sandpaper letters, and alphabet puzzles.

Procedures.   Help students to become familiar with the letters in the English alphabet as they examine, sort, and manipulate letters in a variety of hands-on games and activities. Manipulatives, such as plastic or wooden letter tiles, magnetic letters, sandpaper letters, and alphabet puzzles, can be used by students to match, sort, trace with their fingers, and spell simple words. Each time students handle the letters, their shapes become more familiar. The manipulative activities provide contexts for students and teachers to discuss and describe letter names and sounds, what is "right side up," and a burgeoning sight-word vocabulary ("Is that a real word?" "Look, it's my mommy's name." "Teacher, I made a word from our word wall.").

Alphabet puzzles are a good example of what can be done with letter manipulatives. The simplest of puzzles require students to match a letter to its own shape. Often, the puzzle piece itself is shaped like the letter. The puzzle may be practiced over and over, and students are encouraged to say the letter names or sing the alphabet song as they work to put it together. Students can work with a partner to complete the task, thereby encouraging literacy-related conversation (and partners can supply the names of unknown letters). Give students individual puzzle pieces and ask them to find other examples of that letter around the classroom. More complex alphabet puzzles may require students to match an uppercase letter to its lowercase counterpart, or a letter shape to a word that starts with that letter. The repeated practice of identifying each letter and matching it to its picture or letter pair provides English learners with much needed visual support and reinforcement.

Letter Hunts 4–31

Materials.   A print-rich classroom or area with charts, labels, signs, and so on for students to look for letters and words; books and magazines with print big enough for students to work with; notetaking paper, writing materials, and highlighter pens.

Procedures.   To help students recognize letters and see that they are everywhere, send students on a letter hunt. Have them search for examples of the first letter in their names, or a letter featured in your shared reading or writing activity. They can look on classroom walls, on labels and packages, and in big books or chart stories. Have students write the letter on a small piece of paper each time they find one, or they can write words they find that contain that letter. Students can also use highlighter markers to spotlight the focus letter in printed materials such as old workbooks or outdated magazines with big print.

Sharing Alphabet Books 4–32

Materials.   There is an incredible range of excellent alphabet books on the market that can support your language and literacy teaching for emergent English learners of all ages. ABC books from the simplest wordless books to those using complex content-area vocabulary are described here. Let the artistry of master wordsmiths and illustrators support your English learners' attempts to recognize the English alphabet, build their vocabularies, and engage in meaningful conversations. Please see the reference list of suggested literature featured at the end of this book for additional titles. Alphabet books are coded "ABC" at the end of selected references. Books for specific activities are listed in procedures.

Procedures.   Wordless alphabet books and other concept books show rather than tell, and provide a platform for student participation in storytelling activities. For example, *Alphabet City* (Johnson, 1995) features realistic paintings of objects in New York City that resemble letter shapes. *A* is the side view of a sawhorse, *B* a set of fire escape stairs, and so on. While the book is simple, it is not "babyish." Both young and older emergent learners profit from discussing where in the picture the letter is represented, what object is depicted, what the object does, and what words could be used to describe the pictures. Use this and other wordless books to elicit content-based conversation from your students.

Some alphabet books focus on the sounds that letters make in funny ways. Two examples include *Achoo! Bang! Crash! The Noisy Alphabet* (MacDonald, 2003) and *Talk to Me About the Alphabet* (Raschka, 2003). MacDonald's book provides sounds in nature as well as the sounds of words to narrate a humorous picture for each letter of the alphabet. For instance, the *K* page shows a knight who has been ejected from his horse while walking over a dragon. The text says "Klank! Klang! Klop! Klip! Ka-pow!" (MacDonald, 2003, p. 11). Second-language learners may think that the English language sounds like a bunch of noise, and this book is one way to have fun with that idea! *Talk to Me About the Alphabet* works its way through each letter, incorporating words and sounds the letter represents. Even if students do not understand the meaning of every word, the repetition of sounds provides a connection to learning the written code of English.

Read these alphabet sound books to your students aloud in an energetic and theatrical way. Exaggerate the sounds that are illustrated in the texts. On repeated readings have students echo read the "noisy" lines. Let your students become the chorus of sounds as each page is read. Have students pick their favorite pages and lead the group in chanting the rhythmic and onomatopoetic lines such as "Click! Crackle! Clap! Crunch! Clank! Crash! Crack! Cackle!" (MacDonald, 2003, p. 3).

Many simple alphabet books serve as learning tools that can help build your students' basic vocabulary in English. For example, *Alphathoughts* by poet Lee Bennett Hopkins (2003) simply but eloquently describes a series of common and useful words. The beautiful illustrations help English learners connect the word and poem to an easy-to-understand visual. Read this book over and over, each time clarifying or informally checking that students understand the use of words and their meaning. Ask students to share what they know about individual words or topics.

Other simple definition-type alphabet books focus on specific content areas such as a kind of animal, a job, or a place. *Alphabeep: A Zipping, Zooming ABC* (Pearson, 2003) involves vehicles and road signs that might be seen as you drive. Use a book like this when you want to build vocabulary related to a unit on transportation or the city. Build on the book by learning the names of various kinds of vehicles; cut out pictures of traffic signs and vehicles from magazines; sort these pictures in multiple ways such as by their appearance or function; or have students create their own transportation books. Using content-area alphabet books in thematic units integrates letter–sound awareness within meaningful vocabulary development and conceptual learning.

Alphabet books provide opportunities to create a supportive climate for multicultural and multilingual experiences in the classroom. ABC books such as *Ashley Bryan's ABC of African American Poetry* (Bryan, 1997), *Gathering the Sun: An Alphabet in Spanish and English* (Ada, 1997), and *Handsigns* (Fain, 1995) add to students' understanding of the English alphabet while broadening their knowledge of specific cultures and languages. Guide students to dialogue in class about the many ways in which people express themselves; this often helps them feel more comfortable about sharing their own experiences. As students share their personal background experiences, consider ways to bridge your classroom curriculum to their languages and cultures. Look for the "ABC" code in the children's literature references at the end of this book for additional examples.

Variations.   Older emergent English learners will appreciate alphabet books that use humor or more grown-up themes to elucidate the letters. In *Z Goes Home* the letter Z maneuvers through an ABC of obstacles to reach home at the end of the day (Agee, 2003). While using a very simple text line—each letter is represented by only one word—the illustrations and continuity of the story are appealing to students of many ages. It is a fun book for mature students just beginning to develop letter knowledge and vocabulary in English. Another humorous book for students with more advanced English vocabularies is *What Pete Ate from A–Z (Really!)* (Kalman, 2001). The text describes a mischievous dog that eats his way through people's personal items. The bold and silly illustrations are especially engaging to upper-grade students, and lend themselves to extension activities and discussions. Imagine having students create their own alphabet books of "What Pete Ate" as they expand their English vocabularies.

Sorting Alphabet Books 4–33

As your classroom collection and group experiences with alphabet books grow, consider using the books you have shared to conduct open or closed sorts.

Materials.   Gather a stack of 8 to 10 alphabet books you have previously shared with your group.

Procedures.   Spend a few minutes reminiscing about the storyline, content, or artwork in the books. For open sorts, invite students to think about all of the books, and share ways that the books might be grouped by commonalities. For instance, students might suggest grouping books by the kind of illustrations they use (photographs, collage, drawings, etc.); students may notice letters being displayed in certain styles of fonts; or they may want to classify books by how they were used in your classroom ("We read these ones when we studied about animals."). For closed sorts use a key picture card to represent your category. Invite students to review and discuss which books belong in each group. On one sort, your categories might relate to each book's theme or topic, such as ABC books about animals, school, the community, or a specific habitat.

Another sort might involve sorting books by how much text is presented for each letter: Is the book wordless; does it have single-word descriptions, short phrases, one-sentence, or more complex texts? Still another sort might involve having students sort the alphabet books by their level of sophistication: What age-group audience would most appreciate each book, and why do they think that? Make up categories that fit your classroom studies and students' interests!

Hands on the Alphabet 4–34

Materials.   Begin a collection of magazine pictures or small objects to keep in small containers for each letter of the alphabet. For example, the *A* box may include pictures or mini-versions of an apple, an acorn, an alligator, an armchair, an astronaut, and so on. Many educational supply companies sell these sets ready made. It is also fun to have students contribute to the collection.

Procedures.   Work with one or two letters at a time. Use the objects or pictures to teach students the names of words. Mix up two letters worth of items and see if students can correctly sort them into the appropriate container. Give one item each to students and ask them to form themselves into two lines depending on their letter. Students will need to know the name of their item, and remember to attach it to the appropriate letter in order to do that. Always begin with two letters that have very different sounds!

Variations.   You can use the pictures or objects to play guessing games. Give one item from a specific letter group to each student to keep hidden. Have the student give clues about what the object is until other students have identified it. You can also play a memory game by laying out all of the objects from a certain letter on a tray. Ask students to close their eyes while you remove one object. Students will need to use their memory and vocabulary skills to identify which object is missing.

Sorting with Alphabet Strips 4–35

Materials.   Obtain enough alphabet strips from educational materials stores for each student in your group to have his or her own piece. These can be purchased as rolls of stickers (which can be attached to cardstock) or as individual desktop alphabets with a key illustration for each letter. Photographs as illustrations are especially helpful for English learners who may find some caricatures or drawings difficult to decipher.

Procedures.   Desktop alphabet strips are a useful tool to aid in letter recognition and sorting. Use these alphabet strips to have students touch each letter as they say it, or as they sing the alphabet song. Have students "quiz" a partner on the names of letters. Mix up an alphabet set of letter tiles for students to place under the correct letter on the strip. In small-group discussions, encourage students to identify letters and describe their shapes and sizes. Invite students to sing or chant their way through the alphabet to find the names of unknown letters.

Variations.   Extend these tasks by giving students small word cards with the names of their fellow students on them, and guide them to put each name below the letter on the alphabet strip according to its first letter. As students learn new sight words, have them demonstrate how the first letter of the word they learned matches a letter on the alphabet strip, and line it up below that letter.

Many Kinds of Alphabets 4–36

Materials.   Make copies of some of the sample alphabets from the Appendix of this book.

Procedures.   Emergent students of all ages will enjoy looking at and comparing the alphabets of many languages. Let students examine the various alphabets, and ask them to share their perceptions. What does the writing remind them of? How does it compare to English? Can students distinguish the English alphabet from the others? Try to make some letters from other languages by tracing through a thin layer of salt on a shallow tray.

Variations.   Discuss key ideas about why people from a variety of cultures have created writing systems. You may want to share portions of books that highlight writing in a variety of languages, such as *Scripts of the World* (Bukiet, 1984), or *Day of Ahmed's Secret* (Parry, 1995). Invite in a classroom parent or community member who can share a different writing system with the students. Show examples of how students' names might be written in this other language. Let this be an opportunity to validate the diversity of written languages in the world, and help students to make connections to background knowledge they bring from their primary languages.

Comparing Picture Books in Different Languages 4-37

Materials.   Begin to build a collection of picture books from many languages to share with your students. The most effective of these will be books that have simple text-to-picture matches and clear print. It is also helpful to have bilingual books in which the text is printed in both English and another language. A list of sources for bilingual books is included at the end of this book.

Procedures.   Introduce a bilingual book to your students by showing the cover of the book and pointing out how the text looks in both English and the other language. For example, *My First Book of Proverbs = Mi Primer Libro de Dichos* (Gonzalez & Ruiz, 1995) puts the English print and Spanish print in separate banners across the page. Read the text in English, and then point to the words in Spanish. If you are not bilingual in the language presented, do your best to sound out the words, and ask your students to help you say them. If the text uses a script you cannot read, point it out anyway, and ask students who speak the language to make a prediction about what the text might say. Encourage students to share vocabulary words that relate to the picture, which they could teach to the rest of the group. For instance, in *My First Book of Proverbs* one of the pages quotes a Mexican proverb, "Una abeja no hace una colmena" (One bee doesn't make a hive). Students who are learning English, but do not speak Spanish, can be guided to describe the picture and share words in their primary language that relate such as *bee, flowers,* and *tree.* Help students understand the moral behind the proverb, and ask how this might be expressed in their home languages.

Variations.   If you have bilingual support staff, colleagues, parents, or community members who can share bilingual books with students, build in time for them to come in on a regular basis. Students who have heard a book in their primary language will be able to understand and appreciate the English version much better. If your guest does not speak English, the sharing of a bilingual book can be a team affair! Look for translations of popular children's books from your grade level to include in your classroom library. Students can compare the scripts, make oral language to print connections with their primary language, and pull these books out for bilingual visitors who may be able to read them to individuals informally.

Bilingual Picture Alphabets 4-38

Materials.   Make copies of the bilingual picture alphabet for the letters in Spanish and English from the Appendix of this book. The same illustration represents each letter in both languages.

Procedures. Bilingual picture alphabets help English learners make connections among their home oral language, oral English, writing in their home language, and written English. Bilingual picture alphabets also provide a common vocabulary with which teachers can explain letter–sound correspondences in English by relating these to the language students already know.

Use the Spanish-English picture alphabet to teach vocabulary: "*B* is for *boat*, or *barco* in Spanish; *boat–barco*, they both start with *B*." Let the bilingual alphabet be a scaffold for helping students find letters as they are learning English key words: "Point to *tortuga-tortuga* starts with the letter *T*."

Variations. As you learn more about the background languages of your students, begin to collect resource materials to share in class and consider creating bilingual picture alphabets in numerous languages. Some of these resources may already be available from educational publishers or on the Internet (see resource list at the end of this book). These activities build an appreciation and interest in languages and literacies among monolingual-English speakers. Have students share the names of illustrations in their home languages. Ask students or their parents if the English letters are used in the script of their home language. Use an affirming manner and open inquisitiveness to discuss commonalities and differences among languages in your multilingual community.

Learning My Letters Game 4-39

Use simple games to help students practice the names of letters.

Materials. Copy the blank game board from the Appendix. Choose four or five letters to focus on, and fill in one letter per space, in random order throughout the board. You will also need the same letters on plastic or wooden tiles, and a cup to draw from.

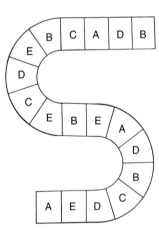

Procedures. Put four or five letter tiles in a small cup—let's say you picked *A, B, C, D,* and *E*. Students take turns picking one letter from the cup and moving to the next spot where that letter appears. Students must say the name of the letter before advancing. The first person to reach the end wins (see Figure 4-7).

Variations. Many variations can be devised for the *Learning My Letters* game. As students become more proficient with recognizing the letters, letter tiles can focus on similar shaped letters such as *c, o, d, b,* and *p*. You can make the game more difficult by having the letter tiles be uppercase versions, and the game board letters lowercase. Or, have students work with the vowels only. As students' language development progresses, you can ask students to think of a word that starts with the letter before they may advance to each new space. It is always helpful to have a copy of the alphabet or simple picture dictionaries handy when creating more complex variations of this game.

FIGURE 4-7 A Sample "Learning My Letters" Gameboard

The Winning Letter Game 4-40

Here is a game to build letter recognition and encourage discussion about the alphabet.

Materials. Choose six letters you want to reinforce with your students. You will need a blank die that you can write letters on for this game. If this is not available, put a small sticker on each side of a numbered die—one letter per side. Each student has a sheet of paper that contains a grid with six rows and five columns. Label each row with the name of one of the letters.

Procedures.   Students take turns rolling the die, coloring in one square on the associated letter row each time. The first person to color in five boxes for the same letter has "The winning letter!"

The Piñata Game 4–41

Materials.   You will need two sets of letter tiles, or one set of uppercase and one set of lowercase letters for students to match. The piñata can be a cup or other small container that holds letters.

Procedures.   This is a letter-matching game. It is a fast game, just like a race for candy in a real piñata. Students take turns tipping the piñata. When the letters fall to the ground, all students quickly find as many matches as they can, and pair them up in their work space. When all of the letters have been partnered, students share the letter names and see who has the most pairs. Then, put the letter tiles back in the piñata and play again.

Sound Boards 4–42

Materials.   Make copies of the sound boards for beginning consonants in English or Spanish from the Appendix in this book.

Procedures.   Sound boards visually help students connect sounds to a key picture. They are exceptionally helpful in giving students a consistent visual key for the sounds of English letters. Keep these sound boards handy for English learners. Students can have their own copies to paste them to the inside cover of their Personal Readers or writing folders. Review the key word pictures so that students can make an oral language connection to the letter and word.

Variations.   Your Spanish-speaking students connect the letters to words in their home language by using the Spanish sound board. Even if you do not speak Spanish, and your students do not have the opportunity to learn to read and write in Spanish, the sound board will facilitate an understanding of the alphabetic principle that smoothes the path to learning letters in English. Encourage your students to point to the consonants and say the name of the associated picture in each box. Chant the sounds along with the word, such as "B-b-b, barco."

Use the same phonemic awareness games and activities with the Spanish key words as you would with English words. Remember, learning to play with and distinguish individual sounds in words is a skill that transfers across languages!

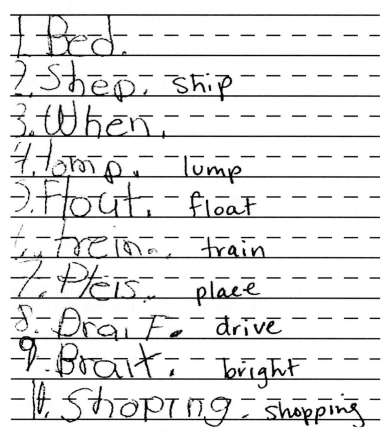

FIGURE 5-2 Middle to Late Letter Name–Alphabetic Spelling by Teresa, a Spanish Speaker

distinctions among sounds. Begin with larger contrasts and then sort for finer gradations that focus on the specific confusions that students experience between sounds in their first language and in English. For example, although students may not pronounce the /v/ sound completely correctly, we do expect them to hear that /v/ is distinctive from other sounds such as /b/ or /f/.

Students use their primary language literacy. Students use what they know about phonics in their primary languages to spell, but the letter–sound relationships in their first languages are not always the same as they are in English. For example, students who speak Spanish may turn to the /ch/ sound to pronounce the /sh/ sound in English because there is no /sh/ sound in Spanish. You will find word study activities in this chapter that compare /ch/ and /sh/, an activity to select when the student writes CH for /sh/ or vice versa.

Students' primary languages support their literacy development. With early letter name–alphabetic beginning readers, vocabulary from students' first language assists students as they make the transition to learning solely with English texts. For example, when students are asked to draw pictures of words that begin with the /t/ sound, students may include words from their primary language that begin with this sound.

Throughout word study, students include words from their primary language when they brainstorm words related to the content studies. For example, when students add concepts to match a food theme they may include terms from their first language such as *pan* or *mkate* (*bread* in Spanish and Swahili, respectively).

Word Study is another way students can learn about oral English.

Vocabulary is a partner in all sorts. Though there is an emphasis on phonics instruction with letter name spellers, vocabulary instruction is a partner in each word study lesson. Use pictures like those in the Appendix of this book to assist in vocabulary instruction. The activities for this stage begin with concept picture sorts that are good for learners of all ages. These sorts set a tone for making meaning and encourage discussion, thinking, and concept development. Vocabulary learning supports all three of these actions. In word study routines like those presented in Chapter 3, students are repeatedly exposed to important vocabulary words. Choose words that have high utility and can be used easily in conversation.

In word study lessons, many older English learners will want to keep a short list of words they see or hear and want to learn. Often, the key content vocabulary is what students bring to the table, as well as some of the academic and descriptive language and vocabulary (e.g., *weather forecast, reverse, subtract*). Students in this stage who are in the intermediate elementary grades may not be able to read many of the words in their content texts, and they may point to key terms they cannot read. Vocabulary lessons become student directed as they search for meaning in the key vocabulary in their texts. Students' knowledge of the content vocabulary and academic language frames the gateway to their school success. In word study, teachers help students hammer vocabulary onto a sturdy frame, and provide some of the student motivation to push on the hinge to swing open the gates to school success.

Pictures are a part of many sorts during this stage.

During the letter name stage, the sorts teachers use are a blend of pictures and words, starting with mostly pictures at the early part of the stage. Early on, students collect sight words from the familiar materials they read. By the time students have mastered beginning consonant sounds, they have learned enough sight words to use mostly words in sorting. Pictures are often included for vocabulary instruction.

Word study instruction for English learners varies with the depth of each student's vocabulary knowledge. Word study can be a vehicle for oral language learning.

Sort with known words and pictures.

To create sorts, teachers must have a good sense of the words students can read. Students' word knowledge is confirmed each day as they sort, read, and write. The few words students do not know are set aside and are discarded from the sort if, after a few days, they remain unknown. If, after supported practice reading the words in a sort, there are more than four words students cannot read, choose a slightly easier sort. Remember to check that students know the meaning of words, even if they can read them.

Letter name-alphabetic spellers are beginning readers.

Beginning readers read slowly and prefer to read out loud. Students who can understand some letter–sound correspondences and who have learned some sight words will have a concept of word. They will be able to read appropriate leveled texts with good accuracy and at a good rate, especially with repeated practice. Their reading skills may be a bit ahead of their understanding of English. Parents and teachers may say, "Students read the words but do not comprehend what they read." This ability to read and not comprehend is related to their language and vocabulary skills that grow through both oral and written language use. Because some students read with accuracy and fluency, they may surprise us in what they do not understand. Vocabulary knowledge is a factor in their understanding. Take time to focus on comprehension activities even when students seem fluent in their reading.

Understanding is the key to successful reading.

What we want to concentrate on is what students do understand and help them to be motivated to have integrity while they read; by integrity, we mean that students are able to keep a *vigil to understand* what they read (cf. Deese, 1969). It is the skill of thinking while they read that we want

Teach students to keep a vigil for understanding in reading and word study.

to promote in all of the students' essential literacy activities, whether in a *Read To* or *Word Study* activity. Students learn to talk about the words they do not know, and they ask their classmates and teachers for clarification.

Concept sorts encourage discussions.

How do teachers know if students understand the meanings of the words they read and sort? One way to assess students' understanding of the words is to have them talk about why they sorted the way they did. To encourage verbal interaction, students sort words conceptually. For example, in a Go

For the English learner, distinguish between being able to read a word and knowing what it means.

Fish format, students call out a request: *"Find two words in this sort that are colors."* (black/red) *or "Find two words for things that you would find in your house"* (lamp, bed). In open concept sorts, students develop their own categories and talk about the concepts that underlie the words.

CHARACTERISTICS OF ORTHOGRAPHIC DEVELOPMENT FOR ENGLISH LEARNERS IN THE LETTER NAME–ALPHABETIC STAGE

The Letter Name Strategy, Reliance on Articulation, and the Alphabetic Principle

In reading and spelling, students in this stage approach words in three ways:

1. They use the names of the letters to understand the alphabet.
2. They use how sounds are articulated in the mouth to understand how words are spelled.
3. They master the principle that the letters of the alphabet represent individual sounds.

With these three ways of examining words, students partner unfamiliar sounds and letter sounds in English with the sounds and letters of their first language. As students use information about articulation, they compare *where* sounds are made (point of articulation) and *how* they are made as air is forced through the mouth and nose (manner of articulation).

Descriptions of how sounds are made in the mouth are presented in Table 5-1. This table helps explain why students may experience difficulty discriminating among specific sounds in English. Minimal pairs are sounds that differ in only one minor way. For example, in saying the words *food* and *vote*, one can feel the similarities and slight difference in the beginning consonants as the two words are said. As can be seen in Table 5-1, /f/ and /v/ are articulated the same way: They are both made with the air coming between the top teeth and bottom lip (see Nilsen & Nilsen, 2002 for additional information). The biggest difference is *how* the sounds are made: /f/ is voiceless and /v/ is voiced. *Feel* how the vocal cords are engaged when saying /v/ and not in saying the /f/ sound. *The way sounds are made is as important as the actual sounds the students hear.* This is why students say the words as they sort. Many of the substitutions in the spelling of English learners are phonetic, letter–sound substitutions according to minimal pairs. This is why it is common for students to substitute F for *v* as in FAFRIT for *favorite*.

Why would a student spell *boat* as POT and not BOT? How can the substitution of *b* for *v* be understood? Refer to Table 5-1, and draw a line from the /b/ to the /v/. Both sounds are voiced, but differ slightly in both *how* they are made—as a stop or **plosive** with a continuing air flow—and *where* they are made—between the lips and teeth. They are similar, however, and this may be experienced by saying *very* for *berry* several times. Feel the slight difference in the shape of the lips as you say the words. Someone who speaks only Spanish will not recognize the difference in these two sounds. (In Spanish spelling, the meaning layer with its Latin origins determines the spelling of *b* and *v*.) In these words, *bola, iba, vale, invitar,* the *b* and *v* are pronounced in the same way (Dalbor, 1997), and even in Spanish, beginning writers will substitute B for *v* or V for *b*. Spanish-speaking English learners may confuse both the pronunciation and spelling of *b* and *v*; *very* may be said "berry" and *berry* may be spelled VERY.

Instruction for English learners at this stage begins with easy contrasts and gradually works toward these more difficult comparisons between minimal pairs. What are the sounds that English learners find difficult? This will depend on the languages students speak. For this book, 15 languages were examined for the sorts and contrasts to study, and a series of sorts for English learners was developed based on the contrasts that linguists have described.

Consonants and the English Learner

The number and types of consonants varies from language to language. The consonants and vowels of English are arranged into syllables. **Open syllables** end in vowels. More common are **closed syllables,** which end in a consonant sound. Spanish, in comparison,

---

The voiced/voiceless distinction explains many of the logical substitutions spellers make.

Plosive Sounds
Plosives are made by closing the air flow and creating a puff of air (/b/, /p/, /t/, /d/, /k/, /g/).

Open Syllable
A syllable that ends with a vowel as in **pi**lot, **rea**son.

Closed Syllable
A syllable that ends with a consonant sound as in **bat**tle, **rack**et.

TABLE 5-1 Where and How Sounds Are Made and Feel in the Mouth: Manner and Point of Articulation for Consonants

HOW MANNER OF ARTICULATION/FLOW OF AIR	WHERE POINT OF ARTICULATION							
	Bilabial—two lips	*Labiodental*—top teeth/bottom lip	*Interdental*—tongue tip/top teeth	*Alveolar*—tongue tip/tooth ridge	*Retroflex or alveolar flap or tap*—tongue tip/hard palate	*Palatal*—tongue mid/hard palate	*Velar*—tongue back/soft palate	*Glottal*—not localized
STOPS/PLOSIVES *a closing of air flow and a puff of air*	**b** ball p pen			**d** donkey t tail			**g** gate k kite	
CONTINUANTS/FRICATIVES *continuing air forced between two places in the mouth*	**w** water hw which	**v** view f file	**ð** then θ thank	**z, y, l** zipper yellow lake s sun	r rain	ž measure š ship		h hen
NASAL CONTINUANTS *air forced through nasal passage*	**m** mat			**n** night			**ŋ** sing	
AFFRICATES *stop + air flow made with some friction between two places in the mouth*						**j** Jim č chip		

Key: Nonbolded words are voiceless
Bolded words are voiced.

is composed mostly of open syllables. As a result, students from languages with a predominantly open-syllable structure may not hear or articulate some final sounds of words. For example, Chinese, Korean, and Spanish speakers may not hear the final consonant sounds of closed syllables or they may add a final sound that they expect to be there (Helman, 2004; Yang, 2005).

To pronounce and spell sounds that do not exist in the primary language, students locate a nearby consonant sound in English that is closest to a sound in their primary language. For example, in Spanish, Mandarin, and Cantonese Chinese, words that end with an /n/, /m/, or /ng/ sound are confused. Often, while deleting final sounds, students produce a slight **glottal** or unreleased sound when they say words that end with a /g/ or /k/, as in the final sound in *dug* or *clock*. This may be heard as a slight /k/ sound and almost like a partial-breath pause.

Glottal Sound
A sound made using the vocal cords or the area around them—the glottis.

Tables 5-2 and 5-3 summarize some of the multiple contrasts for students from different languages. To illustrate the levels of analysis to look for, two sounds and how these sounds are spelled are presented: <u>b</u>e<u>ll</u>, tu<u>b</u>, and <u>sh</u>ell, <u>sh</u>ine, <u>sh</u>ovel, and pu<u>sh</u> by students from various language backgrounds. The first column presents key words for these sounds. The second column lists how students may say these key words. The third column presents the language backgrounds that might create this contrast with English. The fourth column summarizes the characteristics of the contrasts that English learners experience. Table 5-1 showed the manner and point of articulation for these sounds. There are many pictures in the *Pictures for Sorts and Games* section of the Appendix that you can use to help your students practice these contrasts such as *ball, bike, cab, globe, shoe, ship, trash,* and *fish*.

The p for b contrast (written as p/b) in the beginning position (<u>b</u>ell) is less common than for final sounds. The /l/ sound also causes confusions for students with the /r/. As can be seen in Table 5-1, these two sounds are right next to each other; how and where they are made are quite similar. Students match the sounds in English with their primary languages and find the closest sounds as well as the accompanying letter–sound correspondences that they know in their primary written languages.

TABLE 5-2	Beginning and Final /b/ in English Contrasts Across Languages		
Sound and Key Word in English	**May Be Said in This Way**	**May Be Difficult for Speakers of**	**Characteristics, Contrasts, Minimal Pairs**
/b/ *b*<u>ell</u>	/p/ pehr behr	Chinese, Hmong, Vietnamese	/b/ (voiced) may be said more like /p/ (unvoiced). /r/ can substitute for /l/; final /l/ sounds are hard to pronounce.
	bar, ball	Chinese, Hmong, Vietnamese	The short ĕ may be pronounced more like a short ă.
<u>tu</u>*b*	tup, tu	Arabic, Chinese, Hmong, Navajo, Korean, Spanish, Vietnamese	/b/ is not found in final position; /b/ may be omitted or substituted with /p/ in final position.
	to, top	Chinese, Spanish, Vietnamese	The short ŭ may sound more like a short ŏ.

How the /b/ sound is made: puff of air.
Where the /b/ sound is made: between the lips (bilabial).

TABLE 5-3	Beginning and Final /sh/ in English Contrasts Across Languages			

Sound and Key Word in English	May Be Said in This Way	May Be Difficult for Speakers of	Characteristics, Contrasts, Minimal Pairs
/sh/	/ch/ /j/	Spanish, Vietnamese,	/sh/ does not exist in many languages. /ch/ and /j/ substitutes in English for /sh/.
_sh_ell	chell, jell	Korean, Chinese,	
_sh_ine	chine, chy	Arabic	/ch/ substitutes for /sh/; /n/ is a difficult final sound.
_sh_ovel	chovel, chob		/v/ substitutes for /b/.
pu_sh_	puch, buch, pooch		/ch/ substitutes for /sh/ and vice versa.

How the /sh/ sound is made: air continues through a small channel of the mouth.
Where the /sh/ sound is made: tongue tip on hard palate.

TABLE 5-4	Examples of Challenging Consonant Sounds for English Learners		

English Sound		May Be Pronounced	Example Spelling Error
d _as in_	den	then	DEM (them)
j	joke	choke	GOB (job)
r	rope	(rolled r) rope, wope	WAIPEN (ripen)
v	van	ban	SURBING (serving)
z	zipper	sipper	SIVALAIS (civilize)
sh	shell	chell	CHED (shed)
th	thick	tick	TENK (think)
zh	treasure	treachure	CHESHER (treasure)
final rd	hard	har	HAR (hard)
final st	toast	tos	TOS (toast)
final ng	serving	servin'	SIRVIN (serving)
final sk	ask	as	AS (ask)
final z	prize	price	PRAES (prize)
final t	that	tha	THA (that)
final oil	spoil	es-poy-yo	EXPOLLO (spoil)
final mp	bump	bumpa	BAMPA (bump)

Table 5-4 presents some of the more challenging sounds in English, how they may be pronounced, and common spelling errors. The sorts that follow the basic introduction of the letter–sound correspondences focus on these and other challenging sounds.

Vowels and the English Learner

The vowels in English are often different from the vowels in students' primary languages.

Most languages have between 5 and 7 vowels, and vowel combinations. Spanish, Hebrew, and Japanese have 5 vowels; Romanian, 6; and English, 12. With diphthongs, like the vowels in _say, fine, boy, so,_ and _cow,_ there are 40 ways in which vowels can be combined in English. The Spanish vowels are also much more consistent than English across the various dialects and forms of Spanish (e.g., Mexican, Puerto Rican); in English different speakers around the world will pronounce vowels in different ways (e.g., American, British, Indian English), and even regionally as seen in differences in vowels from Vermont to California (Dalbor, 1997).

English learners use the letters from their first language to spell vowels in English. This is what Teresa did when she spelled long *a* with the letter–sound relationships from Spanish, her first language (train = TREIN and place = PLEIS). Figure 5-3 presents the vowel phonemes for American Spanish and English as they are made in the mouth. As noted in Figure 5-3, there are three areas laterally (front, center, and back) and three areas vertically: *high* with the mouth closed, *mid* with the mouth slightly open, and *low* with the mouth open. The five Spanish vowels are underlined. The vowels in blue with arrows beside them are glides that combine two vowels. You can sense the two vowels as you say the vowels in the middle of these words slowly: *bait, bite, boy, how,* and *boat.* Spanish speakers do not have an equivalent for the following vowels in English: short *a* in *bat,* the short *e* in *bet,* the short *i* bit, the short *u* in *but,* or the *oo* in *book.*

What students do is match the sounds in English to the closest sounds in Spanish. Table 5-5 presents some comparisons between English vowels and contrasting letter–sound correspondences in Spanish. These comparisons between the vowels of English and Spanish explain students' spelling errors and their strategies for examining words.

When students are learning a new set of vowels, they may segment the vowel sound more thoroughly than English speakers. For example, the long *a* and long *i* of English are diphthongs that involve a movement from one vowel sound to another: *ĕ* and *ē* for the long *a,* and short *o* and long *e* for the long *i,* a fact that may not be evident to English speakers but may show up in the spellings of English language learners. By saying words and sounds slowly as described in the next section, teachers come to understand how English learners analyze the vowels of English.

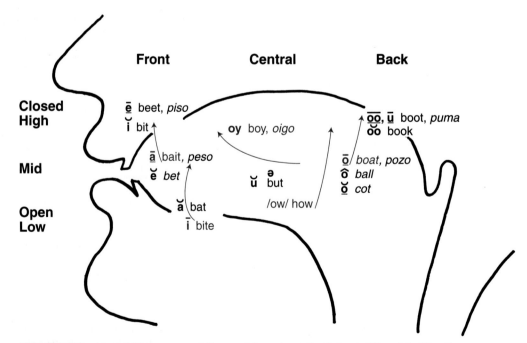

FIGURE 5-3 Vowel Phonemes of General American English and Spanish. The five underlined phonemes exist both in American Spanish and English. The Spanish word examples are written in italics. The phonemes marked in blue with an arrow (↑, ←) designate vowels that are glides with two or more sounds.

TABLE 5-5	Vowel Sounds in English and Spanish and Spelling Errors			
English Letter and Word		**Comparable Spanish Letter and Word**		**Example Spelling Error**
ā *as in*	rake	e *as in*	hecho	CHEK (*shake*)
ē	green	i	ido	PIC (*peek*)
ī	bike	ai	aire	BAIT (*bite*)
ō	rope	o	ocho	FLOUT (*float*)
ŏ	top	a	ajo	TAP (*top*)
ū	June	u	usted	FLUT (*flute*)

The Sequence of Word Study Instruction with English Learners

Students in the letter name–alphabetic stage learn the basic letter–sound correspondences for consonants and short vowels. The sequence of word study presented in Table 5-6 includes the correspondences that are made when English is influenced by the sound system of students' primary languages. The scope and sequence for this stage has been divided into three parts: early, middle, and end of the stage.

Letter name–alphabetic spellers match the sounds in words to the letters they know that may represent these sounds. Separating the speech stream of words into individual sounds is the focus of word study at this time. Beginning consonants using picture sorts are the first area of study for early letter name–alphabetic spellers. After students learn beginning consonants, consonant digraphs are introduced with picture sorts. The goal is for students to appreciate that these digraphs make one sound; that is, ch, sh, th, or wh. Mastery of these sounds will take some time, and should be revisited in the study of word families and short vowels.

Students at the middle of this stage study word families; their attention focuses on the onset, the beginning consonant sound, and the rime, or family (e.g., b-at or b-ell). After examining one vowel and its rimes, students compare words across word families to make generalizations about each short vowel; for example, that the *a* in *sad* sounds and feels much the same as the *a* sound in *fan*. Final sounds are emphasized in word study with English learners, beginning with the large final sound contrasts (*tan/top*) to finer ones (the /d/ and /t/ sounds in *mad/fat*).

Parallel to the study of word families, students study English consonant blends and digraphs in words. Words that are difficult to depict in picture sorts are now accessible because students can read words with word family patterns; that is, -an in *plan*, -in in *spin*. Many languages, including Russian, Spanish, and the eight Chinese languages, do not share English blends and digraphs. English learners benefit from seeing the written words to cue them to differences in articulation among the contrasting sounds.

After the study of word families, students study short-vowel sounds beyond word families. They make generalizations about the short vowels in English. For instance, students become confident that the words *fan, bad, map,* and *pat* sound alike in the middle, especially when these words are sorted next to words like *fin, hid, lip,* and *pit.* Blends and digraphs are again included here and expand the number of words students can spell and read.

In the late letter name stage, students are introduced to the first pattern, the consonant–vowel–consonant (CVC) pattern. This is the first time students have analyzed the syllable structure of English, and from here on, the study of patterns in English will incorporate all three layers of the orthography: sound, pattern, and meaning. As part of this study, they see that words like *spin* and *club* represent the CVC pattern. The

Preconsonantal Nasal
A nasal sound
(/m/,/n/,/ng/) that occurs
before a consonant as in
bump and *sink*.

study of this pattern expands the short vowel to include some of the consonants that color the vowels, as in the *r*- and *l*-influenced vowel sounds in words like *purr, car, pull,* and *call.* Final consonant blends and digraphs are studied in words like *fast* and *dish.* At the end of this stage, students sort words by **preconsonantal nasal** endings as they hear and see them in words like *camp, stamp, blend,* and *stump.* Each step along the way, contrasts that are important and useful to English learners as they study the distinctive sounds of English are featured.

TABLE 5-6	**Sequence of Word Study for English Learners in the Letter Name–Alphabetic Stage in English**	
Features	**Examples**	**Instructional Notes**
Early		
Beginning and ending consonant sounds with pictures	Sort by beginning sounds *log/man/tire/pan* *ball/call, cup/lip*	Students' pronunciation of letter names is influenced by the sound contrasts in the primary language
Letter–sound correspondences	Match pictures with letters and sight words	(e.g., *very* pronounced *berry; zipper* pronounced *sipper*).
Short- and long-vowel sounds with pictures	<ball> B b/*ball*	Final sounds may not be perceived and are omitted in pronunciation and spelling.
Consonant blends and digraphs	Sounds of consonant blends and digraphs are introduced Picture sorts with *th, sh, ch, wh* Contrasts between substituted and target sounds are made in picture sorts (e.g., *sh/ch*). Picture and word sorts with known words *broom/book/ rock, truck /table/ rain* Vocabulary instruction with pictures used in sound sorts.	Consonant blends and digraphs in English may not exist in the students' primary language (e.g., several languages do not include *s* blends: *sl, sm, st*). Names of the pictures of words that begin with blends and digraphs are often unknown and are used for vocabulary instruction that includes concept sorts and accompanying discussion.
Middle		
Word families and ending sounds	Separate/segment beginning sounds from rime among word families. *sad/man/cat* *can/cat, jam/sad* During sorts, student practices pronouncing final sounds of words. Sight words are used to make generalizations about sounds and to aid pronunciation.	Ending sounds of CVC words may not be pronounced or may be confused with a similar sound that exists in the primary language. Final sounds /d/, /t/, /n/ may be omitted or replaced with similar sounds in students' primary language (*call, bed, pan*).

TABLE 5-6	Sequence of Word Study for English Learners in the Letter Name–Alphabetic Stage in English		
Features	**Examples**		**Instructional Notes**
Short vowels sounds and spelling: ă ŏ ĕ ĭ ŭ	Picture sorts to compare and contrast short- and long-vowel sounds.		Vowel confusions reflect unfamiliarity with English vowels.
Sounds within each vowel	*can/cat/cat* *picture sorts cat/ cake, not/note*		Correct spelling may reflect sound–symbol matches in the primary language and not in English.
Sounds across vowels CVC pattern	Compare and contrast short-vowel sounds and patterns *cat/hot, net/sit, cut/hot, cat/hot/ net/sit/cut* Concept sorts with pictures, and objects		Word reading and sight vocabularies may be more advanced than students' understanding of letter–sound correspondences. Unknown vocabulary words interfere with reading comprehension.
Consonant blends and digraphs	Teach specific blends that are confused in sorting and writing (especially *s* blends) sort of final sounds (*-ck, -ch, -tch, -sh, -mp, -nd, -nk, -nt*)		Students may be unfamiliar with final sounds in words if the primary language has mostly open syllables. More difficult beginning and final consonants are learned at this time as sight vocabularies contain more digraphs and blends.
Late			
Continued letter–sound associations within and across short vowels	Picture and word sorts that compare and contrast vowel sounds influenced by the final sounds *bar/bat, ball/bat can/set/hid*		Continue to learn to pronounce and spell ending sounds and difficult beginning sounds. Unfamiliar sounds may be over pronounced; e.g., the individual letters of a blend may be sounded out with a vowel, especially the *s* blends spelled out as syllables (CALIP for *clap*). /r/, /l/, and /w/ may be difficult for English learners to pronounce and substitutions are made based on the closest sounds in their primary language.
Less frequent and complex consonant blends and digraphs	*black, catch, bump, stand, sing*		Final sounds are still being learned and students substitute similar features; e.g., *back* (unvoiced) spelled BAG (voiced), *bump* (unvoiced) as BUMB (voiced).

COMPONENTS OF LITERACY INSTRUCTION AT THE LETTER NAME–ALPHABETIC STAGE

The framework of instruction for letter name–alphabetic spellers is built on five areas of literacy activity described as RRWWT: *Read To, Read With, Write With, Word Study,* and *Talk With* activities. RRWWT covers a full range of literacy activities for students in this stage. Conceptually, RRWWT comes in handy as we consider the integration of word study across literacy instruction.

Talk With

Talking with students is crucial to language learning. Many of the activities presented in the emergent stage apply to beginning readers as well. They need to be given time to share ideas and stories. The "sharing stories" routine described in Chapter 4 in Activity 4–24 is an excellent way to encourage students to talk. Clearly, when teachers tell short stories to students, students in turn are more likely to tell their own stories.

Concept sorts with pictures and objects are engaging, and while students sort next to their classmates they talk about what they are doing. Before putting away a sort or independent activity, students are taught to explain to a classmate what they did.

All creative activities including painting, drawing, sculpting, or arranging blocks should incorporate talking with others. Structure formats so that students can share what they created with classmates. Play areas in the room might include sets for cooking in a restaurant, working in an office, having telephone conversations, shopping for groceries, tending a baby, or building an airport. Literacy props should be included in all sets so students can be shown how to make lists and menus, write letters, answer incoming calls, discuss flight plans, and so forth.

Teachers select key vocabulary words within thematic units and *Read To* experiences. These words should be discussed and used in lessons systematically so that they become familiar to students. Repeated exposures to key vocabulary words provide a model for students, and motivate them to use these words to express themselves.

Creative dramatics is a way for students to use physical characterization along with the level of language with which they are comfortable. The repeated enactment of short scenes from a story gives English learners the practice they need to learn vocabulary. For example, groups of three to five students dramatize one scene from a story without props or rehearsal. The repeated lines of a good story serve as the script, and students improvise as they use the refrain they remember in the story: "I'll huff and I'll puff, and I'll blow your house in." Some students may just huff and puff, and others may repeat one phrase, "I'll huff," and make the gesture. As in concept sorts, in creative dramatics all students have a way to participate and to be supported.

Read To

Read To activities provide access to rich language structures developed by real writers. Comprehension and interest are supported by the pictures and the reader's voice. *Read To* activities allow beginning readers to hear literate language that stimulates thinking and teaches them vocabulary and structures of English grammar. They can listen to stories that they may not be able to read, and they come to appreciate the phrasing and rhythm of language as they are soothed and challenged intellectually.

For older English learners, the stories they read at an instructional level may not be of intellectual interest, and may not teach them the content vocabulary and information they need to participate in class discussions. *Read To* activities provide an opportunity to challenge and motivate students to think and to expose them to the content and vocabulary of their grade-level studies.

There are also cultural differences between what students hear and what they experience in their own lives. Folktales from students' home cultures are a way to engage some students, and, they are written with repetitive themes and language that support memory.

Pictures are a springboard for expanded explanations of concepts and vocabulary, and students can point to pictures to clarify what they say. The repeated use of vocabulary in meaningful ways makes learning possible for many English learners. Asking students to point to the picture of their favorite parts is a way for them to participate and for the teacher to model important vocabulary words. Teachers may ask students to show the group the pictures as a way of responding to a question about the text. Students also draw their own pictures, and the drawings support a beginning

Students use pictures in texts to support what they say.

conversation. The picture is a prop, like show and tell, that helps students explain what they think of a story or have learned from content materials.

Literature ideas are included in this chapter's activities section for specific consonants and vowel sounds so that teachers can review phonemic awareness and teach letter–sound correspondences. These selections have literary value and may be used as *Read To* activities. Language play activities with consonants are also incorporated in jump rope and clapping games.

To keep close tabs on comprehension, use teaching practices that encourage some form of student response. Monitor comprehension while the reading is ongoing instead of waiting until the end of the reading to see if students are making meaning with the text.

Perhaps the most useful activity for teaching and monitoring comprehension is the **Directed Listening–Thinking Activity,** the DL-TA. To prepare for the DL-TA, find three or four stopping points in a book where you can pause and ask students what they think is going on, and what they believe is going to happen next. The following questions are asked of students in *Read To* activities for narrative and expository materials. Notice how the questions change according to the materials that are read:

- *Narrative DL-TA:* (1) Predict: "What do you think will happen?" (2) Read to the students to the next stopping point. (3) Check predictions and make a new round of predictions: "What do you think will happen next?"
- *Content DL-TA:* (1) Predict what the text will be about: "What do you know about this topic?" and "What do you want to know?" (2) Read to the next stopping point and check for what was learned: "Did we find out what we wanted to know?" "What did we learn?" (3) Predict again: "What will we learn next?" and "What do we want to know?"

In both types of DL-TAs, comprehension is monitored throughout the reading. Students' discussions of what they hear are a way to teach them to think and question as they read. For students who are not able to communicate much in English, the teacher gives a few choices and has students choose among the possibilities.

Read With

For *Read With* activities, particular reading materials and support reading practices are used with students.

Read With activities with beginning readers include support reading practices in concert with support reading materials. Support reading activities include choral, echo, repeated, guided, partner reading, and follow-along reading activities of all kinds. These are described in the activities that follow. Support reading materials include easy rhymes, leveled and decodable texts, dictations, short poems or ditties, and songs.

Personal Readers are used to collect materials that students reread for practice for fluency and word recognition. Rhymes and dictations are the texts that are most commonly included in Personal Readers with early and middle-level beginning readers.

Dictations are an incredible tool for teachers to use with English learners of all ages at this developmental level. The teacher records on a chart or a page in the Personal Reader what the student dictates as an account of an experience or thought.

Why do we collect dictations from beginning readers? There are several reasons why Personal Readers contain individual dictations even when many leveled or decodable texts are available. Consider these uses of dictations:

1. *Authorship.* Students compose texts of greater length and coherency than they might have if they were writing on their own. Dictations are a bridge to independent writing and reading.
2. *Creation of interesting materials.* There is an inherent interest in what they themselves create. Dictations are an ideal way to create reading materials for English learners in the beginning reading stage.

3. *Harvest words for word banks.* By rereading their dictations, students acquire a store of words they can recognize automatically or by sight, but it is important also to take the words out of context to examine in isolation. Words that students have learned are written on cards to store in a **word bank** for review over time. These known words can also be used in word study activities such as sorts and word hunts. Word banks can be discontinued when students are in the middle part of the letter name–alphabetic stage and have a sight vocabulary of 150 words or more. Studying word families will add to this number.

4. *Rereading dictations promotes reading fluency and expression.* Memory and the familiar language patterns promote fluency for beginning readers.

5. *Support in content-area studies.* When students dictate about a subject they have been studying in class, they strengthen their understandings of the subject matter.

6. *Opportunities for sharing.* Students reread their dictations to their classmates. With content to share, students' motivation increases and their interest in literacy and new ideas grow.

Word Banks
A collection of known sight words students collect for word study.

FIGURE 5-4   Personal Reader with Word Bank

As can be seen in the illustration of the Personal Reader in Figure 5-4, Personal Readers can include lists of what students read, sight word lists, and student copies of little books for rereading.

The Personal Reader Activities in the Activities section include a variety of activities to develop Personal Reader routines. Bilingual dictations are a special adaptation of the step-by-step process described in the activities at the end of this chapter.

This way of creating reading materials is also an informal assessment of students' oral language resources (Bear & Barone, 1998). When students dictate their language experiences, oral language development works hand in hand with its written production. For students who are just learning English, bilingual readers that contain dictations written in both the home language and in English are presented with the activities.

Write With

Beginning readers and writers should write every day and often draw pictures to accompany what they write. Sit with students as they write to support them as they shape their ideas, and help them as they find the letters for the words. With the support of sound boards (Appendix, p. 238), show students the letters and their sounds.

In addition to helping students talk about what they want to write, teachers provide support in *Write With* activities by suggesting writing frames for which students fill in just one or two words. In this way, reading materials are created because so much of the text is already printed on the page, and there is less of a burden on the students to write. Some of the patterns found in picture books are easily adapted; students enjoy making their own versions of *Brown Bear, Brown Bear* (Martin, 1970) by just changing the animals. More complex patterns to draw on are found in picture books and in poetry guides like Kenneth Koch's *Wishes, Lies and Dreams* (Koch, 1999). A more complex frame is *I used to be . . ., but now I am . . . .*

As with speech, writing in two languages is a way in which some students increase their writing production. There is great vitality in bilingual writing that increases the clarity of expression. When teachers respect students' bilingual writing, students mature and grow, and are able to express themselves in many **registers** as they master standard usage and mechanics. The important thing in writing with English learners is to get them to do plenty of it and to focus on meaningful topics. Separate activities geared to writing mechanics can be built from meaningful pieces of writing and, in editing sessions, students can work on specific features such as capital letters at the beginning of sentences and ending punctuation.

Given the reciprocal relationship between reading and writing, reading makes students better writers, and their vocabulary and spelling knowledge also grow as they read. Reciprocally, writing improves reading as students become more thoughtful readers. In the area of orthographic knowledge, opportunities to write improve students' word knowledge in reading. Among beginning readers, growth in word recognition means that students' reading rate improves substantially: They grow from being word-by-word readers to reading in phrases.

Interactive writing in small groups is a way to teach many composing and spelling skills. The teacher guides the writing lesson on a chart or whiteboard as students dictate or come forward to contribute to the chart writing. Students can be given their own whiteboards or sheets of paper on which to record the developing text. This is more meaningful than copying the sentences later because they are an active part of constructing the message.

Sometimes the student and teacher trade off between writing and dictating. Some writing projects start well with students dictating the first two sentences, and then taking the writing over themselves. Another quick-write type of activity is one in which students pass the writing back and forth with a partner as the two create a short story. These activities are discussed in detail in the Personal Reader activities later in this chapter.

Word Study

1. *Sort for sound before sorting by sight.* Picture sorts during this stage focus attention on the sounds in the words. Student's phonemic awareness will continue to develop throughout the letter name stage as they listen for blends and **medial vowels.** Too often, when sorting words, students use visual cues to sort before thinking through the sound similarities among words. For example, when students hunt for words that sound like *cake,* at the beginning they may choose a word like *cents* from their word bank simply because *cents* begins with a *c.*

Sound sorts are important to students learning about vowel sounds. After students establish a solid understanding of the common short-vowel families, have them study the more difficult vowel contrasts. In English, the sound contrasts between short vowels are subtle and some contrasts are harder than others. When students read through a sort like the one presented in Figure 5-5, they hear themselves and their classmates say the words, and this helps them make generalizations about sounds in English. The visual differences lead students to think about sound differences.

2. *Students say the words as they sort.* During this stage, articulatory information is quite useful to students. It is also useful for teachers to hear how students pronounce words. Sounds omitted in pronunciation may not be attended to when sorting. Listen for how students say the words and listen for particular sounds that are hard to pronounce.

3. *Develop routines to identify and teach word meanings over repeated lessons with each new sort.* Sorts begin with naming the pictures or reading the words in the sort. Independently or with the teacher, students set aside words they do not know (and

Registers
The way language systems like prosody, syntax, semantics, and pragmatics present a specific style in social situations for a particular effect. Baby talk, high society, legaleze, and gangsta registers are just a few examples.

Medial Vowels
Vowels located in the middle of a syllable.

top	*sat*	*?*
dot	hat	ball
pot	can	do
mop	mad	

FIGURE 5-5   Short ŏ and Short ă Word Family Sort

ideally there should just be a few words set aside). These two or three words are revisited after the initial sort. The repeated sorting of the pictures can help students learn the names the words.

English learners and other students may not know the meaning of words in a sort, yet be able to complete the sort using the visual patterns in the words. If they read the words accurately, it may be difficult to know what meanings they do not know. In their reading of connected texts, students demonstrate through phrasing and expression their understanding of the text and word meanings, but in isolation it is more difficult to detect the words they may not understand. Throughout the week, use the meanings of several of the words in the sorts. Repeated use in word study activities helps students learn the meaning of many of the words, even words that they can already read.

Routines for sorting on a weekly basis are presented in Chapter 3.

As you sort with students, ask them what words they do not know, and choose a few words to study that are unknown and can be taught through repeated uses of the word. Choose words that can be surrounded by conversation. Ask students to use the words in a sentence, write the word in a sentence on a chart, or use in an individual dictation.

4. *Teach word meanings through multiple exposures.* To plan for multiple exposures, consider these questions: How many times will students hear and use the words that are being taught? Will students hear the word every day? Will the word be used in a made-up sentence or in natural conversation? Is there a body movement or a part of the characters' activities that can be acted out? Can students draw something that incorporates some of the words? Will students have a chance to use the words in a partner or small-group activity? At this level of development, it is important to teach the words that students will use frequently and encounter in their reading.

Enlist all students as *Word Watchers* who find ways to teach new vocabulary. Students develop an eye and ear for new words, for where they saw and heard the words. What better way to learn about a word than through examples from friends? Second-grade students in this stage write the words on charts with classmates when they hunt for words independently and in small groups.

5. *Pacing word study instruction.* As students work through the numerous sorts in this chapter, choose a level of pacing that fits each group. Three levels of pacing can be considered: introductory, moderate, and fast.

At the introductory level, the number of categories is reduced and students start with large contrasts. Once the larger contrasts are made, finer discriminations are presented. For example, with beginning consonants, a large contrast would be to sort pictures that begin with the /b/ and /s/ compared to a picture sort for the beginning sounds of /b/ and /p/.

At a moderate pace, students start with large contrasts and more quickly sort for two- and three-column sorts. At a fast pace, students already can make the larger contrasts and are ready to begin the finer contrasts that are needed for English learners.

Word Study Lesson Plan Format

Lesson Plan Format: Demonstrate, sort and check, reflect, extend.

Four steps comprise the word study lesson plan format. Follow this lesson plan format for word study as you introduce sorts.

The many word study activities and games presented in the upcoming Activities section incorporate this lesson plan format.

Demonstrate

The teacher demonstrates the sort to the students, and enlists their participation with a demonstration sort (Figure 5-6). Talk through each step along the way, and explain to

FIGURE 5-6 Teacher Demonstrates the Sort

students the key picture or word at the top of each column. Show them how to first say the word to sort, and then compare it to the first key picture or word, and then do the same for each column. With word families, you may want to sort the word by the visual pattern and then read down from the top to identify the word.

Begin by introducing students to basic routines, such as how to cut apart their words or pictures and store them in a baggie or envelope. For identification, students draw three colored lines (students should use a different color from others in their group or at their table) down the back of the sorting page before cutting. Instruct students to shuffle or mix up the word cards after they have cut them up and before sorting. Often the words are in order from the previous sort, and without shuffling, the sort is too easy. Students then try out the sort on their own as time allows. Finally, the sort is bagged and ready for the next day. Some teachers have multiple copies of sorts ready for students to sort when they gather in their small groups.

Sort and Check

Students or student pairs have a set of word or picture cards to sort. After they sort, they read through each column of the sort to check their sort and to make changes.

Reflect

Students explain why they sorted the way they did. To explore meaning, selected words are chosen to incorporate in conversation and interaction.

In the reflect step, students explain or show why they sorted the way they did. Teachers ask: *"Tell us what you have here in your sort. Why did you sort the pictures this way?"* Students are guided to show and tell the group why they sorted the way they did.

This is also when students use the words in the sort in conversations that are teacher and student initiated. Interaction with the meanings of words can begin with students hunting for words; for instance, hunting for a word in a sort that is *"a place to put a present, a square container that can hold many things inside. It has a top"* (box).

Extend

For repeated practice, students sort again at their seats or in centers; enter the sort in their word study notebooks; hunt for related words; play games together; chart collections of related words and pictures for sound, spelling, and meaning; and practice the sort and play word study games at home.

The rest of this chapter outlines numerous activities for use in your word study program: picture and word sorts, multi-use games and activities for working with words and sounds, and Personal Readers.

Activities for English Learners in the Letter Name–Alphabetic Stage

Thirty-three activities are provided for this stage that complement the fundamental activities presented as *RRWWT*. The activities are numbered and organized under the following basic headings: Multi-use Sorting Activities, Picture Concept Sorts, Working with Words and Sounds, Personal Reader Activities, and Picture and Word Sorts and Related Games for Developmental Features.

MULTI-USE SORTING ACTIVITIES

The following activities serve as a foundation for the sorts discussed in this chapter. These activities are integral to word study because they give students the practice they need to learn the principles that underlie the picture and word sorts in this chapter.

Build, Blend, Extend 5–1

This is an activity to reinforce words studied through sorts and introduce blending as a decoding strategy.

Materials. Make two types of cards—letter cards with initial consonant sounds such as *s* or *b*, and word family cards such as *ip* and *ill* for students to manipulate. Specific letter and word family cards will vary depending on the focus of your lesson. The teacher should have an enlarged set of the cards to demonstrate with during the lesson and students should have their own set to build, blend, and extend. These cards are also available in Johnston, Bear, and Invernizzi (2004).

Procedures. Words are *built* with letter and family cards; each word is said slowly to *blend* the sounds, and then related words are made in a similar fashion to *extend* learning. For example, the teacher might show the *-ip,* and *-ill* word family cards with a collection of initial sounds such as *s, b, m, l, tr,* and *sl.* The teacher calls out a familiar word like *sip* and asks a student to build the word with the cards. She might then change the beginning sound to /l/ and ask students to blend the sounds together.

After numerous words have been built with the word families, individual letter cards can be used to help students understand sound contrasts to clarify pronunciation and spelling. For example, after studying the short *a* word families, the contrast between words that end with *t* and *d* can be made (*hat/had*).

After doing the *Build, Blend, and Extend* activity with the teacher, students play this in a rotating game format, and ask each other to make words: For instance, "*Make the word cap.*"

Extension. Extend the activity to consonant blends such as *tr* and *sl,* or other sounds that were not part of students' word study sorts. Magnetic letter boards and white boards can be used in this activity after the students make words with the cards or as an alternate activity.

112

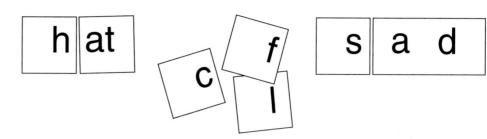

FIGURE 5-7 Build, Blend, Extend

Literature Links 5-2

Throughout the activities, literature links are presented. These links are sometimes the center of the activity, and at other times the literature is for the pleasure of the students' ears. This word play reinforces phonemic awareness and phonics instruction. Literature links are also presented in Table 5-8.

Word and Picture Hunts 5-3

These are the easiest and some of the most enjoyable word study activities. Simply, students hunt for words that are related, either by their common sound, spelling, or meaning. Students hunt for words in their word banks or in familiar reading materials. They may hunt for pictures in magazines in the classroom. The words can be written on cards and added to sorts, or pictures and words can be pasted to a bulletin board as a group activity.

Word Study Notebooks 5-4

These notebooks are ongoing individual collections of sorts students have completed. In the early part of the letter name–alphabetic stage, the notebooks may be collections of pages on which students have pasted the pictures from their sort as a culminating activity, or a collection of pictures students have drawn, or words from their words banks that sound alike (e.g., at the beginning, end, or middle). Later in the stage, word study notebooks are a place to write the words in categories that have been sorted. These notebooks include students' collections of word families (*can, fan, ran*), and later can include short vowel words across families (*can, bat, nap*). Words that students find in word hunts are also recorded in the appropriate categories. If students write their sorts in a word study notebook, the words they find in their word hunts are added to the correct column in the sort.

Word Watchers 5-5

English learners and their teachers watch for interesting and important words to learn or teach. Knowledge of word meaning is not taken for granted—teachers ask students what words they do not know, and they encourage students to ask for the meaning of the unknown words they hear or see. The selected words may be common, everyday words or they may be words related to content areas. Picture concept sorting is a good way to introduce vocabulary. English learners can easily participate in concept sorts as they learn new English vocabulary.

Writing Sorts 5-6

Writing sorts are excellent sorts for students from the middle of this stage onward. Instead of using the letters in *Build, Blend, Extend*, students write the words on their own.

can	stand	stamp
tan	band	

FIGURE 5-8
Example
of a Writing Sort

The sort begins with the teacher writing the key words on a whiteboard for the students to copy. The teacher or a partner calls out a word and the students write the words underneath the correct key word and column.

PICTURE CONCEPT SORTS

Concept sorts are for learners at all ages if the concepts are interesting and relevant to students. The directions for the first sort, the occupation sort, illustrate in detail how to present sorts. Teaching notes are included for the other picture concept sorts. Be sure to introduce the process of sorting with an easy sort with just two columns: pictures of objects that fit the pattern and those that do not.

Picture concept sorts do not require reading, and students may complete the sort without knowing English. Everyone can participate. Concept sorts are particularly effective with older English learners because they are conceptual. The activities to extend are also adaptable to adult interests and learning needs. Through concept sorts students share their ideas, and through discussions and explicit instruction students learn new content vocabulary.

Occupation and Tool Concept Picture Sort: Librarian, Construction Worker, Doctor 5–7

This sort features a collection of vocabulary words associated with occupations and the tools they use. Students sort objects associated with being a librarian, construction worker, and doctor. The completed sort using the key words should look something like Sort 10, Appendix p. 279.

Materials. Make copies of the pictures needed for the occupation and tool concept sort from the pictures in the Appendix, pages 244–276. Scissors and baggies are needed for preparation and storage of sorts. Have students cut the figures apart and place them in envelopes or small plastic bags.

Demonstrate. Review the pictures with the students prior to the actual sort. Students can also review the picture cards with a partner before they begin. Choose three or four highly useful unknown pictures to introduce as new vocabulary.

Introduce the key or guide pictures. Use a few examples from each category to demonstrate the sort explaining why you sorted the way you did through a think-aloud.

Sort, Check, and Reflect. Students shuffle their pictures and repeat the sort under your supervision. Students check their sorts by naming the occupation and the pictures in the column underneath.

Students explain why they sorted the way they did. Students make connections between the items and occupations; for example, a librarian checks out books.

Students draw a picture that shows how the object is related to the occupation. After drawing, students label the occupation and tools and write a sentence or caption to go with the picture.

Extend. There are many activities to accompany this sort that give repeated exposure to the vocabulary and concepts presented: Some of these activities can be supported with Sample Sort 3: Occupations Picture Sort on p. 304 of the Appendix.

Letter Name–Alphabetic Stage

- Students hunt through magazines and newspapers for pictures of people involved in occupations and workplaces. They cut them out and paste them on a poster board with their classmates or create a page of their own; for example, collections of furniture for a furniture store, groceries for a grocery story.
- Students hunt through their word bank and familiar reading materials for words that are related to occupations; for example, car, mother, doctor.
- In pairs or small groups, students research additional occupations. New sorts can be created based on their findings.
- Encourage home and school connections by having students research their parents' or family members' occupations.
- Extend by inviting guest speakers to share the tools from their professions; for example, office staff, car repair, plumbing.
- Provide occupation-related informational texts for students to skim through to add additional items to the list.
- Provide visual dictionaries appropriate for the age group.
- Search online for occupation-related information and pictures.
- Here are a few occupations for students to explore as appropriate to their age and experience: accountant, auto worker, baker, cashier, clergy, designer, farm and agriculturally related occupation, food and beverage occupation, guard, homemaker, landscaper, medical-related professions, mining, painters, roofers, teachers, tile setters, truck drivers, upholsterers.

Sorting Matter Concept Picture Sort: Light, Medium, Heavy Sort Activity 5-8

This sort features a collection of vocabulary words associated with matter and weight. The pictures can be sorted by weight using the "Goldilocks rule": light, medium/just right, and heavy.

Demonstrate, Sort, and Check. Select a variety of pictures from the pictures beginning on page 244 in the Appendix. Arrange these pictures on a sorting template using the blank template for sorting on page 341 of the Appendix. Introduce the guide words and ask students to name objects in the classroom that are light, medium/just right, or heavy. Have students work with partners to sort and check.

Reflect and Extend. After sorting, discuss the weight of the objects; for example, "I know a feather is light because my baby sister can pick it up." Students can add to the list by hunting for magazine pictures that illustrate light, medium/just right, and heavy objects. Students reflect by drawing a picture to illustrate the amount of muscle needed to lift an object. Students extend by thinking of their own examples of comparisons and opposites; for example, a balloon is light and a television is heavy. Encourage home-school connections by having students make a list of examples of each category in their homes.

Electricity Concept Picture Sort: Uses or Does Not Use Electricity Sort 5-9

This sort features a collection of vocabulary words associated with tools that require or do not require electricity. Use sample Sort 1 or 6 in the Appendix, p. 302 or p. 307 for a selection of items to discuss and sort.

Discuss the tools and whether or not they require electricity; for example, "A vacuum needs electricity to run because I have to plug it in before I use it."

WORKING WITH WORDS AND SOUNDS

Collecting Sight Words for My Word Bank 5-10

Students enjoy being involved in sight word record-keeping activities. This activity includes a chart to help students to keep track of the words they learn.

Students develop a word bank, or collection of words on cards, on which the teacher has written the words students know at sight. A list of these sight words is kept on a record page with lines spaced appropriately to the age of your group. These sight words can come from many places, but they frequently come from students hunting through familiar reading materials found in the school and in their Personal Readers.

Use the teaching chart in Figure 5-9 to show students how we know words. The three steps of the teaching chart show students that reading and knowing the meaning of words are important parts of harvesting sight words. The pictures on this chart cue students to the process of learning sight words.

Words that are recognized quickly and easily as sight words are written onto word cards, or "chips." These words are also written onto a record sheet of word bank words. Create a *Words in My Word Bank* record sheet to help students record and review their sight words. If kept carefully, this record sheet is a way to monitor progress.

The record sheet can be kept in the front of students' Personal Readers, and periodically students review these sight words. The teacher records the date on which she/he hears students read through their words. After several such sessions, students can check each other as they review sight words in their word bank.

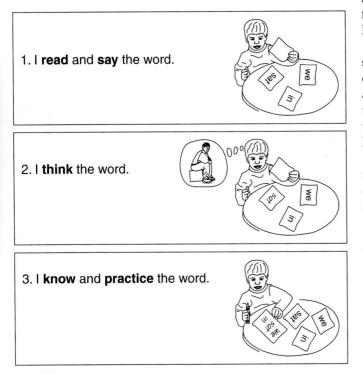

1. I **read** and **say** the word.

2. I **think** the word.

3. I **know** and **practice** the word.

FIGURE 5-9   Teaching Chart to Add Words to the *Words in My Word Bank* Record Sheet

Names I Know 5-11

The Names I Know activity gives students practice with names they know how to read. These words are then written onto students' lists of known words. Say a name and ask students to focus on the beginning sound of the name: "What letter do you hear or feel at the beginning when you say the name?" Show them how to write the word and place it on the chart.

Students use two reference charts to look for names they recognize. On the first chart, the Our Names chart, list students' names in alphabetical order. A pocket chart or Velcro board accommodates changes in the class roster and shows various ways to group words when needs arise. A second way to reference names could be a seating chart with the names of the students positioned where each child sits. This is also a good way to help students learn about mapping.

Students hunt for names that begin or end with the same letters as in their own names. Baby naming books hold special fascination for many learners at school and home, especially when there is a new arrival in someone's family.

Sound Board Activities 5–12

Sound boards are used widely during the letter name–alphabetic stage to introduce and review letter–sound correspondences. Students use the sound boards in their word study and in their writing when they look for letter–sound correspondences to spell.

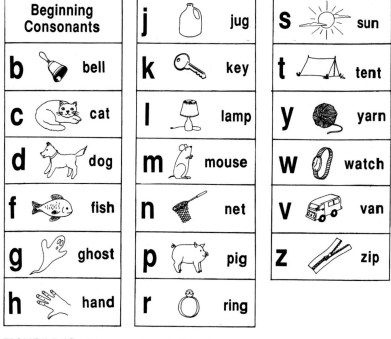

FIGURE 5-10   Reduced Sound Boards

Materials. Sound boards for beginning consonants, consonant digraphs and blends, and vowels are found in the Appendix on page 238. Enlarge, color, and post these charts at eye level for students to refer to in word study and writing.

Teachers can also make reduced-sized copies of the sound boards students are currently studying and attach them to desks in the reading group area, or have students paste their own copies inside their Personal Readers. Reduce the sound boards on a copy machine to 3 inches by 5 inches (Figure 5-10).

Procedures. Introduce sounds and pictures for sorting. The sound board is a place to introduce letter–sound correspondences. For example, the following sentence frame introduces the letter *L*: "Let's find the letter *L*. We see the key picture is a picture of a lamp. Let's say lamp *l-l-lamp*. What's the first sound? Yes, the word lamp begins with the /l/ sound."

This is also a good time to introduce the pictures that will be used for /l/ in sorting, helping English learners develop vocabulary. From here there are any number of sound contrasts and word hunts to pursue. Sound sorts are included in this chapter and in Chapter 4. Extend the sound within the words while showing the pictures to the students.

Two-Finger Pointing. Sound boards are used to show contrasts to students. For example, after studying the /r/ and /l/ sounds separately, students contrast these sounds at the beginning and end of words.

To examine the sounds at the beginning, students use two fingers to point to contrasts as they hear them: "I am going to say two words. If they sound the same, put both fingers on the same letter. If you hear two different sounds, put a finger on each sound. Let's try one. Listen for the beginning sounds. Where will you put your fingers? Ray/rabbit. Yes, both fingers would be on the *r* with the picture of the ring. Now let's try another. Ray/lake. Yes, one finger is on the picture of the ring and the other is on the picture of the lamp." In a short period, the students may make 10 to 12 contrasts.

Place a reduced copy of the most relevant sound board in students' Personal Readers and have copies available during small-group reading activities.

PERSONAL READER ACTIVITIES

Personal Readers are a place for students to store familiar materials that they read on their own and that they use in word study activities. Review the *Read With* activities section earlier in this chapter for guidelines for using Personal Readers with English learners.

The Activities included here provide instructions on how to collect and read the materials. Four types of Personal Reader entries are presented in Activities 5–13 through 5–17: (1) familiar rhymes, poems, and easy readings; (2) student dictations about personal experiences as illustrated in Salad Bowl (Activity 5–15); (3) bilingual Personal Readers and dictations; and (4) content dictations to summarize informational material.

Teach Students How to Help Each Other During Partner Reading. Explain to students that in choral reading, the helping partner reads alongside in a soft voice. When the reading slows with many errors, the helping partner uses a stronger voice. In support reading, the helping partner listens and gives support as needed. We suggest that helping partners wait for 3 seconds before telling their readers the word. In support reading, the reader can tap the helping partner on the arm when assistance is requested. In practice sessions, brainstorm with students what they would do to help a classmate who is having difficulty. These same practices can be used at home; encourage students to teach their family members to give them the type of support that has been modeled in class.

Routine Activities with Personal Reader Selections 5-13

Here are 12 ideas to encourage repeated reading of familiar materials with the dictations and familiar rhymes in students' Personal Readers. These suggestions will help you to develop a repertoire of Personal Reader activities.

1. As you collect contributions to a group experience chart, encourage students to share a sentence that adds a new idea to the chart. A description of this process is presented in Chapter 4.
2. Make three copies of each new entry in the Personal Reader: one for the Personal Reader, one for the student to take home, and one as a backup or to use after students cut stories up to rearrange and reread.
3. Allow time for students to read their dictations to two different partners in the small group to improve fluency and rate.
4. Have students keep a tally at the bottom of each page to record every time they read a selection.
5. As a group, use waxed sticky strips or highlighters to underline interesting words. Focus on features related to students' development. For example, emergent and early beginning readers focus on beginning consonants.
6. Sometimes students like to write their own word bank cards. Make a clean set of blank cards for the students. Students can write their own word cards to use at their desks or at home.
7. What do we do with the word cards in students' word banks that they cannot read? Unknown words that are not harvested can be deposited in a *class word bank,* a home for unknown words.
8. As you read chorally, modulate your voice through volume and pacing so that you give students the support they need to reread the materials with modest fluency.
9. Students use the entries in their Personal Readers to collect sight words for their word banks.
10. Word hunts within the Personal Readers are the most common word study activity with early and middle-level beginning readers.
11. Develop a checking system for home reading. Family members listen to the student read, then do one of the following: Sign the sheet in the front of the Personal Reader; put their initials on the back of the page read; or make a tick mark on the bottom to show it was reread.
12. Give students two copies of their dictation typed in very large type. Students cut apart the words of one copy and match them to the intact copy.

Rhymes and Poems 5-14*

Here is a 4-day cycle for using rhymes and poems within Personal Readers. It is important for materials to be at students' instructional reading levels so they can reread the materials independently after a few practice sessions.

Materials. An easy poem, rhyme, or ditty is selected according to students' instructional levels. Enlarge the text to or type the text in a 26-point font size. For early beginning readers, the text ranges from one or two lines to selections that are several lines long and may be the equivalent of two stanzas. Bilingual texts offer tremendous support to students as they learn English. A book like *Pío Peep!* (Ada, et al., 2003) has traditional poems from Spanish language cultures that include rhymes and songs with great appeal. A middle letter-name speller can read a poem like Sendak's "For September" in *Chicken Soup with Rice* (1991).

Procedures. Make adjustments according to the developmental levels of the students. The adjustments are related to the length and complexity of the materials. Transitional readers use these materials to practice fluency and expression.

Day 1. Introduce the poem and read it to students, enjoying the rhythm and rhyme. Read the poem from a chart, pointing to the words as you read. Give students their own copy of the poem so the students can follow along, pointing to the words as you read together chorally. Discuss the meaning of no more than three or four unknown words. They may also choose words that they found fun to say or that had an interesting meaning.

Late beginning and early transitional readers practice reading one stanza together in pairs. On subsequent rereadings, students lead the group on the stanzas they practiced and dramatize them.

Days 2–4.

1. Reread the poem as students follow along on their own copy. Work on expressive reading according to the mood and tone of the poem using different voices: a happy voice, sad voice, an upset voice, whisper voice, and so forth.
2. For early letter name spellers, cut the poem into sentence strips and have the students rebuild it in a pocket chart. Individual copies can also be cut into strips.
3. Go on a word hunt. With a partner, students find words in the poem that fit the sounds or patterns they are studying for word study. Ask students to find high-frequency words and underline words they want to add to their word bank.

*Carol Caserta-Henry co-authored this activity in the *Nevada REA Personal Reader Project.*

Group or Individual Dictations: Salad Bowl, an Example of Student-Dictated Personal Experience 5-15

Salad Bowl is an example of a student language experience activity. In individual and group dictations, students dictate to the teacher about an experience they have had, such as cutting up fruit to make a salad. After the language experience with the fruit or vegetables, students dictate something about the experience while the teacher records it. Salad Bowl is a flexible activity that can include many ways to examine vegetables and fruits. Vary the length of the dictations from one sentence for early letter name–alphabetic spellers to two paragraphs for middle letter name–alphabetic spellers. The steps to follow for this activity encourage memorable dictations and can be adapted for the other experiences.

Materials. Vegetables or fruits for the salad. Materials to record students' dictations written on a chart, on an individual page, or typed on a word processor in 26-point font.

Procedures.

Day 1.

- Have the experience and take the dictation. In Salad Bowl, the experience is making the salad with students. There are many fruits and vegetables students have not eaten and find new to touch and taste. Discuss the tastes and textures of the food. Separate groups with specific responsibilities: washing, cutting, dressing, and serving. Have the experience and discussion for 10 to 15 minutes.
- Read one of the many versions of *Stone Soup* to students. Salad Bowl can be a new version of the classic folktale, a story of resourcefulness and cooperation in which townspeople bring food to a soup that begins with only a stone. Many parts are easy to dramatize without props and preparation.
- Decide on the length and medium for the dictation. For early beginning readers, consider using a group experience chart and take individual sentence dictations like Ms. Atchison did at the very beginning of this chapter. Keep the overall length to three or four sentences. Bilingual entries can be made to help students transition from the primary language to English. For longer dictations, consider typing the student's account on a word processor. It is easy to make multiple copies from this word-processed version, and volunteers can be taught how to take dictations in readable segments as they work at a word processor.
- Ask the students to talk about the experience. You may want to elicit one sentence from each student if the group is small enough. Say each word slowly as you record the students' ideas and then reread the sentence to the student as you point to the words.
- Shape the account into a coherent whole by helping the students sequence their ideas. Parts of the dictation can be edited into standard English if the student can reread the dictation with the slight modification. This is a time when students learn phrasing and vocabulary. You may choose to use a patterned sentence frame such as "Rosa liked the pineapple. Josh liked the bananas. Carl liked the apples." These simple language patterns will make it easier for students to reread the dictation and will reinforce English syntax and vocabulary.
- Make a copy of the dictation for each student and reread it as they follow along. Students can be asked to illustrate their copy. A copy can be added to students' Personal Readers.

Day 2. Reread the dictation and look for words that have certain features (*Can you find a word that starts with /f/ or the letter f?*). This is the time to decide if this is a text that the student will be able to reread with support. Adjustments can be made by focusing on a few sentences instead of the whole text, rephrasing a sentence or two in ways that the student will be able to reread.

Day 3. Have students underline words in their dictations that they know by sight and that they want to place in their word banks. The teacher points to words randomly, and words that are recognized quickly are recorded on word cards and record sheets.

Days 3–7. Over time, students reread their dictations and other familiar materials in their Personal Readers. Students often reread their selections at the beginning of the day, as well as during small-group reading sessions.

TABLE 5-7	Dictation Starters: Experiences that Lead to Group Experience Charts and Individual Dictations		
Activities to Encourage Talking	**Animals**	**Foods and Food Activities**	**Brief Activities**
favorite music	frogs	pineapple	dissecting flowers
family photographs	turtles	cracking nuts	mixing colors
pictures from weekly magazines	lizards, snakes	different fruits	playing instruments
concept sorts	dogs, cats	examine and cut up gourds	going on field trips
flannel board story	hermit crabs	making soup	sharing collections
response to a video of a story	birds	counting seeds	having worm races
response to picture books	worms	tasting a variety of any	conducting science
pattern blocks	spiders	food type: apples, potato	experiments
	bunnies	chips	going on nature
	gerbils/hamsters	tasting spices—compare and	walks
	crickets	contrast sweet and sour	working with clay
	fish	making pancakes	making salt-flour
			dough animals
			guessing what is in
			the box

Source: From Bear, Caserta-Henry, and Venner (2004).

Extend.

- Students draw or hunt through newspapers and magazines for pictures of foods to go in a salad.
- Students draw pictures by each line to help support what they are reading.
- Students write about the experience, spelling as best they can.
- A copy of the Personal Reader entry goes home and the student finds someone to read to. Afterward the listeners at home add their initials and date to the bottom of the page.
- A comprehensive and categorized list of possible experiences is presented in Table 5-7. For additional ideas see Bear, Caserta-Henry, Venner, 2004.

Bilingual Dictations 5–16

Bilingual entries are important additions to Personal Readers that assist students to transfer what they know about literacy to English. The process of taking the dictation is the same as that described in Activity 5–15 except that a translation of what the student has said is written underneath.

Most of us need assistance to collect dictations in other languages and then to translate the dictation into English. The people who help take dictations include English language development teachers, parents, school mentors, and literate students from the same language background. As a bridge activity, bilingual dictations are usually brief, and the words chosen and sentence structures are easy.

The examples in Figure 5-11 are from three Spanish-speaking children in a first- and second-grade combination class. After the experience of mixing dyes in water, they dictated these accounts in Spanish. Both Eduardo and Alma knew just a little English. Eduardo was a recent arrival and was very limited in his knowledge of English. His dictation in Spanish is illustrative of his age-appropriate language competence in Spanish.

Alma was born in Mexico and attended kindergarten in the United States the previous year. When she dictated in Spanish, she used the English word *yellow* and said later

Alma:	Hice un color rojo y yellow.
	I made the color red and yellow.
Viviana:	A mí me gusta hacer diferentes colores.
	Y me gusta el color rojo, azul y amarillo.
	I like to make different colors.
	I like to make red, blue and yellow.
Eduardo:	Me gustó hacer los colores, porque se hacían de otro color.
	I like to make the colors because they make other colors.

FIGURE 5-11 Bilingual Personal Reader Samples

that she did not know the Spanish word for *yellow* (*amarillo*). This mixing of languages is common and is a sign of her learning at school. Viviana was a fluent speaker in Spanish, and though her dictation is concise, she was the most advanced English speaker among the English learners.

Content Dictations Based on Informational Books and Textbooks 5–17

Content dictations are used with older English learners and are a powerful tool for middle and late letter name–alphabetic and early within-word pattern stage spellers who find their textbooks too difficult to read and understand. The two- to four-paragraph-long dictations help to teach students the vocabulary and concepts that underlie their content studies. This technique extends the use of dictations to transitional reading and within-word pattern stage readers who, though they are beginning to read in easy chapter books, still do not read well enough to read their textbooks. Until there are relevant reading texts written at students' levels, the content dictations make it possible for students to learn the vocabulary and concepts in the text by listening and then summarizing the materials.

One to three students listen to a selection from their textbooks read to them by the teacher, a tutor, or a table partner. At strategic points, students dictate a summary of what they heard. The dictations are typed in 14- to 18-point font for these students and may run over to a second page. In some secondary settings, students have used content dictations to create their own version of the materials, from how-to guides to summaries of key points in the text.

The example in Figure 5-12 is a content dictation based on an informational book about sand sharks. This dictation summarizes what Lucas learned by listening to an informational picture book.

Content dictations are exceptionally useful to help students who cannot read their textbooks at an instructional level. Students listen to a section of a text and then dictate a summary of what they heard. Teachers often need to help students construct coherent dictations. As in all dictations, it is essential that students understand and can reread their dictations.

Sand Sharks

Sand sharks look vicious, but they are not really vicious. Sand sharks mistake humans for prey because they don't have a sense of us. Sand sharks eat squid, other sharks, and shellfish. Sand sharks' teeth are made to hold, not to tear. They hold on with their teeth, and their teeth are not jagged. If their teeth were jagged, the prey could get away. The teeth are circular like pegs. This keeps the prey inside.

FIGURE 5-12   A Content Dictation about Sand Sharks

The length of dictations reflects what each student can say orally, and reread successfully. Lucas was a middle level beginning reader in the third grade. He reread his dictation several times, and by the third rereading, Lucas read this 75-word dictation in 40 seconds, with no errors, with an excellent rate of 107 words per minute.

The materials in the Personal Readers of late beginning and early transitional readers include passages for students to practice phrasal and expressive reading. Two- and three-stanza poems are added to Personal Readers, and the teacher conducts fluency lessons that focus on reading with expression and thinking through the ways comprehension is embedded in the prosodic reading. Examples of instructional materials for fluency and expression include poems from Shel Silverstein, Jack Prelutsky, and from books like *101 Science Poems and Songs for Young Learners* (Goldish, 1999), as well as selections from students' reading series.

For repeated practice, students receive the support they need in partner reading in mixed-ability groups, or with a tape recording. Teach partners, tutors, and parents how to choral read with students. These instructions will change with development: Early beginning readers need choral support, and sometimes *phrase guiding* in which the teacher or table partner reads a little ahead when word recognition slows reading to a crawl.

Content dictations with older students present a way for them to compose without the burden of writing. The teacher, tutor, or partner can start by taking dictation, and then after a few sentences or a paragraph, turn the physical writing over to the student. After the first few sentences, some of the difficult words have been introduced. You can also move back and forth between dictation and having the students write a sentence.

PICTURE AND WORD SORTS AND RELATED GAMES FOR DEVELOPMENTAL FEATURES

Beginning Consonant Picture Sorts 5–18

The beginning consonant picture sorts in this section help students identify and discriminate among more obvious beginning sound contrasts. Students work through a sequence of sorts divided into five groups: /s/, /m/, /b/, /l/; /t/, /p/, /c/, /n/; /d/, /f/, /r/, /g/; /h/, /k/, /j/, /w/; and /v/, /y/, /z/; however, the series can be taught at an introductory, moderate, or fast pace, depending on the developmental needs of the group. Beginning Consonant Picture Sorts are sorts 11–30, and are listed on pages 279–280 of the Appendix. Sort 11 is provided as a sample sort in the Appendix p. 311.

Demonstrate. Prepare a set of beginning consonant pictures for this sort. The first sort is included in the Appendix (p. 311). Thereafter, you will need to find and copy the pictures from the picture section of the Appendix. Copy and cut apart the pictures you will need for the sort. For example, you will begin with a sort contrasting /s/ and /m/. Before doing the teacher-guided sort, hold up each picture card and ask students to give its name. Consider teaching the names of up to five unknown items. Additional unknown items can be set to the side for another time. Proceed through the sort by holding up each picture, and sharing your thinking in the following way: *"Here is a picture of a sink. Does* sink *sound like* sun *at the beginning or like* monkey? *Right! I'll put* sink *under the card with* S *and the sun on it. Now, you help me sort the rest of these pictures."* Continue with the children's help to sort all of the pictures. Model how to isolate, identify, and then categorize the beginning sound in each word.

FIGURE 5-13 A Sample beginning Consonant Picture Sort

Sort and Check. Give each student (or pair of students) a set of the pictures to sort. Now have the students repeat the sort under your supervision using the same key pictures as headers. You may want to have students work with partners, mix up the pictures and take turns drawing a card, saying the picture's name out loud, and sorting it in the correct column. After sorting, remind students to check their sort by naming the words in each column to be sure the beginning sounds are the same. A portion of the completed sort should look something like Figure 5-13.

Reflect. Ask students to reflect about how the words in each column are alike. Have them share their comments with others in the group, or ask each other questions about the words. These are excellent ways for students to use English vocabulary in real conversations.

Extend. Some students may only need a fast-paced review of consonants, studying four sounds at a time in the sequence suggested here. Others will benefit from a slow pace contrasting two or three sounds at a time and tying in literature links that are outlined in Table 5-8. Add letter cards or use magnetic letters or write letters on whiteboards to support the phonics being learned in these beginning consonant picture sorts. When students have sorted the pictures several times, they may paste them onto pages, creating beginning sound books. They can also draw pictures of words that begin with these beginning consonant sounds. Students use the familiar reading materials and the word banks described in the Personal Reader activities to hunt for words that begin with the same beginning consonants.

TABLE 5-8   Literature Links

A

Read *Annie and the Wild Animals* by Jan Brett (1985). In this book, Annie hopes to replace her cat that has gone missing by feeding muffins to the wild animals of the forest. Jan Brett creates additional text by framing each page with the story of the missing cat and the animals yet to appear in the story. Use the story as a springboard to create a classroom book of animals and objects that begin with the short *a* sound as in *Annie* and *animals,* using a variety of letter *a* fonts to frame each page.

B

Read *Brown Bear, Brown Bear, What Do You See?* By Bill Martin (1970). Have students use the pattern in this story to create their own *b* books, such as *Bunny, Bunny, what do you see? I see a button looking at me.*

C

Read *Good-Night Owl!* by Pat Hutchins (1972). Dramatize /c/ sounds such as the cuckoo and the squirrel cracking and crunching nuts. Practice the sound of /c/ through the chant in *Who Stole the Cookie from the Cookie Jar.* Begin by singing the first line of the song, then in the second line insert a name of one of the students in the classroom, to which that student denies "stealing the cookie" and chooses someone else to accuse of stealing the cookie from the cookie jar. This pattern is repeated until all the children in the classroom have had a turn.

Teacher and Class: Who stole the cookie from the cookie jar?
Teacher: Rosa stole the cookie from the cookie jar.
Rosa: Who me?
Class: Yes you.
Rosa: Couldn't be.
Class: Then who?
Rosa: *Chooses another name*, stole the cookie from the cookie jar.

D

Read *A Dark, Dark Tale* by Ruth Brown (1998), and add special emphasis to *dark* and any other words that begin with /d/.

Teach students a fun and memorable chant for the /d/ sound, *Double double this.* Vocabulary knowledge for the word *double* and some of the *d* words are learned. For articulation, the /d/ and /th/ contrast is a good one. Many students will say the /d/ as a /th/. Return to this ditty when /d/ and /th/ are contrasted later in the series.

Double double this this,
Double double that that,
Double this, double that,
Double double this that.

Instructions: Hold out your hands as if you are showing someone your favorite ring. As you are saying the chant turn your hands in the following ways: Whenever you say "double" palms should face up, and as you say

any other word palms face downward. Practice this hand game until you get very fast at it!

Variations: Exchange any words for *this* and *that.* For example:

Double double dirty dirty,
Double double dish dish,
Double dirty, double dish,
Double double dirty dish.

E

Read *Never Ride Your Elephant to School* (Johnson, 1995), a hilarious book about taking an elephant to school. Encourage students to think of other problems that an elephant could create.

F

Read and act out the rhyming and repeating text *Four Fur Feet* by Margaret Wise Brown (1993).

G

Read *Flower Garden* by Eve Bunting (2000). With the support of a picture dictionary, have students think of /g/ words to add to this little rhyme:

Let's go, go, go to the garden
Where some silly things do grow
In our /g/, /g/ garden
There's a (goat, goose, globe, game, or other /g/ word) I know!

Read *Little Gorilla,* by Ruth Bornstein (1986), a story of a little gorilla loved by all in the jungle, even after Little Gorilla grows up to be Big Gorilla. Following the story, the class can join you in a cheer for Big Gorilla. Cheers are a favorite for students and these cheers can be accompanied with word and letter cards that students hold up. Go gorilla, go, go Gorilla, G-O-R-I-L-L-A Goooooo, Gorilla!!!

H

Recite *Humpty Dumpty* together and have students stand up each time they hear a word that begins with the /h/ sound in Humpty.

Humpty Dumpty
Humpty Dumpty sat on a wall.
Humpty Dumpty had a great fall.
All the King's horses and all the King's men, Couldn't put Humpty together again.

I

Read *The Icky Bug Alphabet Book* (Pallota, 1993), an informational text on insects and spiders. To tie in the sound of short *i* have students draw pictures of their favorite "icky" bug on a 3-inch by 3-inch piece of paper. Present a variety of pictures and words, with half of the pictures or words beginning with the short *i.* Each time students hear a word that begins the same as *insect,* they show their "icky" bug card.

(continued)

| **TABLE 5-8** | **Literature Links (continued)** |

J

Practice the /j/ sound with two favorite nursery rhymes. *Jack and Jill* and *Jack Be Nimble, Jack Be Quick.* Have students look at the variety of pictures available that illustrate these rhymes, and, of course, have them act the rhymes out!

> Jack and Jill went up the hill
> To fetch a pail of water.
> Jack fell down and broke his crown,
> And Jill came tumbling after.
>> Jack be nimble.
>> Jack be quick.
>> Jack jump over the candlestick.

K

Read *Katy No Pocket* (Payne, 1973), a delightful tale about a mother kangaroo who does not have a pocket for her baby Freddy, so she asks other animals how they carry their babies. Have students create their own paper kangaroos with a pocket to collect and store pictures and words that begin with the /k/ sound.

L

Read *Leo the Late Bloomer* by Robert Kraus (1994). Play an oral language game by having students complete the sentence, "Leo likes _____ (things that start with /l/)."

Recite the nursery rhyme *Mary Had a Little Lamb* with students and have them raise both hands each time they say a word that begins with the /l/ sound. Picture cards placed on the easel or on the table will cue students who need vocabulary support.

M

Read *Mud Puddle* by Robert Munsch (2001). After reading the story have students play a game of Mud Puddle, Activity 5–19.

N

Read the story *Noisy Nora* by Rosemary Wells (1973) for a springboard to explore the /n/ sound. With the help of a picture dictionary, guide students to think of "Noisy Nora" words that start with /n/ such as *nail, nurse, nose, newspaper,* and *nest.* Then say a word out loud to the group and ask them if it is a "Noisy Nora" word or not.

Play *Nut Butter,* an extension of the Mud Puddle activity presented in Activity 5–13.

O

Read *Old MacDonald Had a Farm* by Carol Jones (1998) or another illustrator. Have students sing along and notice the vowel sounds in E-I-E-I-O. Think of words that start with short and long *o*'s to add to MacDonald's farm.

P

Read one of the Pig Pig books by David McPhail, such as *Pig Pig Gets a Job* (1990). Have students think of words that begin with /p/ that Pig Pig might like to use in his adventures.

Q

Read *Five Little Ducks* by Raffi (1989). Students dramatize both verbally and physically the /q/ sounds as they read "Quack, quack, quack."

Read *Q is for Duck* (Elting & Folsom, 2005), a guessing game alphabet book. Create other questions related to Q such as "Why is Q for money?" (quarter) "Why is Q for sleeping?" (quilt) "Why is Q for fairy tale?" (queen) "Why is Q for library?" (quiet).

R

Practice the /r/ sound in the following nursery rhymes:

> *Rain on the green grass, and rain on the tree,*
> *rain on the rooftop, but not on me.*

> *If all the raindrops, were lemon drops and gum drops,*
> *oh what a rain that would be,*
> *standing outside,*
> *with our mouths open wide.*

> *Row, row, row your boat,*
> *Gently down the stream,*
> *Merrily, merrily, merrily,*
> *Life is but a dream.*

S

Read *The Very Busy Spider* by Eric Carle (1985). Act out what the spider does from the story. Play a variation of *Simon Says* called "Spider says," in which students take turns giving directions to the group.

Chant *A sailor went to sea, sea, sea,* a favorite /s/ chant:

> A sailor went to sea, sea, sea,
> To see what he could see, see, see,
> But all that he could see, see, see,
> Was the bottom of the deep blue sea, sea, sea.

Students clap with a partner in a crossover manner. Each time they say the word *see* they place a hand on their forehead above their eyes to simulate that they are looking for something.

T

Read *The Teeny Tiny Teacher* (Calmenson, 2002) and accentuate the /t/ sound.

> Learn the jump rope chant:
> Teddy Bear, Teddy Bear, turn around.
> Teddy Bear, Teddy Bear, touch the ground.
> Teddy Bear, Teddy Bear, tie your shoe.
> Teddy Bear, Teddy Bear, how old are you?
> 1, 2, 3, 4, ...

Have students practice this chant as they jump rope or do other exercises.

U

Read *Ugly Duckling* by Hans Christian Anderson and Jerry Pinkney (1999). Help students hear the short *u*

TABLE 5-8	**Literature Links (continued)**

sound in the words *ugly* and *duckling*. Play a listening game where students try to hear whether a word has the short *u* sound in it. They put thumbs up if they hear the sound, and thumbs down if it does not have the short *u* sound. For example: *fun*—thumbs up; *ride*—thumbs down.

V

Read and discuss *V Is for Vanishing: An Alphabet of Endangered Animals* by Patricia Mullins (1997). Practice saying and/or acting out lip-tickling /v/ words such as *vanishing, vacuum, vanilla, vase, van, vegetable, vest, vibrate, violin,* and *vulture.*

W

Read *Where the Wild Things Are* by Maurice Sendak (1963) or *Watch William Walk* by Ann Jonas (1997). Have students participate in rereadings of the text, and use a whisper voice each time you come to a /w/ word.

X

Investigate the clever ways that X has been illustrated in alphabet books, including those listed as [ABC] in the resource list in the Appendix.

Y

Investigate the clever way that Y has been illustrated in alphabet books including those listed as [ABC] in the Appendix.

Z

Read *My Visit to the Zoo* by Aliki (1999). After reading the book and discussing zoos, have children contribute names of animals they know by adding to the following chant.

There's a /z/, /z/, zebra at the zoo, zoo, zoo.
There's a /l/, /l/, lion at the zoo, zoo, zoo.
There's a /b/, /b/, bear at the zoo, zoo, zoo.
There's a /c/, /c/, camel at the zoo, zoo, zoo.

Letter Name-Alphabetic Stage

Mud Puddle Game 5-19

In this game for 2 to 4 players collect picture cards that begin with the /m/ sound.

Materials. A collection of 30 to 50 picture cards is needed. Just over half of the cards should begin with the /m/ sound, and the rest of the picture cards should represent consonants that have already been studied. Each player has a mud puddle; a puddle can be made by cutting out a round piece of brown construction paper.

Procedures. Shuffle the picture cards and place them face down. The first player draws a card from the deck, says the name of the picture, and if the picture name begins with the /m/ sound, places the picture in his or her mud puddle. If the picture does not begin with the /m/ sound the card is placed in the discard pile. The first player to collect eight picture cards wins.

Extend. Adapt the Mud Puddles game to a Nut Butter game. An outline of a piece of bread replaces the puddle, and the game is played with a collection of 30 to 50 picture cards. Just over half of the cards should begin with the /n/ sound, and the other picture cards should represent consonants that have already been studied.

Focused Picture Sorts to Contrast Beginning Consonants 5-20

These picture sorts focus on contrasts that most English learners benefit from comparing after the previous sorts. For example, the /b/ and /p/ sort comes after the /p/ /t/ (pig/tire) sort.

Demonstrate. The sorts can be demonstrated with pictures in a pocket chart. These picture sorts are presented in the Appendix on pages 280–281, Sorts 31–48. Compile the sorts from the pictures presented in alphabetical order on pages 244–276 in the Appendix.

Sorts and word study activities teach students to make important contrasts among the sounds of beginning consonants in English.

Sort, Check, and Reflect. The students can then sort their own pictures with a partner. After checking their sorting, students tell each other why they sorted the way they did, as they reflect on the sort.

Extend. To extend, students can play board games with these pictures and go on picture hunts through preselected pages from magazines.

Focused Picture Sorts to Introduce and Contrast Beginning Consonant Digraphs 5-21

The sequence of sorting beginning consonants is presented in the sorting section of the Appendix on pages 281–284 and pages 283–284, Sorts 49–54 and 72–85. Sort 49 is provided as a sample sort in the Appendix, p. 312.

Demonstrate, Sort, Check, and Reflect. Demonstrate the sort with students and have them say the words as you show them the sort. Teach students the vocabulary they do not know before conducting the picture sort. Students then sort and check their sorts. When they are finished, students share their reflections about why they sorted the way they did, and discuss some of the words they have been using.

Extend. The Build, Blend, and Extend Activity (see Activity 5-1) makes the contrasts between beginning consonants and digraphs apparent. An extension activity like Bingo (see Activity 4-19) helps students to listen for these digraphs.

Focused Picture Sorts to Introduce and Contrast Beginning Consonant Blends 5-22

Consonant blends are also introduced in picture sorts but are revisited throughout the stage. Many English learners will find the blends to be new sounds. For example, Spanish speakers do not have *s* blends.

Demonstrate, Sort, Check, and Reflect. Refer to pages 282–283 in the Appendix for Sorts 55–71. Demonstrate the sort with students and have them say the words as you work through the sort. Teach students the vocabulary they do not know before conducting the picture sort, and if there are too many unknown words to learn at once, choose about three to five of the most useful to feature.

Next, give students their own materials and have them do the sort on their own or with a partner. When they are finished, students check their sorts, share their reflections about why they sorted the way they did, and discuss some of the words they have been using.

There are too many beginning consonant blend sorts in the Appendix for students to complete all of them; therefore, it is important to pick and choose among the sorts included. Once students learn some of the *s* blends, they will be able to extend their learning to others.

Extend. Build, Blend, and Extend (Activity 5–1) continues to be an essential activity to teach the new sounds. Picture hunts in magazines and picture drawing are ways for students to practice these sounds.

Final Consonant Picture Sorts 5-23

These pictures sorts introduce many English learners to sounds they are not accustomed to hearing at the ends of words. Pick and choose the final sounds that students do not pronounce or include in their spelling. Commonly, English learners delete the final /t/, /d/, and /n/ sounds at the ends of words.

Demonstrate. Select from the collection of pictures presented in alphabetical order on pages 244–276. A list of words that contrast various ending sounds are included in the Appendix (pp. 284–285, Sorts 86–96). Copy and cut apart the pictures you will use in the ending sound sort, creating a set for each student or pair of students to use. Sort 87 is provided as a sample sort in the Appendix, p. 313.

Sort and Check. Demonstrate the sort with students and have them say the words as you work through the sort. Teach students the vocabulary they do not know before conducting the picture sort, and if there are too many unknown words to tackle at once, choose about three to five of the most useful ones to learn.

Next, give students their own materials and have them do the sort on their own or with a partner. Remind students to say the words aloud and match each picture to the guide word at the top of the column. When they are finished, students check their sorts. After completing the small-group lesson plan in which the teacher demonstrates the sort and has students sort, check, and reflect, students can complete other final sound sorts themselves over several days.

Reflect and Extend. Have students share their reflections about why they sorted the way they did, and discuss some of the words they have been using. Students hunt for words that end with the consonants that represent these ending sounds and add them to their word study notebooks.

Focused Picture Sorts to Contrast Final Consonants 5-24

These sorts build on the previous activity, and compare final sounds that are very similar to each other. For example, in the /m/ and /n/ sort (gu<u>m</u>/te<u>n</u>), students practice feeling the differences between words that are easily confused in pronunciation. Often, these sounds differ only in whether they are voiced, as in /d/ and /t/ sounds (bed/net).

The word lists for which pictures to use in these sorts are noted on page 285 in the Appendix Sorts 97–104. Find the corresponding pictures that are alphabetized in the Appendix beginning on page 244. Be sure that students are confident with the picture sorts from Activity 5–23 before beginning this series.

Demonstrate, Sort, and Check. Demonstrate the sort with students and have them say the words as you work through the sort. Teach students the vocabulary they do not know before conducting the picture sort, and if there are too many unknown words to tackle at once, choose about five of the most useful ones to learn. As the pictures are sorted, enunciate the final sounds.

Next, give students their own materials and have them sort on their own or with a partner. As students sort and check, be sure they say the words out loud. If they do not pronounce the sounds in their conversational speech, they may have difficulty making these discriminations.

Reflect. Students explain why they sorted the pictures the way they did. They may comment that these sounds are hard to hear. Show them the shape of your mouth as you say the words and have them practice after you.

Extend. Various games may be played to reinforce these sounds. Create a Concentration or Go Fish game to reinforce these sounds. Or use the templates in the Appendix on page 343 to make a gameboard that includes pictures with tricky ending sounds. Use the pictures from the sorts to place on the board and for the draw pile. Students use a board game piece to move to the sound that matches the one they drew.

Picture Sorts to Introduce Vowel Sounds 5-25

These sorts introduce the short-vowel sounds with pictures. They should be fairly easy for most English learners. In this sequence of picture sorts, found on page 286, Sorts 105–109 in the Appendix, students contrast long- and short-vowel sounds. Using the pictures presented in the Appendix beginning on page 244, compile these sorts for students to sort by sounds. Sort 105 is provided as a sample sort in the Appendix, p. 314.

Demonstrate. Show students how to compare the short- and long-vowel sounds represented in these pictures. Use the terms *long* and *short* to describe these vowel sounds. Be sure to introduce the names of pictures they do not recognize.

Sort and Check. As students sort, they should say the names of the pictures. Notice the accuracy and speed with which they sort. If the first sort comes easily, they should sort the other short- and long-vowel sorts independently.

Reflect. Students explain their sorts to the person sitting next to them in the group. Ask students to help you sort as they listen for the sounds in the middle of these words.

Extend. Choose books from the literature listed in Table 5-8 that explore the short vowels. Students can draw pictures of the sounds they hear in these books as entries in their word study notebooks.

Same-Vowel Family Picture and Word Sorts 5-26

Sorts 110–130 in the Appendix on pages 286–287 present a sequence of same-vowel family sorts beginning with a single vowel and then students compare the sounds across vowels. Sorts combine pictures and words at first, and later just words.

Demonstrate, Sort, and Check. Prepare the set of pictures and words for the vowel family sort you will be doing by copying the pictures and writing the words onto a blank sorting grid. (Appendix p. 341). Sort 110 is provided as a sample sort in the Appendix on p. 315. Before doing the teacher-guided sort, hold up each picture and word card and ask students to give its name. Check that students know the names of pictures and understand the meanings of the words. Consider teaching the names and meanings of up to five unknown items. Additional unknown items can be set aside for another time. Ask your students if they notice anything about the words. Ask about the vowel sounds in the middle of the words. Do they all have the same vowel sound?

Introduce the word family symbols and their key pictures on the headers. Model the onset-rime segmentation process involved in isolating and identifying each vowel family; for example, "*In* cat *we hear /c/, /at/. In* dad *we hear /d/, /ad/.*" Demonstrate the sorting process by saying each of the other words and pictures and comparing them each to the guide words. Have your students join in as you continue to model the isolation, identification, and categorization of the vowel family. It is critical that your students say the words out loud and enunciate their sounds rather than simply sorting by the visual pattern present. As you sort, tell students that even though they are now using words, they are to still listen for sounds and not just rely on how words look alike. Remind students to set aside words they do not read accurately or understand. This extra attention is helpful so that English learners can focus on final consonant sounds they are not accustomed to pronouncing.

Reflect. In the reflection part of the word study lesson plan format, see if students can generate their own examples of the sounds and word families that are studied.

Extend. Build, Blend, and Extend (Activity 5–1) is an ideal activity at this time. Students make many words by substituting letters and word families. They see how many words they can make with the *-at* family, and how many words they can make by changing just the vowel. Gradually, the consonant blends and digraphs are reexamined as students see how the beginning and later the ending blends and digraphs are part of these word families (*cat, brat, chat*).

Students may hunt for words that fit the sound pattern and write them in their word study notebooks.

Continue to use a combination of words and pictures, play Concentration-type games to match words and pictures, and then move on to only words as students' reading and vocabulary grow.

Other extension ideas include the following:

1. Build, Blend, and Extend activity
2. Literature links
3. Word hunts
4. Word study notebooks
5. Word Watchers
6. Writing sorts.

Mixed Short-Vowel Word Family Sorts 5–27

In Sorts 131–139 found on page 288 in the Appendix, students study short vowels across families. Knowing the families, they concentrate on the sound differences among short vowels, as in the *e* and *o* in *net* and *not*.

Demonstrate. Prepare the set of pictures and words for the mixed short-vowel families you will be teaching (Appendix, p. 288; Sort 131 is provided as a sample sort in the Appendix, p. 316.). Before doing the teacher-guided sort, hold up each picture and word card and ask students to give its name. Check that students know the names of pictures and understand the meanings of the words. Consider teaching the names and meanings of up to five unknown items. Additional unknown items can be set aside for another time. Ask your students if they notice anything about the words. Ask about the vowel sounds in the middle of the words. Do they all have the same vowel sound?

Demonstrate the first sort in this series as described in Activity 5–26. Highlight how the words end the same and how the vowels change. Students should find this sort fairly easy and can help you match the words as you sort. It may be possible for many students to move through this series of sorts at a fast pace.

Sort and Check. If this is an easy sort, have pairs of students complete a different sort instead of the same one you modeled. Have the pairs explain their sorts to another pair of students in the group.

Reflect. Have students discuss their sorts. They will notice that they are all short vowels and that within each sort, the final sounds remain the same.

Extend. Games like Go Fish and Bingo are played to practice listening and saying these short vowels.

Focus on Word Sorts to Contrast Final Consonants 5–28

These seven sorts, Sorts 140–147 are found on pages 288–289 in the Appendix. Previously, students contrasted the sounds of final consonants with pictures. Now, with words, students are cued by letters to articulate a difference between contrasting sounds. For example, students sort words that end in *d* from words that end in *t*: *bed, red, fed, said / met, step, led, red.* Sort 146 is provided as a sample sort on p. 317 of the Appendix.

Demonstrate, Sort, and Check. Show students how to complete the first sort as described in Activity 5–26. Progress through these sorts rapidly. Students say the words as they sort and match the written word with the key picture at the top of each column. Before placing a word in a column, have them say the word they want to sort and then the key word at the top of each column; for example, *jet* to the picture of the bed ("jet–bed") and then contrast the word *jet* to the key picture, *net* ("jet–net"). After following the lesson plan format for the first sort in this series, students can complete the other sorts with partners and record them in their word study notebooks. In small groups, students brainstorm additional words that fit with these sorts.

Reflect. Students explain why they sorted the way they did. Have them discuss any "tricky" parts to the sort.

Extend. To extend, word hunts are particularly effective with these sorts. Students hunt through their readings for words that end with the same sounds and enter them in their word study notebooks, organizing them in columns by their ending consonant.

CVC Short-Vowel Word Sorts 5–29

These word sorts, Sorts 148–157 (Appendix, pp. 289–290) compare short vowels beyond word families. Making the generalization from rimes to the short-vowel sound is important so that students do not overrely on rhyming in English. This series of sorts begins with easier contrasts and ends with finer contrasts (short *i* and short *e*).

Demonstrate, Sort and Check. Prepare the set of words for the short-vowel sorts you will be doing by writing in the selected words on a blank grid copied from the Appendix (p. 342). Teachers should be able to predict the words that students can read at sight and these are the words that should be included in the sorts. Create copies of the sorts for students to use on their own or with a partner.

Before doing the teacher-guided sort, hold up each word card for students to read. Check that students can both read and understand the meanings of the words. Consider teaching the meanings of up to five unknown items; additional unknown items can be set aside for another time. Ask your students if they notice anything about the words. Ask about the vowel sounds in the middle of the words, and the consonants at the end of the words. Do they all have the same vowel family?

Demonstrate the first sort in a manner similar to that outlined in Activity 5–26. Highlight how the words in this sort have the same vowel, but not the same ending sound. Have students say the words along with you as you sort. Help them to pronounce the vowels and ending sounds in the words. Next, have students do the sort on their own or with a partner. When they finish, they check their sort to make sure the words have been correctly sorted. The completed sort should look something like Figure 5-14.

Reflect. Students observe that the words in each sorted column sound alike in the middle. Students may have difficulty understanding how they sound alike in the middle and yet they end with different sounds. This activity helps them to see the CVC pattern. Students are encouraged to share their questions about this pattern, and what might be "tricky" for them.

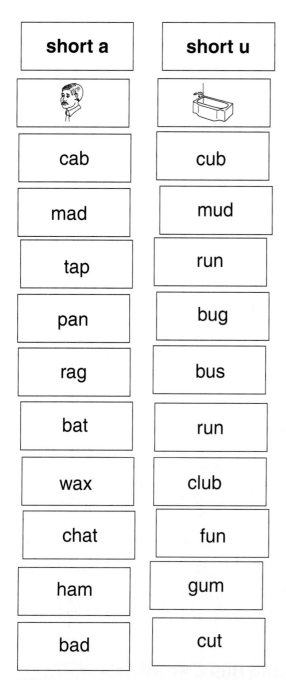

short a	short u
cab	cub
mad	mud
tap	run
pan	bug
rag	bus
bat	run
wax	club
chat	fun
ham	gum
bad	cut

FIGURE 5-14   Sample Short-Vowel Word Sort

Extend. In perhaps the final use of word banks, students hunt through their sight words for words with short vowels, and then they begin to examine the sound and spelling of these words. For example, students hunt for words that have a short *a* sound like in the middle of *cat* and list these words on a page that is later inserted into word study notebooks.

Students play many games with the words from these sorts, including Go Fish, Bingo, and the Racetrack board game that uses the template found in the Appendix on page 343. Their word study notebooks contain pages dedicated to each of the short vowels. As their skills advance, words with beginning and ending blends and digraphs become more frequent as entries in word study notebooks.

This is the time to name the consonant–vowel–consonant (CVC) pattern. Students have many sight words and, having studied short vowels across word families, it is a perfect time to introduce students to their first pattern, the CVC pattern.

Beginning Consonant Digraph and Blend Word Sorts 5–30

In Sorts 158–198, Appendix pages 290–292 students see that digraphs and blends may be seen as one unit and they begin to pronounce them together, without a vowel between the consonants (formerly, the word *split* might have been pronounced "espalitah") and without an ending vowel (formerly, *lump* might have been pronounced "lumpuh").

Demonstrate, Sort, and Check. Refer to the list of consonant digraph and blend sorts outlined in the Appendix (pp. 290–292). Sort 158 is provided as a sample sort in the Appendix, p. 318. After selecting the set of words you will work on, write the words on a blank grid copied from the Appendix (p. 342). Before doing the teacher-guided sort, hold up each word card and ask students to read it. Check that students can read and understand the meanings of the words. Consider teaching the meanings of up to five unknown items; additional unknown items can be set aside for another time. Ask your students if they notice anything about the words. These words have more letters in them than the simple CVC words. Can students identify the digraphs and consonant blends?

Demonstrate the first sort in a manner similar to that described in Activity 5–26. Highlight how the words include more than one consonant together.

Next, have students complete the sort with a partner in a small group. If the students are progressing at a rapid pace, pairs can sort different words that have the same digraphs and blends. When finished, they can read and share their words with other pairs of students.

Reflect. Have students share their understanding of the short-vowel patterned words. Point out that the short vowels follow a CVC pattern when the consonant digraphs and blends are considered as one consonant unit.

Extend. Pictures that have the sounds of the consonant digraphs and blends can also be included in these sorts. Have students conduct writing sorts or word hunts with their partners for independent study at their seats.

Focused Sorts to Contrast Beginning Consonant Digraphs 5–31

These sorts build on the previous activity, and compare consonant digraphs that are very similar to each other. For example, in the /sh/ and /ch/ sort, students practice feeling the differences between words that are easily confused in pronunciation. There are often only slight variations in how these sounds are produced in the mouth, as can be seen in Table 5-1.

Demonstrate, Sort, and Check. Sorts 199–212 in the Appendix (pp. 292–293) present consonant digraph contrasts. After selecting the set of words you will work on, write the words on a blank grid copied from the Appendix (p. 342). Before doing the teacher-guided sort, hold up each word card and ask students to read it. Check that students can read and understand the meanings of the words. Consider teaching the meanings of up to five unknown items; additional unknown items can be set aside for another time. Ask your students if they notice anything about the words. These words all have consonant digraphs like those we have been studying. But now, these digraphs have almost the same sound. Be aware that some of these digraph sounds may not exist in students' home languages.

Demonstrate the first sort in a manner similar to that described in Activity 5–26. Highlight the digraphs and their respective sounds.

Next, have students complete the sort with a partner in a small group. When finished, have them check their sorts together, and read their words to other pairs of students.

Students have already studied these sounds, and the pace can be fast if students easily discriminate among the sounds in the sorts in their speech. Some students may not be able to articulate these sound differences clearly, and these sorts help to clarify how the sounds vary.

Reflect. After sorting, have students explain their sorts to a table partner. Students may discuss how these sounds are the same in their primary languages.

Extend. Word hunts are effective in expanding students' vocabularies and give them practice in how to pronounce these sounds. Students record the words they find in their word study notebooks.

Final Consonant Digraph and Blend Word Sorts 5–32

Digraphs and blends are studied at the ends of words along with short vowels. The study of these final sounds continues into the next stage when long vowels are studied. The following sorts also include preconsonantal nasals (-*ump*, -*unk*, -*ink*, -*ang*) at the end of words.

Demonstrate. Select an easy sort from Sorts 213–227 found in the Appendix, pages 293–294. Have students participate in the demonstration by distributing the word cards that students will use to take turns sorting with the group.

Sort and Check. Students follow the demonstration by sorting independently. Extending and overpronouncing the final sound is common as students learn how to pronounce the final sounds, sounds that may not exist in their primary languages.

Reflect. Students explain their sorts and they often comment on how similar the final sounds are. Show students that even words with final blends and digraphs still follow the CVC, short-vowel pattern.

Extend. Students extend these sorts in a number of ways as they sort the words by vowels, by beginning and ending consonant digraphs and blends, in parts of speech, and in meaning. Writing sorts are popular as independent activities as students take turns calling out the words for their partners to record in the correct column.

Shrimp Camp 5–33

In this game, players move around the track and examine words with preconsonantal nasals as in *shrimp, camp,* and *stand.*

Materials. Use the *-imp/-amp/-and* words from previous sorts to play this game.

> Four playing pieces
> One racetrack, found in the Appendix (p. 343)
> A number spinner or a single die to move players around the track.

Procedures. This game for two to four players is played on an oval track divided into 18 spaces. Different words containing preconsonantal nasals are written onto 11 of the spaces. Seven of the spaces are designated for each of the shrimp events: 100-yard dash, one-mile run, triple jump, high jump, hurdle, pole vault, and weightlifting.
    For example, *shrimp, camp, stamp, limp, band, tend,* and *stand* could be used on the game board. After the racetrack has been constructed, the game board can be decorated with pictures of actual track events.

1. The person who rolls or spins the highest number goes first. Players and play proceed(s) in a clockwise direction.
2. Playing pieces are placed anywhere on the board.
3. First player rolls or spins and moves the piece that many spaces. If the player lands on a word space, he or she must read the word. If the word is read correctly, the player earns one point. If the player lands on an event space, he or she must think of a word that is not on the board that contains a preconsonantal nasal. If successful, the player earns two points.
4. Play then proceeds to the next person.
5. The person to earn the most points wins.
6. Set a time limit for this game.

Variations.

1. The person who rolls or spins the highest number goes first. Players and play proceed(s) in a clockwise direction.
2. Playing pieces are placed anywhere on the board.
3. The first player rolls or spins and moves the piece that many spaces. If the player lands on a word space, she or he reads the word, then every player must write a word that contains the same word family. For example, if a player lands on *shrimp,* players would write an -imp word. Each player then reads the word that was written and players who wrote the same word receive 1 point, and players who wrote a different word receive 2 points.
4. If a player lands on an event space, he or she may choose one player and take a point away from that person's score.
5. The player with the most points at the end of the game wins.
6. Set a time limit for this game.

Letter Name-Alphabetic Stage

6 Word Study with Transitional English Learners in the Within-Word Pattern Stage

Mrs. Hester's second-grade class is bubbling with happy chatter as the students settle in for the day. It is January, and the first week back to school after the winter break. She has planned to spend the week reconnecting with the thematic unit the class was working on in December, reviewing their word study lists, and revisiting some of the standard literacy block routines and practices.

The classroom is chock-full of books. Bookshelves near Mrs. Hester's teaching table hold sets of leveled books to use in her guided reading groups. On one of her bookshelves she has a collection of easy reference materials such as picture dictionaries, alphabet books, and laminated cards she has found to illustrate and label specific content areas such as zoo animals, the solar system, colors, weather words, and so on. She asks students to refer to these when they are searching for vocabulary. At the front of the room, three tubs are filled with thematic books related to the current unit of study—matter.

Print is displayed around the room in many ways. One bulletin board announces the class to be "Matter Detectives" and displays pictures and labels of items that are solids, liquids, and gases. Nearby there is a display of related words in a word bank for students to refer to; the display includes *air, water, ice, steam, heavy, light, flow,* and *rise*. Another large bulletin board area displays individual photographs of the students, with their edited writing posted underneath. Labels around the room let students know where classroom materials belong. Charts are displayed all around as well—they include alphabet and sound charts, charts of the daily schedule and center rotations, charts of adjectives to use in writing, and charts of directions such as "What to do if you finish early."

Mrs. Hester hands out baggies with word cards inside that feature the long o sound as in *rope*. She says, "We've been away from our word study for quite a while now, so let's get our brains warmed up by remembering what we were doing before the break. Sort your words into the three patterns we've discovered so far that make the long o sound. If you find a word that doesn't have the /o/ sound, set it aside."

Mrs. Hester writes CVCe, CVVC, and CV on the board. "Find these three cards in your bag to help you set up your columns." She listens to make sure that students are saying the words aloud as they sort. Soon, the students' desks are covered with the words they have sorted—words like *home, vote, stone,* and *globe* under the CVCe column; *boat, coast,* and *loaf* under the CVVC column; and *so* and *no* under the CV column. When students have finished this sort, Mrs. Hester asks them to read their words to a partner. "Partners, check to make sure that the words are sorted according to the guide cards!"

Next, students are invited to "think of another way to sort your words." Students mix their words up and make their own categories. One student is sorting her words by whether they start with a single letter, a blend, or a digraph. Another student is counting how many letters each word contains.

When the sorting time is over, Mrs. Hester asks the students to replace their words in the baggies and return them to a plastic tub. She takes a few minutes to reflect orally with the group about what they learned from the experience. Students share that it was fun, because they already knew about these word patterns. When asked if their brains are ready to learn more, the group calls out an enthusiastic "Yes!"

The vignette about Mrs. Hester's classroom illustrates many key ideas about effective literacy instruction for students at the transitional stage of development. Her classroom is like a greenhouse—she provides the structures, materials, and experiences to nurture students' growing skills. Mrs. Hester also holds the expectation that students will soon develop into independent, self-directed readers and writers, and provides many experiences to help them try this out. Mrs. Hester has set up the physical environment in her classroom with lots of meaningful print and plenty of reading and writing materials for students to access. She knows the developmental level of her students and plans activities accordingly, building on students' natural enthusiasm and organizing opportunities for students to interact with others.

Transitional students are becoming independent readers and writers.

This chapter focuses on literacy development and instruction for students at the transitional stage of reading and the within-word pattern (WWP) stage of spelling, like many of the students in Mrs. Hester's class. We describe how the essential literacy activities of *Read To, Read With, Write With, Word Study,* and *Talk With* (RRWWT) work together to provide a cohesive learning environment for English learners. We also share examples of specific word study lessons so you can get a picture of how an effective teacher is explicit, and still challenges students to think at higher levels.

LITERACY INSTRUCTION FOR ENGLISH LEARNERS AT THE TRANSITIONAL/WITHIN-WORD PATTERN STAGE

The term *transitional* as used in this chapter refers to the stage of reading development that occurs between the beginning and intermediate levels, as described in Chapter 1 of this book. It is not to be confused with the period of *transition* that is referred to in the bilingual field when a student moves from instruction in a home language to instruction in English.

Students at the transitional stage of literacy development are beginning to gain fluency in their reading and writing. They recognize a large number of words by sight, and can represent all the sounds they hear in words with reasonable letter–sound correspondences. Their advancing skills and large bank of sight words give them the ability to read longer texts, such as early chapter books, and students also write more easily. Some words in their writing will be spelled correctly while others will be phonetically close and readable. (Bear, Invernizzi, Templeton & Johnston, 2004; Ehri, 1997)

During the transitional stage of reading and within-word pattern stage of spelling, students move beyond a reliance on individual sounds as the only decoding tool. Students begin to look at chunks in words, or their patterns, before attempting to pronounce them. In their reading, students differentiate between short- and long-vowel patterns, such as when reading the words *bit* versus *bite*. In their writing, within-word pattern spellers begin to mark the long-vowel pattern, sometimes incorrectly, such as when they spell *paid* as PADE.

The transitional stage of reading is an especially crucial crossroads for English learners as they consolidate their literacy skills. The complexity of phonics patterns can be overwhelming to students who are just learning the meanings of words, and have not had as many experiences hearing or reading them. English learners who bring literacy skills from a home language that is much more phonetically regular than

The CVC pattern is a crucial foundation for understanding more complex vowel patterns.

English are oftern shackled to the idea that sounds should be represented in print in more of a one-by-one manner. It is important that (1) students have a strong foundation in understanding CVC patterns, (2) they have clear and systematic instruction when moving to more abstract patterns, and (3) that new learning builds on what students know. Otherwise, learners are likely to become overloaded and even unsure of how to spell short-vowel words.

The following big ideas are important to keep in mind when designing appropriate instruction for English learners at the transitional stage (Diaz-Rico & Weed, 2002).

Be Pattern Puzzlers

Help students make sense of the ever-more-complex orthographic system of English. What they have learned up to now about the writing system is still true; an additional layer of understanding is just being added. This is growth! Students can become step-by-step "pattern puzzlers," as they work first with comparing short and long sounds and spellings for a specific vowel, and then later as they compare spelling patterns in each vowel. Be positive and be systematic. Follow the scope and sequence we have outlined in this book. Take the instructional time needed for students to thoroughly understand the concept you are working with, and always check that you are at your students' developmental levels before moving ahead.

Include Vocabulary Instruction

With expanding reading and writing abilities, the amount and kinds of words that students encounter in their texts will greatly increase. This means that, in addition to learning the *process* of reading more complex words and sentence structures, students will also face many new vocabulary words. Reading materials and word study activities at this stage become less dependent on picture cues, which in the past have supported students' vocabulary development. It is very important to include explicit vocabulary instruction within literacy activities such as word sorts, concept sorts, and small-group reading instruction. Find ways to check for students' understanding of the content and structure words you are using in your lessons. Be ready to provide explicit instruction when students do not know common words that you hadn't realized were problematic (Dutro & Moran, 2003).

Wide Reading Supports Oral and Written Language Development

Give students many opportunities to read a wide variety of materials at their instructional level. Wide reading helps them become more fluent and automatic; it also provides students with frequent encounters with high-frequency words. The more that English learners recognize and practice reading the patterns within words that they are studying, the more they will develop an inner sense for "what looks right." This exposure will also help students build the background knowledge to associate the correct spelling patterns of common **homophones** such as *cheap* and *cheep* that are studied at this stage.

Homophones
Words that sound the same but are spelled differently, such as *deer* and *dear*.

Another benefit of reading lots of easy materials is that it helps English learners to fine-tune distinctions in sound that may have been tricky for them to distinguish aurally. For example, some English learners pronounce the short *i* sound as a long *e* ("seat" for *sit*). With exposure to more and more words in texts, inquisitive readers and spellers now begin to associate spelling patterns with pronunciation differences. Thus, texts support this phonetic awareness.

Sounds Play a Role at the Within-Word Pattern Stage

For English learners at the within-word pattern stage, sounds will continue to play a role in word study instruction. Help students differentiate closely-related sounds when vowel patterns are explored. Can students hear the distinctions in contrasting vowel sounds? If they cannot, the activity becomes a random guessing game. To avoid this, begin with picture sorts for vowel sound contrasts as a way to assess students' phonological discrimination. Then, work with the patterns the sounds represent. If students from specific language backgrounds have difficulty with a certain vowel contrast, find a different vowel to begin with. Follow the guidelines in this book to help you predict which students may experience difficulty with certain sounds.

In the within-word pattern stage, students have enough sight words, know enough about sound–symbol correspondences, and understand long- and short-vowel patterns sufficiently well to attend to sound differences among short vowels. For example, Spanish-speaking students in this stage begin to identify differences between the vowels in words like *hat* and *top*. They also come to recognize that the *a* in *father* may be more like the short *o* sound than the short *a*. The ability to detect subtle sound differences develops at this time for students who speak a regional dialect; students are able to manipulate language to shift speech styles as they wish. Interestingly, as students progress through the within-word pattern stage, changes in their own pronunciation of the short vowels are noticeable.

As discussed in the preceding chapter, blends and ending sounds can also require extra support for English learners. Continue to be aware of the relationship between sounds and spelling patterns for transitional students. This is a great time to help students verbalize their understanding of the sound–pattern connection in English words, and to compare it to their home languages.

CHARACTERISTICS OF ORTHOGRAPIC DEVELOPMENT FOR ENGLISH LEARNERS AT THE WITHIN-WORD PATTERN STAGE

During the within-word pattern stage of development, students expand on their knowledge of short-vowel patterns to experiment with how to spell the long-vowel sounds. Students now understand that TRAN does not spell *train*, but they may attempt to spell the long sound by adding a silent *e* to the end, as in TRANE. As students progress through this stage, they explore the varied long-vowel patterns, the influence of *r* on vowels, and the spelling of other complex or ambiguous vowel patterns. They also expand on their understanding of digraphs and consonant blends. By the end of the within-word pattern stage, students work with homophones and homographs and get an introduction to how the meaning layer of the orthography plays a role in spelling.

Adriana is a good example of an English learner at the within-word pattern stage. Figure 6-1 shows the developmental spelling samples from an inventory she was given in class. Adriana correctly spelled all of the short-vowel words, including *bump*. When tackling long-vowel words, she correctly spelled *train* and *beaches,* but spelled *chase* as CHAS, and *float* as FLOT. In the multisyllable words on the list, Adriana gave her best guess on words such as SQUERREL for *squirrel,* and CATLE for *cattle*. It is interesting to see how syllables are omitted as in FOATCH for *fortunate,* and PUNKCH for *puncture*. It is also important to note how she has plugged in a known word for a difficult word: PLAYER for *pleasure*. As a within-word pattern speller, it would be important for Adriana to begin a systematic study of long-vowel patterns, so she develops a deep understanding of these before moving on to two-syllable word patterns.

The representation of vowel sounds in English is very complex. Although the short-vowel sounds may pose some difficulty for English learners because many of their sounds are not present in students' home languages, in general the short vowels represent a one-sound to one-letter match. When students move into the within-word pattern

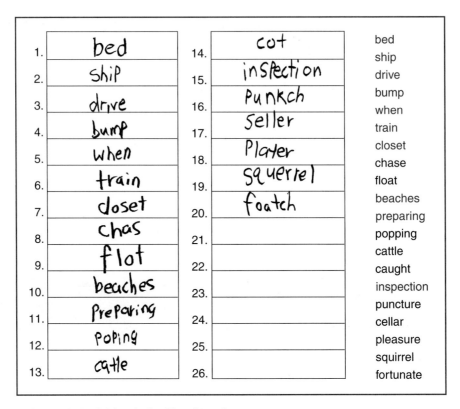

1.	bed	14.	cot	bed
2.	ship	15.	inspection	ship
3.	drive	16.	Punkch	drive
4.	bump	17.	seller	bump
5.	when	18.	Player	when
6.	train	19.	squerrel	train
7.	closet	20.	foatch	closet
8.	chas	21.		chase
9.	flot	22.		float
10.	beaches	23.		beaches
11.	Preparing	24.		preparing
12.	poping	25.		popping
13.	catle	26.		cattle
				caught
				inspection
				puncture
				cellar
				pleasure
				squirrel
				fortunate

FIGURE 6-1 Adriana's Spelling Sample

stage of development, they must use more abstract thinking; they not only need to identify the sounds they hear in words, students must also understand and choose from a variety of vowel and consonant patterns that involve silent letters; that is, they are no longer dealing with a one-to-one match!

Within-word pattern spellers come to realize several key ideas:

Representing vowel sounds in English can be very complex for English learners.

- English has many more vowel sounds than letters. Vowels are used in numerous ways on their own and in combination to represent various sounds.
- There is often more than one possible way to spell a given vowel sound. Even as students learn the logic of "marking" a long vowel with a silent *e* or vowel team (*plane, plain*), they need to become familiar with the correct spelling of specific words. For instance, although it would be logical for a student to spell *boat* as BOTE, that would not be correct.
- English has many "oddball" words that do not match the patterns being studied. These words should not be ignored, but rather discussed in the context of how they are different from the norm. Students need to have the support of enough positive examples of the pattern, however, so that they can get a good sense of how vowel and complex consonant patterns work.
- English learners who have literacy experiences in a language that is more phonetically transparent come to understand the qualitative differences between English and their home language. Discussions and comparisons allow students to bring the similarities and differences among languages to a greater level of consciousness.

The job of students at the within-word pattern stage of orthographic development is to understand the *whys* and *hows* of patterns with vowels and complex consonants. This time of transition builds on the sound layer that students have relied on previously, and ultimately connects them to the meaning layer that guides advanced spelling.

Sequence of Word Study for the Within-Word Pattern Stage

Table 6-1 shares the sequence of word study for English learners at the within-word pattern stage. The first two columns outline important features that are studied, and give specific examples. The final column highlights aspects of these features that may require special attention or instruction for English learners.

Patterns
The second layer or tier of English orthography in which letter sequences, rather than individual letters themselves, represent vowel sounds.

Students first spend time comparing the sounds of the short and long sounds in each vowel using pictures to make these distinctions. Next, students examine the **patterns** of single-syllable words beginning with the CVC and CVCe patterns. While students begin to look at patterns, instruction also includes continued study of the contrasts between the sound system of students' home languages and English; for example, *cab* may be pronounced "cob". What is important is that students recognize a sound contrast between the sound of the *a* in *cab* and the long *a* in a word like *name*; if they can make this sound difference, then they can also see that there is a spelling difference, a first step to dividing the words by pattern (CVC/CVCe).

After students are familiar with the sound differences within a vowel, words using the common vowel patterns of CVCe and CVVC are included in the sorts (e.g., *make* versus *paid*). Students spend a significant chunk of time working on these common long-vowel patterns with one vowel in depth; when they understand the patterns, their study extends to other vowels. It is hoped that by studying one vowel in depth, perception of the CVCe and CVVC patterns will develop easily and quickly with subsequent vowels.

After students become comfortable with the most common long-vowel patterns across all five vowels, they move to exploring less common long-vowel patterns such as the ending vowel sounds in *play* and *chew*, and VCC patterns such as *kind* and *high*. These diverse sounds and spelling patterns challenge students to continue to grow as "pattern puzzlers." It is the job of the teacher to help English learners see and understand the regularities in the writing system, and to build on what students know.

R-Influenced Vowel Patterns

In the middle within-word pattern stage, students examine the influence that certain consonants, such as *r*, have on vowel sounds. For instance, *r* changes the sound of the vowel in what should be short-vowel words, making it difficult to know how to spell words such as *her, first, word,* and *turn*. English learners from many languages find the sound of the English *r* hard to pronounce, and this adds to the spelling challenge. *R*-influenced word study activities compare words that contain the *ar, er, ir, or,* and *ur* chunks, and their long-vowel counterparts, and support English learners to clarify their knowledge base relating to this feature. Word study of *r*-influenced vowels continues through the middle and late portions of the within-word pattern stage.

Diphthongs

Diphthongs are complex sounds in which two vowel sounds slide into each other within the same syllable, such as in the word *boy* or *cloud*. As students in this stage work to master vowel patterns, diphthongs are an important feature for them to learn. Students examine the spelling patterns of these sounds, and consider how the position of the diphthong within a word influences its spelling, such as in *joy* versus *join*. Because two sounds can be heard in a diphthong, English learners often find them easier to learn.

Other Ambiguous Vowel Sounds

Continuing to build on vowel patterns, within-word pattern spellers work with what may be called "other ambiguous vowel sounds"—sounds that are neither short nor long.

TABLE 6-1	**Sequence of Word Study for English Learners in the Within-Word Pattern Stage**	
Features	**Examples**	**Instructional Notes**
Early		
Short and long sounds of each vowel using pictures	*Cat/cake; desk/cheese; pig/pie; clock/coat; sun/soup*	Sound may not occur in home language, so perceiving its pronunciation is difficult. It is most important that students hear a distinction between the long and short sound, not that their pronunciation of these sounds is exact.
Short- and long-vowel sounds (CVC/CVCe) in words and pictures	*Mad/made; hot/hose; drum/cute*	See above. Also, students who bring literacy skills from a shallow orthography may have difficulty understanding more complex vowel representations.
Middle		
Long-vowel sounds using the CVCe and CVVC patterns	*Mice, huge, rain, toad*	Different letter patterns spell the same long-vowel sounds. In-depth vocabulary is needed to distinguish different spellings for the same pronunciation and to attach an appropriate spelling pattern. Students may attempt to use diphthongs for the long-vowel sounds in a and o (AYTE for *ate*, HOUME for *home*).
Less common long-vowel patterns	*Play, chew*—ending vowel sound *Kind, fold*—VCC *High, right*—VCC (igh)	Students who bring literacy skills from a shallow orthography may have difficulty understanding the range and complexity of vowel representations in English.
R-influenced vowel patterns	*Far/fare; her/hear; fir/fire; more/work; purr/pure*	Many languages do not have *r*-influenced vowels, so perceiving their pronunciation and attaching the correct spelling pattern is difficult.
Diphthongs	*Boil, boy; ground, growl*	Vowel sounds may not be combined in this way in students' home languages.
Other ambiguous vowel sounds	*Moon, book; draw, cause; wash; fall; bought*	Sounds may not occur in students' home languages, so perceiving their pronunciation, differentiating them from similar vowel sounds, and attaching the correct spelling pattern are difficult tasks.
Late		
Beginning complex consonants and consonant clusters	*Knife*—silent beginning consonants *Scrape*—triple *r* blends *Three*—consonant digraphs plus *r* blends	These sound and spelling patterns may not exist in students' home languages, which can make attaching spelling patterns more difficult.
Contractions	*Here's, they'll, couldn't*	In-depth vocabulary and verbal flexibility are needed to associate contractions with their longer forms.
Homophones with long-vowel patterns	*Plane, plain; meat, meet; write, right; doe, dough; due, do, dew*	In-depth vocabulary is needed to distinguish different spellings for the same pronunciation and to attach an appropriate spelling pattern.
Introduction to two-syllable words	*Afraid, belong*	Spelling two-syllable words increases the cognitive difficulty for students. Unstressed vowels that take on the schwa sound can be especially difficult to represent.
Introduction to inflectional endings with plural and past tense	*Girls (-s), boxes (-es); Cleaned, walked, treated*	Verb forms and plurals may be constructed differently in home languages or these forms may not occur. Perceiving the pronunciation of *-ing* at the end of a word may be difficult.

These include vowel sounds such as those in the words *book, saw, caught, tall,* and *cough.* Differentiating these sounds from their short- and long-vowel counterparts and attaching the correct spelling pattern for a great variety of words are indeed critical features to master at this stage.

Complex Single-Syllable Words

By the later portion of the within-word pattern stage of spelling, students take on a deeper analysis of consonant clusters and digraphs. Although students have learned to work with consonant clusters from late in the letter name stage, they now investigate silent beginning consonants such as in *knife* and *gnat,* blends with three letters such as in *scrape* and *stream,* and blends involving digraphs such as *three* and *shrink.* This word work involves multiple layers, as students are asked to discriminate a series of complex consonant sounds (e.g., /s/-/c/-/r/) as well as attach the appropriate vowel pattern (e.g., *ape*) in words like *scrape.* Taking the time to work closely with English learners on these features can serve multiple purposes. First, it helps students explicitly identify the types of clusters possible in English. In many of the students' home languages these complex clusters of consonants simply do not exist. Second, this word work gives students a chance to review both the vowel patterns and the vocabulary of complex, single-syllable words, such as *shrub* and *strike.* These words use a multiplicity of vowel patterns from short, to long, to diphthongs and other ambiguous vowel sounds. Working with a variety of complex, single-syllable words allows students to put together the sum of their learning about consonants and vowel patterns prior to taking on multisyllable words.

Introduction to the Spelling–Meaning Connection and to Two-Syllable Words

As students become proficient at spelling the vowel patterns and consonant clusters in complex, single-syllable words, their word study focus expands. A simple first step in discussing the idea that spelling and meaning are often connected begins with a focus on contractions. Discuss with students the meaning, spelling, and the grammatical usage of contractions. English learners will need to practice these words orally, understand how each component word contributes to the contraction's meaning, and practice reading and writing contractions in authentic contexts.

Another introduction to the spelling–meaning connection occurs when students investigate homophones. Homophones are word partners that sound the same but are spelled differently, such as *plane* and *plain,* or *for, four,* and *fore.* Late within-word pattern spellers combine their knowledge of vowel patterns with an expanding oral and written vocabulary to begin to understand that what a word *means* relates to how it is spelled (Templeton, 1983). For example, students come to understand that although *sea* and *see* are pronounced in the same way, only one is correct in the sentence "I want to *see* the movie." Activities to help English learners attach the appropriate spelling to specific words will involve talking explicitly about the meaning of homophones, having lots of opportunities to see these words while reading, and getting feedback during the writing process.

Late within-word pattern spellers have developed a firm foundation in their understanding of a multitude of one-syllable words. Now, they prepare to transition into the upper levels of orthographic development and to focus on multisyllable words. This advancement begins with an exploration of high-frequency, two-syllable words such as *ago, belong,* and *until.* Now that students are comfortable with single-syllable words, these words are not hard to spell.

One final feature addressed at the end of the within-word pattern stage is an introduction to plural and past tense inflectional endings such as in *boxes* and *cleaned.* Inflectional endings are studied in great depth during the upper levels of word study (see Chapter 7), but it is helpful for students in the late within-word pattern stage to be introduced to them conceptually with words that do not require any adjustments. For instance, adding *-s, -es* and *-ed* to create words such as *girls, wishes,* and *helped* is straightforward and allows English learners to develop a conceptual understanding of the grammatical process.

Studying High-Frequency Words with English Learners

Encouraging English learners to memorize high-frequency words is a tempting way to approach spelling instruction. Many students who have limited oral skills seem to succeed at remembering words visually. In the end, however, this approach does not help students understand the logic of the English writing system, and when students have memorized all they can, they will be left without a road map for their literacy journey. While some limited time studying high-utility words may be appropriate during the early stages of development, this study should not replace the developmental scope and sequence outlined in this book. Words should be analyzed in systematic ways, by features. This helps students make sense of the writing system and construct categories to support long-term memory. Students must memorize the "oddballs," but must see them as simply that—different from the usual pattern.

COMPONENTS OF LITERACY INSTRUCTION AT THE TRANSITIONAL STAGE

Students at the transitional stage of reading need many experiences with the essential literacy activities of *Read To, Read With, Write With, Word Study,* and *Talk With* to fortify their expanding reading and writing abilities. Here are some suggestions for implementing the essential literacy components with English learners at the transitional stage.

Talk With

At this level, students' oral language skills are advancing, and they are trying out longer, more syntactically complex sentences. If the classroom climate allows them, students will become oral language resources for each other, and help one another practice their developing vocabulary and grammar. Teachers can help students to interact orally throughout their literacy activities in many important ways:

- Discuss everything—words, phrases, sentences, lists, poems, stories, books! Help students connect what they say to written language by keeping charts of featured words, poems, directions, dictations, and other notes. Find ways for students to practice the words they are learning in a meaningful context. When working with a large group of students, stop at frequent intervals for partner sharing activities. For example, ask students to turn to the person next to them and "share a time when you felt *productive.*"

- Use discussion to check for understanding about the lesson. Ask students to "use that word in a sentence," "share what just happened in the story in your own words," or "tell me how all of those things are alike."
- Now that students can write longer pieces of text, help them develop their ideas ahead of time by talking with fellow students or the teacher. Encourage them to jot down big ideas on a **mind map** or other graphic organizer so they can hold onto these thoughts throughout the writing process.
- Think out loud with students about how speech varies, but print remains consistent. As their oral language and literacy skills advance, students begin to be more aware of variations in spoken dialect, and connecting those to written language. Students' developing reading proficiency helps them use the support of print to fine-tune their pronunciation. For example, the short *i* and short *e* distinction will become clearer as students learn many written words such as *pen/pin, red/rid,* and *beg/big,* and attempt to refine their pronunciations.
- Engage in **Reader's Theater** and other performance and rereading activities to help students focus on expression in reading and speaking.

Mind Map
Starting with a central idea, and extending rays outward, a mind map is a visual way of brainstorming and showing connections.

Reader's Theater
A simple form of dramatics in which students take roles and read from a script or a story.

Read To

Students at the transitional level of reading are finding a greater range of materials to read on their own, but this does not mean you should stop reading *to* them. By listening to stories, nonfiction texts, and other pieces that are too hard for them to read on their own, students learn about unfamiliar topics, hear new vocabulary words and sentence structures, and are motivated to explore an array of reading materials. So, for your read-aloud lessons, choose texts that excite, enthrall, and open new doors to students. As you read, be expressive and dramatic, so that students hear fluent models. Pick materials that appeal to students from different cultural backgrounds, and to both boys and girls. Inspire your students to become connected personally with books.

The vocabulary in books at this level is becoming more abstract at a rapid pace, and is likely to be less familiar than the language of oral conversations. Technical words in nonfiction texts such as *microscopic, decomposition,* or *organism* will demand some visual support and discussion. Even narrative texts use less common words and possibly unfamiliar concepts such as *previously, annual,* or *loyal.* Preview your read-aloud texts to be sure the vocabulary is at the listening comprehension level of your students. If you doubt that the English learners in class will understand the vocabulary completely, consider providing ways to give extra support. You might preview the content in a small group; provide pictures; find an outlet for students to ask clarifying questions about the material; let students listen to the text on tape after hearing it read aloud; discuss their ideas with peers in their home language; or you may make the decision to select a text that is more connected to students' background experiences and language level.

Reading To students can also be a bridge to creating instructional-level reading materials for students in content dictations as described in Activity 5-17. If your textbook or content resource material is too difficult for students to read on their own, read it to them. Take time to clarify confusing vocabulary, answer questions, and share visuals relating to the topic. After reading, ask students to dictate to you what they learned from hearing this material. Their dictations can be typed up and used as *Read With* text at other times of the day.

Provide vocabulary support for the texts you read aloud in class.

Read With

Students at the transitional level are beginning to read easy chapter books; they are reading more fluently in phrases, no longer word by word. Transitional readers need lots of opportunities to read material that is not too hard for them in order to become automatic, rhythmic, and expressive in their reading. Make available to students as many easy-to-read texts as you can.

Schedule multiple opportunities within the school day for students to read on their own, in small, teacher-guided groups, and with peers. Even though students can now read a greater range of materials on their own, they still need regular time in small instructional groups at their developmental level. During these lessons, teachers help students by previewing materials, providing support for vocabulary and more complex decoding skills, developing strategies for comprehension, and assessing that reading materials are at the appropriate level of difficulty.

Book Clubs
In-class structures in which groups of students select, read, and discuss books.

The transitional stage is a good time for teachers to set up social structures, such as **Book Clubs** (Raphael, Pardo & Highfield, 2002) within the classroom. Book Clubs provide formats for groups of students to read the same texts and discuss them. English learners profit from engaging in these small-group activities because it is less intimidating to speak up in a small group, and it is expected that all members contribute. Reading becomes part of a social interaction, and this is highly motivating. Partner reading activities also give students an opportunity to read material of interest at their level and to interact with a peer about it. Reading skills grow, language is developed and practiced, and motivation to read is enhanced—a winning combination all around!

During *Read With* activities, have students reread materials aloud, and focus on their pace, expression, and clarity. While an improving words-per-minute rate is to be commended, it is not the only goal. Students should notice and work on clustering together meaningful phrases; they should read at a normal pace; and their intonation should match the text's meaning. For instance, in the phrase "down the dark, scary hallway" there would be a slight pause between *dark* and *scary*, and the phrase might be read in a low or trembling manner. There are numerous ways for students to reread materials aloud for a meaningful purpose such as: in Reader's Theater, where students use a short text as a dramatic reading; through the shared reading of poetry from group charts or overhead projections, especially if they will have an occasion to read the poem for an audience; in **Author's Chair,** where students have opportunities to read their personal writing to other students; and by practicing and reading simple picture books to younger students in a "big buddy" type relationship. Students can also be asked to reread some of these materials to family members at home for homework.

Author's Chair
Opportunities for students to present their own writing in class.

Write With

As in all stages of spelling development, students' unedited writing shows teachers their understanding of the orthographic system. With advancing abilities to put more down in writing with less effort, the writing of students at the within-word pattern level also gives teachers a window into their proficiency with the syntax and vocabulary of English. In other words, by looking at students' first draft writing, teachers can get a good idea of what spelling features, sentence structures, and words students need to work on next. Based on common needs within the classroom, teachers can set up mini-lessons for individuals and small groups of students to address these goals. These lessons will be highly effective for students, because they focus on students' current understandings and confusions.

Writer's Workshop
A time in class for students to focus on various aspects of the writing process including pre-writing, drafting, writing, revising, sharing, and publishing.

Write With time will progress along a couple of avenues. First, students should be encouraged to write freely in journals, personal narratives, note taking, and so on. In many of these cases, content will override form, and students should not feel the pressure of "having to write it correctly." The message of what students are saying should be valued unconditionally. Processes such as **Writer's Workshop,** in which students work through a series of steps from prewriting through final editing and publishing, can be used with students on selected writing projects. Feedback from peers and teachers about the message and voice of the writing will help students see themselves as writers, and value the importance of what they have to share, but attention is also given to mastering the conventions of good writing.

Write With activities should also involve explicit instruction in the structures of specific writing forms such as letters, essays, stories, and reports. By using support strategies—modeling, providing visuals, guided practice, graphic organizers, and the like—teachers provide a scaffold for students to follow at first, and then to expand on as their skills and understandings grow. Explicit guidelines allow English learners to be successful at writing projects even as they are developing oral and written language proficiency.

Word Study

Use the results of your developmental spelling assessments (see Chapter 2) to identify and cluster students into instructional groups. As the year progresses, continue to informally assess students and adjust groupings according to students' development. When you have identified students who are at the within-word pattern stage, look at their spelling carefully to place them at the early, middle, or late stage, and also to inform yourself about the features within this stage that they are using correctly and those they are just beginning to try out. The activities presented later in this chapter progress from early to late in this stage, and can be selected according to the needs of your specific groups of students. The suggestions outlined next are general enough to apply to students throughout the within-word pattern stage.

Build a curiosity for word learning.
The increasing complexity of the orthographic system through the within-word pattern stage might tempt you as a teacher to throw up your hands and say, "English spelling is very confusing!" This response will provoke overwhelming feelings of confusion in your students, too. Instead, consider fostering a climate of confidence and curiosity about words in your classroom. Let your students know that you will be their guide on a journey of discovery as they learn about the wide range of patterns in the writing system, moving from simple to more complex. Frame your word study lessons around the idea that all students are "pattern puzzlers" who explore words to look for commonalities and variations. Marvel at the abundance of interesting patterns you find, and talk about the oddballs that do not seem to fit. Learn with your students, and enjoy this adventure!

Connect the patterns being learned to their sounds.
It is important for English learners to continue to work with pictures, to say words aloud as they sort, and not just to memorize visual patterns. Connecting words in print and speech allows word study to support oral language development and aids in deeper learning. Sounds and patterns go together, and speaking words helps learners to read and spell words.

Develop a consistent and comprehensive routine for word sorts.
As you work with students in their instructional-level word study groups, follow a set format that includes *demonstrate, sort, check, reflect,* and *extend.* Check that the words or pictures are known, and only teach a small number of new words at a time. Teaching three to five new words is usually sufficient. Model and talk through the sort with the group the first time through. Then, have students do the sort on their own or with a partner under your supervision. Have students check their sort with you or a peer before putting it away. Take the time to share reflections about what was learned in the sort. Extend the sort throughout the week using techniques described in Chapter 3 such as word hunts, speed sorts, no-peeking and writing sorts, and related games.

Integrate phonics, spelling, and vocabulary learning.
With increasingly complex vowel patterns to explore at this stage, there may be a tendency to focus only

on the form or structure of words. It is so easy to get intrigued by the ways that vowel sounds get expressed, such as the long *u* sound in *tune, cruise, clue, brew, food,* and *through,* that the meaning of these words may be assumed or overlooked. English learners need to know not only *how* the writing system operates, but also what the words *mean.* Word study should not be done with unknown words unless meaningful vocabulary instruction is included. Set up procedures that ensure that students understand the words being used in sorts and games: Check their background knowledge; teach them to self-monitor their comprehension and ask clarifying questions about words they do not know; use the words in sentences and other meaningful contexts; and have them set aside words they do not know before sorting.

Help students learn and apply vocabulary from content-area studies.

As students transition from the "learning to read" stage to the "reading to learn" stage, the importance of academic language takes on even greater prominence. Students are required to understand a growing body of technical vocabulary in their textbooks and reference materials. Word study activities such as the concept sorts included later in the Activities section can help students learn new vocabulary and apply it to their classroom units of study. After you have tried out some of the concept sorts in this book, consider doing the following:

- Develop your own concept sorts based on the thematic units or content-area studies in your classroom. Create cards with related words that students can read, or pictures if the word is too difficult for them to decode. Conduct open and closed sorts using these cards.
- Use a pocket chart, bulletin board, or chart paper to create vocabulary word banks related to the key content words in the unit of study. Find pictures to clarify these terms, or ask student volunteers to illustrate them.
- Help students create personal dictionaries with vocabulary from content-area studies. These can be used as a reference for the pronunciation, meaning, and spelling of important words.
- Include nonfiction reading materials at the students' instructional levels relating to the content area you are studying.
- Make connections to what students are reading. Have students discuss interesting words that come up in their daily reading, and connect these to word study lessons or concept sorts.
- Include writing projects that ask students to use specific vocabulary words relating to key concepts. On some occasions, you may want to provide frame sentences for students to build on such as "Electricity can make *(name of thing) (action)*." For example, "Electricity can make refrigerators get cold."

Make the most of word study notebooks.

Word study notebooks are mentioned throughout this book (see Chapters 3, 5, and 7). At the within-word pattern stage, word study notebooks serve several purposes: To document or reflect on a learning activity; to categorize and keep lists of related words; and to use as a reference tool for spelling patterns and vocabulary. Create word study notebooks by adding lined paper to a three-pronged paper folder or using a single-subject composition book. Add tabs for the sections you want students to access, such as "Reflections," "My sorts," "Homophones," or "Vocabulary Words." Include the categories that fit with your word study lessons and students' needs. Add new pages or tabs as needed.

Make the word study notebook a working document and reference source. Bring it out for word study activities, and reflect on it at the close of your daily lesson. Use the notebook to list words that follow specific patterns as students discover them throughout the day and during word hunts. Encourage students to "look it up" in their word study notebook if they have questions about spelling patterns or vocabulary. If you and your students at the within-word pattern stage are explorers on a learning adventure, let the word study notebook be your travel log to record the journey!

The preceding general ideas presented a framework for the specific lessons you use with within-word pattern spellers in word study. The rest of this chapter describes numerous specific sorts and games sequenced from least to most difficult for English learners at the within-word pattern stage of development. These activities can be used to guide students into the world of complex vowel and consonant patterns, and help them negotiate the increasing demands of content-area study. Participating in these activities helps your students *transition* into a more advanced understanding of words that will frame their literacy development into the future.

Activities for English Learners in the Within-Word Pattern Stage

Throughout the following activities, students will have many opportunities to work with words and pictures that may be new to them. Activities are sequenced according to *early, middle,* or *late* within-word pattern. Table 6-1 is a good reference for this sequence.

The series of sorts described in the activities section that follows are listed as Sorts 227–261 in the Appendix, (pp. 294–298). Several of the concept sorts are presented as full-page sorts in the *Sample picture and word sorts* section of the Appendix. For most of the sorts described, you will need to refer to the outline in the Appendix, write the words onto a copy of the blank sorting grid (Appendix p. 342), and make multiple copies for student use. When pictures are called for, find the appropriate pictures that are laid out alphabetically in the *Pictures for sorts and games* section of the Appendix (pp. 243–276), copy them, and add them to your sort.

TEACHING NEW WORDS

Here are some ideas for how to teach new vocabulary as you sort and play.

Materials. Depending on the sort or game you are doing, plan to have multiple copies of the words and pictures. They should be cut apart and in separate envelopes for student use. Students might be assigned to cut these up when they first come in so that they are ready for sorting later. At times you will want students to have their word study notebooks available to keep track of words, or you may ask them to create a personal picture dictionary. Other support materials that are helpful include commercially produced picture dictionaries, simple encyclopedias, topical reference materials, and reference cards (often sold as laminated pages with pictures and labels).

Procedures. As you begin to work with a group of students in a word study activity, set the context for how the words or pictures are related. For example, if all of the words relate to a thematic unit, such as the community, introduce the words by letting students know the connection. If the words are not related by content, but rather by a spelling pattern or grammatical feature, encourage students to be "pattern detectives" to see how the words are similar. You will not use all of the following steps in any one lesson, but consider the ideas as a resource list for your vocabulary instruction:

1. As a group, read through the set of picture or word cards in the sort or game. If students do not know how to read a certain word or its meaning, set it aside for the time being.
2. Select a limited number of new vocabulary words to teach at a given lesson; three to five is usually a good number. Choose useful and important words that students will hear in their ongoing academic work and content-area studies.
3. Identify the new vocabulary words or pictures, say the names out loud, and have students repeat them. Use the words in simple sentences.
4. Ask students to try using the new words in sentences, or to say what they know about the words.
5. Encourage students to translate the words or pictures into their home language. Let them discuss the term with fellow students who may not understand it yet.
6. When possible, find pictures of the words that are unknown. This book has numerous simple pictures in the Appendix to use for reference. You may also want to expand your library of picture cards, picture dictionaries, reference charts or cards, and simple informational texts so you can use these as support materials.
7. Let students practice saying and using the new words with partners or in small groups before doing the sort or game.

Variations. If you want to teach a bigger group of new words or pictures, consider some active games such as those presented in Chapter 4 in the *Games Using Concept Picture Sorts* section.

WORD STUDY ACTIVITIES AT THE EARLY WITHIN-WORD PATTERN STAGE

Picture Sorts Contrasting the Short and Long Sounds of A, O, U, I, E 6-1

This is a series of five picture sorts that draw students' attention to the short and long sounds of each of the vowels. The first sort will be described here in detail and the others should be done in a similar fashion. The letter *a* is a good vowel to start with for English learners. The short *e* sound is a very difficult sound to produce and differentiate for many English learners so it is saved for last. Using these picture sorts will ensure that students are really hearing the differences between the long and short sounds, as opposed to relying on letter cues.

Demonstrate. Prepare a set of short *a* and long *a* pictures for Sort 227. You will need to find and copy the following pictures from the appendix section *Pictures for sorts and games* (Appendix pp. 243–276): *grass, man, bat, gas, plant, bath, mask, pants, flag, can, graph, train, snake, skate, tape, cane, whale, grapes, chain, wave, nail, cave.* These items are listed as Sort 227, in the Appendix on p. 294, as they might appear in a completed sort. Copy a set of pictures for each student or pair of students. Before doing the teacher-guided sort, hold up each picture card and ask students to give its name. Consider teaching the names of up to five unknown items. Additional unknown items can be set aside for another time. Set up *hat* and *rain* as the guide pictures at the top of your columns. Proceed through the sort by holding up each picture, and sharing your thinking in the following way:

> *Here is a picture of snake . . . Snn—aaaa—kk; I hear the letter a say its name in the middle. When we hear a vowel say its name in the middle, we call it a long-vowel sound. I hear a long a in the middle of* snake. *Snake has the same sound as* rain *in the middle, so I will put it under the picture of rain. This is a picture of a bat. Bb—aaa—tt has a short a in the middle—the ǎ sound like in the middle of the word* hat. *I'll put bat under hat because they both have the ǎ sound, the short a sound in the middle. Now, you help me sort the rest of these pictures.*

Continue with the children's help to sort all of the pictures. Model how to divide words into individual phonemes to isolate, identify, and then categorize the medial vowel sound in each word. If students do not pronounce the vowel sounds exactly as you do, don't worry. What is important is that they differentiate between the short and long sounds. Refined pronunciation will come with time.

When all the pictures have been sorted, check the sort. Name all of the pictures in each column and check to make sure they all have the same vowel sound in the middle. *Do all of these words sound alike in the middle? Do we need to move any?*

Sort, Check, and Reflect. Give each student (or pair of students) a copy of the set of pictures for guided practice. Now have the students repeat the sort under your supervision using the same key pictures as column headers. You may want to have students work with partners to mix up the pictures and take turns drawing a card, saying its name out loud, and sorting it in the correct column. English-speaking partners can supply the vocabulary for English learners. After sorting, remind students to check their sort by naming the words in each column to be sure the vowel sounds are the same. Ask them to reflect about how the words in each column are alike. Have them share their comments with others in the group. What did they find easy or difficult about this sort?

Extend. Give each student a plastic bag or envelope in which to store the pictures for independent sorting over several days by themselves or with a partner. As they sort, ask students to separate a word into its individual sounds, and to explain why they placed a particular picture in a column. Have them restate the sounds of the vowels on which they are working.

Follow the same procedures for picture sorts contrasting the short and long sounds of *O, U, I,* and *E*. These sorts are outlined in the Appendix, p. 295, Sorts 228–231.

Concept Sort: Community 6-2

Make copies of the community concept sort page in the Appendix, p. 319, cut the cards apart, and place them in envelopes or small plastic bags. To help keep multiple sets organized, consider using various colors of paper or putting a small colored dot or number on each card so that it can easily be reorganized if multiple copies get mixed up.

Demonstrate. This sort features a collection of vocabulary words associated with communities. Introduce the key words (guide cards) and ask students to name places, persons, and objects in a community to activate their prior knowledge. Use several words from each category to demonstrate the sort, explaining your rationale through a think-aloud. For example, you may pick *factory, harvest,* and *drawbridge* to discuss together. In which environment does each item belong? Review all of the picture and word cards with the students to make sure they can both read and understand the meaning of each term. You may also want to have students review the picture and word cards with a partner. The completed sort should look something like the one listed as Sort 232, Appendix p. 295.

After sorting, discuss how the places and objects relate to each other within a concept: *A farmer stores grain in a silo.* Some words such as *barge* and *irrigation* may be unknown to students. Provide outlets for students to learn the meanings of these words, such as in explicit lessons, by asking classmates and teachers, and by using picture dictionaries, informational texts, and online reference materials.

Sort, Check, and Reflect. Students should shuffle their cards and repeat the sort under your supervision. Have them check their sorts by explaining their rationale to a partner or to you. Encourage students to reflect by asking them to write a few sentences or draw a picture about one or all of the communities. For picture reflections, individual items can be labeled with terms from the sort.

Extend. Have the students work in pairs or small groups to create a detailed illustration of their own community or a nearby community, identifying parts of the community presented in the sort and adding components that were not represented but could be included in the sort.

Word Sort Contrasting Short and Long Sounds of A, O, U, and I 6-3

This is a set of four sorts that direct students' attention to the CVC and CVCe spelling patterns for the short and long sounds of *A, O, U,* and *I.* E is not included because there are so few words that have the pattern. Some of these will be included in a later sort. See Sorts 235–238 in the Appendix, p. 295. Several pictures are included in these sorts to ensure that students are focusing on sound differences, as opposed to relying only on letter cues. You will need to find and copy the pictures noted in parentheses to include with these sorts. Pictures are located in the *Pictures for sort and games* section of the Appendix, pp. 243–276.

Demonstrate. Prepare the set of pictures and words for short *a* and long *a* to use with Sort 235, Appendix p. 295. Before doing the teacher-guided sort, hold up each picture and word card and ask students to give its name. Check that students know the names of pictures and understand the meanings of the words. Consider teaching the names and meanings of up to five unknown items. Additional unknown items can be set aside for another time. Ask your students if they notice anything about the words (they all have an *a* in them). Ask about the vowel sounds in the middle of the words. *Do they all have the same vowel sound?*

Introduce the short ă symbol and the long ā symbol and their key pictures on the headers. Model the phoneme segmentation process involved in isolating and identifying each vowel sound; for example, "*In* hat *we hear /h/, /a/, /t/. In* rain *we hear /r/, /ai/, /n/.*" Demonstrate the sorting process by saying each of the other words and pictures and comparing them each to the guide words. Have your students join in as you continue to model the isolation, identification, and categorization of the medial vowel sound. It is critical that your students say the words out loud and segment their sounds rather than simply sorting by the visual pattern present. The completed sort should look something like Sort 235, Appendix p. 295.

When you are finished sorting, ask the students how the words in each column are alike and how they are different from the other words. Check the sort by naming all of the pictures and words in each column to make sure they all have the same vowel sound in the middle. *Do all of these words sound alike in the middle? Do we need to move any? What do we notice about the spelling of the words?* Add the CVC and CVCe cards to the top of the appropriate column and encourage students to discuss the role that the silent *e* has in creating the long-vowel sound.

Sort, Check, and Reflect. Give each student or pair of students a copy of the sort for guided practice. Now have the students repeat the sort under your supervision, using the same key pictures as column headers. Tell your students to say each word aloud as they sort. You may want to have students work with partners to mix up the words and take turns drawing a card, saying its name out loud, and sorting it in the correct column. After sorting, remind students to check their sort by naming the words in each column to be sure the sounds are the same in the middle. If a student does not notice a mistake, guide him or her to it by saying, *"One of these doesn't fit. See if you can hear which one as I read them all."* Then read each word card, being careful to enunciate each vowel sound clearly. Ask students to reflect on how the words and pictures in each column are alike. Have them share their comments with others in the group. You might have students write how the words in one column are alike and how they are different from the words in the other. What did they find easy or difficult about this sort?

Extend. Have students store their words and pictures in an envelope or plastic bag so they can reuse them throughout the week in individual and partner sorts. Students should repeat this sort several times. See the list of routines for word sorting in Chapter 3 to plan follow-up activities to the basic sorting lesson. It is important to introduce the no-peeking sort now that students are working with visual patterns. Model it before sending students off to do it with partners.

Follow the same directions to contrast long and short *o, u,* and *i* sounds by using Sorts 236–238, Appendix p. 295.

WORD STUDY ACTIVITIES AT THE MIDDLE WITHIN-WORD PATTERN STAGE

Word Sorts Contrasting Spelling Patterns for Long A and O 6-4

This sort focuses students on two common long-vowel patterns, CVCe and CVVC. This sort supports students in learning the most common patterns that create the long-vowel sound.

Demonstrate. Prepare the set of long *a* words to use with Sort 240, Appendix p. 296. Before doing the teacher-guided sort, hold up each word card and ask students to read it. Check that students know the words and their meanings. Consider teaching up to five unknown items. Additional unknown items can be set aside for another time. Ask your students if they notice anything about the words (they all have an *a* in them). Ask about the vowel sounds in the middle of the words. Do they all have the same vowel sound?

Introduce the CVCe and CVVC column header cards. Ask students to tell you what these letters stand for, and to think of example words. Model the process of looking at one of the long-vowel words and labeling its components: Make *has a consonant, a vowel, another consonant, and the letter* e. So, make *follows the CVCe pattern.* Paid *has a consonant, vowel, another vowel, and a final consonant.* So, paid *follows the CVVC pattern.* Demonstrate the sorting process by analyzing each of the other words and comparing them to the header cards. Have students join in as you continue to model this process. Note that a blend or digraph can also be considered as a consonant in this pattern (e.g., *claim* = CVVC). It is critical that your students say the words out loud even as they look for visual patterns for sorting. The completed sort should look something like the one listed as Sort 240, Appendix p. 296.

When you are finished sorting, ask the students how the words in each column are alike, and how they are different from the other words. Check the sort by rereading the words aloud and visually noticing the spelling patterns. *Do all of these words follow the CVCe or CVVC pattern? Do we need to move any?*

Sort, Check, and Reflect. Give each student or pair of students a copy of the sort for guided practice. Now have the students repeat the sort under your supervision using the same column headers. Tell your students to say each word aloud as they sort. You may want to have students work with partners to mix up the words and take turns drawing a card, saying its name out loud, and sorting it in the correct column. After sorting, remind students to check their sort by naming the words in each column and reviewing the spelling pattern. If a student does not notice a mistake, guide him or her to it by saying, *"One of these doesn't fit. See if you can notice the spelling pattern that is different."* Ask students to reflect on how the words in each column are alike. Have them share their comments with others in the group. You might have students write how the words in one column are alike and how they are different from the words in the other. What did they find easy or difficult about this sort?

Extend. Have students store their words in an envelope or plastic bag so they can reuse them throughout the week in individual and partner sorts. Students can also go on a word hunt to find long **a** words that match the CVCe and CVVC patterns to add to their word study notebooks.

Use the same directions for the long *o* sound, using Sort 241 found in the Appendix on p. 296.

Word Sort Contrasting Sounds and Spelling Patterns for Long A and O 6-5

This sort starts by differentiating words with the long *a* or long *o* sound, and then asks students to notice the spelling patterns across both long vowels. It is a good review and provides an opportunity for students to reflect on what they are learning with the CVCe and CVVC patterns.

Demonstrate. Prepare the set of long *a* and *o* words for Sort 242, Appendix p. 296. Before doing the teacher-guided sort, ask students to read the words aloud and check to see that they know the meanings of the words. Consider teaching up to five unknown terms. Additional unknown items can be set aside for another time. Set up *nail* and *goat* as the guide words at the top of your columns. Demonstrate the sorting process by saying each of the words and comparing them to the guide words: *Does* take *sound like* nail *or* goat *in the middle?* Have your students join in as you continue to model the isolation, identification, and categorization of the medial vowel sound. It is critical that your students say the words out loud and segment their sounds rather than simply sorting by the visual pattern present.

When you are finished sorting, ask the students how the words in each column are alike and how they are different from the other words. Check the sort by naming all of the words in each column to make sure they all have the same vowel sound in the middle: *Do all of these words sound alike in the middle? Do we need to move any? What do we notice about the spelling of the words?*

Sort, Check, and Reflect. Give each student or pair of students a copy of the sort for guided practice. Now have the students repeat the sort under your supervision using the same key words as column headers. Tell your students to say each word aloud as they sort. You may want to have students work with partners to mix up the words and take turns drawing a card, saying its name out loud, and sorting it in the correct column. After sorting, remind students to check their sort by naming the words in each column to be sure the sounds are the same in the middle. If a student does not notice a mistake, guide him or her to it by saying, *"One of these doesn't fit. See if you can hear which one as I read them all."* Then read each word card, being careful to enunciate each vowel sound clearly. Ask students to reflect on how the words in each column are alike.

Extend. In the second part of this sort, ask students to subdivide each of the columns in their sort by the spelling pattern for the words. Use the CVCe and CVVC header cards under each long vowel to sort the words according to spelling pattern. Your completed sort will look something like the one outlined as Sort 242, Appendix p. 296.

When you are finished sorting, ask the students how the words in each column are similar to and different from the other words. Encourage students to write this sort into a page of their word study notebook and add to it as they find more related words.

CVCe/CVVC Word Sort with Long A, O, and E 6–6

This sort asks students to separate long-vowel words into the spelling patterns of CVCe or CVVC. Because three different vowels are used, students are guided to generalize the pattern into larger contexts.

Demonstrate. Prepare the set of long CVCe and CVVC words for Sort 243, Appendix p. 296). Before doing the teacher-guided sort, ask students to read the words aloud and check to see that they know the meanings of the words. Consider teaching up to five unknown terms. Additional unknown items can be set aside for another time. Set up *nose* and *soap* as the guide words at the top of your columns. Ask students to tell you which column the CVCe card goes with, and which column is for CVVC words. Demonstrate the sorting process by saying each of the words and comparing them to the guide words: *Does* globe *have the CVCe pattern like* nose *or the CVVC pattern like* goat? Have your students join in as you continue to model the identification and categorization of the correct pattern. It is critical that your students say the words out loud even as they visually discern the pattern.

When you are finished sorting, ask the students how the words in each column are alike and how they are different from the other words. The completed sort should look something like Sort 243, Appendix p. 296. Check the sort by naming all of the words in each column and visually reviewing their spelling patterns. *Do all of these words have the same spelling pattern? Do we need to move any? What do we notice about the sounds in the words?*

Sort, Check, and Reflect. Give each student or pair of students a copy of the sort for guided practice. Now have the students repeat the sort under your supervision using the same key words as column headers. Tell your students to say each word aloud as they sort. You may want to have students work with partners to mix up the words and take turns drawing a card, saying its name out loud, and sorting it in the correct column. After sorting, remind students to check their sort by naming the words in each column to be sure the spelling patterns are the same. If a student does not notice a mistake, guide him or her to it by saying, *"One of these doesn't fit. Which one looks like it doesn't have the same spelling pattern?"* Ask students to reflect on how the words in each column are alike.

Extend. This is an excellent opportunity to have students go on a word hunt to find other CVCe and CVVC words with the long sounds of *a, e,* and *o.* If students find words with these patterns that do not have the long sound, such as *said,* discuss them and put them into an "oddball" category. Students may write this sort and other found words into their word study notebooks.

Word Sort Contrasting Spelling Patterns for Long I 6–7

This sort works on two common patterns for the long *i* sound: CVCe (as in *like*), and CV (as in *by* or *tie*).

Demonstrate. Prepare the set of long *i* words to use with Sort 244, Appendix p. 296. Before doing the teacher-guided sort, hold up each word card and ask students to read it. Check that students know the words and their meanings. Consider teaching up to five unknown items. Additional unknown items can be set aside for another time. Ask your students if they notice anything in common with all the words (they all have a long *i* sound in them). Ask if all the words have the same letter to represent that sound.

Place the CVCe and CV header cards at the tops of the columns, along with the guide words *like, by*, and *tie*. Note that -y and -ie both can make the long *i* sound, and might be described as a CV (consonant-vowel) pattern. Proceed through the sort by looking at the long-vowel words one at a time, and labeling their patterns as you have done in previous sorts such as Activity 6–4. Have your students join in as you continue to model this process. The completed sort should look something like Sort 244, Appendix p. 296.

When you are finished sorting, ask the students how the words in each column are alike, and how they are different from the other words. Check the sort by rereading the words aloud and visually noticing the spelling patterns. *Do all of these words follow the CVCe or CV pattern? Do we need to move any?*

Sort, Check, and Reflect. Give each student or pair of students a copy of the sort for guided practice. Now have the students repeat the sorting, checking, and reflecting under your supervision.

Extend. Have students store their words in an envelope or plastic bag so they can reuse them throughout the week in individual and partner sorts. Students can also go on a word hunt to find long *i* words that match the CVCe and CV patterns to add to their word study notebooks.

Leaves on a Tree Game 6–8

In this game, two players compare visual long *e* vowel patterns.

Materials. You will need two paper or cardboard trees without leaves, 10 construction paper leaves, and word cards representing the long *e* vowel pattern. Here are some examples of long *e* words:

e	e-e	ea	ee	ie
he	eve	bean	seek	chief
be	scene	reach	sheet	field
me	theme	steal	cheek	piece
she	these	teach	deep	thief
		steam	sleep	belief
		plead	queen	grief
		beast	creep	brief
		feast	greed	shriek

Within-Word Pattern Stage

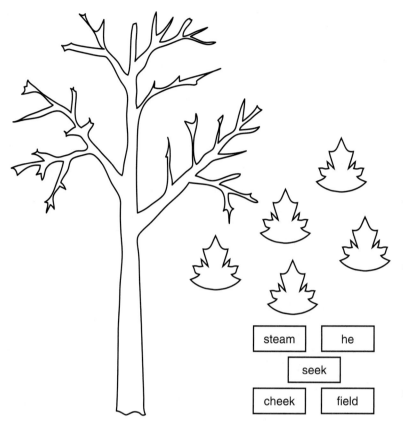

Procedures.

1. One player shuffles and deals five cards and five leaves to each player.
2. Remaining cards are placed face down for the draw pile.
3. Each player puts down pairs that match by pattern. For example, *reach/steal* would be a pair, but *eve/chief* would not. Each time a pair is laid down, the player puts one leaf on his or her tree.
4. The dealer goes first, says a word from his or her hand, and asks if the second player has a card that has the same pattern.
5. If player 2 has a card that matches the pattern, player 1 gets a leaf; if not, player 1 must draw a card. If the player draws a card that matches any word in his or her hand, the pair can be discarded, and a leaf is earned. Player 2 proceeds in the same manner.
6. The player using all five leaves first wins. If a player uses all the cards before earning five leaves, the player must draw a card before the other player's turn.

Variations. Upon using all five leaves, a player must correctly pronounce his or her words. If a word is mispronounced, the player loses a leaf and the game continues.

Word Sort Contrasting Spelling Patterns for Long U 6–9

This sort works on two common patterns for the long *u* sound: CVCe (as in *use*), and CVVC (as in *fruit* or *food*).

Demonstrate. Prepare the set of long *u* words to use with Sort 245, Appendix p. 296. Before doing the teacher-guided sort, hold up each word card and ask students to read it. Check that students know the words and their meanings. Consider teaching up to five unknown items. Additional unknown items can be set aside for another time. Ask your students if they notice anything in common with all the words—which is a trick question this time, because some of the words that make the long *u* sound do not have a *u*. They have a double *o* instead! Ask if all the words have the same vowel sound. Help them hear that the /oo/ in *food* is the same sound as in *fruit*.

Place the CVCe and CVVC header cards at the tops of the columns, along with the guide words *use*, *fruit*, and *food*. Note that *oo* and *ui* both can make the long *u* sound, and might be described as a CVVC pattern. Proceed through the sort by looking at the long-vowel words one at a time, and labeling their patterns as you have done in previous sorts. Have your students join in as you continue to model this process.

Students may want to include the words *juice, bruise,* and *cruise* in the column of CVCe words, because they end with an *e*. If this comes up, you can explain that the *e* at the end of these words is not the same kind of silent *-e* that makes a vowel "say its name."

The *e* at the end of *cruise* and *bruise* tells us that the *s* is pronounced like a /z/ instead of an /s/; the *e* at the end of *juice* tells us to pronounce the *c* with an /s/ sound. The vowel patterns in these words are CVVC. When you are finished sorting, ask the students how the words in each column are alike, and how they are different from the other column. The completed sort should look something like Sort 245, Appendix p. 296. Check the sort by rereading the words aloud and visually noticing the spelling patterns. *Do all of these words follow the CVCe or CVVC pattern? Do we need to move any?*

Now sort by patterns as well: *u-e, ui, oo*.

Sort, Check, and Reflect. Give each student or pair of students a copy of the sort for guided practice. Now have the students repeat the sorting, checking, and reflecting under your supervision.

Extend. Have students store their words in an envelope or plastic bag so they can reuse them throughout the week in individual and partner sorts. Encourage students to chant the words so the long *u* sound in all of these patterns is reinforced. For added practice, ask students to do a speed sort to see how fast they can go!

Concept Sort: Matter 6–10

Make copies of the matter concept sort, Sort 234, Appendix p. 295, cut them apart, and place them in envelopes or small plastic bags. To help keep multiple sets organized, consider using various colors of paper, or putting a small colored dot or number on each card so that it can easily be reorganized if multiple copies get mixed up.

Demonstrate. This sort features a collection of vocabulary words associated with matter, and can be used when your class is studying this science topic. Introduce the key words (guide cards) and ask students to tell you what they know about solids, liquids, and gases to activate their prior knowledge. Use several words from each category to demonstrate the sort, explaining your rationale through a think-aloud. For example, you may pick *ice, water,* and *air* to review together. How does each item represent its category? Review all of the picture and word cards with the students to make sure they can both read and understand the meaning of each term. You may also want to have students review the picture and word cards with a partner. Then, work your way through the sort as a group.

The completed sort should look something like Sort 234, Appendix p. 295.

After sorting, discuss the similarities within each category and the differences among the categories. For example: "*Statue and steel are similar because they both take up space and hold their own shape. Ice and steam are different because ice is a solid—it takes up space and holds its own shape; whereas steam is a gas because it does not hold its own shape and it takes the shape of its container.*" The vocabulary words found in the solid and liquid categories may be understood without too much difficulty, but should be reviewed to be sure. Students may experience more difficulty with the concept of gas, and will likely need support to understand some of the more abstract terms. Provide outlets for students to learn the meanings of these words, such as in explicit lessons, by asking classmates and teachers, and by using picture dictionaries, informational texts, and online reference materials.

Sort, Check, and Reflect. Students should shuffle their cards and repeat the sort under your supervision. Have them check their sorts by explaining their rationale to a partner or the teacher. Encourage students to reflect by asking them to draw a picture of a solid, liquid, or gas. The example may or may not be from the actual sort.

Extend. Create a classroom chart for each state of matter: solid, liquid, and gas. Add to the chart over time by finding examples of each from the surrounding environment. For

Within-Word Pattern Stage

example, a student may ask to include *hamburger, grill,* and *propane:* "I ate a hamburger which my dad cooked on the propane grill—hamburger *and* grill *are examples of a solid, and* propane *is an example of a gas.*"

Word Sort with A_E, AI, AY 6–11

This sort adds another common spelling pattern to students' repertoires for long *a* words—*ay.*

Demonstrate. Prepare the set of long *a* words to use with Sort 246, Appendix p. 296. Before doing the teacher-guided sort, hold up each word card and ask students to read it. Check that students know the words and their meanings. Consider teaching up to five unknown words. Additional unknown items can be set aside for another time. Ask your students if they notice anything about the words (they all have an *a* in them). Ask about the vowel sounds in the middle of the words. Do they all have the same vowel sound?

Show students the A_E, AI, and AY header cards. Remind students that they have worked previously with long-vowel patterns that follow the CVCe and CVVC pattern. In this sort, you will be adding a new pattern for long *a* words—*ay.* Show the guide words for each column and match them to the corresponding pattern, *name* with A_E, *rain* with AI, and *day* with AY. Model the process of looking at one of the long-vowel words and figuring out which pattern it belongs with: Make *has a consonant, a vowel, another consonant, and the letter* e. So, make *follows the A_E pattern.* Paid *follows the AI pattern.* Play *follows the AY pattern.* Demonstrate the sorting process by analyzing each of the other words and comparing them to the header cards. Have your students join in as you continue to model this process. It is critical that your students say the words out loud even as they look for visual patterns for sorting. The completed sort should look something like Sort 246, Appendix p. 296.

When you are finished sorting, ask the students how the words in each column are alike, and how they are different from the other words. What ideas do they have about why some words are spelled with *ai* while others are spelled with *ay*? Check the sort by rereading the words aloud and visually noticing the spelling patterns. *Does each column of words match the pattern of its header? Do we need to move any?*

Sort, Check, and Reflect. Give each student or pair of students a copy of the sort for guided practice. Now have the students repeat the sorting, checking, and reflecting under your supervision.

Extend. Have students store their words in an envelope or plastic bag so they can reuse them throughout the week in individual and partner sorts. Students can also go on a word hunt to find words with *ay* to add to their list of long *a* words in their word study notebooks.

Word Sort with O_E, OA, OW 6–12

This sort adds another common spelling pattern to students' repertoires for long *o* words—*ow.*

Demonstrate. Prepare the set of long *o* words to use with Sort 247, Appendix p. 296. Before doing the teacher-guided sort, hold up each word card and ask students to read it. Check that students know the words and their meanings. Consider teaching up to five unknown words. Additional unknown items can be set aside for another time. Ask your students if they notice anything about the words (they all have an *o* in them). *Do all of the words have the same vowel sound?*

Show students the O_E, OA, and OW header cards. Remind students that they have worked previously with long-vowel patterns that follow the CVCe and CVVC pattern. In this sort, you will be adding a new pattern for long *o* words—*ow*. Show the guide words for each column and match them to the corresponding pattern, *bone* with O_E, *soap* with OA, and *low* with OW. Model the process of looking at one of the long-vowel words and figuring out which pattern it belongs with: "Home *has a consonant, a vowel, another consonant, and the letter* e. *So,* home *follows the O_E pattern.* Roam *follows the OA pattern.* Grow *follows the OW pattern.*" Demonstrate the sorting process by analyzing each of the other words and comparing them to the header cards. Have your students join in as you continue to model this process. It is critical that your students say the words out loud even as they look for visual patterns for sorting.

When you are finished sorting, ask the students how the words in each column are alike, and how they are different from the other columns. The completed sort should look something like Sort 247, Appendix p. 296. Check the sort by rereading the words aloud and visually noticing the spelling patterns. *Does each column of words match the pattern of its header? Do we need to move any?*

Sort, Check, and Reflect. Give each student or pair of students a copy of the sort for guided practice. Now have the students repeat the sorting, checking, and reflecting under your supervision.

Extend. Have students store their words in an envelope or plastic bag so they can reuse them throughout the week in individual and partner sorts. Students can also go on a word hunt to find words with *ow* to add to their list of long *o* words in their word study notebooks.

Word Sort with U_E, EW, UE 6–13

This sort adds more common spelling pattern to students' repertoires for long *u* words—*ew* and *ue*.

Demonstrate. Prepare the set of long *u* words to use with Sort 248, Appendix p. 296. Before doing the teacher-guided sort, hold up each word card and ask students to read it. Check that students know the words and their meanings. Consider teaching up to five unknown words. Additional unknown items can be set aside for another time. *Do all of the words have the same vowel letters? Do all of the words have the same vowel sound?*

Show students the U_E, EW, and UE header cards. Remind students that they have worked previously with long-vowel patterns that follow the CVCe and CVVC pattern. In this sort, you will be adding two new patterns for long *u* words—*ew* and *ue*. Show the guide words for each column and match them to the corresponding pattern, *tube* with U_E, *new* with EW, and *blue* with UE. Model the process of looking at one of the long-vowel words and figuring out which pattern it belongs with: Rule *has a consonant, a vowel, another consonant, and the letter* e. *So,* rule *follows the U_E pattern.* Grew *follows the EW pattern.* True *follows the UE pattern.* Demonstrate the sorting process by analyzing each of the other words and comparing them to the header cards. Have your students join in as you continue to work through this process. It is critical that your students say the words out loud even as they look for visual patterns for sorting.

When you are finished sorting, ask the students how the words in each column are alike, and how they are different from the other columns. The completed sort should look something like Sort 248, Appendix p. 296. Check the sort by rereading the words aloud and visually noticing the spelling patterns. *Does each column of words match the pattern of its header? Do we need to move any?*

Sort, Check and Reflect. Give each student or pair of students a copy of the sort for guided practice. Now have the students repeat the sorting, checking, and reflecting under your supervision.

Extend. Have students store their words in an envelope or plastic bag so they can reuse them throughout the week in individual and partner sorts. Students can also go on a word hunt to find words with *ew* and *ue* patterns to add to their list of long *u* words in their word study notebooks.

Word Sort with *I_E*, *IGH*, *Y* 6–14

This sort adds another common spelling pattern to students' repertoires for long *i* words—*igh*.

Demonstrate. Prepare the set of long *i* words to use with Sort 249, Appendix p. 296. Before doing the teacher-guided sort, hold up each word card and ask students to read it. Check that students know the words and their meanings. Consider teaching up to five unknown words. Additional unknown items can be set aside for another time. *Do all of the words have the same vowel letters? Do all of the words have the same vowel sound?*

Show students the I_E, IGH, and Y header cards. Remind students that they have worked previously with long-vowel patterns that follow the CVCe and CV pattern. In this sort, you will be adding a new pattern for long *i* words—*igh*. Show the guide words for each column and match them to the corresponding pattern, *line* with I_E, *high* with IGH, and *my* with Y. Model the process of looking at one of the long-vowel words and figuring out which pattern it belongs with: Like *has a consonant, a vowel, another consonant, and the letter* e. *So*, like *follows the* I_E *pattern*. Might *follows the IGH pattern*. By *follows the Y pattern*. Demonstrate the sorting process by analyzing each of the other words and comparing them to the header cards. Have your students join in as you continue to work through each word. It is critical that your students say the words out loud even as they look for visual patterns for sorting.

When you are finished sorting, ask the students how the words in each column are alike, and how they are different from the other columns. The completed sort should look something like Sort 249, Appendix p. 296. Check the sort by rereading the words aloud and visually noticing the spelling patterns. *Does each column of words follow the pattern of its header? Do we need to move any?*

Sort, Check, and Reflect. Give each students or pair of students a copy of the sort for guided practice. Now have the students repeat the sorting, checking, and reflecting under your supervision.

Extend. Have students store their words in an envelope or plastic bag so they can reuse them throughout the week in individual and partner sorts. Students can also go on a word hunt to find words with *igh* patterns to add to their list of long *i* words in their word study notebooks.

Star Light, Star Bright Game 6–15

In this game, two players compare long *i* vowel pattern words.

Materials. Create a basic follow-the-path game board from the U-game boards found in the Appendix, p. 344, and color the squares yellow, green, blue, and red. You will also need a collection of at least 24 words with long *i* vowel patterns written on yellow, green, blue, and red paper or tag board stars. Designate a space at one end as the starting point and a space at the other end as the finish line. At the "finish" create a picture depicting nighttime sky. A number spinner or a single die is used to move players along the path. Here is a list of words for you to include on the word cards:

i-e	ie	y	igh
like	pie	sky	high
nice	tie	fly	light
ride	lie	try	night
time	die	my	bright
white		spy	flight
mile		spry	sight
pride		dry	right
slice		cry	fright
strive			might
glide			

Procedure.

1. Each player rolls the die or spins the spinner to see who goes first. The player with the highest roll or spin will start, and play proceeds in a clockwise manner.
2. Shuffle the word cards and place them face down on the game board.
3. The first player draws a card, reads the word, and designates the vowel pattern. If the player reads the word correctly and identifies the vowel pattern, he or she moves to the first colored space that matches the color of the word card.
4. The winner is the first one to get to the end of the path.

Variation.

1. Each player rolls the die or spins the spinner to see who goes first. The player with the highest roll or spin will start, and play proceeds in a clockwise manner.
2. The second player draws a card from the stack of words placed face down. The player reads the word aloud to the first player who must spell the word aloud. If the player spells the word correctly, he or she moves to the first colored space that matches the color of the word card.
3. The winner is the first one to get to the end of the path.

Note: This game board can be used for any vowel patterns as long as the word cards are color coded.

Homophone Personal Picture Dictionaries 6–16

This activity will take place over time, and helps students create a personal reference book of homophones that can be used for many purposes.

Materials. Use composition folders with paper or make construction paper notebooks with at least one page for each letter of the alphabet. Make copies of the example homophone word list to follow. Students can also add to their homophone dictionaries as they find words in their reading. Have pens, markers, and other art materials available for students to use as they illustrate their homophone picture dictionaries.

Procedures. Write the words *no* and *know* on chart paper for students to see. Ask them to read both of the words. Do they sound the same? Do they mean the same thing? How do we know when to use which word? Tell students that these words are homophones, they sound the same but have different meanings. What we mean to say when using one of these words helps us know how to spell it correctly. Write a sentence using *no*, and another using *know*. Discuss the meaning of the word in each sentence. Have students make up their own sentences orally using these words.

Remind students that they have been studying lots of vowel patterns. Sometimes, there is more than one pattern to express a certain vowel sound; for instance *ai* and *a_e* both make the long *a* sound. Because of different spelling patterns, many homophones can be formed. Share homophone pairs such as *tail/tale, maid/made, sail/sale,* and *plain/plane*. Discuss the meanings of these pairs, and ask students to use them in a sentence. Finally, ask students to choose one of the homophone pairs to write and illustrate in their personal homophone picture dictionary. The words should be written on the appropriate letter page according to their first letter.

Continue coming back to the picture dictionary over time, exploring other patterns that create homophones. Use the example homophones (sample below) to have students match words that sound the same. Focus on specific homophone pairs for vocabulary and spelling development in ongoing lessons. Encourage students to note homophones they discover, write them in their dictionary, and illustrate them during free time. Refer to students' homophone picture dictionaries when spelling confusions arise among words.

to	eye	bear	ate	pour	cheap
one	deer	great	aunt	sun	sale
add	bore	not	boar	I	lead
male	sell	dye	browse	pole	won
four	plane	two	hi	mail	meat
aisle	wee	prey	steak	cell	heal
brows	bored	in	cheep	jeans	grate
ant	high	heel	past	tied	ad
pray	stake	for	pore	role	roll
son	I'll	tide	genes	too	prays
passed	led	meet	praise	poll	fore
bare	die	eight	knot	dear	board
sail	made	we	plain	inn	maid

Example homophones

Variations and Extensions. Use the example homophone list as a resource to make larger cards for games such as Rummy, Go Fish, and Concentration. Read books that feature jokes using homophones such as *The King Who Rained* (Gwynne, 1988), *How Much Can a Bare Bear Bear?* (Cleary & Gable, 2005), and *The Moose Is in the Mousse* (Scheunemann, 2002). See if students can make up their own homophone word plays, and construct a class book of their individual pages.

Find the Gold Game 6–17

This board game reviews long-vowel words that follow the VCC pattern such as *find* and *gold*. Make a literature connection by playing this game after you have read *That's What*

Leprechauns Do by Eve Bunting (2005), about three mischievous leprechauns who must dig up their pot of gold before the rainbow comes to point it out.

Materials.

1. Prepare a game board using a U-game board template from the Appendix (p. 344). Write a few words from the book as well as VCC words such as the following:

find	blind	gold	fold	post	stroll
kind	grind	cold	roll	sold	volt
child	hind	hold	scold	bold	jolt
climb	sign	most	bolt	colt	poll
mind	bind	old	folk	host	scroll
wild	wind	told	ghost	mold	

2. You will need a spinner with numbers 1 through 4, playing pieces to move around the board, and a pencil and small piece of paper for each player.

Procedures.

1. After reading *That's What Leprechauns Do* and sorting words with the VCC pattern, players move to the board game and place game markers at the start position.
2. One player spins and moves that number of spaces on the board.
3. The player reads the word on the space. A player moves back a space if he or she reads the word incorrectly. Students "add a piece of gold to their pot" by drawing a circle on their note paper and writing in a word that rhymes from the game board.
4. Players take turns. The player wins who reaches the finish line first or who has the greatest number of gold pieces.

Variations.

1. Players can move two or three times around the board.
2. Students hunt for these words or words that follow the same patterns in other texts and record them on a rainbow.

Word Sort with Long-Vowel *R* Words 6–18

This sort examines words with *r* that retain their long-vowel sound.

Demonstrate. Prepare the set of long-vowel *r* words for Sort 250, Appendix p. 296. Before doing the teacher-guided sort, ask students to read the words aloud and check to see that they know the meanings of the words. Consider teaching up to five unknown terms. Additional unknown items can be set aside for another time. Set up *A, E, I, O,* and *U* as the guide letters at the top of your columns. Demonstrate the sorting process by saying each of the words and comparing them to the guide letters. *Does* care *have the long a pattern or another long-vowel sound?* Have your students join in as you continue to model the identification and categorization of the correct long-vowel sound and place the word in the appropriate column. It is critical that your students say the words out loud even as they visually discern the letters in the words. The completed sort should look something like Sort 250, Appendix p. 296.

When you are finished sorting, ask the students what makes the words in each column alike. Check the sort by naming all of the words in each column and visually reviewing their spelling patterns. *Do the words in each column have the same vowel sound? Do we need to move any? What do we notice about the spelling patterns in the words?*

Sort, Check, and Reflect. Give each student or pair of students a copy of the sort for guided practice. Now have the students repeat the sorting, checking, and reflecting under your supervision using the same vowel letters as column headers.

Extend. Have students brainstorm other words that rhyme with the words in this sort. Do the words they thought of follow the same spelling patterns?

R-Influenced Word Sort 6–19

In this sort, *r*-influenced words using all five vowels are explored for sound differences.

Demonstrate. Prepare the set of *r*-influenced words for Sort 251, Appendix p. 297. Before doing the teacher-guided sort, ask students to read the words aloud and check to see that they know the meanings of the words. Consider teaching up to five unknown terms. Additional unknown items can be set aside for another time. Set up *ar, er, or, ur* and *ir* as the guide patterns at the top of your columns. Demonstrate the sorting process by saying each of the words and comparing them to the guide patterns. *What pattern does the word* car *have? Yes. the* ar *pattern.* Have your students join in as you continue to model the identification and categorization of the correct *r*-influenced pattern and place the word in the appropriate column. It is critical that your students say the words out loud even as they visually discern the letters in the words.

When you are finished sorting, ask the students what makes the words in each column similar. The completed sort should look something like Sort 251, Appendix p. 297. Check the sort by naming all of the words in each column and visually reviewing their spelling patterns. *Do the words in each column have the same spelling pattern? Do we need to move any? What do we notice about the sounds in the words?* Discuss with students the fact that when the *r* combines with some of the vowels, it is so strong that the words sound alike. The /er/ sound in *er, ir* and *ur* words sound just the same. This makes spelling them more difficult!

Sort, Check, and Reflect. Give each student or pair of students a copy of the sort for guided practice. Now have the students repeat the sorting, checking, and reflecting under your supervision using the same letter patterns as column headers.

Extend. Pronouncing and spelling *r*-influenced words can be quite a challenge for many English learners. Provide lots of opportunities for students to review the sorts and practice reading and spelling the words. Encourage students to work with a partner, read each other the *r*-influenced words, and predict the spelling pattern without looking.

Within-Word Pattern Stage

Her First Word Turn Game: The Spellings of *ER* 6–20

This Tic-Tac-Toe variation explores the variety of spelling patterns for the /er/ sound.

Materials. You will need a stack of cards with words printed on them that have the /er/ sound. Here is a list of suggested words:

Her: herd, perch, fern, germ, clerk, term, per, jerk
First: bird, chirp, girl, dirt, shirt, third, birth, firm, stir, fir, thirst, squirt, swirl, whirl, twirl
Word: work, worm, world, worth, worse
Turn: burn, hurt, curl, purr, burst, church, chum, curb, hurl, burr, blurt, lurch, lurk, spur, surf

Each student will need scratch paper and a pencil to make his or her personal *Her first word turn* (tic-tac-toe) boards.

her	first	word
turn	her	first
word	turn	her

turn	her	first
word	turn	her
first	word	turn

Procedures.

1. Place the /er/ word cards in a small bag or tub and mix them up.
2. Each student makes a Tic-Tac-Toe grid, and writes the words *her, first, word,* or *turn* in each of the spaces. The student may begin on *her* or any of the other words, but should write each word in sequence without skipping or repeating. For example, a student may choose to begin on the word *turn,* but should then write the remaining words in sequence as in *turn, her, first, word, turn, her, first, word, turn.*
3. One student is the "caller," or students take turns with this job. The caller pulls a card out of the bag, reads it to the group, and spells it. Students looks at their game board for a word that has the same/er/ spelling, and put an X on it. If more than one words works, they choose the word that will most likely give them three in a row. If students no longer have a word that matches the spelling pattern of the called word, they do nothing.
4. The first person to get three in a row across, down, or diagonally, wins.
5. Make another game board and play again!

Variations. Instead of getting three in a row, play until all of the words on the board are crossed out. Or, try playing *Her first word turn* without peeking. See if students can figure out the spelling patterns of the called words without looking at the card first.

Word Sort with Diphthongs 6–21

This sort features the diphthongs *oi/oy* and *ou/ow.* Diphthongs are vowel sounds that move from one position to another within the same syllable.

Demonstrate. Prepare the set of diphthong words for Sort 252, Appendix p. 297. Before doing the teacher-guided sort, ask students to read the words aloud and check to see that they know the meanings of the words. Consider teaching up to five unknown

Within-Word Pattern Stage

terms. Additional unknown items can be set aside for another time. Set up *oi, oy, ou,* and *ow* as the guide patterns at the top of your columns. Demonstrate the sorting process by naming each of the words and comparing them to the guide patterns. *What pattern does the word* oil *have? Yes, the* oi *pattern.* Have your students join in as you continue to model the identification and categorization of the correct diphthong spelling and place the word in the appropriate column. It is critical that your students say the words out loud even as they visually discern the letters in the words.

When you are finished sorting, ask the students what makes the words in each column similar. The completed sort should look something like Sort 252, Appendix p. 297. Check the sort by naming all of the words in each column and visually reviewing their spelling patterns. *Do the words in each column have the same spelling pattern? Do we need to move any? What do we notice about the sounds in the words?* Discuss with students the fact that the *oi* and *oy* have the same sound, and *ou* and *ow* do, too. Why do students think the letters might be different for different words?

Sort, Check, and Reflect. Give each student or pair of students a copy of the sort for guided practice. Now have the students repeat the sorting, checking, and reflecting under your supervision using the same letter patterns as column headers.

Extend. Provide additional opportunities for students to review the sort and practice reading and spelling the words. Go on a word hunt to find further examples of words with these spellings. Do *ou* and *ow* always get pronounced as a diphthong?

Word Sort with Ambiguous Vowel Sounds 6–22

This sort contrasts an array of related, open vowel sounds similar to the *a* in *draw*. The sort features the spelling patterns short *o, aw, au, al, w+a,* and *ough.*

Demonstrate. Prepare the set of ambiguous vowel words for Sort 253, Appendix p. 297. Before doing the teacher-guided sort, ask students to read the words aloud and check to see that they know the meanings of the words. Consider teaching up to five unknown terms. Additional unknown items can be set aside for another time. Set up *o, aw, au, al, w+a,* and *ough* as the guide patterns at the top of your columns. Demonstrate the sorting process by naming each of the words and comparing them to the guide patterns. *What pattern does the word* cloth *have? Yes, the short* o *pattern.* Have your students join in as you continue to model the identification and categorization of the correct ambiguous vowel spelling and place the word in the appropriate column. This is a difficult sort because of the variety of spelling patterns and the similarity among the sounds in the words. It is critical that your students say the words out loud even as they visually discern the letters in the words. The completed sort should look something like Sort 253, Appendix p. 297.

When you are finished sorting, ask the students what makes the words in each column similar. Check the sort by naming all of the words in each column and visually reviewing their spelling patterns. *Do the words in each column have the same spelling pattern? Do we need to move any? What do we notice about the sounds in the words?* Think aloud with the group about what is tricky in spelling these words.

Sort, Check, and Reflect. Give each student or pair of students a copy of the sort for guided practice. Now have the students repeat the sorting, checking, and reflecting under your supervision using the same letter patterns as column headers.

Extend. Provide numerous opportunities for students to review the sort and practice reading and spelling the words. Go on a word hunt to find further examples of words with these spellings. Create lists of rhyming words to put in word study notebooks so that students have a chance to review common spelling patterns.

Ambiguous Vowel Sound: Jeopardy 6-23

This guessing game helps students learn and practice words with ambiguous vowel sounds. Students have to guess the right word based on a clue, so it is also a good way to get vocabulary practice.

aw	W + a	ough	au	oo
100	100	100	100	100
200	200	200	200	200
300	300	300	300	300

Example game board

Point value	aw	w+a	ough	au	oo
100	crawl	watch	bought	caught	book
200	squawk	swat	fought	fault	wood
300	thaw	swap	cough	launch	hood

Words used in sample game

Materials. You will need dice, a game board, and clue cards. A poster board or open file folder is divided into five columns with three boxes each. A clue card worth 100, 200, or 300 points is placed on each space. Cards should be color coded or labeled by their category so they are placed in the appropriate column.

Following is a list of possible words and point values for you to get started. You can add new words to this game over time, but remember to find words that are concrete, so that English learners can predict them from short clues. The words should also represent an ambiguous vowel word that they have worked with in the past.

Answers for clue cards:

aw
100: A baby moves this way.
200: A loud cry or scream, like a goose might make.
300: This means to melt.

w+a
100: Something you wear to tell time.
200: This means to hit, like you would a fly.
300: This means to trade things, like friends might do.

ough
100: You spent money. You _____ things.
200: They had a fight yesterday. They _____.
300: When you are sick you might sneeze or _____.

au
100: When they threw the ball to him, he _____ it.
200: When someone is to blame, it is his or her _____.
300: What is done to make a rocket take off.

oo
100: Something to read.
200: We get this from the trunks of trees.
300: This part of your jacket covers the head.

Procedures.

1. One player is the game host. The others roll the dice to determine who goes first.
2. The game begins when the first player picks a category and an amount for the host to read, for example, *"I'll take* aw *for 100."* The host reads the clue and the player must respond by phrasing a question and spelling the word. For example:

   Host:　"A baby moves this way. "
   Player:　"What is crawl? c-r-a-w-l."

3. The player receives the card if the answer is correct. This player chooses another clue. (A player can only have two consecutive turns.) If the player misses, the player to the left may answer.
4. The game continues until all the clue cards are read and won, or left unanswered. Players add their points, and the one with the highest number of points wins.
5. Depending on the English proficiency level of your students, adjust the difficulty level of words and clues.

WORD STUDY ACTIVITIES AT THE LATE WITHIN-WORD PATTERN STAGE

Word Sort with *SCR, STR, SPR* 6–24

This sort is the first to examine complex consonant clusters with students. Explicit attention and practice to blends such as *scr, str,* and *spr* help English learners to discriminate and represent these sounds more effectively.

Demonstrate.　Prepare the set of *scr, str,* and *spr* words for Sort 254, Appendix p. 297. Before doing the teacher-guided sort, ask students to read the words aloud and check to see that they know the meanings of the words. Because many of the words sound very similar to each other (e.g., *scrap* and *scrape*), students may need extra support in the pronunciation aspect of this new learning. Make saying these words fun—like working with tongue twisters! Consider teaching up to five unknown terms. Additional unknown items can be set aside for another time. Set up *spr, str,* and *scr* as the guide patterns at the top of your columns. Demonstrate the sorting process by discussing each of the key words and comparing them to the guide patterns. *What cluster does the word* spray *have? Yes, the* spr *cluster.* Have your students join in as you continue to model the identification and categorization of the correct consonant cluster, and place the word in the appropriate column. This is a difficult sort because of the similarity among the sounds in the words. Keep the mood playful and supportive. It is critical that your students say the words out loud even as they visually discern the letters in the words. The completed sort should look something like Sort 254, Appendix p. 297.

When you are finished sorting, ask the students to compare the words in each column. Check the sort by naming all of the words in each column and visually reviewing their spelling patterns. Make the checking fun by chanting or adding rhythm to the rereading of the words. *Do the words in each column have the same consonant cluster? Do we need to move any? What do we notice about the sounds in the words?* Think aloud with the group about what is tricky in spelling these words.

Sort, Check, and Reflect. Give each student or pair of students a copy of the sort for guided practice. Now have the students repeat the sorting, checking, and reflecting under your supervision using the same letter patterns as column headers.

Extend. Have students make up fun, tongue-twister sentences using several words from this sort such as "I scratch *and* scream *crossing the* strong stream." Can they say the sentence quickly several times?

Word Sort with SQU, THR, SHR 6–25

This sort continues to examine complex consonant clusters with students, in the format of Activity 6–24, but this time with the blends of *squ, thr*, and *shr*.

Demonstrate. Prepare the set of *squ, thr*, and *shr* words for Sort 255, Appendix p. 297. Before doing the teacher-guided sort, ask students to read the words aloud and check to see that they know the meanings of the words. Because these words contain blends that are complex or may not exist in students' home languages, extra support and practice may be called for here. Keep the atmosphere light and supportive—don't fixate on minor pronunciation problems. First check to see if students can read and understand the meanings of the words. Consider teaching up to five unknown terms. Additional unknown items can be set aside for another time. Set up *squ, thr*, and *shr* as the guide patterns at the top of your columns. Demonstrate the sorting process as described in Activity 6–24. The completed sort should look something like Sort 255, Appendix p. 297.

When you are finished sorting, check the sort as described in Activity 6–24.

Sort, Check, and Reflect. Give each student or pair of students a copy of the sort for guided practice. Now have the students repeat the sorting, checking, and reflecting under your supervision.

Extend. Have students illustrate some of the interesting words in this sort, such as *squish* or *shriek*. Collect their illustrations to create a class book or wall display.

Triple Threat Racetrack Game 6–26

In this game, two players match words in their hand with words on the track. This is a great way to examine triple *r* blends and digraphs with *r* blends.

Materials. Use the Racetrack game board template found in the Appendix, p. 343. Reproduce the two sides of this game board, glue together on a file folder, and write a different word on each space that begins with a triple *r* blend, or a digraph and *r* blend (e.g., *thrill*). Draw a star in two of the spaces. Triple *r* blend words include *stripe, scream, scrape, stream, spring, threat, thread, through, throughout, sprout, spring, sprint, stripe, threw, throat, string, street, struck, strand, strict, strike, string, stream, phrase, shrimp, thrill, spray, scram, screech, screw.* You will also need 40 to 50 cards prepared with words that share the same beginning consonant cluster patterns as the game board words. A number spinner or a single die is used to move players around the track.

Procedures.

1. Shuffle the word cards and deal six to each player. Turn the rest face down to become the deck.

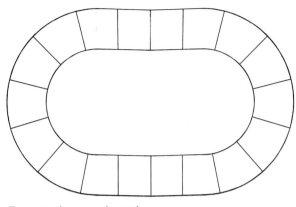

Racetrack game board

2. Playing pieces are placed anywhere on the board and moved according to the number spinner or die.
3. When players land on a space, they read the word and then look for words in their hand that have the same pattern. For example, a player who lands on *scream* may pull *screech* and *screw* from his hand to put in the winning pile. If he moves to a space with a star, he chooses a pattern to lay down.
4. The cards placed in the winning pile are replaced by drawing the same number from the deck before play passes to the next player.
5. A player who has no match for the pattern must draw a card anyway.
6. The game is over when there are no more cards to play. The winner is the player with the most word cards in his or her lay-down pile.

Word Sort with Endings *DGE, GE* 6–27

This sort examines words that end with the final /j/, spelled with *dge* or *ge*. Students learn how specific letters such as *r, l,* and *n*, as well as the vowel sounds in these words, influence their spelling.

Demonstrate. Prepare the set of *dge, ge,* and *r, l, n + ge* words for Sort 256, Appendix p. 297. Before doing the teacher-guided sort, ask students to read the words aloud and check to see that they know the meanings of the words. Many of the words may not be familiar to English learners (e.g., *surge* and *bulge*), so students may need extra support in learning the vocabulary. Consider teaching up to five unknown terms. Additional unknown items can be set aside for another time. Set up *dge, ge,* and *r, l, n + ge* as the guide patterns at the top of your columns. Demonstrate the sorting process by discussing each of the key words and comparing them to the guide patterns. *What ending does the word* dodge *have? Yes, the* dge *cluster.* Have your students join in as you continue to model the identification and categorization of the correct ending spelling pattern, and place the word in the appropriate column. It is critical that your students say the words out loud even as they visually discern the letters in the words. This helps them articulate the *r, l,* or *n* sound in addition to the /j/ that they all end with. The completed sort should look something like Sort 256, Appendix p. 297.

When you are finished sorting, ask the students to compare the words in each column. *Do the words in each column have the same consonant cluster? Do we need to move any? What do we notice about the sounds in the words?* Next, ask the students to consider the vowel sound in each word: *What do you notice about the vowel sounds in the* ge *column? Why do you think these words have a long vowel sound? Do the words in the* dge *column have a long or a short sound? Why do you think there is a* d *in their ending spelling pattern? How are the words in the* r, l, n + ge *column the same or different?* (When you hear a short-vowel sound, use dge, unless you hear an *r, l,* or *n* before it.)

Sort, Check, and Reflect. Give each student or pair of students a copy of the sort for guided practice. Now have the students repeat the sorting, checking, and reflecting under your supervision using the same letter patterns as column headers.

Extend. These interesting words can be used for vocabulary development activities and as cards in word study board games.

Within-Word Pattern Stage

Word Sort with Endings *TCH*, *CH* 6–28

This sort examines words that end with the final /ch/ sound, spelled with *tch* or *ch*. As in the previous sort, students learn how specific letters such as *r*, *l*, and *n*, as well as the vowel sounds in these words influence their spelling.

Demonstrate. Prepare the set of *tch, ch,* and *r, l, n + ch* words for Sort 257 (Appendix p. 297). Before doing the teacher-guided sort, ask students to read the words aloud and check to see that they know the meanings of the words. Many of the words may not be familiar to English learners (e.g., *clutch* and *pouch*), so students may need extra support in learning the vocabulary. Consider teaching up to five unknown terms. Additional unknown items can be set aside for another time. Set up *tch, ch,* and *r, l, n + ch* as the guide patterns at the top of your columns. Demonstrate the sorting process by discussing each of the key words and comparing them to the guide patterns. *What ending does the word* catch *have? Yes, the* tch *cluster.* Have your students join in as you continue to model the identification and categorization of the correct spelling pattern, and place the word in the appropriate column. It is important that your students say the words out loud even as they visually discern the letters in the words. This helps them articulate the *r, l,* or *n* sound in addition to the /ch/ that the words end with. The completed sort should look something like Sort 257, Appendix p. 297.

When you are finished sorting, ask the students to compare the words in each column. *Do the words in each column have the same spelling pattern? Do we need to move any? What do we notice about the sounds in the words?* Next, ask the students to consider the vowel sound in each word: *What do you notice about the vowel sounds in the* tch *column? Why do you think these words have a short-vowel sound? Do the words in the* ch *column have a long or a short sound? If we think that they should have a long-vowel sound, which words would be "oddballs"? What about the words withn the* r, l, n, + ch? *What vowel sound do they have? Why do you think this is so?*

Sort, Check, and Reflect. Give each student or pair of students a copy of the sort for guided practice. Now have the students repeat the sorting, checking, and reflecting under your supervision using the same letter patterns as column headers.

Extend. Encourage students to quiz each other on the meanings and spellings of these interesting words. Have students practice the sort over time to gain fluency.

Introduction to Two-Syllable Words 6–29

This sort gives a peek into the world of multisyllable words by exploring some of the most high-frequency two-syllable words. It is a first opportunity to discuss the "uh" or schwa sound that occurs in unaccented syllables.

Demonstrate. Prepare the set of two-syllable words for Sort 258, Appendix p. 297. Before doing the teacher-guided sort, ask students to read the words aloud and check to see that they know the meanings of the words. These words are very common and highly used, so if any of the words are unknown, consider taking the time to teach them. Tell students that now that they have learned so much about all kinds of one-syllable words, they are ready to start exploring longer words. You might say something like, *"Today we are going to work with longer words. The words we are using are all around the room—on our signs, in our books, and in your writing. I have seen that many of you have trouble spelling some of these words. Let's see why."* Set up *a-, be-,* and *other* as the guide cards at the top of your columns. Demonstrate the sorting process by naming each of the words and comparing them to the guide cards: *What letter does the word* across *start with? Yes, the* a. *What about the word* really? *That doesn' start with* a-, *or* be-, *so let' put it in the* other *column.* Have your students join in as you continue to model the identification and categorization of the beginning letter, and place the word in the appropriate column. The completed sort should look something like Sort 258, Appendix p. 297.

When you are finished sorting, ask students to check the sort by naming all of the words in each column and making sure they are in the correct column. *Have you ever had trouble spelling any of these words? What has been tricky for you?* Reread the *a-* words with the group, and ask them to notice the first sound they hear: *The "uh" sound happens because it is not in the strong syllable. Sometimes it is hard to know how to spell that "uh" sound.* Ask students if they notice any "uh" sounds in the other columns of words. What can they do to help spell these words in the future?

Sort, Check, and Reflect. Give each student or pair of students a copy of the sort for guided practice. Now have the students repeat the sorting, checking, and reflecting under your supervision using the same column headers.

Extend. Provide numerous opportunities for students to review the sort and practice reading and spelling the words. Encourage students to write these high-frequency words in their word study notebooks or personal dictionaries. These are also good words to include on a classroom word wall.

Word Sort with Contractions 6–30

This sort explores common contractions and the words that work together to create their meaning. It serves as an initial foray into the world of the spelling–meaning connection.

Demonstrate. Prepare the set of contractions for Sort 259, Appendix p. 297. You might introduce this sort by asking students to use some of the following words in a sentence: *don't, isn't, you're,* and *I'll.* You can model by saying something like, *"I'll be going to the store on my way home from school today."* As students contribute sentences, think aloud about which two words are put together to create the contraction they are using: I'll *comes from the two words* I *and* will. *So, instead of* I'll, *we could also say,* "I will *be going to the store on my way home from school today."* Explain to students that you will be working on words like these today that are called contractions. Contractions are two words that have been put together, with a letter or letters taken out. An apostrophe has been added to show where the letter(s) are missing. Students will have likely heard and worked with contractions before, but this may be the first time that they have explored their spelling–meaning connection in depth.

Share the headers *not, are, is,* and *will.* Now, discuss each of the key words to show how they connect with one of the headers: Don't *means do not. It belongs in the* not *column.* Demonstrate the sorting process by naming each of the words and comparing them to the guide cards: *What two words make up* you're? *Yes,* you *and* are. You're *goes under the* are *column.* Have your students join in as you continue to model the identification and categorization of the contractions with their component word, and place the contraction in the appropriate column. The completed sort should look something like Sort 259, Appendix p. 297. When you are finished sorting, ask students to check the sort by naming all of the words in each column and making sure they are in the correct column. Have students point out where the letter is missing in each contraction, and what the component words are.

Sort, Check, and Reflect. Give each student or pair of students a copy of the sort for guided practice. Now have the students repeat the sorting, checking, and reflecting under your supervision using the same column headers.

Extend. Provide numerous opportunities for students to review the sort and practice reading and spelling the words. Encourage students to write these contractions in their word study notebooks or personal dictionaries. For oral language development, practice using the contractions in storytelling or writing.

Concept Sort: Ecosystems 6-31

Make copies of the ecosystem concept sort in the Appendix, p. 321, cut the cards apart, and place them in envelopes or small plastic bags. To help keep multiple sets organized, consider using various colors of paper, or putting a small colored dot or number on each card so that it can easily be reorganized if students get multiple copies get mixed up.

Demonstrate. This sort features a collection of vocabulary words associated with ecosystems. Introduce the key words (guide cards) and ask students to name any plants and animals that may live in ponds, oceans, and deserts to activate their prior knowledge. Use several words from each category to demonstrate the sort, explaining your rationale through a think-aloud. For example, you may pick *sagebrush, seaweed,* and *reeds* as plants that live in different ecosystems. Review all of the picture and word cards with the students to make sure they can both read and understand the meaning of each term. You may also want to have students review the picture and word cards with a partner. The completed sort should look something like Sort 235, Appendix p. 295.

After sorting, discuss the relationships between the plants and animals in each of the ecosystems: *A frog sits on a lily pad waiting to catch a dragonfly as it flies by.* The words will range in difficulty based on their abstractness and on students' background knowledge. Much of the vocabulary should be reinforced in ongoing activities related to your hands-on study of this science unit. Provide outlets for students to learn the meanings of these words, such as in explicit lessons, by asking classmates and teachers, and by using picture dictionaries, informational texts, and online reference materials.

Sort, Check, and Reflect. Students should shuffle their cards and repeat the sort under your supervision. Have them check their sorts by explaining their rationale to a partner or the teacher. Encourage students to reflect by asking them to draw a picture of one or all of the ecosystems, label each concept, and write a few sentences that describe the ecosystem(s).

Extend. Have students work in pairs or small groups to research additional plants and animals and create food chains or food webs for each of the ecosystems.

Word Sort for Plural Endings 6-32

This sort is an introduction to how *-s* and *-es* are added to words to create plurals. It serves as a foundation for sorts that will be conducted in later stages.

Demonstrate. Prepare the set of *plural ending* words for Sort 260, Appendix p. 298. Play some language games with students to make plural words orally: *Today we will be working with words that mean more than one. For instance,* trees *means more than one tree. I'll say a word, and you tell me how to say more than one of it. Ready? Car; paint; name; fox, witch.* If students have any trouble making plurals, work with them orally before beginning the sort. Next, ask students to read the words in this sort aloud and check to see that they know the meanings of the words. Consider teaching up to five unknown terms. Additional unknown items can be set aside for another time. Set up +*s* and +*es* as the guide patterns at the top of your columns. Demonstrate the sorting process by discussing each of the key words and comparing them to the guide patterns: *You'll have to think carefully about each word, and how it is spelled before it becomes more than one.* Work with a whiteboard to show students the original word and its plural if students are confused. Have your students join in as you identify and categorize each of the words as to whether an -*s* or -*es* was added. It is important that your students say the words out loud even as they visually discern the letters in the words. This helps them hear the words that have one or two syllables. The completed sort should look something like Sort 260, Appendix p. 298.

When you are finished sorting, ask the students to compare the words in each column. *Which words needed* -es *to be added? Why? When was* -s *only needed?* Reread the sort as you check the words, and notice how many syllables each word has. *Are words like* friends *and* tests *harder to say because they are only one syllable?*

Sort, Check, and Reflect. Give each student or pair of students a copy of the sort for guided practice. Now have the students repeat the sorting, checking, and reflecting under your supervision using the same column headers.

Extend. Have students go on a word hunt for plural words. How many words can they find or think of? What else do they learn about adding -*s* or -*es* to words?

Word Sort for Past Tense Endings 6–33

This sort is an introduction to how -*ed* is added to words to show how something has already happened. It is modeled with simple forms, and serves as a foundation for sorts that will be conducted in later stages.

Demonstrate. Prepare the set of *past tense endings* words for Sort 261, Appendix p. 298. Play some language games with students to help them understand the concept of past tense: *Today we will be working with words that tell you that something has already happened. For instance,* rained *means it already happened. I'll say a word, and you change the word to mean that it already happened. Ready? Plant, paint; show; help, start.* If students have any trouble putting words into the past tense, work with them orally before beginning the sort. Next, ask students to read the words in this sort aloud and check to see that they know the meanings of the words. Consider teaching up to five unknown terms. Additional unknown items can be set aside for another time. Set up /d/, /id/, and /t/ as the guide patterns at the top of your columns. Tell students that when you add *ed* to a word to make it the past, it can be pronounced in different ways: *Today you will be comparing the different sounds that* -ed *makes.* Demonstrate the sorting process by discussing each of the key words and comparing them to the guide patterns: Mailed *means that something has already been put in the mail. What does the* -ed *sound like in* mailed? *Right, it sounds like a* /d/. *It goes under the card with the* /d/ *sound.* Have your students join in as you identify and categorize each of the words as to what sound the -*ed* makes. It is important that your students say the words out loud so they can accurately identify the sound. Listen carefully and help your students if they mispronounce the words. The completed sort should look something like Sort 261, Appendix p. 298.

When you are finished sorting, ask the students to reread the words in each column. *Did they all get placed in the correct sound column?*

Sort, Check, and Reflect. Give each student or pair of students a copy of the sort for guided practice. Now have the students repeat the sorting, checking, and reflecting under your supervision using the same column headers.

Extend. Have students go on a word hunt for other words that mean something has already happened. How many words can they find or think of?

7

Word Study with English Learners in the Syllables and Affixes and Derivational Relations Stages

Ms. Thompson's fourth-grade class is well organized and emanates a sense of purpose. Student desks are clustered into table groups, and there is an open floor space for community meetings. Tubs of books are everywhere you turn: this way, a bookshelf filled with chapter books, including collections of mysteries and series such as *The Boxcar Children* and *Cam Jansen;* that way, bins of nonfiction books labeled with a content area such as *U.S. History and Government, Famous People, Math*, or *Land Animals.*

The bulletin boards hold useful directions and reference materials for students. On one bulletin board there is a word wall with high-frequency words that students often misspell. Another wall houses a *math word bank* that displays vocabulary words related to the math curriculum; the letter D is represented by the words *difference, division, decimal*, and *deposit*. Various charts capture previous group brainstorms, such as "Choosing new books," "When to abandon a book," and "Possible topics for letters." Easy-to-read charts outline when each of the Book Clubs will meet, and who is working at each center on Monday, Tuesday, Wednesday, and Thursday.

During literacy center time Ms. Thompson's multilingual and multiethnic class is active, but not chaotic. Four students are working at the state history center, using resource materials to write the text for their individual state books. Three students are playing a word study game together in the rug area. Six students are at an independent reading center, either reading to themselves, or completing entries in their reading response journals. Two students are cooperatively engaged in a computer game, and four other students are listening to books on tape at tape players around the room. Ms. Thompson knows it is important for English learners to have repeated opportunities to come back to interesting texts as they build their oral language skills, so she has many books available on tape or on the computer, along with a number of listening stations around the room.

On the rug in the meeting area, Ms. Thompson and a group of six English learners are gathered around a small chart stand with paper. The group is brainstorming words related to families, the topic of today's reading text. There are many common words on the list already, such as *brother, sister, mom, dad*, and *grandma*. Now the group is moving into more complex words and concepts, such as *stepsister, stepbrother*, and *stepfather*. The students are asking questions, and Ms. Thompson helps them to clarify their understanding of these relationships.

After brainstorming a list of about 25 family-related words, Ms. Thompson moves to her word study focus of the day—the use of the plural *s* versus *'s* for the possessive. She begins with a teacher-led word sort with the key words *mothers* and *mother's*. The group discusses in which column *aunts, brother's, cousins*, and a dozen other words belong. Ms. Thompson asks students if they can use the words in a sentence to clarify the meaning.

When the word sort is done, the students get out their book for the day. It is a nonfiction text about families written at a late second-grade level, which is the students' instructional reading level. She walks them through the book, noting some of the key vocabulary. Students point out to her that there are one or two family-related words that are missing from the group's brainstorming chart, so these are added to the list. The group is guided to make predictions, then read the first five pages and stop for a brief discussion to check for understanding. In this way, Ms. Thompson provides practice time for her students to read at their instructional level while supporting their language development and comprehension of the text. By explicitly working with the plural and possessive *s*, she integrates grammar, spelling, and vocabulary development into the language arts lesson.

Ms. Thompson's lesson models many of the guiding principles we have focused on throughout this book. In the preceding vignette, students received explicit and systematic instruction when they had opportunities to discuss content-related words with teacher support; the teacher used reading materials at students' instructional levels, and provided opportunities for guided practice in reading and sorting. A supportive, small group context engaged students within a learning community. Ms. Thompson helped students make connections in numerous ways—by writing their oral language on chart paper, by helping them connect the schema for family words in English, by matching a word study lesson to the theme of the book being read, and by eliciting their background knowledge during the brainstorming. Finally, she provided opportunities for the active construction of knowledge when students participated in sorting the family words, coming up with their own sentences, and having time to talk in a small group setting.

This chapter takes an in-depth look at helpful support strategies, the characteristics of development, and the content of instruction for English learners at the intermediate and advanced levels. We describe how the essential literacy activities of *Read To, Read With, Write With, Word Study,* and *Talk With* (RRWWT) work together to provide a cohesive learning environment for English learners. We share examples of word study conversations so you can get a picture of how an effective teacher is both explicit and challenges students to think at higher levels. Ideas for organizing word study activities that accommodate students from a range of developmental levels within a single classroom are also presented. The chapter concludes with dozens of hands-on sorts, games, and activities to use with your students as they progress through the intermediate and advanced stages of word knowledge in English.

LITERACY INSTRUCTION FOR ENGLISH LEARNERS IN THE SYLLABLES AND AFFIXES AND DERIVATIONAL RELATIONS STAGES

Students at the upper levels of word study, such as the syllables and affixes or derivational relations stages, may be mature in age and social skills while operating at earlier literacy levels. They may be ready to quickly translate their previous literate experiences into English, or they may be confounded by vocabulary and content that are totally unfamiliar. It will be important for you to keep a host of factors in mind as you design lessons for your students: their developmental spelling level, students' previous literacy experiences in another language, their oral language proficiency in English, their level of background knowledge about the content of the material, and their social maturity. The following ideas will guide you in designing appropriate instruction for English learners at the upper levels:

Adapt and tailor lessons to students' background knowledge and experiences.

1. Cluster students into word study groups based on the results of their developmental spelling inventories. Do not assume that age or grade level equals understanding.
2. Find out who your students are: What languages do they speak at home? What literacy skills do they have in their first language? What background experiences do they have that relate to the content of the lesson? What do current language proficiency tests show about students' oral language skills in English? Use this knowledge to adapt your lesson and tailor questions to individual students as you go.
3. While you may need to simplify instruction to address the language and literacy levels of your students, try to do so with materials that match the social maturity of your students.
4. Be as explicit as needed in your word study instruction. English learners do not have a large reservoir of vocabulary words to pull from during lessons. Provide lists and simple dictionaries for them to refer to as you work together. Help them by sharing simple words that can be connected to new vocabulary.
5. Make every lesson a language-learning event. Move from what students can say, to putting it into writing. Incorporate daily opportunities for talking about words and texts. Assume that much of the vocabulary in your lesson will need to be taught and worked with. Oral discussions about words are critical so that students are bathed in language—they hear it spoken and use it to share experiences, discuss issues, ask questions, and make connections during their literacy lessons.
6. Place meaning-making at the center of each literacy lesson, even if you are focusing on a skill. Help students to self-monitor and speak up when they do not understand what is going on.
7. Connect spelling, vocabulary, and grammar study. Words that are featured in word study must also become vocabulary words, and should also be used and analyzed in conversational speech and connected text as a part of the lesson.
8. Don't overemphasize pronunciation. Students at the upper levels of word study understand distinctions in letter–sound correspondences, even if they cannot pronounce them perfectly. Pronunciation will continue to be refined by students' interactions with printed materials over time.
9. Give extra support to students who have more limited English language skills. This may include working with a partner, having a peer translator, or seeing physical examples of projects.

CHARACTERISTICS OF ORTHOGRAPHIC DEVELOPMENT FOR ENGLISH LEARNERS IN THE SYLLABLES AND AFFIXES AND DERIVATIONAL RELATIONS STAGES

Students with more advanced word knowledge in English are ready to learn about the *deep* characteristics of English orthography. As Venezky (1999) expressed it, in English spelling "Visual identity of word parts takes precedence over letter–sound similarity" (p. 197). So, students who have learned similar deep orthographies have a supportive mindset for learning how English orthography works. On the other hand, students who are literate in a home language that is highly regular phonetically may find this orthographic complexity surprising and confusing. Making connections and comparisons between other writing systems and English can be very helpful to both sets of students at this time.

A fundamental aspect of intermediate students' developmental word knowledge is learning about **morphology,** the processes by which meaningful word parts, called **morphemes,** combine, such as when we put *un-* + *break* + *-able* together to form *unbreakable*. These morphemes include base words, prefixes, and suffixes; prefixes and suffixes are

Morphology is the study of word structure.

Morphemes are the smallest meaningful units in words. The word *walked* has two morphemes—*walk* and *ed* (signaling past tense).

Affixes
are most commonly suffixes or prefixes that are attached to base words, stems or roots. *Pre-* is an affix in the word *predict*.

collectively referred to as **affixes.** Importantly, understanding these processes will support students' spelling *and* vocabulary development. Two related but distinct areas of spelling are also explored at this level: (1) learning about spelling conventions where syllables join; for example, when consonants are doubled or left alone, as in *sun/sunny, dine/diner,* or when a final *y* changes to *i* before adding a suffix, as in *supply/supplier*; and (2) spelling patterns in unaccented syllables, for example, cur*tain* and ta*ble*.

Because of the aspects of word structure that students explore at this phase, we refer to students' word knowledge at the intermediate phase of literacy development as *syllables and affixes.* Table 7-1 outlines the sequence of word study for English learners at the syllables and affixes stage. The first two columns share important features that are studied, and examples of those features. The final column highlights aspects of this study that may be difficult for students learning English.

TABLE 7-1 Sequence of Word Study for English Learners in the Syllables and Affixes Stage

Features to Study	Examples	Instructional Notes
Early		
Inflectional ending/suffix *-ing*	*running*—short vowel + double consonant *standing*—short vowel, no change *writing*—long vowel, e-drop *dreaming*—double vowel, no change	Verb forms may be constructed differently in students' home language, or this form may not occur. Perceiving the pronunciation of *-ing* at the end of a word is difficult. Spelling changes in the base word add a layer of complexity to the process.
Inflectional ending/suffix *-ed*	*talked* /t/; *begged* /d/; *shouted* /ed/ *wanted*—short vowel, no change *hopped*—short vowel + double consonant *hoped*—long vowel, e-drop *dreamed*—double vowel, no change	Past tense may be constructed differently in students' home language. Perceiving and producing the pronunciations of *-ed* may be difficult. Spelling changes in the base word add a layer of complexity to the process.
Plural endings *-s* and *-es*	*plants* /s/; *dog* /z/; *places* /ez/ *wishes*—es after *sh, ch, ss,* and *x* *parties*—change *y* to *i* + *es*	Plurals may be formed differently in students' home language. Perceiving and producing the pronunciations of *-s* and *-es* at the end of a word may be difficult.
Compound words	*downtown, bookworm*	Morphology in the home language may not involve compounding.
Unusual plurals	*knife/knives; mouse/mice; goose/geese*	Learning the small subset of nouns, verbs, and adjectives that involve an internal sound/spelling change.
Syllable patterns: *V/CV* vs. *VC/CV*	*silent* vs. *happen, basket*	Students' home language may not signal change in pronunciation through spelling; English signals long or short vowel through number of consonants at the syllable juncture that follows the vowel.

TABLE 7-1   Sequence of Word Study for English Learners in the Syllables and Affixes Stage

Simple prefixes and base words: *re-* (again), *un-* (not), *dis-* (opposite, not), *mis-* (wrong)	*re*do, *re*make; *un*happy, *un*wrap; *dis*like, *dis*agree; *mis*behave, *mis*spell	Morphology in students' home language may not occur by combining different morphemes.
Ambiguous vowels in one-syllable words	p*aw*, th*ough*t	Sounds may not occur in the home language, so perceiving their pronunciation and attaching the correct spelling pattern is difficult.

Middle

Familiar vowel patterns in accented syllables	p*ai*nter, *a*wake; n*i*nety, de*light*; al*o*ne, s*oa*py	Different pronunciations of accented and unaccented syllables. Students may use vowel sound instead of schwa in unaccented syllables.
Less familiar and ambiguous vowels in two-syllable words	f*ou*ntain, p*ow*der; empl*oy*, embr*oi*der	Sounds may not occur in students' home language, so perceiving their pronunciation and attaching the correct spelling pattern is difficult.
Final unaccented syllables *-er*, *-or*, *-ar*	moth*er*, doct*or*, sug*ar*	*R*-influenced vowel does not provide clue to spelling
Initial hard and soft *c* and *g*	*c*ircle, *c*enter vs. *c*orrect, *c*ustom *g*entle vs. *g*ossip, *g*arden	Same letter has different sounds.

Late
Simple suffixes and base words

Comparatives *-er/-est*, *-ier/-iest*	calm*er*/calm*est*; happy/happ*ier*/happ*iest* change y to i before suffix	Comparatives must be both understood conceptually and then distinguished aurally. These forms may be constructed differently in students' home language.
-y, *-ly*	cloud*y*, slow*ly*	These forms may be represented or constructed differently in students' home language.
		In addition, morphology in home language may not be signaled by spelling/orthography; morphology may not occur by combining different morphemes, but rather by tonal changes.
Less frequent one-syllable homophones Two-syllable homophones	aisle/isle; cruise/crews allowed/aloud; principle/principal	In-depth vocabulary needed to distinguish different spellings for same pronunciation, and attaching appropriate spelling pattern.
Less frequent one-syllable homographs Two-syllable homographs	bow wound **pres**ent/pre**sent**; **ob**ject/ob**ject**	In-depth vocabulary needed to interpret correct pronunciation for words with the same spelling.
Introduction: spelling–meaning connection	nation/national sign/signature	Morphology in students' home language may not be signaled by spelling/orthography; morphology may not occur by combining different morphemes, but rather by tonal changes.
Introduction: concrete and frequently occurring Greek and Latin word roots	*spect* (to look), in*spect*; *struct* (to build), *struct*ure; *tele* (distance), *tele*vision	

Some of the components of Table 7-1 are not new for learners at this phase. What is new is applying this understanding, developed through the earlier examination of one-syllable words, to two-syllable words.

Inflectional Endings

Students first explore the conventions of consonant doubling—when you do and when you don't—in the context of adding simple inflectional suffixes such as *-ed* and *-ing* to base words. Students' learning builds on their within-word pattern understanding of long- and short-vowel patterns in single-syllable words. For example, adding *-ing* to *hop* or *hope* requires different spelling adjustments: *hop/hopping, hope/hoping*. Students learn that whether you double a consonant depends on the vowel pattern in the base word—is it short or long? In the case of *hoping*, a CVCe pattern, the *e* is dropped before adding *-ing*. In other patterns (CVCC, CVVC), there is no change: *land* + *-ing* = *landing*; *soak* + *-ing* = *soaking*.

For students whose first language includes a Latinate component, they may already be familiar with these types of morphological processes of word formation—adding prefixes and suffixes. For instance, in Spanish *ir* is dropped from *vivir* and *iendo* is added to change *live* to *living*. So, extending this knowledge to English should be easier than learning it from scratch. It is important, however, to determine whether English inflectional suffixes are perceptible to students: For many English learners, it is initially difficult to perceive auditorally the *-ed* suffix, much less discriminate among the three different ways in which it can be pronounced: /t/ as in *hoped*; /ed/ as in *wanted*; /d/ as in *climbed*. For this reason we have included many activities in this chapter to support students' oral language development in the context of word study.

Understanding the conventions of adding inflectional suffixes to base words provides the foundation for learning explicitly about *syllable patterns*. For example, students learn that whether we double consonants at the juncture of syllables in words such as *dinner* and *human* depends on the vowel sound we hear in the first syllable of the word: If the sound is short, there are usually two consonants; if the sound is long, there is a single consonant at the juncture.

As part of their developing understanding of morphological processes that underlie word formation in English, intermediate students also begin to learn about the *spelling–meaning connection*: Words that are related in meaning often resemble each other in spelling as well, despite changes in sound (Templeton, 1979, 1983, 2004). In English, we tend to spell similarly the parts of words that are similar in meaning, so that although their sound may be different, their spelling visually preserves the meaning relationship they share. For example, notice the change within the pronunciation of *nation* when *-al* is added: *nation/national*; the spelling of the base, however, does *not* change. Ask students, "*When you sign your name, what is that called?*" You can then point out how the spelling of the letters s-i-g-n does not change, even though the pronunciation does: We go from a long-vowel sound in *sign* to a short-vowel sound in *signature*, and the "silent" *g* in *sign* becomes pronounced in *signature*. Other examples include what happens in the third syllable of *similar* and *personal* when the suffix *-ity* is added: In *similarity* and *personality*, the accent now falls on the third syllable and the sound of the syllable changes, but the spelling remains the same. Students' awareness and understanding of this relationship between spelling and meaning—how the visual identity of word parts takes precedence over letter–sound relationships—becomes a powerful foundation for more advanced spelling knowledge and lays the groundwork for their understanding of the critical role of Greek and Latin word parts in English. This period also invites an exploration of cognates among languages—words that came from the same root and have a meaningful connection across languages. For example, consider the words *airport* and *aeropuerto*, *tecnología* and *technology*. Cognates allow students to make connections to other languages they know, and provide a tool for hypothesizing the meaning of new words.

Compare word formation in English to students' home languages.

Derivational Suffixes

Spelling–meaning exploration also helps develop students' understanding of English syntax and grammar. As students explore spelling–meaning relationships, we point out how adding certain suffixes—such as *-ity* to *similar*—changes the part of speech from the base word to the derived word. In addition to *-ity*, there are a number of other **derivational suffixes** that have this effect: *-ly, -y, -ment, -al, -ion/-tion/-ation*. Derivational suffixes are the "workhorses" of morphology, allowing us to *derive* several additional words from a single **base** or **root**. When we help students to understand the meaning of these derivational suffixes and how they affect the base to which they are attached, we simultaneously build students' awareness of syntax and relationships among words. For languages that do not have a Greek and Latin component and therefore do not share many cognates with English—Asian languages, for example—it is especially important to focus on the processes of suffixation in English: first, inflectional suffixes such as *-ed* in *stopped*; next, derivational suffixes such as *-ment* in *government*. These suffixes occur so often that they become a visual "hook" for English learners. By exploring how suffixes affect the base words to which they are attached, and how they usually change the part of speech of the word, students not only learn the structure of English, they also develop a foundation for learning the Greek and Latin component of English. As Corson (1997) pointed out, learning the specialist vocabulary that is constructed from Greek and Latin roots then becomes easier. This occurs through two instructional emphases: First, point out words that are visually similar in structure—and therefore in meaning. Second, help students learn to analyze words in order to locate their meaningful *parts*—prefixes, suffixes, and bases and roots.

As indicated in Table 7-1, it is important that students in the late syllables and affixes phase of development be *introduced* to spelling–meaning relationships and, later, to concrete and frequently occurring Latin and Greek word roots. These students have the cognitive sophistication to learn how spelling can represent meaning or *morphological* relationships in English, and can understand these relationships in the context of familiar words. As with native English speakers, more *systematic* and extensive exploration of these features will occur when English learners become advanced readers and writers and derivational relations spellers.

To ensure that students are given a strong foundation of examples in putting word parts together, provide them with these opportunities:

1. Begin with teacher-guided sorts that include a thorough discussion of vocabulary issues, and make time for students to ask questions.
2. Provide opportunities for students to partner with proficient English speakers to support their oral language and vocabulary development.
3. Have students say the words aloud, and check in frequently for understanding.
4. Repeat sorts until students are able to do them quickly and accurately.
5. Have students record their words and word meanings in a word study notebook for future reference.
6. When students have internalized a wide variety of base words and affixes, plan learning activities for them to hunt for additional examples independently or in small groups.

FIGURE 7-1 Supporting English Learners in Word Analysis

Instructional Implications

Many students come from countries and/or cultures in which classroom instruction is primarily direct, lecture based, and has a strong emphasis on memorization. As we noted in Chapter 3, these students need time to learn and negotiate the more socially interactive contexts characteristic of so many American classrooms. The implications for word study, however, are critical: At first, we immerse students in numerous, clear examples of regular word construction. In addition, it is important to provide more direct instruction for these students, when appropriate, to help them understand the logic of word structure. After many guided experiences, we provide opportunities for students to explore and search for patterns on their own. Figure 7-1 provides suggestions for instructing students who are learning English and need support in understanding how English words are constructed.

Students at the advanced phase of literacy development explore the morphological aspects of English much more extensively. They probe further the relationship between spelling and meaning as they learn additional prefixes and suffixes and explore in more depth the Greco-Latin component of the language. Although there are not as many students at the advanced phase in the intermediate grades, it is important to know the content of word study at this level because there is some overlap with word study for syllables and affixes spellers, and it shows us where our students are heading.

The Greco-Latin component of English includes *roots*, the part of a word to which affixes may be added but which cannot stand alone as a word. For example, *tract* in *attraction* and *spect* in *inspection* are the roots in these words and are the foundation for families of related words that share these roots: *tract* (meaning "to draw or pull") is at the heart of the words *retract, traction*, and *subtract; spect* (meaning "to look") yields the family of words including *inspect, retrospect*, and *spectacle.* Many English learners, particularly those whose first language is Spanish, will notice the visual/spelling similarity between roots in English and in their home language, such as *foto/photo* and *dictador/dictator*.

COMPONENTS OF LITERACY INSTRUCTION AT THE SYLLABLES AND AFFIXES AND DERIVATIONAL RELATIONS STAGES

At the upper levels of literacy learning, we continue to structure our teaching around the essential literacy activities of *Read To, Read With, Write With, Word Study,* and *Talk With,* although at this level the activities will look different from those at the early grades.

Talk With

English learners at all ages need many opportunities to engage in instructional conversations, and this is still the case at the upper levels of literacy development. Students at the syllables and affixes and derivational relations stages will be presented with challenging content-area vocabulary and complex written texts at school. Provide outlets for students to dialogue with each other and instructors every day. *Talk With* activities can be integrated throughout the day, and in the other four essential literacy activities. For example, stop during your read-aloud time to have students make predictions about the text, share personal connections, comment on interesting words, or ask questions. If you have students share with a partner or in small groups, more students will get a chance to speak.

Read With activities also provide an important venue for integrating conversation. Have students share their impressions of what they are reading with fellow students in Book Clubs (Raphael, Pardo, & Highfield, 2002) or other structured group formats. Provide English learners with a graphic organizer or other note-taking guide so they have something to refer to as they speak to the group. Teachers will not only help develop students' verbal abilities, but they will also get important informal assessment information from discussing what students are reading with them in a small group setting. Getting students to talk in such activities as *Reader's Theater* and sharing book reviews are also good ways to connect *Talk With* and *Read With* activities.

Write With can become a socially-interactive time if students are allowed to read their drafts to others, provide or request feedback, and present their finished writing aloud to the group. Students can be encouraged to suggest interesting words, ask thoughtful questions about a peer's writing, or create translations for each other to make a bilingual book. Speaking and writing are activities that can support each other for those developing literacy skills in a new language. Encourage students to write before sharing, and discuss with others before writing.

Numerous opportunities to integrate talking into word study are outlined in great detail later in this chapter. In word study lessons students sort with partners, play games, go on word hunts, brainstorm word derivations, and discuss interesting or tricky words. All of these activities get students talking and learning together. In addition, *Word Study* becomes a key time to analyze and discuss content-area words that are critical so that students understand the curriculum in their classroom. For instance, before having English learners read about the solar system they will profit from discussing and trying out words such as *rotation, gravity, orbit* and *atmosphere.*

Read To

Reading aloud to students at the upper levels can serve a number of purposes. It is a good way to share content information that may be too difficult for your students to read independently. You can connect your read-aloud text to a thematic unit you are studying, and include schema-building discussion activities such as charting, listing, or sorting the information that has been presented. A read-aloud session is also a good way to present, clarify, and discuss new vocabulary with students. Learning a term like *magnetism* or *compassion* may be facilitated by a book that illustrates its meaning and provides a gateway to discussion.

Reading to students lets them hear a fluent and expressive reader, and presents words that are not common in conversational language. English learners need as many opportunities as possible to listen to a variety of words used in context, as long as they are able to comprehend what is being said. Books on tape are helpful, but even better is a real teacher who can help clarify words that are not understood by the student. Some books on computer may also provide students with the ability to have words repeated or clarified as many times as needed.

As for all students, read-aloud time provides motivation for expanding into unknown and exciting texts, and to reinforce the interpersonal relationship between teacher and students. If your classroom has a wide variation in the listening comprehension levels of your students, you may need to tailor your text to a vocabulary level that most students will understand. Provide support for students with limited English proficiency in some of the following ways: Allow bilingual peers to fill students in on details in the book; meet with students before or after reading to answer their questions about what has been read; provide books on tape for them to review; provide copies in their home language for them to read or listen to; or, find simpler books related to the theme to read to them at a different time of the day, or with an available volunteer.

Read With

Students at the upper levels of literacy development are now reading silently in longer texts on their own. It is critical for them to have lots of time to read material that is not too difficult to decode or comprehend. After assessing your students, form groups with similar needs in terms of reading level and vocabulary development. Find engaging texts that support your goals for the students, offering choices for them when possible. Structure time throughout the week to meet with the groups to scaffold vocabulary development, discuss the text, and partner read for oral practice. You can "listen in" as students read together, or pull students out periodically to assess if the text is at their instructional level (93% or above accuracy, with good comprehension).

If you have students in your upper-grade classroom who are still beginning or transitional readers, you will want to meet with them in teacher-led instructional reading groups on a daily basis. To do this, you may try to enlist any teaching help you have from support personnel such as ESL, literacy, or resource teachers, or community volunteers from the university, students' families, or elsewhere.

Write With

Students at the upper levels are now able to write longer pieces with greater fluency. They have the stamina to participate in the writing process, from rough drafts to final editing. They are able to revise their work based on teacher or peer feedback. *Writing With* projects at this stage will likely focus on expanding students' repertoire or genre, developing their voice and style, and using increasingly descriptive vocabulary. Example activities include expository content-area reports, letters, and personal or fictional stories.

English learners at this stage need guidance in a number of ways during *Write With* time. Some support strategies may be presented to the class as a whole, such as when you provide models for various writing genres, discuss how writers express their voice, or expand students' written vocabulary. For example, you may lead a group lesson in how to write a consumer letter, post a chart-sized model for the class, and have students write their own letter based on a product they use. You may also have the whole class participate in an activity to brainstorm other ways to say "said," "nice," or "happy." These lists of words can be posted on the wall or printed on large cards for students to refer to during writing. Another activity that develops written vocabulary is to have students take a number of descriptive words and place them on a continuum so that they can see subtle variations in meaning. For example, consider the following words: *mad, upset, angry, irritated, bothered, infuriated, aggravated,* and *incensed.* Help students discuss how they might arrange these words from least to most strongly felt. They can save their lists in a word study notebook or on a chart in class.

On other occasions, it will work better to conduct small-group mini-lessons with students who could use help in specific areas. You will discover these needs by examining students' unedited writing, or as you work with them in your instructional reading groups. English learners may make grammatical errors in their writing because they are learning English syntax, or because they are representing the structure of their home language in their English writing. For example, Ms. Phillips noticed that several students in her class were omitting "do" or "did" in their questions, such as in "How you get to school?" This signaled to her a grammatical error that she could take time to clarify and practice correctly in a small group. Unedited writing is a wonderful informal assessment of how to guide students' oral and written language development.

English learners will find it helpful to have reference materials close at hand, so consider helping students create a writer's notebook, or expanding their word study notebook to include vocabulary lists, personalized dictionaries or thesauruses, and/or lists of synonyms, antonyms, or homophones. The notebook might also contain a personal list of writing ideas or story starters that the student can draw from over the course of the year.

As in other instructional activities, English learners need opportunities to talk about their writing both as they develop ideas, and after they have created a first draft. Writing conferences with the teacher and in peer groups allow students to engage in meaningful conversations about words, sentences, and whole pieces of text. Conferences also help students learn new words to express ideas, and provide a forum for contributing their insights to others' work.

Word Study

Students' spelling lists should be based on their developmental level. Polysyllabic theme words that relate to your content-area study can be used in reading and discussion and added to a vocabulary section of their word study notebooks.

After assessing students using the Elementary Spelling Inventory (Appendix p. 217), form groups of students who cluster at similar developmental levels as described in Chapter 2. Spelling lists and word study instruction should be based on the features that students are using but confusing in their assessment. To make your classroom organization manageable, you may need to work with groups that span a range of levels at one time, and tailor words and activities to students' specific needs. For instance, Mr. O'Brien was able to cluster his fifth graders into three groups for word study: a late syllables and affixes group, an early syllables and affixes group, and a middle within-word pattern group. He also had two late letter name–alphabetic students who were newer to English reading; he asked them to meet with the within-word pattern group, but provided differentiated word lists and support for them within that group.

Fostering a Climate for Word Learning

While working in word study groups, students will do the sorts and activities described throughout this book and in other *Words Their Way* publications. In addition to these small-group and individualized activities, there are many ways to foster an interest in words with the class as a whole. Talk with students about interesting words in the books they are reading and listening to. Make a place for interesting words on your classroom walls and in word study notebooks. Point out and discuss words that tie into students' language and relate to their lives, hobbies, and activities. Investigate blended words such as *smog* and *Internet*, clipped words such as *gas* and *cab*, or abbreviations and acronyms such as *radar* and *PC*. What other examples can they think of? Find creative ways to work with idioms like "apple of my eye"; when explicit, these discussions will give English learners a greater understanding of the subtleties in the language. Use texts that include **codeswitching,** such as Gary Soto's *Chato* series (Soto, 1997, 2004) to delve into the richness of words in different languages.

> **Codeswitching**
> Moving between two or more languages or dialects in a conversation when people have more than one language in common.

Students become excited about word study when the teacher models an inquiring stance. Show students that you wonder about where words come from, what the logic is behind a certain spelling, or how English compares with students' home languages. Explore how the vocabulary from your thematic unit may share meaningful word parts, such as *cycle, bicycle, tricycle,* and *motorcycle*. Even though students may not yet be spelling these words correctly, this exploration will set a foundation for future word work.

Walking Through Words with Students

"Walk through words" with students both in your developmental groups and, from time to time, on a class-wide basis. Using the scope and sequence outlined in Table 7-1, we offer three examples of a teacher introducing how the concept of morphemes—prefixes, suffixes, bases, and word roots—works within words. We begin with the most concrete and frequently occurring prefixes (*un-* and *re-*) and walk through how they combine with concrete, well-understood base words. Next, we address concrete and frequently occurring suffixes (*-y, -ly*) and walk through their combination with concrete base words. Later, we move to the exploration of concrete, frequently occurring word roots (for example, *tele*, meaning "distant," and *rupt*, meaning "break").

In each example, the teacher combines a written or visual representation of words and elements with an oral conversation/discussion with the students, and then involves the students in talking about their understandings. This allows her the opportunity to respond as necessary to confirm, clarify, or extend.

The Prefixes re- *and* un-

- Writing the word *do* on the overhead, the teacher says "I wonder: When you *do* a chore, what does that mean? [Students respond.] Yes, like cleaning up after you and your friends make sandwiches. If it's still a mess after you finish, though, we say you will have to *re*do that chore. [Adds the prefix *re-* to the base word *do*.]"
- Writing the word *make* on the overhead, the teacher continues, "If your mother tells you to *make* your bed and she doesn't like how you've made it, she'll have you *re*make the bed. [Adds the prefix *re-* to *make*.]"
- "If you *fill* a glass with water, what does that mean? [Students respond.] If you are very thirsty and want to put more water in the glass, we can say you will [pause briefly, waiting to see if students will apply *re-* to *fill*]. Excellent! Yes, we say you *re*fill your glass."

OR...

If students respond with something like "You put more water in it" rather than responding with *refill*, the teacher may in turn respond: "That's right. Now, remember when we said you *re*make your bed if it isn't done right? So, another way of saying you put more water in your glass when you *fill* it again is to say you . . . [pause for the students to respond]." With this additional clarification, students usually will reply "refill." If they still do not, however, the teacher would go ahead and supply the correct word: "Just like when you *make* your bed but your mother tells you to do it again, you *re*make it. So if you fill your glass and need to do it again, we say you *re*fill it."

- The teacher helps students pull together the understandings from each of her examples to realize what *re-* means: She writes the words *do, make*, and *fill* on another transparency. Pointing to each word as she says it, she continues: "Let's go back over what we did when we said we had to *do, make,* or *fill* something again. When we had to *do* the chore again, we had to [pause]. That's right! We had to *re*do it [adds *re-* to *do.*]. When we had to *make* our bed again, we had to . . ." and so forth.

  On the overhead, the teacher writes the sentence *Johnny had to rewrite his paper.* She asks the students to read the sentence with her; she pauses at the word *rewrite* to see if the students will identify it. If they have difficulty, she covers the prefix *re-* to see if they know the base. She then uncovers the prefix; they finish reading the sentence. She asks the students, "So, what do you think Johnny had to do. . . . How do you know? So, whenever we see the word part *re-* added to a word, what do you think it will mean?" If the students are uncertain or hesitant to respond, the teacher says, "The word part *re-* will mean 'to do again.' We call word parts that are added at the beginning of a word, like *re-*, *prefixes*. We will be learning about other prefixes over the next several days."

- The teacher has the students write the words and their meanings in their word study notebooks. She provides the model for this, based on what she has written on the transparency:

  redo = "to do again"
  remake = "to make again"
  refill = "to fill again"
  The prefix *re-* means "to do again."

- The next day the teacher would review the *re-* prefix with the students, drawing out their own explanations. She will then introduce the prefix *un-* in the same fashion, using the words *happy, wrap, do*, and *selfish.*

The Spelling–Meaning Connection

- Attention to the spelling–meaning connection is especially important because spelling helps English language learners become aware of the *morphology* of the language. Meaningful units, or *morphemes*, are usually spelled consistently, despite changes in sound. Because of this consistency, they become visual cues to students that help them notice important meaning elements in English such as prefixes, suffixes, base words, and word roots.

- The teacher writes the following words on the overhead:
  nation
  national
  She asks the students, "Are these words similar in meaning?" She gets the students to discuss the relationships, and encourages them to use each of the words in a sentence.

- The teacher then points out: "When we add the suffix *-al* to the base word *nation*, do you notice how the sound of the base word *nation* changes?" She encourages the students to talk about *how* it changes. If necessary, she will point out that the sound that the letter *a* stands for changes, from a long **a** sound in *na*tion to a short *a* sound in *na*tional. She comments, "But notice that we don't *spell* these sounds with different letters, do we?"

- Next, she writes the following words on the overhead:
    human
    humanity
  Again, she asks the students: "Are these words similar in meaning?" She continues, "When we add the suffix -ity to the base word *human*, do you notice how the sound of the base word *human* changes?" Again, she encourages the students to discuss how it changes; if necessary, she points out how the sound that the letter *a* stands for changes from a schwa sound in *human* to a short *a* in *humanity*.
- The teacher summarizes the spelling–meaning connection as follows: "This is a very important thing about the way we spell most words in English: While every *sound* isn't spelled with its own letter all of the time, words that share similar *meanings* are *spelled* similarly."

Word Roots

- The teacher reminds the students that they have discussed base words, prefixes, and suffixes. She continues, "There is another very important word part that we will learn about today, called a *word root*. If you remove all of the prefixes and suffixes from a word and what remains is no longer a word, you have discovered what we call the word *root*.

    "For example, let's look at the word *inspect* [writes *inspect* on the board]. When you *inspect* something, what does that mean?" It is fairly easy to draw out the students' ideas about the word because it is one that they know. "How about *inspection*?" Again, the students are able to discuss this word fairly easily.

    "Good! Now, let's find the word root in each of these words. The word *inspect* has the prefix *in-*, meaning 'into.' When we take it off, what's left? Right! *Spect*. Now, is *spect* a word? No, it isn't. It is the word *root*, and it has a meaning. As we'll learn, word roots come from Latin and Greek and occur in thousands of words in English. The word root *spect* comes from a Latin word that means 'to look.' So, when we put the prefix *in*, meaning 'into,' and the word root *spect*, meaning 'look,' together, we get the meaning 'to look into' — and that is what you've already said *inspect* means!

- "How about the word *inspection*? Do you see a word root in it? Right! We take off the prefix *in*, meaning 'into,' and the suffix *-ion*, meaning 'the act of,' and we find *spect* again. Now, put the word parts back together: *-ion* meaning 'the act of,' plus *spect* meaning 'look,' and *in* meaning 'into.' *Inspection* literally means '*the act of looking into.*' And isn't that what happens in an *inspection*?"

- "We will be learning the most important word roots in English and thinking about how they combine with prefixes and suffixes. Your understanding of this process of combination will help you learn new words in your reading and help your spelling as well."

These examples of walking through words with students show how you can teach directly about word meaning and structure in the classroom. Throughout this process, teachers check for understanding via students' verbal responses and body language. Documenting this new word learning on classroom reference charts or in students' notebooks will provide a way for them to remember the meanings of word parts, and to use this knowledge to learn new words independently.

Now that we have presented some overarching ideas of how to organize and introduce word study with your class, it is time to share the specific word sorts and activities that you will use at the upper levels of development. The rest of this chapter outlines a number of specific sorts and games sequenced from least to most difficult for English learners at the syllables and affixes and derivational relations stages. These activities can be used in teacher-directed, guided, and independent activities with students.

Activities for English Learners in the Syllables and Affixes and Derivational Relations Stages

The following activities are sequenced according to *early, middle* or *late* syllables and affixes stage. Table 7-1 is a good reference for this sequence. The series of sorts described in the activities section are listed as Sorts 258–287 in the Appendix pages 297–301. The cognate game (Activity 7-31) is presented as a full-page sort in the *Sample Picture and Word Sorts* section of the Appendix. For most of the sorts described, you will need to refer to the outline in the Appendix, write the words onto a copy of the blank sorting grid (Appendix p. 342), and make multiple copies for student use.

WORD STUDY ACTIVITIES AT THE EARLY SYLLABLES AND AFFIXES STAGE

Adding -*ing* to Words with VC and VCC Patterns 7-1

Demonstrate. Prepare the words for Sort 262 Appendix p. 298. Students should find these words easy to read, but it is helpful for them to say them aloud to themselves before beginning the sort. Assist with pronunciation questions as needed. Put up the headers VC and VCC. Pull out the base words and have the students help you sort them into two categories starting with *let* and *call.* Explain to the students that these are *base words.* Ask them if there is anything they notice about all the base words: They all have one vowel that is usually short. Some end in one consonant (*let* = CVC) and some end in two (*call* = CVCC). They are all verbs. Then match the -*ing* form of the word to each base word. Ask the students what happened to the base word *let* before the -*ing* was added. Repeat with several more words in the column. Introduce the term *double* and explain that when a base word ends in one vowel and one consonant we must double the final consonant before adding -*ing.* Put the header *double* above the word *letting.* Then ask students what they notice about the -*ing* words in the other column. Guide them to notice that the -*ing* was just added without any change because there are already two consonants after the vowel. Add the header *nothing.* The completed sort should look something like Sort 262, Appendix p. 298.

Sort, Check, and Reflect. After modeling the sort with the group, have students repeat the sort under your supervision using the same column headers and key words. Have them check their sort by looking for the pattern in each column. Encourage the students to reflect by asking them how the words in each column are alike and what they have learned about adding -*ing* to base words. Have the students put the rules into their own words. You may want to write down this rule on chart paper and post it for reference. Leave space for the additional rules and revisions that will develop over the weeks to come.

Extend. Students should repeat this sort several times and work with the words using some of the weekly word study routines described in Chapter 3: buddy sorts, blind sorts, writing sorts, and timed sorts. Word hunts will turn up lots of words that can be added to these categories but students will find many words that do not fit either of them. Tell them to add these words to a third column (oddballs) and challenge students to see if they can discover the rule that governs these other words in anticipation of the sort for next week.

Students might be encouraged to share contrasting sentences (orally or in writing) for the base word and its *-ing* form. For example, *I plan to go to the beach. I have been* planning *my trip all month.* Ask students to share sentences using the *-ing* form and ask them if they notice anything (using *-ing* as a verb often requires helping verbs such as *am, have been, was,* etc.).

Give students additional words and ask them to apply the rule. Some suggested transfer words are *rest, hunt, swim, kick, stir, mop, run, quit, wish, sit, guess,* and *smell.*

Adding *-ing* to Words with VCe and VVC Patterns 7–2

Demonstrate. Prepare the set of words for Sort 263, Appendix p. 298. Introduce this sort in a manner similar to that for Activity 7–1. Ask students what happened to the base word *like* before the *-ing* was added. Look at the other words under the VCe column to see how the *e* is gone in each word. Introduce the term *e-drop* and put it at the top of the column. Explain that when a base word ends in silent *e* we must drop the *e* before adding *-ing.* Guide them to notice that the *-ing* was just added without any change to the VVC words. The completed sort should look something like Sort 263, Appendix p. 298.

Sort, Check, Reflect, and Extend. Students should repeat the sort using the same column headers and key words. Encourage the students to reflect by asking them how the words in each column are alike and what they have learned about adding *-ing* to base words. Review what they learned in the previous sort and add to the chart. Give students additional words and ask them to apply the rule. Some suggested transfer words are *ride, need, close, use, eat, smile, vote, meet, mail, clean, turn, speak.*

Adding *-ed* to Words with Double, E-Drop, and No Change 7–3

Demonstrate, Sort, Check, and Reflect. Prepare the set of words to use with Sort 264, Appendix p. 298. You might begin this sort by asking your students to spell *hopped* and then *hoped.* Ask them to justify why they spelled them as they did. Explain that students often have trouble with these words and that the sort for this week will help them learn and remember the rules that govern the addition of *-ed* just as they did for *-ing.* Begin with a teacher-directed sort using the headers *hopped* and *hoped* and proceed in a manner similar to that of Activity 7–1. Again you may want your students to underline the base word to help them identify the pattern, especially in words like *hoped* and *moved.* Help the students see that the rules are similar to the rules for adding *-ing* and can be summed up as "double, drop, or nothing." Talk about the fact that adding *-ed* means that something has already happened and that such words are said to be in the "past tense." Have students use some example words in a sentence to check for understanding of meaning.

Extend. Also challenge your students to sort these words by the sound of the *-ed* ending as shown here. No headers are provided for this sort but are indicated here for clarity. Ask students if there is anything they can discover about the words in each column. They might notice that certain consonants precede certain sounds (*p* before /t/, *d* and *t* before /ed/) and that the words in the last column have added a syllable to the base word.

/t/	/d/	/ed/
asked	hugged	hated
walked	rhymed	spotted
picked	fanned	floated
slipped	rained	twisted
cooked	jailed	traded
	mailed	
	poured	
	begged	
	named	
	phoned	
	sneezed	
	shaved	
	slammed	

Ask students to apply their knowledge by adding *-ed* to additional words: *dream, march, plan, nod, step, drop, save, close, like, lived, tame, beg, clean, wave, boil, clip, scoop, pet, talk, climb, snap, melt, score, shout, wait,* and *help.*

Language in Use: Present and Past Tense 7-4

Talk with your students about the concept of actions taking place in the present or the past. Brainstorm a list of what they did yesterday, and write these words on a chart: *ate, walked, dressed, studied, helped, rode a bike,* etc. Circle the words on the chart that end with *ed.* As they know from the previous lesson, adding *-ed* is one way to show that something happened in the past. Ask students to change the words into actions that they might be doing today—*eat, walk, dress, study,* etc. Note any difficulties that arise for your students so that you can support them in the future.

To close the lesson, do a group sort of past tense versus other *-ed* words. With a list of words such as <u>walked</u>, <u>rented</u>, <u>bed</u>, <u>named</u>, <u>shred</u>, <u>worked</u>, <u>seaweed</u>, and so on, have students decide which of the words happened in the past and which did not.

Unusual Past Tense: Card Games 7-5

If you previously charted past tense words in Activity 7–4, review your brainstormed list to find the words that do not end in *-ed* (e.g., *ate, rode*). If you did not already brainstorm a list, ask students to talk about what they have done in the past week. Write down any past tense verbs they mention. Remind students that we often show that something already happened by adding *-ed.* There are also many words in English that indicate the past in unusual ways. Create word cards from the Unusual Past Tense list that follows. Introduce the word cards in this lesson, and ask students to use the words in a sentence. Clarify the meanings of any unknown words.

Procedures. Five cards are dealt to each player and the remaining cards are placed in the middle as a draw pile. The first player asks any other player for a match to his or her hand: "I have *leaf*. Do you have *leaves*?" A player may also request the singular word, such as "I have *geese*. Do you have *goose*?" If the player is uncertain of the singular or plural word to request, he or she may ask for assistance from another student.

If the player receives the requested card, he or she may put the pair down and ask for another card. If the other player does not have the card requested, that player tells the first player to "Go fish," which means that the first player must draw a card from the draw pile. The first player's turn is over when he or she can no longer make a match.

Play continues around the circle until one player runs out of cards. Points can be awarded to the first person to go out and to the person who has the most matching cards.

Syllable Juncture in VCV and VCCV (Doublet) Patterns 7-10

Demonstrate. Prepare the set of VCV and VCCV words for Sort 267, Appendix p. 298. You might introduce this lesson by asking your students to spell *hoping* and *hopping*. Ask them to tell you why they spelled the words as they did. Assure them that the sort you are doing will help them understand what is going on with such words. Resist the temptation to explain to students what is taking place in these words. They will learn so much more if they are allowed to figure this out as you work through the sort. Tell students that you will be looking at patterns in a different way and introduce the headers VCV and VCCV and remind them that V stands for vowel, and C for consonant. Put the key words *hoping* and *hopping* under the headers. Underline the letters in these key words and label them: VCV represents the *o, p,* and *i* in *hoping,* while VCCV represents the *o, p, p,* and *i* in *hopping.* Notice that one or more letters—or no letters—can come on either side of the juncture. Model how to sort several more of the word cards, then begin to involve your students in the sorting process. Show the group one of the word cards and ask students where it should be placed. Continue with their help to sort all the words into columns under each header. The completed sort should look something like Sort 267, Appendix p. 298.

Now read down each column of words and ask your students to listen to the vowel sound in the first syllable. They should notice that in each word of the VCV column the vowel is long. Explain that these first syllables that end with a long-vowel sound are called *open.* You might demonstrate how to break the word into two syllables by drawing a line between the two syllables as in *ho/ping.* Remind them that they have studied open syllables in words such as *go, row,* and *blue.* Next read the other column to find that the vowel is short in the first syllable. Again you might draw a line between the syllables (*hop/ping*) and explain that these syllables are called *closed* because they end with a consonant.

Sort Check, and Reflect. Now, have students repeat the sort under your supervision. To reinforce the idea of the syllables, you might ask students to draw a line between them. They could also divide the words into syllables on small chalkboards or whiteboards or in their word study notebooks. Have them check their sorts by looking for the pattern in each column. Encourage the students to reflect by asking them how the words in each column are alike and what they have learned. Help the students to articulate a generalization such as "*A syllable that ends in a vowel usually has a long-vowel sound, and a syllable that ends in a consonant usually has a short-vowel sound.*"

More Syllable Juncture in VCV and VCCV Patterns 7-11

Demonstrate. Prepare the set of VCV and VCCV words for Sort 268, Appendix p. 299. This sort reinforces the patterns from the previous sort but adds words that have different consonants at the juncture (e.g., *carpet*) in addition to the words with the same consonant at the juncture or "doublets" (e.g., *funny*). Introduce the sort in a manner similar to that of Activity 7–10, but this time ask students to notice what is different about the consonants among the VCCV words (some are doublets and some are different). Set up the column headers and key words, and model several of the words. Guide students to notice how many consonants there are at the syllable juncture. If there are two, are they both the same or are they different? Think aloud as you sort the words with student help. After students are comfortable with the patterns, have them do the sort on their own or with a partner. Your final sort will look something like Sort 268, Appendix p. 299.

Extend. Students should work with the words using some of the weekly routines that have been previously outlined, such as writing them in their word study notebooks, using them in card games, or going on word hunts. A word hunt will turn up many words as well as oddballs that are open syllables but do not have a long-vowel sound. Have them put oddballs into a fourth column and keep them handy for further reference.

Prefixes (*re-*, *un-*) 7–12

Demonstrate. Prepare the set of prefixes for Sort 269, Appendix p. 299. See the example of how to "walk through words" with students on page 299 of this chapter before doing this sort with students. For teacher-directed modeling, display a transparency of the words on the overhead or hand out the sheet of words to the students. Ask them what they notice about the words and get ideas about how the words can be sorted. Students might note that the words all contain smaller words and remind them of the term *base words* that was used in the study of inflected endings. Put up the column headers and key words and then sort the rest of the words. During this first sort the oddballs *under* and *reader* might be included under *re-* and *un-*. They are there to help students see that these letters do not always spell a meaningful prefix added to a meaningful base word. Praise students if they notice this on the first sort!

After the first sort discuss the word meanings with students. What do they notice about all of the words under the *re-* column? Start with *reuse*. Ask students for the base word. Explain that a prefix has been added to the base word and that it changes the meaning of the word. Ask students what *reuse* means. (To use something over again, as in *We had to reuse the party hats at every birthday.*) Repeat this with the other words under *re-*, talking about the meaning of each word: *Repay* means to pay again. *Recount* means to count again, etc. The word *reading* does not mean to do something again and should be transferred to the oddballs. Then explain that a prefix has a meaning of its own and ask them what *re-* means in all the words. (It means to do something again.) Repeat this with the words in the *un-* column to determine that the prefix means "not" in words such as *unbroken*, or *unkind*, but something more like "the opposite of" in words like *untie* and *uncover*. *Under* will be moved to the oddballs because it does not have a prefix or base word and does not mean the opposite of anything. Students might be asked to write the meaning of the prefix on the headers (for example, *re-* = again). The completed sort should look something like Sort 269, Appendix p. 299.

Sort, Check, and Reflect. Students should repeat this sort several times and work with the words using some of the weekly routines such as writing them in their word study notebooks, word hunts, and using words in sentences. When students write these words in their word study notebook, they might be asked to underline the prefix in each one and write the meaning of the prefix.

Extend. Word hunts will turn up lots of words that begin with *re-* and *un-* including more oddballs that look like they might have a prefix until the meaning and base word are considered. Word hunts will also reveal other subtle variations in meaning for the prefix *re-* as well as words with no clear base words. While studying these prefixes, you can also encourage students to see how these morphemic changes take place in their home languages. For example, in Spanish *re-* has a similar meaning, and is used in words like *repasar* (review) or *representar* (represent). In Spanish, *un-* often takes the form of *des-* such as in *desafortunado* (unlucky) or *deshacer* (undo).

Prefixes (*dis-*, *mis-*) 7–13

Demonstrate. As in Activity 7–12, help students see spelling–meaning connections in the words in this sort, which you will find as Sort 270 on page 299 of the Appendix. You might begin by asking students how to spell the word *misspell* (a word that is often misspelled). Have them speculate about why there are two *s*'s in the word. If students come up with an explanation, talk it through with them. If they look confused, divide the word between *mis-* and *-spell*, and ask them if one of those pieces looks like a whole word. Then, encourage them to look at the rest of the words in the sort. Do they see other whole words before *mis-* or *dis-*? Remind them about what a prefix means, and tell them that today you will be working with two new prefixes.

Sort the words into two columns under the headers. The completed sort should look something like Sort 270, Appendix p. 299. When the words have been sorted, discuss the meaning of each word in the *dis-* column. Help students discover that *dis-* means "the opposite of." Next, examine the *mis-* words. Help them determine that *mis-* means to do something "wrongly."

Have students examine the words *dishes, missed,* and *mishmash.* They should be able to see that in those three words there is no base word whose meaning is changed by the prefix. Create an oddball category for them. After discussing the meaning of the prefixes and how the prefixes change the meaning of the base word, revisit the word *misspell.* Ask students again about the spelling of the word. Can they explain to you that one *s* is part of the prefix and the other is part of the base word, so both must be there?

Extend. As in the previous sort, students can investigate cognates for prefixes in other languages such as Spanish. Have them use a bilingual dictionary to see if they come up with a common way to express the concept of *mis-* or *dis-*. Activities 7–12 and 7–13 can also be put together as a larger collection of words for students to use in speed sorts alone or with a partner. Encourage word analysis skills by having students look up words in the dictionary that begin with *mis-, dis-, re-,* and *un-* to see if they can find out how the prefix changes a given word's meaning.

WORD STUDY ACTIVITIES AT THE MIDDLE SYLLABLES AND AFFIXES STAGE

Accented Syllables: Jeopardy Game 7–14

In this game, a small group of students recall and spell words that follow familiar long-vowel patterns in accented syllables. Students have to guess the right word based on a clue, so it is also a good way to get vocabulary practice.

Materials. You will need dice, a game board, and clue cards. A poster board or open file folder is divided into five columns with four boxes each. A clue card worth 100, 200, 300, or 400 points is placed on each space—cards should be color coded or labeled by their category so they are placed in the appropriate column. A list of possible words and point values follows that will help you get started. You can add new words to this game over time, but remember to find words that are concrete, so that English learners can predict them from short clues. The words should also represent the given long-vowel sound in an accented syllable.

Point value	Long *a*	Long *e*	Long *i*	Long *o*	Long *u*
100	today	fifteen	ninety	remote	perfume
200	mistake	reader	polite	lonely	pollute
300	rainbow	repeat	decide	toaster	shampoo
400	escape	compete	surprise	hopeful	toothache

Answers for clue cards:

Long a

100: The past is yesterday, the present is _____.
200: It is wrong; it is a _____.
300: A big arch of colors in the sky.
400: When the house caught on fire, the people ran to _____.

Long e

100: The number after 14.
200: Look at your book list. You are a good _____!
300: To do it again.
400: To try to win against others.

Long i

100: 60, 70, 80, _____.
200: To have good manners.
300: To make a decision.
400: At the party, they jumped out and yelled, "_____!"

Long o

100: Use this to change the channel on the TV.
200: By yourself and feeling sad.
300: Use this to brown your bread.
400: Feeling like it will all work out.

Long u

100: Women use to smell good.
200: To dirty the water or land.
300: Use this to clean your hair.
400: A pain in your mouth.

Procedures.

1. One player is the game host. The others roll the dice to determine who goes first.
2. The game begins when the first player picks a category and an amount for the host to read, for example, *"I'll take Long o for 100."* The host reads the clue and the player must respond by phrasing a question and spelling the word. For example:

   Host: "The past is yesterday, the present is _____."
   Player: "What is today? t-o-d-a-y."

3. The player receives the card if the answer is correct. This player chooses another clue. (A player can only have two consecutive turns.) If the player misses, the player to the left may answer.

4. The game continues until all the clue cards are read and won, or left unanswered. Players add their points, and the one with the highest number of points wins.
5. Depending on the English proficiency level of your students, adjust the difficulty level of words and clues.

Less Familiar and Ambiguous Vowels in Accented Syllables 7–15

Demonstrate. Prepare the set of words for Sort 271, Appendix p. 299. This sort includes a collection of words whose vowel sounds are neither long nor short in the stressed syllable of a two-syllable word. Many of these words have diphthongs, in which the vowel sound "slides" from one sound into another, such as the "ow" sound in *house*. We have combined six types of ambiguous vowels into this sort. It is recommended that if your students have difficulty with these patterns you should pull the individual contrasts out for them to study in more depth.

Begin by reading the words together and discussing their meanings as needed. Show students the bold headers, and put these at the top of your sorting columns. Help students to notice the letter patterns in each word, and say the word out loud as you sort it into the correct column. After several examples, give students responsibility for finding the right column for each new word. Your finished sort will look something like Sort 271, Appendix p. 299.

Sort, Check, and Reflect. After modeling this sort, have students repeat it under your supervision. Have them check their sort by looking for the pattern in each column. Ask students to notice that the focus pattern is part of the accented syllable, such as in *en***joy.** Encourage them to say the words in a chant-like manner to highlight the accented syllable, or to tap their leg or make a hand movement on the strong syllable as they read their finished sorts.

Extend. If you find that your students need more practice on these ambiguous vowel sorts, have them go on a word hunt for additional words to add to the sort. You can focus on specific patterns that are difficult for your students. With these other words, you can also encourage students to do two sorts: (1) to sort by vowel pattern and (2) to sort based on whether the word is accented on the first or second syllable.

Final Unaccented Syllables -*er*, -*or*, -*ar* 7–16

Demonstrate. Prepare the word cards for Sort 272, Appendix p. 299. You might begin this sort with a short spelling test in which you ask students to spell three words: *enter, doctor,* and *polar*. Discuss the problem spellers face when they can hear the sound in the final unaccented syllable but are not sure how to spell it. Show students the words for this sort and read them aloud together. Talk about how the final sound is exactly the same but may be spelled in several ways. Ask them to hypothesize about which one is most common. Proceed with a teacher-directed sort that will end up looking something like Sort 272, Appendix p. 299. Again review the idea of accent or stress by reading the columns of words to find that the final syllables in these words are unaccented. Show students how they can use the dictionary to check how pronunciation of the unaccented syllable is represented.

Sort, Check, and Reflect. After modeling this sort, have students repeat it under your supervision. Let them practice reading and pronouncing the words. Discuss the fact that despite different spellings, the words all sound the same at the end.

Extend. After completing this sort, ask students to find other words that end in the unaccented -*er*, -*or*, and -*ar*. Which pattern is the most common? You can also challenge students to sort the words they find by parts of speech. They will find many adjectives and nouns that will help get them ready for the next sort.

Derivational Relations Stages

Language in Use: Agents and Comparatives
Word Building Activity 7–17

This word building activity highlights how words change to agents (i.e., people or objects that do things) or comparatives (e.g., *fast-faster*) when *-er, -or,* and *-ar* are added. In the second phase of the activity, the transformed words can be sorted in several ways.

Procedures.

1. Begin this activity by writing the word *teach* on the board. Ask students to talk about what it means to teach. Now add *-er* to make *teacher*. How has the meaning of the word changed? Do the same with some additional words such as *farmer, hunter,* and *dreamer*. What kinds of words were created when the *-er* ending was added? Help students understand that these words represent people who do things. Point out that they can be created by adding *-er, -or,* and *-ar* to some words in English. Ask students if they can think of any words that describe a person who does something. Write these words on a group chart.

    Now have students focus on a different thing that can happen when we add *-er* to a word. Demonstrate by adding *-er* to *old* to make it *older*. What happened? Try again with *harder, softer,* and *slower*. Discuss with students that these adjectives, or describing words, have now become words that can be compared, or comparative adjectives.

2. Pass out a set of the word cards to each student (the bolded headers should not be included at this point). Ask students to pair up the words that have been transformed with an *-er, -or,* and *-ar* such as *fast-faster*. When all the words have been paired, ask students to reread them and think about their meanings. Discuss the meanings of any words that are unknown.

    Guide students to look at the spelling of the words. What was added to change the words into an agent or comparative? What changes needed to occur in the base words in some cases? Remind students about the rules they learned when they studied about other endings: Sometimes it is necessary to double consonants, to drop an *e*, and at other times the ending can be added with nothing changed. With the base words close at hand, have students notice the changes that occurred when *-er, -or,* and *-ar* were added.

3. Have students put away the base words from their pairings. Now it is time to sort! In the first round, ask students to sort the words by whether they are people who do things or words to compare. Provide the column headers for these categories. Once sorted, ask students to sort again by whether an *-er, -or,* or *-ar* has been added. The completed sort should look something like this:

People Who Do Things			Words to Compare
teacher	educator	beggar	faster
walker	actor		larger
rider	sailor		younger
jogger			smaller
drummer			hotter
shopper			older
juggler			shorter
diner			
leader			

Derivational Relations Stages

4. Finally, sort the words by how the ending was added. Did the change require doubling a letter, dropping an *e*, or simply adding the ending (nothing)? The completed sort should look something like this:

double	*e*-drop	nothing
beggar	educator	teacher
hotter	larger	walker
shopper	rider	sailor
jogger	juggler	leader
drummer	diner	faster
		younger
		smaller
		older
		shorter
		actor

The words in this sort can be transcribed into students' word study notebooks, and added to as new agents and comparatives are discovered.

Spanish and English Hard and Soft G and C 7–18

Demonstrate. This double set of sorts, found as Sort 273 in the Appendix and later in this activity, has many possibilities, so consider using it over several days. If you have students who speak Spanish, it will provide the opportunity for them to build on vocabulary and spelling patterns in their home language. If your English-learning students don't speak Spanish, consider using the words as examples of how cognates exist between languages, and ask students to brainstorm examples of cognates between their home languages and English.

To begin, take the set of words in English and the set in Spanish and spread them out on a table. If you like, you can have the two sets color coded so it is clear which words go with each language. Ask students if they see any similarities between any of the words. Do they see any words that are spelled almost the same? Have them look for pairs such as *celebrar-celebrate*. Encourage students to share the meanings of the words and their pronunciations if they can. Continue matching the words with their cognates and sharing and discussing the words.

Once the words have been paired up, ask students if they notice anything about the beginning sounds of *c* and *g*. Read some of the words together and notice that the *c* sometimes represents a soft sound as in *circus*, and sometimes a hard sound as in *curve*. *G* sometimes stands for the soft sound as in *giant*, and the hard sound as in *goal*. Give students the labels "hard" and "soft" *g* and *c*. Using the header labels, sort one or two of the *c* words by whether they represent the hard or soft sound. Tell students they will now be sorting the words in this way on their own.

Sort, Check, and Reflect. Depending on the circumstances of your classroom, you can have the students sort either the English words only, the Spanish words only, or all of the words from both sorts. You be the judge of how to best support the success of your

English learners on this task. The completed sort if done in English will look something like the following:

Soft *c*	Soft *g*	Hard *c*	Hard *g*
circus	giant	canoe	goal
celebrate	gem	calendar	guide
cemetery	general	calm	gorilla
center	generous	coconut	garage
ceremony	geography	control	gasoline
cycle	gymnasium	curve	guard

The completed sort if done in Spanish will look something like the following:

Soft *c*	Soft *g*	Hard *c*	Hard *g*
circo	gigante	canoa	gol
celebrar	gema	calendario	guía
cementerio	general	calma	gorila
centro	generoso	coco	garaje
ceremonia	geografía	control	gasolina
ciclo	gimnasio	curva	guardia

Next (whether you are doing the sort in English, Spanish, or both), combine all of the soft *c* and soft *g* words. Ask students if they notice anything about the vowel in these words. Repeat this with the hard *c* and hard *g* words. Suggest that they try sorting the words by the second letter in each word. The final sort will reveal that the hard and soft sounds in both English and Spanish are related to the vowel that follows. Underline or highlight one example of each kind of vowel that follows the *c* or *g* to use as a key word for each column. The sort in English will look something like the following:

Soft *g* and soft *c*			Hard *g* and hard *c*		
center	circus	cycle	garage	coconut	curve
celebrate	giant	gymnasium	gasoline	control	guide
cemetery			calendar	goal	guard
ceremony			calm	gorilla	
gem			canoe		
general					
geography					
generous					

The sort in Spanish will look something like the following:

Soft *g* and soft *c*		Hard *g* and hard *c*		
centro	circo	garaje	coco	curva
celebrar	gigante	gasolina	control	guía
cementerio	ciclo	calendario	gol	guardia
ceremonia	gimnasio	calma	gorila	
gema		canoa		
general				
geografía				
generoso				

Students may notice that Spanish does not use the *y* in the same way to create the soft sound in *c* and *g* words.

Encourage reflections by asking the students how the words in each column are alike and how they are different from the other words. Help students formulate a generalization that goes something like this: *c* and *g* are usually soft when followed by *e, i,* and *y,* and hard when followed by *a, o,* or *u.*

Extend. Students should repeat these sorts several times and record them in their word study notebook. They may also want to create a section in their notebook for Spanish word sorts or cognates. Many additional *c* and *g* words can be found to add to their lists that may or may not be cognates. Let them explore which ones are, and which ones aren't!

WORD STUDY ACTIVITIES AT THE LATE SYLLABLES AND AFFIXES/EARLY DERIVATIONAL RELATIONS STAGES

Comparatives -*er* and -*est* 7-19

Demonstrate, Sort, and Check Prepare the comparative word cards for Sort 274, Appendix p. 299. Introduce this sort by discussing the term **suffix**, a part that is added to the end of a word. Practice adding -*er* and -*est* to some words orally first—what happens when you add -*er* to *brave*? To *close*? What do they mean? How is the suffix -*est* different from -*er*? How are the words *braver* and *bravest* different in meaning? *Closer* and *closest*? Act out the terms to dramatize meaning differences. Other words to help you discuss meaning might also be *calmer/calmest, hotter/hottest,* and *weaker/weakest.* To provide visual support, write some base words such as *calm, hot,* and *weak* on the board and show how the endings are added to create a related word. Now sort the cards in this word sort by -*er* and -*est* and talk about the meaning of the words and what the suffix does to the base word. (When comparing two things -*er* is used. When comparing more than two use -*est.*) Ask students to underline the base words to highlight the fact that in words like *happier* or *happiest* the *y* has been changed. Sort any words that fall into that category under -*ier* and -*iest.* Ask the students to form a generalization that covers these words and remind them of previous sorts. (When a word ends in *y* change the *y* to *i* before adding -*er* or -*est.*) The completed sort should look something like Sort 274, Appendix p. 299.

Extend. To review the rules involved in adding suffixes, sort the words as shown here:

double	e-drop	change y to i	nothing
hotter	finer	happier	faster
bigger	nicer	luckier	cleaner
		angrier	longer
		earlier	
		fancier	
		funnier	

To help students *transfer* their understanding of these rules to new words ask them to add -*er* and -*est* to these words: *few, wet, close, pretty.*

Suffixes -y, -ly, and -ily 7–20

Demonstrate, Sort, Check, and Reflect. Prepare the suffix word cards for Sort 275, Appendix p. 299. This sort builds on some of the ideas in Activity 7–19. Remind students that suffixes are added to the ends of words, and that they change the meaning. *Today you will be looking at the suffixes* -y, -ly, *and* -ily. Present some base words orally first, such as *rain* and *cloud*. What happens when -y is added to these words? Help them come to the understanding that -y turns a noun like *sun* into an adjective that means "like the sun" or "having sun." Now discuss how adding -ly or -ily to words such as *slow* or *happy* changes their meaning. These suffixes turn adjectives (that describe words) into adverbs (that describe the manner in which something is done).

Before beginning the sort go through the word cards and discuss the meanings of the words, and how the suffixes affect the meaning. Once students have a good sense of what the words mean, and the role of the endings, demonstrate the sort to the group. Encourage students to participate as you sort the words into columns for -y, -ly, and -ily. The completed sort should look something like Sort 275, Appendix p. 299.

Have students repeat the sort using the same column headers and key words. To reinforce the idea of the base word you might suggest underlining them. Remind students of how *happy* was changed in previous sorts to make the words *happier* and *happiest*. The same procedure is followed here—words that end in y change to i before an ending is added. Have students write in the base word for the -ily words since they cannot simply underline it. Encourage the students to reflect by asking them how the words in each column are alike and what they have learned about adding -y and -ly to base words.

Extend and Review. To review parts of speech create frame sentences such as *The weather today is* _____ and *He worked* _____. Use such sentences to test words for their part of speech. Ask students to find words that describe the noun *today* and the verb *work*.

Review with students how to add -ing and -ed to words like *dig*. Ask them to find two words in the sort that also had to double before adding a suffix (*runny, glassy*). Point out that the word *bad* did not have to double before adding -ly. Review how to form the plural of words like *party* and *baby* (change the y to i and add *es*) and how to make the past tense of words like *carry* and *fly* (change the y to i and add *ed*). Ask them to find words in the sort that also had to change the y to i (such as *easily*). Help them articulate a new rule about adding -ly to words that end in y.

Give students transfer words to practice applying the rules. Ask them to add -y or -ly to these base words: *fog (foggy), snow (snowy), wind (windy), chop (choppy), rock (rocky), point (pointy), soap (soapy), great (greatly), fair (fairly), deep (deeply), real (really), noisy (noisily), hungry (hungrily)*.

Homophones 7–21

Demonstrate, Sort, and Reflect. The 28 words in Sort 276 on page 299 of the Appendix will likely be a vocabulary challenge to your students and you may want to split them into two groups to work on over time. Homophones are tricky—the words sound alike, but the meaning tells how they should be spelled. Use a simple example of a homophone such as *eye/I* to introduce the topic. Homophones sound alike but mean different things. Take the time to discuss the word meanings in this sort so you are sure that students understand them. Quick drawings, visuals, or using the words in a clarifying sentence may be helpful. For example, you might say, *"I like to put a bouquet of flowers on my table to make it colorful. Another kind of flour is what I use when I make a cake."* (Draw a vase of flowers.) If there are too many unknown words, either put some aside or take another day to learn the words before doing this matching sort.

No column headers are needed since the sorting activity consists of matching word pairs or triplets. Present a pair of words like *principle* and *principal*. Ask students what they notice about them. (They sound alike but are spelled differently.) If students do not know the term, supply the word *homophone*. Continue to pair up words and to talk about what the words mean. Students will typically know one homophone better than the other, but by pairing them up to compare spelling and by discussing their meaning the new words will become more familiar.

Ask students for ideas about how certain spellings can be remembered: *There* has the little word *here* as in "here and there." One of the *s*'s deserted in *desert* and so on.

Extend. Draw small pictures on word cards or in word study notebooks to stimulate memory for the meaning of the word (e.g., draw a strawberry for *berry* and a tombstone for *bury*). Also have students use these words in sentences. Pairs of students might be assigned two to three words and asked to compose sentences. These can be shared with each other orally or made into a group book to be illustrated.

The sorting cards can also be used in a Memory or Concentration game—just remember to remove one of each of the triplets before doing it as a pairing activity.

Homographs 7-22

Demonstrate, Sort, Check, and Reflect. In the homographs for Sort 277 on page 300 of the Appendix, the accented syllable is in bold type. Stressed syllables can also be marked with accent marks or underlined. As with Activity 7–21, you are likely to challenge your students' vocabularies with these words, so take the time needed to clarify and discuss their meanings well. If there are too many new words, set some aside for another day.

Begin by writing a sentence such as *He will permit you to have a permit.* Ask students what they notice about the words *per mit'* and *per'mit*. They should note that the words are spelled the same but sound slightly different. Review with students words that are spelled the same but pronounced differently such as *tear, live,* and *read* and introduce the term **homograph** meaning "same writing" or "same spelling." (You might point out how this term is related to *homophone*, which means "same sound.") Remind students about how some words are nouns and others verbs. As a review, have students brainstorm a few examples of each in the group. Go back to the *permit* sentence and ask students to identify the part of speech for each word and place them under the headers *noun* (**per**mit) and *verb* (per**mit**). Proceed in a similar manner with each set of words. Use them in sentences or invite students to use them and then sort them under the headings. Make sure that the words are being pronounced aloud as they are sorted, and not just examined visually. The completed sort should look something like Sort 277, Appendix p. 300. When all of the words have been sorted, read down each column placing extra emphasis on the accented syllable. Ask students what they notice. (The nouns are accented on the first syllable and the verbs on the second syllable.)

Extend. Students should return to these words several times to practice pronouncing and sorting them and to discuss their meanings. When working with partners, students should be careful to pronounce the words clearly and perhaps use them in a sentence before asking their buddy to sort them by accented syllable. Ask students to work together to create sentences for these words and to record some of these sentences in their word study notebooks. They might also draw small pictures as described for homophones in Activity 7–21.

Cover Your Bases Game 7-23

In this game students study easy base words and add affixes and related words to them.

Materials. You will need a copy of the baseball game card from the Appendix, p. 346 for each student, and a sand clock or timer for the group. Print the base words and cut them apart into small word cards (see the following list). Provide a stack of small, blank word cards to write related words.

Base word cards: *like, see, make, call, look, think, work, cake, help, tell, give, ask, read, form, move, cut, drip, lock, stop, plan, tap, let, owe, rule, rain, feel, load, wait, walk, play, paint, hate, fan, taste, spot, slip, forget*

Procedures.

1. Model ways to add affixes to base words. Here are four examples you can write on the overhead or whiteboard:

fan	rule	feel	call
fanned	rules	feels	calling
fanning	ruler	feelings	called
fans	ruled	unfeeling	calls
	ruling	feelings	recall
	rulings		recalling
	unruly		

2. Choose a method to determine order of play. For example, players draw from the collection of base words and the student with the word earliest alphabetically goes first.
3. The first player's base word is placed in front of the group.
4. Players have one or two turns of the sand clock or 2 minutes to write all the words they can think of that contain this base.
5. Go around the group to share words. The first player says a related word he or she has written and lays it down underneath the base word.
6. Players lay down matches at that time. Students continue to lay down related words. The last player to lay down a word moves all of the words into his or her base.
7. Move on to the base word that was drawn by the next player, and repeat steps 3 through 6.
8. Continue until each player's base word card has been played.
9. The player with the most cards on his or her base at the end wins.

Variations and Extensions.

1. Words and their relations are recorded by students in their word study notebooks.
2. Sort by prefixes and suffixes, past/present tense, singular/plural.
3. In one or two turns of the same clock, players search dictionaries and word study books and write down new base words. A new round of play is made with these new words.
4. Write prefixes and suffixes on word cards and have students combine them with base words.
5. Include in the game directions a list of prefixes and suffixes for players to refer to as they play.
6. Students use the words in sentences.
7. Make a game board with the bases. Students land on a base and have to use the word in a sentence. Explore the multiple meaning of words.

Adding *-ion*, No Spelling Change 7-24

Demonstrate, Sort, and Reflect. Prepare the set of words for Sort 278, Appendix p. 300. Introduce the sort by displaying a transparency of the words on an overhead, or hand out a printed sheet of words to the students. Ask them what they notice about the words, and get ideas about how the words can be sorted. Students will likely notice that the words can be matched up with one word being contained in another, and the other having *-ion*. Point out the pair *prevent/prevention*. Discuss how the meaning of the word is changed when *-ion* is added. When we *prevent* something, we are doing an action. A *prevention* is the result of our action, a "thing." Encourage them to put the meanings into their own words as they discuss what happens when we put *-ion* onto base words. Scaffold their understandings of the following: Putting *-ion* on a base word results in a word that means "the act or result" of the meaning of the base word. For example, if you *predict* that a team will win a game, you have made a *prediction;* the act of subtracting one number from another is called the process of *subtraction*.

Spend some time sharing what students know about the meaning of each of the words in the sort.

Once students have noted the base word/suffixed word distinction, discuss the pronunciation of the base + *-ion* pattern. What happens to the sound of *t* when it is added to the base words? This sound change can make the words trickier to spell. The completed sort should look something like Sort 278, Appendix p. 300.

Extend. Note that sometimes words ending in two consonants add *-ation* as in *adaptation* and *condemnation*. These are easy to spell because we can clearly hear the "ation." In spelling, a common confusion primarily at the syllables and affixes stage but also at the derivational relations stage is the treatment of *-ion*. Students often remember the various spellings but are uncertain about when to use a particular spelling, and whether and how it affects the spelling of the base word. The next sort will examine another application of this feature.

Adding *-ion*, *e*-Drop, and Spelling Change 7-25

Demonstrate, Sort, and Reflect. Prepare the set of words for Sort 279, Appendix p. 300. Ask the students to notice how the words in this sort are related. What similarities do they see? Does this look similar to a sort they have previously done? Discuss the meaning of the words. How does *celebrate* change when it becomes *celebration*? (It changes from a verb to a noun.) Sort the words together so that each base matches up with its suffixed or derived word, and meanings are clarified and contextualized for students. The completed sort should look something like Sort 279, Appendix p. 300. Guide students to compare the words in the first column to those in the second. What happened to the word before the *-ion* could be added? (*e*-drop) Try creating some new *-ion* words with the bases *vacate, relate, rotate, narrate,* and *imitate*.

Extend. Students can be encouraged to go on word hunts to look for words that end in *-ion*. They will find some that fit into the categories that have been studied, and others that will have new patterns such as *production, permission,* and *explosion*. This may whet their appetites for exploring words with related affixation patterns.

Vowel Alternation: Long to Short 7-26

The focus in Sort 280, Appendix p. 300 is the constancy of spelling despite a change in pronunciation of the vowel from the base to the derived word or its derivative. A derivative comes from, or is *derived* from, a base. (This is an appropriate place in word study at the derivational level to begin to use this term.)

Demonstrate, Sort, and Reflect. Ask the students how they might sort the words. They will probably notice that some are base words. Suggest that they sort the words into base words and related suffixed or *derived* words. Discuss the meanings of the base words and derived words as you sort. For instance, how are *wise* and *wisdom* related? What about *decide* and *decision*? Clarify and contextualize the meanings of any words students are unsure of.

The completed sort should look something like Sort 280, Appendix p.300.

Once the related words have been matched up, ask the students if the vowel sounds in the accented syllables of the word pairs change. (Yes, they do.) Does the spelling of the vowel change? (No.) Remind the students that this is because the words are related in meaning; this is the *spelling–meaning connection*. For many English learners, some of the short-vowel sounds can be especially difficult to distinguish. As you review these paired words, if you find that students need additional, explicit instruction, consider using a highlighter pen to mark the vowel sounds you are discussing. You may also want to help students read the focus words in a dramatic voice, accentuating the vowel sound in question.

Vowel Alternation: Long to Short/Schwa 7-27

Demonstrate, Sort, and Reflect. Prepare the word cards for Sort 281, Appendix p. 300. The words in this sort help students contrast the long-vowel/short-vowel alternation pattern with a schwa. We know that a good many spelling errors at this level are in the unaccented syllables of words, so that is why these spelling–meaning patterns are helpful to study. Importantly, this sort will help students attend to accent within words.

Introduce the sort by asking the students if they have ever had to stop and think about how to spell a particular word, such as *competition* or *invitation*. Tell them that thinking of a related word may provide a clue. For example, thinking of the base word *compete* will help with *competition;* thinking of the base word *invite* may help with *invitation*. Tell them that thinking of these spelling–meaning patterns is what they are going to explore in this sort.

Work with students to match up each base word with its derivative. As you do, discuss and clarify word meanings and pronunciations. Explore students' familiarity with the words, and if you find there are too many to learn in one day, work with only a few of the words on the first day. After the words are paired up, have students listen for the vowel alternation. Remind them that in the previous sort they noticed how some derivatives changed from a long to a short vowel. In this sort, some of the derivatives also take on the schwa or "uh" sound. Distinguishing these sounds, especially the schwa sound, may be very difficult for your students. Use a greater level of explicitness and directness if you find that your students cannot hear these differences without your support.

If students do not notice the different type of vowel alternation on their own, ask them to compare the pair *unite/unity* with *compete/competition*. In *unite/unity*, do they hear how the long **i** in *unite* changes to a short *i* in *unity*? Does the long e in *compete* change to a short *e* in *competition*? Not exactly? In *unity*, is the second syllable clearly accented? In other words, does it get most of the "oomph" when we say the word? In *competition*, is the second syllable clearly accented? Not really. Because of this fact —it is not accented— the vowel sound in the second syllable of *competition* sounds like an unaccented "short *u*" sound (the schwa); there's no "oomph" behind it. How might they remember how it is spelled? (By thinking of *compete*.) In most unaccented or least accented syllables, the vowel sound is also unaccented, becoming a schwa. The completed sort should look something like Sort 281, Appendix p. 300. Students may notice that the word *cycle* is spelled with a *y* but becomes a short *i* sound in the word *cyclical*. This is because the *y* is alternating from a long **i** sound.

Extend. Use these words to jump-start your vocabulary discussions. Find out what words hold particular connection or interest to your students, and work with them in greater depth. What related words can you think of? Can they be featured in students' writing? Are there any cognates in students' home languages (examples in Spanish from this list include *preference/preferencia, invitation/invitación, cycle/ciclo, photograph/fotógrafo*)? Build on your students' background experiences and curiosity and see where this exploration takes you!

Greek Roots -*graph*-, -*tele*- 7–28

Demonstrate, Sort, and Reflect. Prepare the Greek roots cards for Sort 282 on page 300 of the Appendix by telling the students that a large number of words contain Greek roots and that these roots usually have a pretty consistent or constant meaning. Most often they do not occur by themselves as words, though on occasion some of them may do so. We want students to think directly about the meaning of each of these elements and to examine, discuss, and understand how these word parts combine to result in the meaning of a word. When they combine with other Greek elements, the resulting meaning of words often becomes decipherable. We encourage you to review the format outlined in the overview of this chapter as an example of how to explicitly "walk through" the words in these meaning-based sorts.

Tell the students that learning the meaning of a number of these roots and understanding how they combine to create words will be extremely helpful to the students in figuring out and learning new vocabulary through their reading as well as in helping them with occasional spelling errors. Begin by writing the familiar words *television* and *telephone* on the board or overhead. Ask students if they see a smaller word within *television* (*vision*)? How about *telephone* (*phone*)? Then, tell them that the word part or root '*tele*'comes from Greek and means "distant." When it combines with *vision*, it literally means "vision from a distance." Discuss why this is, literally, what *television* is and does—it delivers vision from a distance (cable, satellite, antenna). Next discuss that *phone* in *telephone* actually comes from a Greek word that means "sound." When it combines with *tele*, it literally means "sound from a distance."

Have the students sort the words by whether they contain *tele* or *graph*. Note that *telegraph* can go in either column or in between because it contains both parts. The completed sort should look something like Sort 282, Appendix p. 300. Have students review all of the *tele* words. Discuss how the meaning of each results from the combination of *tele* with another word. Elicit definitions and explanations from the students, though you may need to scaffold their explanations for particular words. For example, *telegraph* contains another word that came from Greek, *graph*, which means "writing." They have probably heard about the *telegraph*, but perhaps not thought about the fact that it was, literally, "writing from a distance." As for *telescope*, tell them that *scope* is also a word that originally came from Greek and means "target" or "aim"; what, then, does *telescope* literally mean? Encourage students to contribute their ideas to how *tele* contributes to the total meaning of the individual words, such as in *telecommunication, telecast,* and *telethon*.

Next, look over the *graph* words. Discuss *photography*—literally "writing with light"—because there usually is at least one student who understands the process by which photography works. If not, this may be a good time to mention the process briefly; for example, the lens lets in light that is "written" onto film or a disk (as with a digital camera). A reference book of Greek and Latin word parts will help you and your students find out more about the meaning of these elements, and this will contribute to your investigations and discussions. Another good practice is to photocopy a table of Greek word roots and place it in the students' word study notebooks for ready reference.

Greek Roots -*photo*-, -*auto*- 7–29

Demonstrate, Sort, and Reflect. Prepare the Greek root cards for Sort 283, Appendix p. 301. This sort offers additional opportunities to explore Greek elements, this time words that contain *auto*, meaning "self," and *photo*, which means "light." Remind students that learning the meaning of a number of these roots and understanding how they combine to create words will be extremely helpful to the students in figuring out and learning new vocabulary through their reading as well as in helping them with occasional spelling errors.

Work with the students to sort the words into two columns *-photo-* and *-auto-* as you read and practice saying them aloud. Tell them that after the words are sorted, you will discuss what "light" and "self" might have to do with the meaning in each of the words.

The completed sort should look something like Sort 283, Appendix p. 301.

Now work through each column, examining the word parts. For example, *photo* and *graph* come from the Greek roots for "light" and "write," respectively, as discussed in the previous sort. Make connections to how *tele*, meaning "distant," can help us understand that telephoto lenses are used to take pictures from far away. Photocopiers use light to make copies of documents, and so on. In this way, proceed through the rest of the *photo* words.

In the *auto* column, have students think about how the idea of "self" relates to the word meanings. A camera with *autofocus* does the focusing by itself. An *autobiography* is written by a person, about him- or herself. An *automobile* is powered by itself, unlike a cart that used to require animals to pull it along. Use these words to discuss how to break apart words to get at their meanings. For unfamiliar words, have students discuss what the meaning might be, based on their inference from the combination of the word parts. When in doubt, pull out a reference book on Greek and Latin elements for you and your students to use to explore the meanings of word parts. Discuss how the meaning of the Greek combining forms works to result in the overall meaning of each word.

Extend. How many of these words have cognates in your students' home languages? As you walk through the words, ask students if any look familiar to words they have seen in other languages. For instance, some of your students may notice that words such as *photography* and *automobile* have similar meanings and spellings in Spanish (*fotografía*, *automóvil*). Encourage students to note these cognates in their word study notebooks.

Latin Roots *-spect-*, *-port-* 7–30

Demonstrate, Sort, and Reflect. Prepare the Latin root words for Sort 284, Appendix p. 301. Because this is a beginning sort for Latin word roots, you may wish to begin by walking the students through two or three words, explaining how the elements combine to produce the meaning of the word. (We have outlined a possible teacher script about "walking through words" in the overview section of this chapter that can help you structure your lesson.)

The meanings of the Latin roots in this sort are fairly straightforward, as are the meanings of most of the words in which they combine with other affixes and roots. As with the Greek roots or combining forms in the previous two sorts, these Latin roots occur with some frequency in printed materials from the intermediate grades onward. Remember that for students from Latinate language backgrounds, there may be numerous opportunities for students to connect these words to cognates in their home languages.

Begin by writing the words *inspect* and *transport* on the board or overhead. Ask the students to explain the meaning of *inspect*, and use it in a sentence. Then tell them that the word is made up of the Latin root *spect*, which means "to look at," and the prefix *in-* meaning "into." Now think about it: Given their explanation and definition of *inspect*, do they see that putting these word parts together literally means "to look into" something? Repeat this process with *transport*: Have them discuss what the word means, then show them that the word comes from the Latin root *port*, which means "to carry," and the prefix *trans-*, meaning "across." Now think about it: Given their explanation and definition of *transport*, do they see that putting the root *port* together with the prefix *trans-* literally means "carrying across"? (You may mention *import* as well here: Tell them the prefix *im-* means "in, into." Is it clear how *transport* and *import* are related?)

After the introduction, have students sort the words according to the root in each. The completed sort should look something like Sort 284, Appendix p. 301.

-spect-	-port-
inspect	transport
perspective	deport
retrospective	import
spectator .	exporter
circumspect	report
respect	portfolio
suspect	heliport
spectacle	portable
spectacular	airport
spectrum	carport
unsuspecting	portal
prospect	transportation

Follow up by discussing with students how they think the word parts combine to produce the meaning of each word. Here are some words that you may want to "walk through" with the students after they sort and discuss them: *perspective*, "look through"—when you talk about your *perspective* on an issue or on life you are actually talking about how you have *looked through* that issue; *prospect*, "look forward." Point out to the students that, for a vast majority of words that appear to contain a word root, they can best analyze the words by beginning at the end of the word: Reflect on how you analyzed the words *inspect* and *transport*.

Extend. Several words offer possibilities for generating additional words derived from them by adding *-ion* or *-ation*. Have students see how many derived words they can generate, first discussing whether the derived words really exist or not, and then checking the dictionary to confirm or not. For example, *inspection* or *inspectation? Importation* or *importion?*

Cognate Games 7–31

Materials. Make a copy of the sorting grid of cognates (Appendix p. 322), and cut the pieces apart. If you would like to have students do this sort independently following the guided activity, make additional copies for them to cut apart.

Procedures. Start by showing students the picture cards for this sort along with the English labels for them. Match the words to pictures and spread them out on a table or floor area. Ask students if they know the names of these things in a language besides English. As students respond, listen to see if any of the words they share sound similar to the English versions. If a word does, ask the student to repeat it slowly, and, if possible, to help you write it down.

Explain to students that words with similar spellings and meanings across languages are called cognates. Today you will be sorting some words that are cognates with English. Even though they are written in other languages, they shouldn't be too difficult to figure out. Now bring out the other word cards, and see if students can tell you which picture they go with. If students recognize the words in another language, or if you do, help students practice pronouncing them. The words are written in many other languages including Spanish, Italian, German, French, Norwegian, and Dutch. The completed sort should look something like Sort 285, Appendix p. 301.

Once the sort has been completed, encourage students to share what they notice about the words, and reflect on how cognates may be helpful to them as they learn new languages. They may want to go on an Internet or library hunt to find other cognates for *bank, music, train, park, telephone*, and *computer*. They may also want to try to find cognates for other simple words like *museum, university*, or *tourist*.

Variations. Using the picture cards from the Appendix of this book, give a key word picture to a pair of students and have them research on the Internet, in reference materials, or from multilingual speakers in the class or community how many cognates they can find for the word. Create a classroom dictionary of cognates, or a word wall of cognates to which students can add.

Adding Suffixes: Vowel Alternation, Accented to Unaccented 7-32

Demonstrate, Sort, and Reflect. Prepare the word cards for Sort 286, Appendix p. 301. This sort continues students' exploration of how vowel sounds may alternate across related words, but the spelling remains constant. Students' examination of this type of pattern is very productive because it continues to build a spelling–meaning strategy: If you are uncertain about the spelling of a particular word, thinking of a related word may provide a clue.

Have students match up each base word with its derived word. The completed sort should look something like Sort 286, Appendix p. 301. Using *combine* and *combination* as examples, discuss how accent affects each word: In *combine*, is the last syllable accented? (Yes.) What happens to that syllable when the suffix *-ation* is added? (It becomes unstressed.) If they were uncertain about the spelling of the /in/ syllable at the middle of *combination*, thinking of the word *combine* might help them because they can clearly hear the vowel sound in the second syllable of *combine* and they know how to spell that sound. Because words that are related in spelling are often related in meaning as well, the stressed syllable in *combine* provides a clue to the spelling of the schwa sound in *combination*. Also take the time to discuss the related meanings of the word pair. What is *combine*, and what is *combination*? How can the base word inform students about a derived word's meaning?

Discuss the rest of the word pairs in this same manner. You may also present a misspelling such as CONFADENT, for example, and ask students what word would clear up the spelling of the schwa sound, and why.

Extend. Provide many opportunities for students to revisit this sort with partners to practice pronouncing, comparing, and looking for related words. Encourage students to write translations of words that are similar in their home language such as *combinación/ combination, vacación/vacation*, and *residente/resident*.

Adding Suffix *-ity*: Vowel Alternation, Schwa to Short 7-33

Demonstrate, Sort, and Reflect. Prepare the word cards for Sort 287, Appendix p. 301. Students first dealt with *-ity* in the previous sort, and discussed its effect on the pronunciation of the word to which it is affixed. The derivational suffix *-ity* (state, quality) is very productive, and for that reason its effect on words is examined further in this sort

(Appendix p. 301). In this sort, the unaccented final syllable in each base word, /al/, becomes accented when *-ity* is affixed.

Ask the students how they might sort the words. By now, an obvious suggestion is to put the *-ity* words together in one column and their related words in the other column. Match the words with derivational partners. The completed sort should look something like Sort 287, Appendix p. 301. Ask the students to look at the first few word pairs: What do they notice when *-ity* is added? If they do not mention that they worked with words that end in *-ity* in an earlier sort, remind them of this and mention some of those word pairs (for example, *legal/legality, similar/similarity*). Remind students that words that are related in spelling are often related in meaning as well, and such is the case with these words. For example, the stressed syllable in *personality* provides a clue to the spelling of the schwa sound in *personal*. Also take the time to discuss the related meanings of the word pair. What is *personal*, and what is *personality*? How can the relationships between word parts inform students about a derived word's meaning?

Discuss the rest of the word pairs in this same manner. You may also present a misspelling such as *musicul*, for example, and ask students what word would clear up the spelling of the schwa sound, and why.

Extend. Encourage students to revisit this sort with partners to practice reviewing their meanings and pronunciations. Have them find other words that relate, such as *person, personality, personal, persons, interpersonal, craftsperson, impersonator, personify*, and *salesperson*. This will help students understand that once they learn one new word, they may have a good sense about the meanings of many more as well!

Appendix

This Appendix consists of eight sections. The first section contains the materials you will need for assessments. Most of the Appendix consists of pictures, sorts, lists, and materials that you can use to create your own sets of picture and word cards for the basic sorting activities described throughout the book.

ASSESSMENT MATERIALS FOR CHAPTER 2

Primary Spelling Inventory.

Directions. This is a brief spelling assessment to understand the word knowledge students bring to their reading and spelling. This assessment can be administered multiple times over a year to monitor progress and plan instruction. The words in this inventory are ordered in terms of their relative difficulty. Follow the directions agreed on in your school. If you use the inventory independently, consider calling out just 8 words in kindergarten, 15 words in first grade, and the entire list for students in other grades.

Administer the Spelling Inventory. Call the words as you would for any spelling test. Use the words in a sentence to be sure your children know the exact word, but be aware that this can also be confusing to young spellers, and you may not choose to use the sentences at all or only in the case of some words. Assure your students that this is not for a grade but to help you plan better for their needs. Seat the children to minimize copying or test the children in small groups (recommended for kindergarten and early first grade).

Score and Anayze Spelling with a Feature Guide. Copy a feature guide for each student. For each word, check the features that are spelled correctly. Write in substitutions if you wish. Do not count reversed letters as errors but note them in the boxes. Give credit for features even when other letters might be added. (FANE for *fan* still has a final N and a short A and student should get credit for those features.) Add an additional point in the "words spelled correctly" column if the entire word is correct. Total the number of points under each feature and word; and enter the totals at the top of the page. The total score can be compared over time. If less than the total list was called out, *adjust the totals*.

Study the bottom row for the accuracy of spelling for particular features. *Consider starting the student's instruction in the first place where the student missed more than one feature in a column.* A student who gets only two or three of the seven short vowels needs a lot of work on that feature. If the child did not get any points for a feature, it is beyond his or her instructional range and earlier features need to be addressed first.

To determine what stage a student is in, follow this column to the top row and match the feature to a gradation within a stage: early, middle, or late. Staple the student's paper to the feature guide. See Chapter 2 for further instructions on administration and interpretation.

Class Composite and Classroom Organization Chart. Make one copy of the class composite form on page 224. Arrange students' feature guides from highest total points to lowest total points before transferring the numbers from the bottom row of each student's feature guide to this class composite. To view students' needs and to form groups for instruction, *highlight* students who make *more than one error* on a particular feature.

The Spelling-by-Stage Classroom Organization Chart on page 225 is another tool to organize word study groups. Write students' names under the stage and then organize word study/reading groups for differentiated instruction choosing activities from the instuctional chapters, Chapters 4 through 7.

Sentences to use with the Primary Spelling Inventory

1. fan	I could use a fan on a hot day. *fan*
2. pet	I have a pet cat who likes to play. *pet*
3. dig	He will dig a hole in the sand. *dig*
4. rob	A raccoon will rob a bird's nest for eggs. *rob*
5. hope	I hope you will do well on this test. *hope*
6. wait	You will need to wait for the letter. *wait*
7. gum	I stepped on some bubble gum. *gum*
8. sled	The dog sled was pulled by huskies. *sled*

(You may stop here for kindergarten unless a child has spelled five words correctly.)

9. stick	I used a stick to poke in the hole. *stick*
10. shine	He rubbed the coin to make it shine. *shine*
11. dream	I had a funny dream last night. *dream*
12. blade	The blade of the knife was very sharp. *blade*
13. coach	The coach called the team off the field. *coach*
14. fright	She was a fright in her Halloween costume. *fright*
15. chewing	Don't talk until you finish chewing your food. *chewing*

(You may stop here for first grade unless a child has spelled 10 words correctly.)

16. crawl	You will get dirty if you crawl under the bed. *crawl*
17. wishes	In fairy tales wishes often come true. *wishes*
18. thorn	The thorn from the rose bush stuck me. *thorn*
19. shouted	They shouted at the barking dog. *shouted*
20. spoil	The food will spoil if it sits out too long. *spoil*
21. growl	The dog will growl if you bother him. *growl*
22. third	I was the third person in line. *third*
23. camped	We camped down by the river last weekend. *camped*
24. tries	He tries hard every day to finish his work. *tries*
25. clapping	The audience was clapping after the program. *clapping*
26. riding	They are riding their bikes to the park today. *riding*

Feature Guide for Picture Spelling Inventory

Directions: Check the features that are present in each student's spelling. In the bottom row, total the features spelled correctly. Note the first column of features in which the student missed more than one feature. Check the spelling stage that summarizes the student's development. Begin instruction on the features needed.

Student's Name _____ Teacher _____ Grade _____ Date _____

SPELLING STAGES →	EMERGENT LATE	LETTER NAME–ALPHABETIC EARLY	MIDDLE	LATE		WITHIN-WORD PATTERN EARLY	MIDDLE	LATE	SYLLABLES & AFFIXES EARLY	MIDDLE
Features →	Beginning Consonants	Final Consonants	Short Vowels	Consonant Digraphs, & Trigraphs	Consonant Blends	Long-Vowel Patterns	Other Vowel Patterns	Inflected Endings, Unaccented Syllables, & Consonant Doubling	Feature Points	Words Spelled Correctly
1. bed	b	d	e							
2. lip	l	p	i							
3. drum		m	u		dr					
4. belt			e		-lt					
5. ring	r		i		-ng					
6. cake	c	k				a-e				
7. witch	w			-tch						
8. thumb			u	th	-mb					
9. wheel		l		wh		ee				
10. train		n			tr	ai				
11. knife		f			kn	i-e				
12. chair				ch		ai				
13. whale				wh		a-e				
14. heart	h	t					ear			
15. cheese		s				ee-e				
16. jacket	j		a		-ck			et		
17. tractor			a		-ct			or		
18. window					-nd		ow			
19. zipper	z							er pp		
20. whistle				wh				le		
Circle cells with more than 1 error.	(8)	(9)	(8)	(6)	(9)	(7)	(2)	(5)	(54)	(20)

SPELLING STAGES:

☐ EARLY ☐ MIDDLE
☐ LATE ☐ EMERGENT
☐ LETTER NAME–
  ALPHABETIC
☐ WITHIN-WORD PATTERN
☐ SYLLABLES & AFFIXES

Words Spelled Correctly: /20
Feature Points: /54
Total /74

Words Their Way with English Learners Appendix ©2007 by Pearson Education, Inc.

Qualitative Spelling Checklist

Student _____   Teacher _____

Students' first-draft uncorrected writing can be analyzed for a spelling stage with this checklist. There are three gradations within each stage: early, middle, and late. Spelling examples at each level are in parentheses and are drawn from the Words Their Way Spelling Inventories.

Check for when the bulleted features are observed in students' spelling. When a feature is always present, check "Yes." The last place where "Often" is checked corresponds to the student's stage of spelling development. The spaces for dates at the top of the checklist are used to follow students' progress.

Dates: _____ _____ _____

Emergent Stage

Early
- Does the child scribble on the page?   Yes _____   Often _____   No _____
- Do the scribbles follow the conventional direction? (left to right in English)   Yes _____   Often _____   No _____

Middle
- Are random letters and numbers used in pretend writing? (4BT for *ship*)   Yes _____   Often _____   No _____

Late
- Are key sounds used in syllabic writing? (S or P for *ship*)   Yes _____   Often _____   No _____

Letter Name–Alphabetic

Early
- Are beginning consonants included? (B for bed, S for *ship*)   Yes _____   Often _____   No _____
- Are final consants included (D for bed, P for *ship*)   Yes _____   Often _____   No _____
- Is there a vowel in each word?   Yes _____   Often _____   No _____

Middle
- Are some consonant digraphs and blends spelled correctly? (**ship, when, float**)   Yes _____   Often _____   No _____
- Are there logical vowel substitutions with a letter name strategy? (FLOT for *float*, BAD for *bed*)   Yes _____   Often _____   No _____

Late
- Are short vowels spelled correctly? (*bed, ship, when, lump*)   Yes _____   Often _____   No _____
- Is the *m* or *n* included in front of other consonants? (*lump, stand*)   Yes _____   Often _____   No _____

Within-Word Pattern

Early
- Are long vowels in single-syllable words used but confused? (FLOTE for *float*, TRANE for *train*)   Yes _____   Often _____   No _____

Middle
- Are most long vowels in single-syllable words spelled correctly, but some long-vowel spelling and other vowel patterns used but confused? (DRIEV for *drive*)   Yes _____   Often _____   No _____

Late
- Are the harder consonant digraphs and blends spelled correctly? (spe**ck**, swi**tch**, smu**dge**)   Yes _____   Often _____   No _____
- Are most other vowel patterns spelled correctly? (sp**oi**l, ch**ewe**d, s**er**ving)   Yes _____   Often _____   No _____

Syllables & Affixes

Early
- Are inflectional endings added correctly to base vowel patterns with short-vowel patterns? (*serving, marched*)   Yes _____   Often _____   No _____
- Are junctures between syllables spelled correctly? (*bottle, cellar, carries*)   Yes _____   Often _____   No _____

Middle
- Are inflectional endings added correctly to base words? (chew**ed**, march**ed**, show**er**)   Yes _____   Often _____   No _____

Late
- Are unaccented final syllables spelled correctly? (*cattle, fortunate, civilize*)   Yes _____   Often _____   No _____
- Are less frequent prefixes and suffixes spelled correctly? (**con**fident, favor, ripen, cellar, plea**sure**)   Yes _____   Often _____   No _____

Derivational Relations

Early
- Are most polysyllabic words spelled correctly? (*fortunate, confident*)   Yes _____   Often _____   No _____

Middle
- Are unaccented vowels in derived words spelled correctly? (*confident, civilize, category*)   Yes _____   Often _____   No _____

Late
- Are words from derived forms spelled correctly? (**plea**sure, op**position**, criti**cize**)   Yes _____   Often _____   No _____

Feature Guide for Spanish Spelling Inventory

Directions: Check the features that are present in each student's spelling. In the bottom row, total the features spelled correctly. Note the first column of features in which the student missed more than one feature. Check the spelling stage that summarizes the student's development. Begin instruction on the features needed.

Student's Name _____   Teacher _____   Grade _____   Date _____

ETAPAS DE LA ESCRITURA	EMERGENTE TARDÍA		ALFABÉTICA			PATRONES		ACENTOS Y AFIJOS	DERIVACIONES Y SUS RELACIONES		
			TEMPRANA	MEDIA	TARDÍA	TEMPRANA	TARDÍA				
Características →	Vocal Prominente	Consonante Prominente	Vocales/ Consonantes	Representación de Sonidos	Dígrafos, Sílabas Cerradas	Contrastes, Letras Mudas	Diptongos Homófonos	Tildes, Plurales, Afijos	Raíces	Puntos	Palabra
1. el	e	l									
2. suma	u	s									
3. pan	a	p									
4. red			re	d							
5. campos				os	mp						
6. plancha				pl	ch						
7. brincar			c (k)	ar	n						
8. fresa			sa	fr							
9. aprieto			o	ie							
10. guisante				ante		gui					
11. quisiera				iera		qui					
12. gigante			ga		nt	gi					
13. actrices				tr	ac			ces			
14. voy						v	oy				
15. hierro						h	ie				
16. bilingüe						b	üe				
17. lápices						c		á			
18. extraño				ñ				ex			
19. autobús								ú	auto		
20. haya							h-y				
21. geometría								ía	metr		
22. caimán							ai	án			
23. intangible								ible	tang		
24. herbívoro								í	herb		
25. psicólogo								có	psi		
Totales	(3)	(3)	(5)	(10)	(5)	(7)	(5)	(9)	(5)	(52)	(25)

SPELLING STAGES:

☐ TEMPRANA ☐ MEDIA ☐ TARDÍA

☐ EMERGENTE
☐ ALFABÉTICA
☐ PATRONES
☐ ACENTOS Y AFIJOS
☐ DERIVACIONES Y SUS RELACIONES

Words Spelled Correctly: /25
Feature Points: /52
Total: /77

Words Their Way with English Learners Appendix ©2007 by Pearson Education, Inc.

Classroom Composite for Feature Guide for Spanish Spelling Inventory

Directions: Record students' scores beginning with the student with the highest total feature points. Identify students who missed more than 1 of any feature in a category. In the bottom row, total the number of students in each category who missed more than 1 feature.

Teacher _____ School _____ Grade _____ Date _____

SPELLING STAGES →	Total Features Points & Words	EMERGENTE TARDÍA		TEMPRANA	ALFABÉTICA MEDIA	TARDÍA	PATRONES TEMPRANA	TARDÍA	ACENTOS Y AFIJOS	DERIVACIONES Y SUS RELACIONES
↓ Students' Names		Vocal Prominente	Consonante Prominente	Vocales/ Consonantes	Representación de Sonidos	Dígrafos Sílabas Cerradas	Contrastes Letras Mudas	Diptongos Homófonos	Tildes, Plurales Afijos	Raíces
Possible points →	**77**	**3**	**3**	**5**	**10**	**5**	**7**	**5**	**9**	**5**
1.										
2.										
3.										
4.										
5.										
6.										
7.										
8.										
9.										
10.										
11.										
12.										
13.										
14.										
15.										
16.										
17.										
18.										
19.										
20.										
21.										
22.										
23.										
Number who missed more than 1 feature. →										

中文字听写测验卷

施测指导语. 今天我们听写36个字。这些字有些是大家学过的，有些可能是大家没学过的。请尽量把那些学过的字写正确，遇到不会写的字，尽你最大努力猜一猜，写一个你认为合适的字代替，如果想不出什么合适的字，可以写拼音。请尽量不要留空白，因为空白是没有分数的。我将每一个字读三遍。第一遍单独念这个字，第二遍在一个词中念这个字，第三遍在一个句子中念这个字。比如：妈，妈妈的妈，我爱妈妈的妈。下面我们就开始听写。

Sentences to use with Chinese Spelling Inventory

1.	放	放	我们放学了
2.	教	教	这是我们的教室
3.	进	进	请你进来
4.	信	写	我给爸爸写信
5.	跟	跟	请你跟着我
6.	知	知	我们学了很多知识
7.	评	批	他被老师批评了
8.	码	号	这是我家的电话号码
9.	批	批	他被老师批评了
10.	架	打	请不要打架
11.	健	健	祝你健康
12.	座	座	这个座位空着
13.	改	改	我要改正缺点
14.	勤	勤	我妈妈很勤劳
15.	达	达	我要达到这目的
16.	感	感	我很感谢你
17.	珍	珍	这些东西很珍贵
18.	休	休	星期天可以休息
19.	弹	子	这是一颗子弹
20.	努	努	我们要努力学习
21.	控	控	机器人控制着开关
22.	毕	毕	他小学毕业了
23.	挥	发	他发挥了很大的作用
24.	驶	驾	他会驾驶火车
25.	技	技	我们有先进的技术
26.	庭	家	我做家庭作业
27.	疗	治	有病要及时治疗
28.	潜	潜	潜水艇会潜水
29.	陪	陪	我陪着妹妹玩
30.	链	链	这个链条松了
31.	仗	打	我爱看打仗电影
32.	梁	桥	我想当个桥梁工程师
33.	皱	皱	爸爸脸上有皱纹
34.	赔	赔	损坏公物要赔偿
35.	誉	荣	我们要保持先进班的
36.	赚	赚	他赚了很多钱

Source: Shen, 1997.

Guidelines to Classify and Interpret Spelling Errors on the Chinese Spelling Inventory

Examples of Chinese Spelling Errors by the Nine Error Types

Correct Spelling	Phonological-Based Invented Spelling		Graphemic-Based Invented Spelling				Semantic-Based Invented Spelling		
	PY	HS	NPR	CC	PC	SHS	IUC	IC	SS
1. 等	deng								
2. 绒		容							
3. 歌			哥						
4. 和				口禾					
5. 绩					糸				
6. 眨						贬			
7. 驶							骞		
8. 旺								荣	
9. 独									特

Classification and Frequency of Errors on the Chinese Spelling Inventory by Grade Level

Error Category	Error Type	Grade						Total
		1	2	3	4	5	6	
Phonological	PY	1,429	789	284	155	51	1	2,790
	HS	213	115	69	85	86	17	585
Subtotal		1,642	904	353	240	137	18	3,294
Graphemic	NPR	2	13	19	25	27	14	100
	CC	0	0	0	0	1	0	1
	PC	1	1	0	0	1	0	3
	SHS	103	106	47	59	72	23	410
Subtotal		106	120	66	84	101	37	514
Semantic	IUC	1	26	19	20	26	16	108
	IC	2	13	4	10	33	2	64
	SS	0	2	0	2	7	4	15
Subtotal		3	41	23	32	66	22	187
Total		1,751	1,065	442	356	304	77	3,995

Key to Chinese spelling error types:

PY: Pinyin substitution
HS: homophone substitution
NPR: nonphonetic radical substitution
CC: change in configuration
PC: partial character

SHS: substitution of a shape-similar character
IUC: invention of an unconventional character
IC: substitution of an irrelevant character
SS: synonym substitution

Source: Adapted from Shen, 1996.

SOUND BOARDS AND ALPHABETS

Sound Board for Beginning Consonants and Digraphs

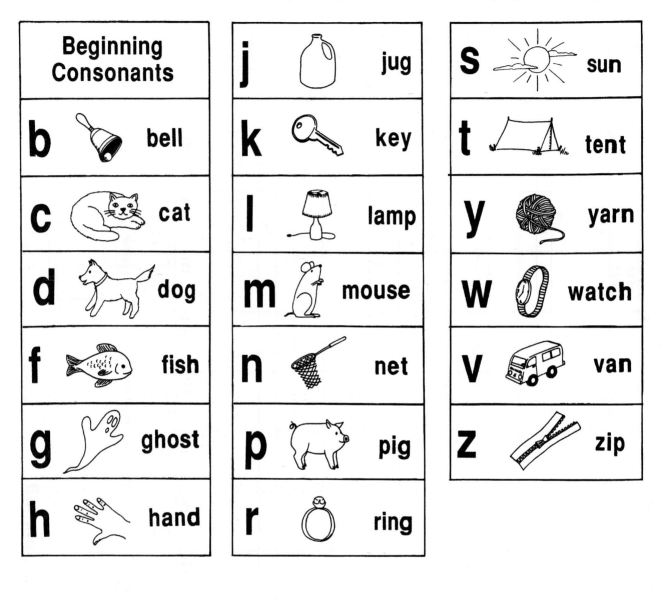

Beginning Consonants			
b bell	**j** jug	**s** sun
c cat	**k** key	**t** tent
d dog	**l** lamp	**y** yarn
f fish	**m** mouse	**w** watch
g ghost	**n** net	**v** van
h hand	**p** pig	**z** zip
	r ring	

Beginning Digraphs	**ch** chair	**th** thumb
	sh shovel	**wh** wheel

Sound Board for Beginning Blends

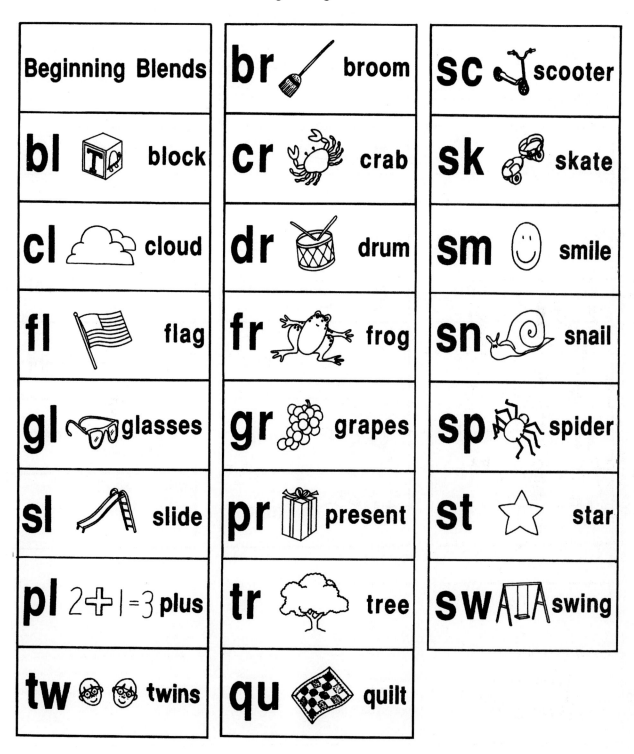

Beginning Blends	**br** broom	**sc** scooter
bl block	**cr** crab	**sk** skate
cl cloud	**dr** drum	**sm** smile
fl flag	**fr** frog	**sn** snail
gl glasses	**gr** grapes	**sp** spider
sl slide	**pr** present	**st** star
pl 2+1=3 plus	**tr** tree	**sw** swing
tw twins	**qu** quilt	

Sound Board for Long and Short Vowels

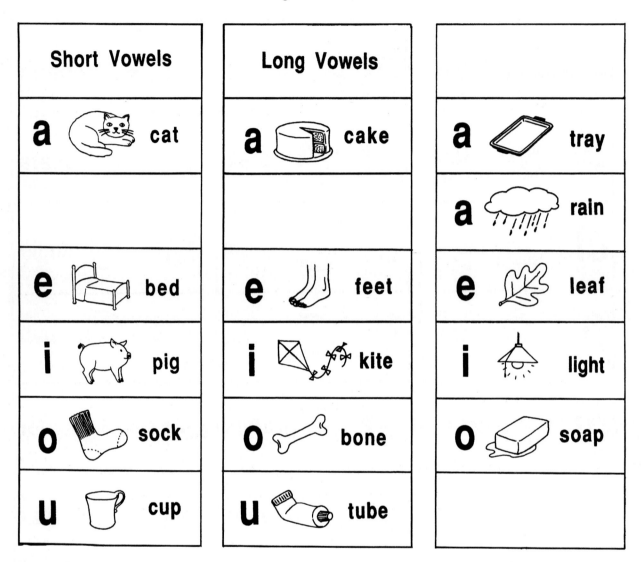

Bilingual Picture Alphabet—English/Spanish

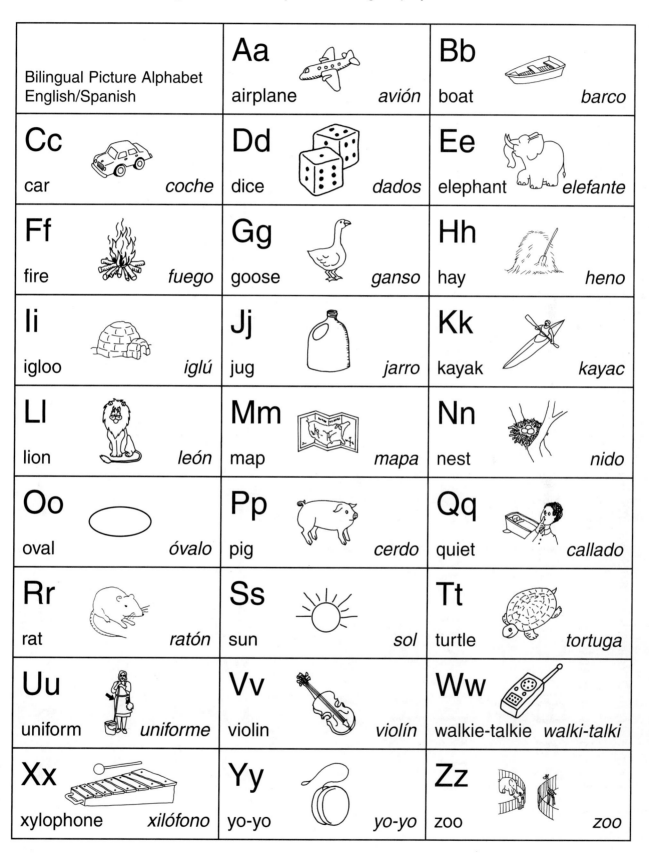

Bilingual Picture Alphabet English/Spanish	**Aa** airplane *avión*	**Bb** boat *barco*
Cc car *coche*	**Dd** dice *dados*	**Ee** elephant *elefante*
Ff fire *fuego*	**Gg** goose *ganso*	**Hh** hay *heno*
Ii igloo *iglú*	**Jj** jug *jarro*	**Kk** kayak *kayac*
Ll lion *león*	**Mm** map *mapa*	**Nn** nest *nido*
Oo oval *óvalo*	**Pp** pig *cerdo*	**Qq** quiet *callado*
Rr rat *ratón*	**Ss** sun *sol*	**Tt** turtle *tortuga*
Uu uniform *uniforme*	**Vv** violin *violín*	**Ww** walkie-talkie *walki-talki*
Xx xylophone *xilófono*	**Yy** yo-yo *yo-yo*	**Zz** zoo *zoo*

Words Their Way with English Learners Appendix ©2007 by Pearson Education, Inc.

Sample Alphabets with Various Scripts

English Alphabet

Aa Bb Cc Dd Ee
Ff Gg Hh Ii Jj Kk
Ll Mm Nn Oo Pp
Qq Rr Ss Tt Uu
Vv Ww Xx Yy Zz

Thai Consonants

ก ข ฃ ค ฅ ฆ ง
จ ฉ ช ซ ฌ ญ ฎ
ฏ ฐ ฑ ฒ ณ ด ต
ถ ท ธ น บ ป ผ
ฝ พ ฟ ภ ม ย ร
ล ว ศ ษ ส ห ฬ อ ฮ

Russian Alphabet

Аа Бб Вв Гг Дд Ее Ёё
Жж Зз Ии Йй Кк Лл Мм
Нн Оо Пп Рр Сс Тт Уу
Фф Хх Цц Чч Шш Щщ
ъ ы ь Ээ Юю Яя

Arabic Alphabet

ء 'Alif	ب Baa'	ت Taa'	ث Th!aa'
ج Jiim	ح H·aa'	خ Xaa'	
د Daal	ذ Thaal	ر Raa'	ز Zaay
س Siin	ش Shiin	ص Saad	ض Daad
ط Taa'	ظ Th:aa'	ع	غ
ف Faa'	ق Qaaf	ك	ل Laam
م Miim	ن Nuun	ه	و Waaw
ي			

PICTURES FOR SORTS AND GAMES

The pictures in this section of the Appendix can be copied on cardstock or glued to card-stock to create a set of pictures for sorting activities. The pictures are organized alpha-betically, and have been referred to throughout the book chapters. The pictures are used with the word and picture sorts outlined in the Word and Picture Sorts by Spelling Stage section of the Appendix, and as materials in various games. The pictures may also be used to create additional sorts and activities appropriate to the teacher's individual needs. A word list of the pictures is included in the Word Lists of Pictures in Book with Translations section of the Appendix, this also includes translations into Spanish, Ara-bic, Chinese, Korean, and Vietnamese.

A list of the picture words and their translations into five languages is located on pages 323–340 of the Appendix.

A list of the picture words and their translations into five languages is located on pages 323–340 of the Appendix.

A list of the picture words and their translations into five languages is located on pages 323–340 of the Appendix.

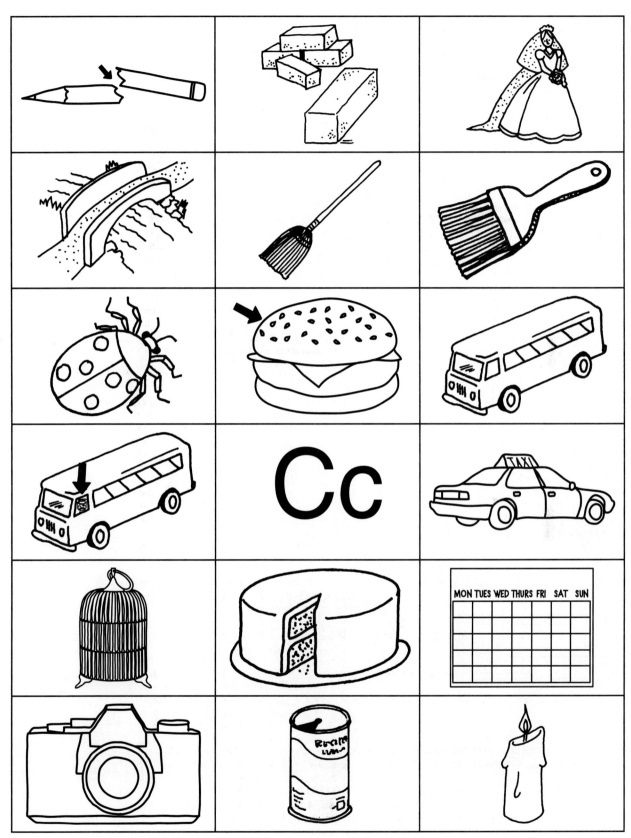

A list of the picture words and their translations into five languages is located on pages 323–340 of the Appendix.

A list of the picture words and their translations into five languages is located on pages 323–340 of the Appendix.

A list of the picture words and their translations into five languages is located on pages 323–340 of the Appendix.

A list of the picture words and their translations into five languages is located on pages 323–340 of the Appendix.

A list of the picture words and their translations into five languages is located on pages 323–340 of the Appendix.

A list of the picture words and their translations into five languages is located on pages 323–340 of the Appendix.

A list of the picture words and their translations into five languages is located on pages 323–340 of the Appendix.

A list of the picture words and their translations into five languages is located on pages 323–340 of the Appendix.

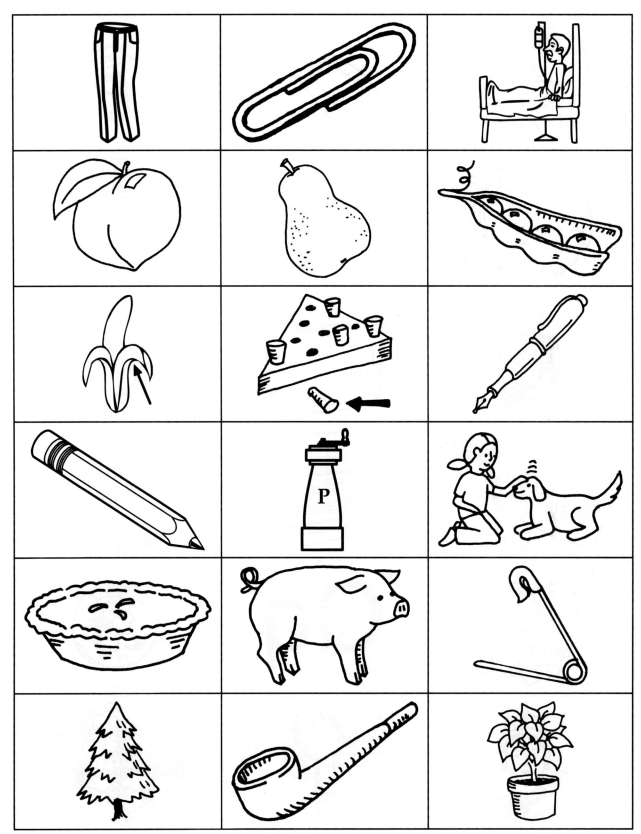

A list of the picture words and their translations into five languages is located on pages 323–340 of the Appendix.

A list of the picture words and their translations into five languages is located on pages 323–340 of the Appendix.

A list of the picture words and their translations into five languages is located on pages 323–340 of the Appendix.

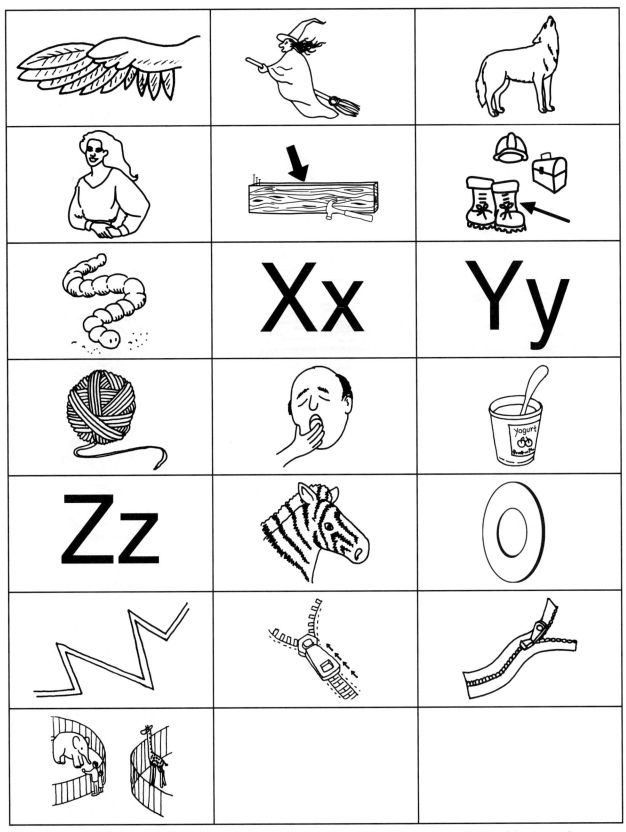

A list of the picture words and their translations into five languages is located on pages 323–340 of the Appendix.

WORD AND PICTURE SORTS BY SPELLING STAGE

The word and picture sorts outlined in this section of the Appendix are arranged by spelling stage, and build on the basic framework set up in each of the instructional chapters of the book. The sorts are numbered sequentially here, and this numbering system is cross-referenced in the instructional activities section of each chapter. For instance, Activity 5–18 in the letter name–alphabetic chapter aligns with Sorts 11 through 30 in this Appendix. In the outline of sorts, pictures are noted in parentheses. Following the comprehensive lists of sorts, 21 sample picture and word sorts are presented in the Appendix. These examples not only provide a ready-made activity for classroom use, they model how teachers will create further sorts on their own. Blank templates for picture or word sorts are included in Section 7 of the Appendix.

Prepare word or picture/word sorts to use with your own students by copying the words on a template such as the one on page 341. Be sure to write the words in randomly so students can make their own discoveries as they sort. Consider the following points as you use these sorts:

1. These sorts are not intended to be a sequence for all students. Chapter 2 will help you match your students to the stages of spelling in relation to their background languages. Each instructional chapter provides numerous suggestions about pacing and selecting word study during each stage. Choose appropriate sorts from among those presented here. Always remember that students need to have the vocabulary for the words and pictures in the sort.

2. This is not an exhaustive list of sorts, but it does give you a starting point for creating your own. You can adapt these sorts by adding, subtracting, or substituting words that are more appropriate for your students. The words were selected because of their high utility and/or the orthographic principles they represent. It is best to focus instructional time with English learners on words that will be important, useful, and help clarify essential word study learning. As you work with your students, you can make words in a sort harder or easier in a number of ways:

   - Common words like *cat* or *horse* are easier than uncommon words like *vat* or *terse*. Use words students know in their oral vocabularies first, and use each lesson to work on a few new vocabulary words. Choose high-utility words so that students will be able to use in their studies right away.

   - As students progress developmentally, choose features in words that keep them challenged. For example, add words with blends, digraphs, and complex consonant units like *ce*, *dge*, or *tch* to make words harder. *Bat* and *blast* are both CVC words, but *blast* is harder to spell.

   - Words that look or sound as though they match the features of a sort, but do not, are included in many of the sorts under an asterisk (*) to mark the oddball category. Adding more oddballs to a sort makes it harder. We have included oddball spellings in this book in a limited manner because we want to scaffold English learners to understand the regularities of the English writing system. As students become familiar with the regularities, more and more oddballs should be included and discussed in the sorts. Oddballs should never, however, constitute more than about 20% of the words in a sort, or students might fail to see the generalizations that govern the majority of words. Also, do not use oddballs that English learners are unlikely to know.

   - As discussed throughout this book, regional dialects and first-language influences on pronunciation may lead you to categorize words differently from those indicated in the sorts. These pronunciations should be honored. Substitute words or change categories as needed.

Emergent Stage Sorts

Pictures from sorts 1 to 9 can be used in connection with activities in Chapter 4.

1. Furniture and Household Item Picture Sort
(This sort is laid out with pictures in a full-page format on page 302 of the Appendix.)

(broom)	(kitchen table)	(dining room chair)	(armchair)
(couch)	(lamp)	(door)	(house)
(kitchen)	(mop)	(rug)	(tub)
(towel)	(vacuum)	(roof)	(window)
(bed)	(closet)	(light switch)	(refrigerator)
(stairs)	(television)	(stereo)	(stove)

2. Living Things Picture Sort
(This sort is laid out with pictures in a full-page format on page .303 of the Appendix.)

(cat)	(dog)	(fish)	(pig)
(oak tree)	(snail)	(bird)	(plant)
(cow)	(woman)	(girl)	(spider)
(duck)	(boy)	(flower)	(grass)
(fox)	(horse)	(vine)	(fruit tree)
(man)	(whale)	(pine tree)	(baby)

3. Occupations Picture Sort
(This sort is laid out with pictures in a full-page format on page 304 of the Appendix.)

(doctor)	(police officer)	(firefighter)	(teacher)	(sales clerk)	(postal worker)	(bus driver)
(mother)	(father)	(artist)	(construction worker)	(custodian)	(soldier)	(librarian)
(farmer)	(cook)	(astronaut)	(gardener)	(banker)	(actor)	(painter)
(veterinarian)	(truck driver)	(taxi driver)				

4. Personal Care Picture Sort
(This sort is laid out with pictures in a full-page format on page 305 of the Appendix.)

(comb)	(brush)	(toothpaste)	(towel)	(washcloth)	(tissue)	(hairbrush)
(glasses)	(soap)	(sink)	(toilet)	(person sleeping)	(bowl of fruit)	(hair dryer)
(shaving cream)	(razor)	(vitamins)	(scarf)	(mittens)	(lotion)	(shampoo)
(floss)	(fingernail clippers)	(Band aid)				

5. School and Office Items Picture Sort
(This sort is laid out with pictures in a full-page format on page 306 of the Appendix.)

(key)	(chair)	(desk)	(pen)	(pencil)	(stapler)	(lined paper)
(drawing paper)	(clock)	(scissors)	(envelope)	(paperclip)	(glue)	(school)
(table)	(tape)	(book)	(map)	(wastebasket)	(markers)	(crayons)
(computer)	(cupboard)	(shelves)				

6. Technology and Numbers Picture Sort
(This sort is laid out with pictures in a full-page format on page 307 of the Appendix.)

(computer)	(keyboard)	(digital alarm clock)	(wall clock)	(thermometer)	(calendar)
(watch)	(checkbook)	(plug)	(remote control)	(video recorder/player)	(camera)
(video camera)	(telephone)	(printer)	(microwave)	(date)	(add)
(subtract)	(dice)	(ruler)	(measuring tape)	(price tag)	(receipt)

7. Toys Picture Sort
(This sort is laid out with pictures in a full-page format on page 308 of the Appendix.)

(block)	(drum)	(board game)	(kite)	(toy car)	(doll)
(jacks)	(ball)	(teddy bear)	(scooter)	(train set)	(Etch-a-Sketch)
(peg game)	(toy boat)	(dinosaur figure)	(Legos)	(sand bucket and shovel)	(paint set)
(model plane)	(toy house)	(comic book)	(baby book)	(rattle)	(puzzle)

8. Transportation Picture Sort
(This sort is laid out with pictures in a full-page format on page 309 of the Appendix.)

(car)	(van)	(motorcycle)	(bus)	(train)	(bicycle)
(skateboard)	(subway train)	(school bus)	(boat)	(airplane)	(horse with rider)
(ship)	(sled)	(skates)	(truck)	(jet)	(sailboat)
(unicycle)	(taxi)	(horse and cart)	(jeep)	(tractor)	(helicopter)

9. Weather and Related Items Picture Sort
(This sort is laid out with pictures in a full-page format on page 310 of the Appendix.)

(sun)	(clouds)	(rain)	(snow)	(wind)	(sunglasses)	(scarf)
(mittens)	(gloves)	(umbrella)	(galoshes)	(sunscreen)	(jacket)	(bathing suit)
(sandals)	(sunrise)	(night)	(fall tree)	(rake)	(snowman)	(raincoat)
(thermometer)	(beach umbrella)	(fan)				

Letter Name-Alphabetic Stage Sorts

Pictures and words from sorts 10 to 227 can be used in connection with activities in Chapter 5.

10. Occupation and Tool Picture Sort (Activity 5–7)

(Librarian)	(Construction Worker)	(Doctor)
(books)	(beam)	(cast)
(bookshelves)	(brick)	(medicine)
(computer)	(goggles)	(thermometer)
(library card)	(hammer)	(hospital)
(bookmobile)	(nails)	(stethoscope)
(scanning wand)	(helmet)	(mask)
(books on tape)	(crane)	(patient)

Beginning Consonant Picture Sorts (Activity 5–18)

11. Beginning Consonant Picture Sorts /s/ /m/
(This sort is laid out with pictures in a full-page format on page 311 of the Appendix.)

Ss (sun)	Mm (monkey)
(seal)	(man)
(socks)	(moon)
(sit)	(mitten)
(soap)	(mat)
(sink)	(milk)
(six)	(mask)
(saw)	(map)
(sail)	(mop)
(scissors)	(mail)
(sack)	(match)
(sad)	(motorcycle)

12. Beginning Consonant Picture Sorts /b/ /l/

Bb (ball)	Ll (lamp)
(bell)	(lip)
(bus)	(leaf)
(beans)	(leg)
(bed)	(log)
(bird)	(lock)
(belt)	(letter)
(book)	(lid)
(bat)	(legs)

13. Beginning Consonant Picture Sorts /s/ /m/ /b/

Ss (sun)	Mm (monkey)	Bb (ball)
(seal)	(man)	(bell)
(socks)	(moon)	(bus)
(suit)	(mitten)	(beans)
(soap)	(mat)	(bed)
(sink)	(milk)	(bird)
(six)	(mask)	(butterfly)
(saw)	(map)	(book)

14. Beginning Consonant Picture Sorts /s/ /m/ /b/ /l/

Ss (sun)	Mm (monkey)	Bb (ball)	Ll (lamp)
(sail)	(mask)	(bat)	(lock)
(suit)	(map)	(baby)	(lip)
(six)	(mop)	(belt)	(leaf)
(sink)	(mail)	(boat)	(leg)
(soap)	(mud)	(box)	(log)

15. Beginning Consonant Picture Sorts /t/ /p/

Tt (tent)	Pp (pig)
(top)	(paint)
(tie)	(pie)
(two)	(pen)
(tire)	(pot)
(toes)	(pipe)
(towel)	(pear)
(turtle)	(pin)
(ten)	(pail)

16. Beginning Consonant Picture Sorts /c/ /n/

Cc (cat)	Nn (net)
(cup)	(nest)
(cow)	(nut)
(cake)	(nine)
(coat)	(nail)
(car)	(nose)
(candle)	(needle)
(corn)	(newspaper)
(can)	(nap)

17. Beginning Consonant Picture Sorts /t/ /p/ /c/

Tt (tent)	Pp (pig)	Cc (cat)
(tag)	(paint)	(carrot)
(toes)	(pie)	(cape)
(tube)	(pen)	(cup)
(ten)	(peas)	(can)
(tub)	(pan)	(comb)

18. Beginning Consonant Picture Sorts /t/ /p/ /c/ /n/

Tt (tent)	Pp (pig)	Cc (cat)	Nn (net)
(turtle)	(pencil)	(cake)	(nest)
(two)	(pot)	(crayon)	(nail)
(tire)	(pipe)	(car)	(nine)
(toes)	(pear)	(candle)	(needle)
(towel)	(pin)	(corn)	(nose)

19. Beginning Consonant Picture Sorts /d/ /f/

Dd (dog)	Ff (fish)
(dice)	(fork)
(deer)	(five)
(doll)	(fence)
(duck)	(fish)
(door)	(fan)
(desk)	(foot)
(dive)	(fox)
(dishes)	(fire)

20. Beginning Consonant Picture Sorts /r/ /g/

Rr (ring)	Gh (ghost)
(roof)	(girl)
(rake)	(goat)
(rug)	(gas)
(rope)	(gum)
(rain)	(gate)
(road)	(game)
(rabbit)	(goose)
(rock)	(gardener)

21. Beginning Consonant Picture Sorts /d/ /f/ /r/

Dd (dog)	Ff (fish)	Rr (ring)
(desk)	(foot)	(road)
(dive)	(fox)	(rabbit)
(dishes)	(fire)	(rope)
(doll)	(four)	(rose)
(dog)	(fin)	(rat)

22. Beginning Consonant Picture Sorts /d/ /f/ /r/ /g/

Dd (dog)	Ff (fish)	Rr (ring)	Gh (ghost)
(dishes)	(fire)	(rock)	(gum)
(dive)	(fox)	(rabbit)	(gate)
(duck)	(fish)	(rope)	(game)
(door)	(fan)	(rain)	(girl)
(desk)	(foot)	(road)	(goose)

23. Beginning Consonant Picture Sorts /h/ /k/

Hh (hand)	Kk (key)
(horse)	(king)
(house)	(kitchen)
(hose)	(kite)
(hook)	(keyboard)
(horn)	(kitten)
(hat)	(kangaroo)
(ham)	(ketchup)
(heart)	(key)

24. Beginning Consonant Picture Sorts /j/ /w/

Jj (jet)	Ww (watch)
(jet)	(web)
(jar)	(worm)
(juice)	(wheel)
(jeep)	(wig)
(jacks)	(window)
(jacket)	(well)
(jewel)	(witch)

25. Beginning Consonant Picture Sorts /h/ /k/ /j/

Hh (hand)	Kk (key)	Jj (jewel)
(hose)	(kite)	(jeep)
(hook)	(kitten)	(jacks)
(horn)	(kangaroo)	(jacket)
(hat)	(ketchup)	(jump)
(ham)	(king)	(jet)
(heart)	(kitchen)	(juice)

26. Beginning Consonant Picture Sorts /h/ /k/ /j/ /w/

Hh (hand)	Kk (key)	Jj (jewel)	Ww (watch)
(horn)	(kitten)	(jacks)	(worm)
(hook)	(king)	(jeep)	(window)
(horse)	(kitchen)	(jet)	(web)
(house)	(kite)	(jar)	(wheel)
(hose)	(key)	(jewel)	(wig)

27. Beginning Consonant Picture Sorts /v/ /y/

Vv (van)	Yy (yarn)
(vine)	(yawn)
(vacuum)	(yogurt)
(vest)	
(vase)	
(volcano)	
(violin)	
(vitamins)	

28. Beginning Consonant Picture Sorts /z/ /q/

Zz (zip)	Qq (quilt)
(zebra)	(quack)
(zero)	(question)
(zoo)	(quarter)
(zigzag)	(quiet)

29. Beginning Consonant Picture Sorts /v/ /y/ /z/

Vv (van)	Yy (yarn)	Zz (zip)
(vine)	(yo-yo)	(zebra)
(vacuum)	(yarn)	(zero)
(vest)	(yawn)	(zoo)
(vase)	(yogurt)	(zigzag)

30. Beginning Consonant Picture Sorts /v/ /y/ /z/ /q/

Vv (van)	Yy (yarn)	Zz (zip)	Qq (quilt)
(valentine)	(yawn)	(zipper)	(quiet)
(vest)	(yogurt)	(zebra)	(quarter)
(vase)	(yarn)	(zero)	(quack)
(volcano)	(yell)	(zoo)	(queen)
(violin)		(zigzag)	(question)

Focused Picture Sorts to Contrast Beginning Consonants (Activity 5-20)

31. Focused Picture Sorts to Contrast Beginning Consonants /b/ /p/

Bb (ball)	Pp (pig)
(bell)	(paint)
(bus)	(pie)
(beans)	(pen)
(bed)	(pot)
(bird)	(pipe)
(bug)	(pear)
(book)	(pin)
(bat)	(pail)

32. Focused Picture Sorts to Contrast Beginning Consonants /t/ /d/

Tt (tent)	Dd (dog)
(top)	(dice)
(tie)	(deer)
(two)	(doll)
(tire)	(duck)
(tub)	(door)
(towel)	(desk)
(turtle)	(dive)
(tag)	(dig)

33. Focused Picture Sorts to Contrast Beginning Consonants /m/ /n/

Mm (monkey)	Nn (net)
(man)	(nest)
(moon)	(nut)
(mitten)	(nine)
(mat)	(nail)
(milk)	(nose)
(mask)	(needle)
(map)	(newspaper)
(mad)	(net)

34. Focused Picture Sorts to Contrast Beginning Consonants /c/ /g/

Cc (cat)	Gg
(cup)	(girl)
(cow)	(goat)
(cake)	(gas)
(coat)	(gum)
(car)	(gate)
(candle)	(game)
(corn)	(goose)
(can)	(gold)

35. Focused Picture Sorts to Contrast Beginning Consonants /g/ /c/ /k/

Gg	Cc (cat)	Kk (key)
(girl)	(cup)	(king)
(goat)	(cow)	(kitchen)
(gas)	(cake)	(kite)
(gum)	(coat)	(kick)
(gate)	(car)	(kitten)
(game)	(candle)	(kangaroo)
(goose)	(corn)	(ketchup)

36. Focused Picture Sorts to Contrast Beginning Consonants /p/ /f/

Pp (pig)	Ff (fish)
(paint)	(fork)
(pie)	(five)
(pen)	(fence)
(pot)	(fish)
(pipe)	(fan)
(pear)	(foot)
(pin)	(fox)
(pan)	(fire)
(paint)	(four)

37. Focused Picture Sorts to Contrast Beginning Consonants /p/ /v/ /f/

Pp (pig)	Vv (van)	Ff (fish)
(paint)	(vine)	(fork)
(pie)	(vacuum)	(five)
(pen)	(vest)	(fence)
(pot)	(vase)	(fish)
(pipe)	(violin)	(fan)
(pear)	(volcano)	(fox)
(pan)		(fin)

38. Focused Picture Sorts to Contrast Beginning Consonants /b/ /d/

Bb (ball)	Dd (dog)
(bell)	(dice)
(bus)	(deer)
(boat)	(doll)
(bed)	(duck)
(bird)	(door)
(bug)	(desk)
(book)	(dive)
(bat)	(dot)
(belt)	(dishes)

39. Focused Picture Sorts to Contrast Beginning Consonants /v/ /b/

Vv (van)	Bb (ball)
(vine)	(bell)
(vacuum)	(bus)
(vest)	(beans)
(vase)	(bed)
(volcano)	(bird)
(violin)	(bug)
(valentine)	(book)

40. Focused Picture Sorts to Contrast Beginning Consonants /f/ /b/ /v/

Ff (fish)	Bb (ball)	Vv (van)
(fork)	(bell)	(vine)
(five)	(bus)	(vacuum)
(fence)	(beans)	(vest)
(fish)	(bed)	(vase)
(fan)	(bird)	(volcano)
(foot)	(bug)	(violin)
(fox)	(book)	(valentine)

41. Focused Picture Sorts to Contrast Beginning Consonants /l/ /r/

Ll (lamp)	Rr (ring)
(lip)	(roof)
(leaf)	(rake)
(leg)	(rug)
(log)	(rope)
(lock)	(rain)
(letter)	(road)
(lid)	(rabbit)
(leaves)	(rock)

42. Focused Picture Sorts to Contrast Beginning Consonants /l/ /r/ /w/

Ll (lamp)	Rr (ring)	Ww (watch)
(lip)	(roof)	(web)
(leaf)	(rake)	(worm)
(leg)	(rug)	(wheel)
(log)	(rope)	(wig)
(lock)	(rain)	(window)
(letter)	(road)	(well)
(lid)	(rabbit)	(witch)

43. Focused Picture Sorts to Contrast Beginning Consonants /d/ /r/

Dd (dog)	Rr (ring)
(dice)	(roof)
(deer)	(rake)
(doll)	(rug)
(duck)	(rope)
(door)	(rain)
(desk)	(road)
(dive)	(rabbit)
(dive)	(rat)
(dishes)	(run)

44. Focused Picture Sorts to Contrast Beginning Consonants /s/ /z/

Ss (sun)	Zz (zip)
(seal)	(zebra)
(socks)	(zero)
(soup)	(zoo)
(soap)	(zigzag)
(sink)	
(saw)	
(six)	
(sink)	

45. Focused Picture Sorts to Contrast Beginning Consonants /j/ /h/

Jj	Hh (hand)
(jet)	(horse)
(jar)	(house)
(jog)	(hose)
(jeep)	(hook)
(jacks)	(horn)
(jacket)	(hat)
(jump)	(ham)

46. Focused Picture Sorts to Contrast Beginning Consonants /w/ /g/

Ww (watch)	Gg
(web)	(girl)
(worm)	(goat)
(wheel)	(gas)
(wig)	(gum)
(window)	(gate)
(well)	(game)
(witch)	(goose)
(wall)	(gift)

47. Focused Picture Sorts to Contrast Beginning Consonants /d/ /j/

Dd (dog)	Jj
(dice)	(jet)
(deer)	(jar)
(doll)	(jog)
(duck)	(jeep)
(door)	(jacks)
(desk)	(jacket)
(dive)	(jump)

48. Focused Picture Sorts to Contrast Beginning Consonants /y/ /h/

Yy (yarn)	Hh (hand)
(yo-yo)	(horse)
(yolk)	(house)
(yawn)	(hose)
(yogurt)	(hook)
	(horn)
	(hat)
	(ham)

Introduction to Beginning Consonant Digraphs and Blends (Activity 5-21)

49. Introduction to Beginning Consonant Digraphs and Blends /c/ /h/ /ch/

(This sort is laid out with pictures in a full-page format on page 312 of the Appendix.)

Cc (cat)	Hh (hand)	ch (chair)
(cup)	(horse)	(chimney)
(cow)	(house)	(chop)
(cake)	(hose)	(chin)
(coat)	(hook)	(check)
(car)	(horn)	(chain)
(candle)	(hat)	(cheese)
(corn)	(ham)	(chick)

50. Introduction to Beginning Consonant Digraphs and Blends /s/ /h/ /sh/

Ss (sun)	Hh (hand)	sh (ship)
(seal)	(horse)	(sheep)
(socks)	(house)	(shirt)
(soup)	(hose)	(shoe)
(soap)	(hook)	(shark)
(sink)	(horn)	(shave)
(six)	(hut)	(shop)
(saw)	(hill)	(shell)

51. Introduction to Beginning Consonant Digraphs and Blends /t/ /h/ /th/

Tt (tent)	Hh (hand)	th (thorn)
(top)	(heart)	(thumb)
(tie)	(house)	(think)
(two)	(hook)	(thimble)
(tire)	(horn)	(thermos)
(toes)	(hose)	(thirteen)
(towel)	(horse)	(towel)
(turtle)	(hat)	(thermometer)

52. Introduction to Beginning Consonant Digraphs and Blends /ch/ /sh/ /th/

ch (chair)	sh (ship)	th (thorn)
(chimney)	(sheep)	(thumb)
(chop)	(shirt)	(think)
(chin)	(shoe)	(thimble)
(check)	(shark)	(thermos)
(chain)	(shave)	(thirteen)
(cheese)	(shop)	(thermometer)
(chick)	(shell)	

53. Introduction to Beginning Consonant Digraphs and Blends /j/ /ch/

Jj	ch (chair)
(jet)	(chimney)
(jar)	(chop)
(jog)	(chin)
(jeep)	(check)
(jacks)	(chain)
(jacket)	(cheese)
(jump)	(chick)

54. Introduction to Beginning Consonant Digraphs and Blends /wh/ /sh/ /th/ /ch/

wh (whale)	sh (ship)	th (thorn)	ch (chair)
(whip)	(sheep)	(thumb)	(chin)
(whistle)	(shirt)	(think)	(cheese)
(whisker)	(shoe)	(thimble)	(chain)
(wheelbarrow)	(shark)	(thermos)	(check)
(wheel)	(shave)	(thirteen)	(chop)

55. Introduction to Beginning Consonant Digraphs and Blends /s/ /t/ /st/

Ss (sun)	Tt (tent)	st (star)
(seal)	(top)	(stamp)
(socks)	(tie)	(stool)
(soup)	(two)	(stir)
(soap)	(tire)	(stem)
(sink)	(toes)	(stump)
(six)	(towel)	(stick)
(saw)	(turtle)	(stop)

56. Introduction to Beginning Consonant Digraphs and Blends /s/ /p/ /sp/

Ss (sun)	Pp (pig)	sp (spider)
(seal)	(paint)	(sponge)
(socks)	(pie)	(spoon)
(soap)	(pen)	(spear)
(six)	(pot)	(spool)
(seal)	(pipe)	(spill)
(sit)	(pear)	(spot)

57. Introduction to Beginning Consonant Digraphs and Blends /st/ /sp/ /sn/ /sk/

st (star)	sp (spider)	sn (snail)	sk (ski)
(stamp)	(sponge)	(snake)	(skate)
(stool)	(spoon)	(snow)	(skull)
(stir)	(spear)	(snap)	(skunk)
(stem)	(spool)	(snowman)	(skeleton)
(stump)	(spill)	(snail)	(skirt)

58. Introduction to Beginning Consonant Digraphs and Blends /sc/ /sm/ /sl/ /sw/

sc (scarf)	sm (smile)	sl (slide)	sw (swing)
(scale)	(smoke)	(slipper)	(swim)
(scout)	(smell)	(sled)	(sweater)
(scarecrow)	(smile)	(sleeve)	(sweep)
(scooter)		(sleep)	(switch)

59. Introduction to Beginning Consonant Digraphs and Blends /c/ /l/ /cl/

Cc (cat)	Ll (lamp)	cl (clouds)
(cup)	(lip)	(clip)
(cow)	(leaf)	(clock)
(cake)	(leg)	(clown)
(coat)	(log)	(climb)
(car)	(lock)	(clothes)
(candle)	(letter)	(clap)

60. Introduction to Beginning Consonant Digraphs and Blends /sl/ /fl/ /pl/

sl (slide)	fl (flower)	pl (plug)
(slipper)	(flag)	(plane)
(sled)	(fly)	(plant)
(sleeve)	(flashlight)	(plate)
(sleep)	(float)	(plus)

61. Introduction to Beginning Consonant Digraphs and Blends /bl/ /cl/ /gl/

bl (block)	cl (clouds)	gl (glue)
(blouse)	(clip)	(globe)
(blade)	(clock)	(glove)
(blindfold)	(clown)	(glass)
(blanket)	(climb)	(glasses)

62. Introduction to Beginning Consonant Digraphs and Blends /b/ /r/ /br/

Bb (ball)	Rr (ring)	br (broom)
(bell)	(road)	(bread)
(bus)	(rabbit)	(brush)
(beans)	(roof)	(bridge)
(bed)	(rose)	(bride)
(bird)	(rat)	(brick)
(bike)	(rug)	(brim)

63. Introduction to Beginning Consonant Digraphs and Blends /b/ /br/ /l/ /r/

Bb (ball)	br (broom)	Ll (lamp)	Rr (ring)
(bus)	(bread)	(leg)	(road)
(bed)	(brush)	(letter)	(rabbit)
(bird)	(bridge)	(leaf)	(rose)
(bike)	(bride)	(lip)	(rug)
(book)	(brick)	(lock)	(rat)

64. Introduction to Beginning Consonant Digraphs and Blends /c/ /cr/ /f/ /fr/

Cc (cat)	cr (crab)	Ff (fish)	fr (frog)
(candle)	(crayon)	(foot)	(freeze)
(cow)	(crackers)	(fox)	(fruit)
(cake)	(crown)	(fire)	(freezer)
(coat)	(crib)	(four)	(fruit tree)
(car)	(cry)	(fan)	(frame)

65. Introduction to Beginning Consonant Digraphs and Blends /g/ /gr/ p/ /pr/

Gg (game)	gr (grapes)	Pp (pig)	pr
(girl)	(grass)	(paint)	(price tag)
(goat)	(groceries)	(pie)	(printer)
(gas)	(grasshopper)	(pen)	(prize)
(gum)	(grill)	(pot)	(pretzel)

66. Introduction to Beginning Consonant Digraphs and Blends /br/ /bl/ /gl/ /gr/

br (broom)	bl (block)	gl (glue)	gr (grapes)
(bread)	(blouse)	(globe)	(graph)
(brush)	(blade)	(glove)	(groceries)
(bridge)	(blindfold)	(glass)	(grass)
(brick)	(blanket)	(glasses)	(grasshopper)

67. Introduction to Beginning Consonant Digraphs and Blends /t/ /tr/ /r/

Tt (tent)	tr (tree)	Rr (ring)
(top)	(triangle)	(road)
(tie)	(truck)	(rabbit)
(two)	(train)	(rag)
(tire)	(tractor)	(rain)
(toes)	(trap)	(rake)
(towel)	(trunk)	(rip)
(turtle)	(track)	(rock)

68. Introduction to Beginning Consonant Digraphs and Blends /ch/ /r/ /tr/ /t/

ch (chair)	Rr (ring)	tr (tree)	Tt (tent)
(chain)	(roof)	(triangle)	(top)
(cheese)	(rake)	(truck)	(toes)
(chop)	(rug)	(train)	(tire)
(chin)	(rope)	(tractor)	(two)
(check)	(rain)	(trap)	(tie)

69. Introduction to Beginning Consonant Digraphs and Blends /d/ /r/ /dr/

Dd (dog)	Rr (ring)	dr (drum)
(dice)	(roof)	(drill)
(deer)	(rake)	(dress)
(doll)	(rug)	(drip)
(duck)	(rope)	(drive)
(door)	(rain)	(dream)
(desk)	(road)	(dragon)

70. Introduction to Beginning Consonant Digraphs and Blends /ch/ /dr/ /tr/ /j/

Ch (chair)	dr (drum)	tr (tree)	Jj
(chain)	(drill)	(triangle)	(jacket)
(cherries)	(dress)	(truck)	(jar)
(chop)	(drip)	(train)	(jet)
(chin)	(drive)	(tractor)	(jeep)
(check)	(dragon)	(trap)	(jog)

71. Introduction to Beginning Consonant Digraphs and Blends /br/ /tr/ /pr/

br (broom)	tr (tree)	pr
(bread)	(triangle)	(prize)
(brush)	(truck)	(price)
(bridge)	(train)	(pretzel)
(bride)	(tractor)	(pray)
(brick)	(trap)	

Focused Picture Sorts to Contrast Beginning Consonant Digraphs and Blends (Activity 5-22)

72. Focused Picture Sorts to Contrast Beginning Consonant Digraphs and Blends /s/ /ch/

Ss (sun)	ch (chair)
(seal)	(chop)
(socks)	(chin)
(sit)	(check)
(soap)	(chain)
(sink)	(cheese)
(six)	(chick)
(saw)	(chimney)

73. Focused Picture Sorts to Contrast Beginning Consonant Digraphs and Blends /sh/ /ch/

sh (ship)	ch (chair)
(sheep)	(chop)
(shirt)	(chin)
(shoe)	(check)
(shark)	(chain)
(shave)	(cheese)
(shop)	(chick)
(shack)	(chimney)
(shell)	(chair)

74. Focused Picture Sorts to Contrast Beginning Consonant Digraphs and Blends /s/ /sh/ /ch/

Ss (sun)	sh (ship)	ch (chair)
(seal)	(sheep)	(chop)
(socks)	(shirt)	(chin)
(soup)	(shoe)	(check)
(soap)	(shark)	(chain)
(sink)	(shave)	(cheese)
(six)	(shop)	(chick)
(saw)	(shell)	(chimney)

75. Focused Picture Sorts to Contrast Beginning Consonant Digraphs and Blends /j/ /sh/

Jj	sh (ship)
(jog)	(sheep)
(jeep)	(shirt)
(jacks)	(shoe)
(jacket)	(shark)
(jump)	(shave)
(jar)	(shop)
(jet)	(shell)

76. Focused Picture Sorts to Contrast Beginning Consonant Digraphs and Blends /j/ /ch/

Jj	ch (chair)
(jog)	(chop)
(jeep)	(chin)
(jacks)	(check)
(jacket)	(chain)
(jump)	(cheese)
(jar)	(chick)
(jet)	(chair)

77. Focused Picture Sorts to Contrast Beginning Consonant Digraphs and Blends /ch/ /y/ /j/

ch (chair)	Yy (yarn)	Jj
(chop)	(yawn)	(jet)
(chin)	(yogurt)	(jar)
(check)	(yarn)	(jog)
(chain)		(jeep)
(cheese)		(jacks)
(chick)		(jacket)

78. Focused Picture Sorts to Contrast Beginning Consonant Digraphs and Blends /y/ /ch/ /h/ //j/

Yy (yarn)	Hh (hand)	Jj	ch (chair)
(yawn)	(horse)	(jet)	(chin)
(yogurt)	(house)	(jar)	(chop)
(yarn)	(hose)	(jog)	(chick)
	(hook)	(jeep)	(cheese)
	(horn)	(jacks)	(chain)

79. Focused Picture Sorts to Contrast Beginning Consonant Digraphs and Blends /j/ /h/ /wh/

Jj	Hh (hand)	wh (whale)
(jet)	(horse)	(whistle)
(jar)	(house)	(whisker)
(jog)	(hose)	(wheelbarrow)
(jeep)	(hook)	(wheel)
(jacks)	(horn)	(whip)
(jacket)	(hat)	(whisper)

80. Focused Picture Sorts to Contrast Beginning Consonant Digraphs and Blends /t/ /th/

Tt (tent)	th (thorn)
(top)	(thumb)
(tie)	(think)
(two)	(thimble)
(tire)	(thermos)
(toes)	(thirteen)
(towel)	(three)
(turtle)	(thermometer)
(ten)	(thirteen)

81. Focused Picture Sorts to Contrast Beginning Consonant Digraphs and Blends /d/ /th/

Dd (dog)	th (thorn)
(dice)	(thumb)
(deer)	(think)
(doll)	(thimble)
(duck)	(thermos)
(door)	(thirteen)
(desk)	(three)
(dive)	(thermometer)
(dig)	(thirteen)

82. Focused Picture Sorts to Contrast Beginning Consonant Digraphs and Blends /d/ /th/ /t/

Dd (dog)	th (thorn)	Tt (tent)
(dice)	(thumb)	(top)
(deer)	(think)	(tie)
(doll)	(thimble)	(two)
(duck)	(thermos)	(tire)
(door)	(thirteen)	(toes)
(desk)		(towel)

83. Focused Picture Sorts to Contrast Beginning Consonant Digraphs and Blends /f/ /th/

Ff (fish)	th (thorn)
(foot)	(thumb)
(fox)	(think)
(fire)	(thimble)
(four)	(thermos)
(fan)	(thirteen)
(fin)	(thermometer)
(fish)	(three)

84. Focused Picture Sorts to Contrast Beginning Consonant Digraphs and Blends /h/ /wh/

Hh (hand)	wh (whale)
(horse)	(whistle)
(house)	(whisker)
(hose)	(wheelbarrow)
(hook)	(wheel)
(horn)	(whip)
(hat)	(whisper)

85. Focused Picture Sorts to Contrast Beginning Consonant Digraphs and Blends /wh/ /qu/

wh (whale)	qu (quilt)
(whistle)	(quack)
(whisker)	(question)
(wheelbarrow)	(quarter)
(wheel)	(quiet)
(whip)	(queen)
(whisper)	(quilt)

Final Consonant Picture Sorts (Activity 5–23)

86. Final Consonant Picture Sorts /-b/ /-m/

-b bib	-m gum
(tub)	(swim)
(web)	(ham)
(cab)	(drum)
(crib)	(stem)
(crab)	(plum)

87. Final Consonant Picture Sorts /-b/ /-m/ /-s/

(This sort is laid out with pictures and words in a full-page format on page 313 of the Appendix.)

-b bib	-m gum	-s bus
(tub)	(swim)	(lips)
(web)	(ham)	(socks)
(cab)	(drum)	(gas)
(crib)	(stem)	(house)
(crab)	(plum)	(horse)

88. Final Consonant Picture Sorts /-b/ /-m/ /-s/ /-l/

-b bib	-m gum	-s bus	-l doll
(crab)	(plum)	(lips)	(towel)
(web)	(ham)	(socks)	(turtle)
(cab)	(drum)	(gas)	(candle)
(crib)	(stem)	(house)	(girl)

89. Final Consonant Picture Sorts /-b/ /-m/ /-x/

-b bib	-m gum	-x box
(tub)	(game)	(fox)
(web)	(ham)	(wax)
(cab)	(drum)	(axe)
(crib)	(stem)	(six)
(crab)	(plum)	

90. Final Consonant Picture Sorts /-t/ /-p/

-t net	-p mop
(hat)	(map)
(foot)	(mop)
(jet)	(top)
(net)	(lamp)
(pot)	(pipe)
(mat)	(rope)
(bat)	(jeep)
(cat)	(lip)
(boat)	(zip)
(belt)	(jump)
(tent)	(cup)
	(soap)

91. Final Consonant Picture Sorts /-t/ /-p/ /-n/

-t net	-p mop	-n fan
(hat)	(map)	(lion)
(foot)	(mop)	(man)
(jet)	(top)	(moon)
(net)	(lamp)	(yarn)
(pot)	(pipe)	(ten)
(mat)	(rope)	(sun)
(bat)	(cup)	(can)
	(soap)	

92. Final Consonant Picture Sorts /-t/ /-p/ /-n/ /-k/

-t net	-p mop	-n fan	-k back
(mat)	(map)	(lion)	(sink)
(foot)	(mop)	(man)	(cake)
(jet)	(top)	(moon)	(mask)
(net)	(lamp)	(yarn)	(book)
(pot)	(pipe)	(ten)	(lock)
	(soap)		

93. Final Consonant Picture Sorts /-d/ /-f/

-d bed	-f if
(hand)	(roof)
(bird)	(knife)
(road)	(scarf)
(yard)	(leaf)
(bed)	(golf)

94. Final Consonant Picture Sorts /-d/ /-f/ /-r/

-d bed	-f if	-r car
(card)	(roof)	(letter)
(bird)	(knife)	(fire)
(road)	(scarf)	(four)
(yard)	(leaf)	(feather)
(add)	(wolf)	(car)

95. Final Consonant Picture Sorts /-d/ /-f/ /-r/ /-g/

-d bed	-f if	-r car	-g dog
(card)	(roof)	(letter)	(dog)
(bird)	(knife)	(fire)	(pig)
(road)	(scarf)	(four)	(log)
(yard)	(leaf)	(feather)	(bug)
(braid)	(cliff)	(car)	(wig)

96. Final Consonant Picture Sorts /-v/ /-z/

-v five	-z (prize)
(dive)	(toes)
(twelve)	(nose)
(drive)	(hose)
(stove)	(rose)

Focused Picture Sorts to Contrast Final Consonants (Activity 5–24)

97. Focused Picture Sorts to Contrast Final Consonants /-d/ /-t/

-d bed	-t net
(road)	(hat)
(bird)	(foot)
(head)	(jet)
(add)	(net)
(bed)	(pot)
(card)	(mat)
(braid)	(bat)

98. Focused Picture Sorts to Contrast Final Consonants /-g/ /-p/

-g dog	-p mop
(leg)	(map)
(bug)	(mop)
(log)	(top)
(pig)	(lamp)
(wig)	(pipe)
(bug)	(rope)
(dog)	(cup)
(bag)	(jeep)
(rug)	(ape)
(wig)	(cape)

99. Focused Picture Sorts to Contrast Final Consonants /-g/ /-k/

-g dog	-k back
(leg)	(bike)
(bug)	(cake)
(log)	(sack)
(pig)	(chick)
(wig)	(brick)
(bug)	(stick)
(dog)	(rock)
(bag)	(check)
(rug)	(lock)
(wig)	(block)
(zigzag)	(sock)

100. Focused Picture Sorts to Contrast Final Consonants /-b/ /-p/

-b bib	-p mop
(tub)	(map)
(web)	(mop)
(cab)	(top)
(crib)	(lamp)
(crab)	(rope)
(globe)	(cup)
(tube)	(ape)
(robe)	(jeep)

101. Focused Picture Sorts to Contrast Final Consonants /-g/ /-n/

-g dog	-n fan
(leg)	(lion)
(bug)	(man)
(log)	(moon)
(pig)	(yarn)
(wig)	(ten)
(bug)	(sun)
(dog)	(can)
(rug)	(fan)
(bag)	(mitten)
(wig)	(corn)

102. Focused Picture Sorts to Contrast Final Consonants /-m/ /-n/

-m gum	-n fan
(thumb)	(lion)
(ham)	(man)
(drum)	(moon)
(broom)	(yarn)
(plum)	(ten)
(stem)	(sun)
(swim)	(can)
(game)	(corn)
(worm)	(mitten)

103. Focused Picture Sorts to Contrast Final Consonants /-g/ /-t/ /-d/

-g hug	-t net	-d bed
(bug)	(foot)	(bird)
(log)	(jet)	(road)
(pig)	(net)	(braid)
(wig)	(pot)	(yard)
(bug)	(mat)	(card)

104. Focused Picture Sorts to Contrast Final Consonants /-p/ /-m/ /-n/ /-b/

-p mop	-m gum	-n fan	-b bib
(rope)	(broom)	(lion)	(tub)
(mop)	(ham)	(man)	(globe)
(top)	(drum)	(moon)	(tube)
(lamp)	(stem)	(yarn)	(crab)
(map)	(plum)	(ten)	(web)

Picture Sorts to Introduce Vowel Sounds (Activity 5-25)

105. Picture Sorts to Introduce Vowel
Sounds /ă/ /ā/
*(This sort is laid out with pictures in a
full-page format on page 316 of the Appendix.)*

ă (cat)	ā (tr<u>ai</u>n)
(hat)	(skate)
(grass)	(snake)
(flag)	(game)
(bat)	(plane)
(mask)	(whale)
(gas)	(shave)
(can)	(rain)
(mat)	(vase)
(pan)	(paint)
(man)	(grapes)

106. Picture Sorts to Introduce
Vowel Sounds /ĕ/ /ē/

ĕ (net)	ē (teeth)
(jet)	(bead)
(pet)	(peas)
(leg)	(beach)
(egg)	(peach)
(bed)	(beak)
(vest)	(feet)
(desk)	(three)
(peg)	(teeth)
(vest)	(bee)
(hen)	(cheese)

107. Picture Sorts to Introduce
Vowel Sounds /ĭ/ /ī/

ĭ (s<u>i</u>x)	ī (sl<u>i</u>de)
(bib)	(bride)
(wig)	(pie)
(pig)	(bike)
(lips)	(knife)
(hill)	(pipe)
(fish)	(kite)
(fin)	(five)
(lid)	(dive)
(six)	(vine)
(crib)	(drive)

108. Picture Sorts to Introduce Vowel
Sounds /ŏ/ /ō/

ŏ (socks)	ō (soap)
(pot)	(stove)
(dot)	(bone)
(mop)	(cone)
(box)	(rose)
(fox)	(robe)
(rock)	(toast)
(top)	(smoke)
(lock)	(coat)
(clock)	(road)
(dog)	(toad)

109. Picture Sorts to Introduce Vowel
Sounds /ŭ/ /ū/

ŭ (b<u>us</u>)	ū (gl<u>ue</u>)
(sun)	(cube)
(nut)	(tube)
(cut)	(mule)
(hut)	(flute)
(gum)	(fruit)
(mud)	(suit)
(bug)	(glue)
(bus)	(two)

Same Vowel Family Picture and Word Sorts (Activity 5-26)

110. Same Vowel Family Picture
and Word Sorts <u>at, ad</u>
*(This sort is laid out with pictures
and words in a full-page format on
page 315 of the Appendix.)*

-at c<u>at</u>	-ad d<u>ad</u>
(hat)	dad
hat	mad
(rat)	had
rat	sad
(mat)	glad
mat	lad
bat	fad
sat	(sad)
cat	(mad)
fat	(add)
flat	pad

111. Same Vowel Family Picture and
Word Sorts <u>at, ad, an</u>

-at c<u>at</u>	-ad d<u>ad</u>	-an m<u>an</u>
(bat)	dad	tan
(hat)	(mad)	pan
fat	had	(fan)
pat	sad	van
rat	glad	(can)
mat	lad	ran
sat	fad	plan

112. Same Vowel Family Picture and
Word Sorts <u>ap, ag</u>

-ap m<u>ap</u>	-ag t<u>ag</u>
(snap)	(bag)
snap	bag
(cap)	(flag)
slap	flag
(clap)	drag
clap	wag
tap	snag
lap	nag
nap	rag
chap	brag

113. Same Vowel Family Picture
and Word Sorts <u>ap, ab</u>

-ap m<u>ap</u>	-ab cr<u>ab</u>
slap	cab
chap	dab
nap	jab
lap	lab
(snap)	tab
(cap)	crab
(clap)	grab
flap	blab
zap	(crab)
trap	scab
tap	stab

114. Same Vowel Family Picture and
Word Sorts <u>an, ag</u>

-an m<u>an</u>	-ag t<u>ag</u>
tan	drag
pan	brag
(fan)	rag
van	nag
(can)	sag
ran	flag
plan	wag
man	snag
can	(flag)
than	(bag)

115. Same Vowel Family Picture and
Word Sorts <u>an, am</u>

-an m<u>an</u>	-am h<u>am</u>
than	dam
fan	Sam
(can)	jam
man	ram
(pan)	yam
ran	clam
tan	slam
plan	(bam)
(van)	(dam)

116. Same Vowel Family Picture and Word Sorts <u>an</u>, <u>ad</u>

-an f<u>an</u>	-ad d<u>ad</u>
than	(sad)
(can)	mad
man	bad
ran	had
plan	glad
than	sad
fan	pad

117. Same Vowel Family Picture and Word Sorts <u>ap</u>, <u>ag</u>

-ap m<u>ap</u>	-ag t<u>ag</u>
slap	drag
tap	brag
nap	rag
lap	nag
cap	sag

118. Same Vowel Family Picture and Word Sorts <u>ip</u>, <u>ib</u>

-ip lip	-ib cr<u>ib</u>
rip	(bib)
dip	fib
ship	rib
(zip)	(crib)
drip	bib
trip	crib
(clip)	
chip	

119. Same Vowel Family Picture and Word Sorts <u>ig</u>, <u>ick</u>

-ig wig	-ick s<u>ick</u>
big	lick
dig	kick
fig	chick
pig	brick
(pig)	(brick)
rig	chick
twig	trick
wig	thick
	(stick)

120. Same Vowel Family Picture and Word Sorts <u>id</u>, <u>it</u>

-id l<u>id</u>	-it s<u>it</u>
bid	bit
did	fit
hid	kit
kid	lit
(lid)	pit
skid	(sit)
slid	spit

121. Same Vowel Family Picture and Word Sorts <u>it</u>, <u>in</u>, <u>ip</u>

-it s<u>it</u>	-in p<u>in</u>	-ip l<u>ip</u>
(sit)	(pin)	(lip)
bit	sin	hip
pit	win	dip
fit	(fin)	sip
kit	tin	rip
hit	kin	(zip)
spit	thin	(ship)

122. Same Vowel Family Picture and Word Sorts <u>ug</u>, <u>ut</u>

-ug b<u>ug</u>	-ut n<u>ut</u>
(bug)	(nut)
dug	but
rug	(cut)
tug	(hut)
(hug)	gut
mug	rut
(plug)	shut

123. Same Vowel Family Picture and Word Sorts <u>ub</u>, <u>up</u>, <u>ud</u>

-ub t<u>ub</u>	-up c<u>up</u>	-ud m<u>ud</u>
cub	pup	bud
grub	up	dud
rub	(cup)	stud
(cub)		(mud)
(tub)		

124. Same Vowel Family Picture and Word Sorts <u>un</u>, <u>um</u>

-un g<u>un</u>	-um dr<u>um</u>
(bun)	bum
fun	(gum)
gun	hum
run	(plum)
sun	(drum)
(sun)	sum

125. Same Vowel Family Picture and Word Sorts <u>ub</u>, <u>ug</u>, <u>ut</u>

-ub t<u>ub</u>	-ug b<u>ug</u>	-ut n<u>ut</u>
tub	bug	nut
(cub)	dug	but
rub	(rug)	(cut)
(sub)	tug	(hut)
club	(hug)	gut
(tub)	mug	rut
grub	(plug)	shut

126. Same Vowel Family Picture and Word Sorts <u>op</u>, <u>og</u>

-op t<u>op</u>	-og d<u>og</u>
top	
hop	(dog)
mop	log
pop	fog
bop	hog
cop	jog
stop	frog
(stop)	(frog)
(mop)	(log)
(chop)	

127. Same Vowel Family Picture and Word Sorts <u>ot</u>, <u>od</u>, <u>ob</u>

-ot p<u>ot</u>	-od n<u>od</u>	-ob c<u>ob</u>
(pot)	nod	bob
cot	clod	job
hot	plod	mob
lot	pod	rob
got	rod	sob
not		blob
spot		snob
(knot)		

128. Same Vowel Family Picture and Word Sorts <u>ob</u>, <u>op</u>, <u>ot</u>

-ob c<u>ob</u>	-op t<u>op</u>	-ot p<u>ot</u>
blob	(top)	(pot)
sob	hop	cot
mob	mop	hot
job	pop	lot
bob	bop	got
rob	cop	not
slob	stop	spot
	(mop)	(knot)

129. Same Vowel Family Picture and Word Sorts <u>ed</u>, <u>en</u>, <u>et</u>

-ed bed	-en h<u>en</u>	-et n<u>et</u>
(bed)	(hen)	(net)
fed	den	bet
led	men	get
red	(pen)	let
wed	(ten)	(jet)
(sled)	when	wet
sped	then	yet

130. Same Vowel Family Picture and Word Sorts <u>et</u>, <u>ed</u>, <u>eg</u>, <u>en</u>

-et n<u>et</u>	-ed b<u>ed</u>	-eg leg	-en h<u>en</u>
(net)	(bed)	beg	den
bet	fed	keg	men
get	led	(leg)	ten
let	sped	peg	(pen)
			(hen)

187. Beginning Consonant Digraph and Blend Word Sorts f, r, fr

Ff fish	Rr rat	fr frog
fad	rust	frog
fan	rush	fresh
fat	rich	frost
fib	rash	fret
fin	run	from
fix	rip	frill
fog	red	frizz

188. Beginning Consonant Digraph and Blend Word Sorts cl, cr, fl, fr

cl clouds	cr crab	fl flag	fr frog
clash	crab	floss	frog
clam	crib	flip	from
clip	crop	flap	frost
clod	crash	flat	fret
club	crest	flop	fresh

189. Beginning Consonant Digraph and Blend Word Sorts cr, fr, gr, pr

cr crab	fr frog	gr grass	pr press
crib	frog	grass	prod
crest	fresh	grim	prep
crop	from	grub	prim
crust	frost	grab	prop
crab	fret	grip	prom

190. Beginning Consonant Digraph and Blend Word Sorts br, bl, gl, gr

br brick	bl block	gl glad	gr grass
brad	blab	glint	grill
brag	blob	glass	grab
brat	blast	glob	grip
brass	blip	glum	grub
brim	black	gloss	grim

191. Beginning Consonant Digraph and Blend Word Sorts t, r, tr

Tt ten	Rr rat	tr trap
tag	rut	truck
tax	run	trim
tent	rod	trip
tip	rim	trot
top	rib	trash
tub	red	trust

192. Beginning Consonant Digraph and Blend Word Sorts ch, r, t, tr

ch chair	Rr rat	Tt tent	tr trap
chip	rib	test	trot
chop	rub	tab	trash
chap	ran	tub	trust
chat	red	tip	trim
chin	rip	tin	trip

193. Beginning Consonant Digraph and Blend Word Sorts d, r, dr

Dd dog	Rr red	dr drum
dog	ran	drip
dig	rib	drag
did	rest	drop
dim	rob	drab
dish	run	dress
dad	rat	

194. Beginning Consonant Digraph and Blend Word Sorts ch, dr, tr, j

ch chip	dr drum	tr trap	Jj jug
chop	dress	trip	jam
champ	drip	trash	jet
chap	drop	trust	jog
chat	drag	trot	job
chin	drab	trim	

195. Beginning Consonant Digraph and Blend Word Sorts br, tr, pr

br brick	tr trap	pr press
brag	trip	prod
brat	trash	prom
brass	truck	prop
brim	trot	prim
brad	trim	prim
brush	trust	prep

196. Beginning Consonant Digraph and Blend Word Sorts dr, fr, gr

dr drum	fr frog	gr grass
drip	frog	grab
drag	fresh	grid
drop	frost	grim
drum	fret	grin
drab	from	grip
dress	frill	grit
drill	frizz	grill

197. Beginning Consonant Digraph and Blend Word Sorts t, w, tw

Tt ten	Ww wet	tw twin
tab	wag	twins
tax	wax	twig
tent	west	twill
tip	win	twist
tub	wig	twit

198. Beginning Consonant Digraph and Blend Word Sorts k, qu, tw

Kk kid	qu quilt	tw twin
keg	quest	twins
king	quack	twig
kit	quit	twill
kick	quiz	twist
kin	quick	twit
kiss	quill	twas

Focused Sorts to Contrast Beginning Consonant Digraphs and Blends (Activity 5-31)

199. Focus on Sorts to Contrast Beginning Consonant Digraphs and Blends s, ch

Ss sun	ch chin
sad	chap
sit	chat
six	champ
sob	chip
sun	chop
such	chum
sum	chest
sub	check

200. Focused Sorts to Contrast Beginning Consonant Digraphs and Blends sh, ch

sh ship	ch chin
shed	chap
ship	chat
shop	champ
shot	chip
shut	chop
shack	chum
shell	chest

201. Focused Sorts to Contrast Beginning Consonant Digraphs and Blends s, sh, ch

Ss sun	sh ship	ch chin
sad	shed	chap
sit	ship	chat
six	shop	champ
sob	shot	chip
sun	shut	chop
such	shack	chum

202. Focused Sorts to Contrast Beginning Consonant Digraphs and Blends j, sh

Jj jug	sh ship
jab	shed
jam	ship
jet	shop
John	shot
job	shut
jog	shack
jack	shell
just	shift

203. Focused Sorts to Contrast Beginning Consonant Digraphs and Blends j, ch

Jj jug	ch chin
jab	chap
jam	chat
jet	champ
John	chip
job	chop
jog	chum
jack	chest
just	check

204. Focused Sorts to Contrast Beginning Consonant Digraphs and Blends ch, y, j

ch chin	Yy yes	Jj jug
chap	yak	jab
chat	yam	jam
champ	yell	jet
chip	yet	jig
chop	yum	job
chum		jog
chest		jack

205. Focused Sorts to Contrast Beginning Consonant Digraphs and Blends y, h, j, ch

Yy yarn	Hh hip	Jj jug	Ch chin
yum	had	jab	champ
yak	hat	jam	chest
yam	hen	jet	chum
yes	him	jack	chop
yet	hit	job	chip

206. Focused Sorts to Contrast Beginning Consonant Digraphs and Blends j, h, wh

Jj jug	Hh hat	wh when
jab	had	whip
jam	hut	what
jet	hum	whack
jig	hug	which
job	hot	wham
jog	hop	
jug	hip	

207. Focused Sorts to Contrast Beginning Consonant Digraphs and Blends t, th

Tt ten	th this
test	thud
tug	them
tub	then
tip	thin
tent	that
tax	than

208. Focused Sorts to Contrast Beginning Consonant Digraphs and Blends d, th

Dd dog	th this
dust	thud
dish	them
dug	then
dog	thin
dip	that
did	than

209. Focused Sorts to Contrast Beginning Consonant Digraphs and Blends d, th, t

Dd dog	th this	Tt ten
dam	thud	tug
dig	them	top
dot	then	tin
dud	thin	tax
dim	that	tan
dad	than	tab
dip	thick	tag

210. Focused Sorts to Contrast Beginning Consonant Digraphs and Blends f, th

Ff fish	th this
fad	thud
fat	them
fib	then
fin	thin
fix	that
fox	than

211. Focused Sorts to Contrast Beginning Consonant Digraphs and Blends h, wh

Hh hat	wh what
had	whip
has	whack
hand	when
hem	which
his	wham

212. Focused Sorts to Contrast Beginning Consonant Digraphs and Blends wh, qu

wh what	qu quilt
whip	quack
whack	quit
when	quiz
which	quick
wham	quill

Final Consonant Digraph and Blend Word Sorts (Activity 5–32)

213. Final Consonant Digraph and Blend Word Sorts -ch, -th, -sh

-ch rich	-th bath	-sh fish
rich	bath	fish
much	math	mesh
which	with	cash
such	cloth	wish

214. Final Consonant Digraph and Blend Word Sorts -s, -t, -st

-s bus	-t net	-st vest
bus	bat	best
gas	cut	cast
yes	fit	lost
class	lot	trust
fuss	nut	chest

215. Final Consonant Digraph and Blend Word Sorts -t, -st, -ft

-t net	-st vest	-ft gift
brat	test	drift
hot	vest	craft
bet	dust	left
vet	list	soft
cat	cost	swift
hit	blast	raft
spit	pest	theft

216. Final Consonant Digraph and Blend Word Sorts -m, -p, -mp

-m gum	-p map	-mp lamp
ham	map	lamp
gum	stop	lump
slam	chap	stomp
him	prop	damp
mom	up	ramp
yam	zip	jump
sum	whip	stamp

217. Final Consonant Digraph and Blend Word Sorts -n, -d, -nd

-n fan	-d bed	-nd hand
clan	thud	stand
tan	glad	land
pin	wed	send
can	pad	wind
bin	mud	end
bun	did	blend
van	bad	grand

218. Final Consonant Digraph and Blend Word Sorts -n, -t, -nt

-n fan	-t net	-nt tent
bin	sat	dent
can	pit	runt
gun	spot	stunt
man	shut	print
run	cot	pant
win	hat	ant
then	nut	vent

219. Final Consonant Digraph and Blend Word Sorts -d, -t, -nd, -nt

-d bed	-t net	-nd hand	-nt tent
nod	hot	hand	dent
bed	cot	pond	ant
did	gut	sand	runt
bud	rut	wind	lint
had	sit	end	tent

220. Final Consonant Digraph and Blend Word Sorts -mp, -st, -nd, -nt

-mp lamp	-st vest	-nd hand	-nt tent
dump	just	wind	vent
lamp	vest	hand	bent
stamp	pest	band	chant
camp	just	lend	ant
plump	mist	spend	punt

221. Final Consonant Digraph and Blend Word Sorts -n, -g, -ng

-n fan	-g pig	-ng wing
thin	bug	bang
skin	fog	hang
clan	peg	king
run	bag	sting
on	wig	song
hen	slug	prong
bun	drag	cling

222. Final Consonant Digraph and Blend Word Sorts -ang, -ing, -ong, -ung

-ang fang	-ing wing	-ong gong	-ung lung
clang	ring	prong	hung
fang	wing	gong	lung
gang	sing	long	rung
hang	sting	song	sung
bang	king	bong	
	swing		

223. Final Consonant Digraph and Blend Word Sorts -n, -k, -nk

-n fan	-k sock	-nk sink
pan	black	bank
ten	stack	dunk
chin	check	honk
when	neck	junk
sun	thick	pink
fun	brick	stink
grin	rock	blank

224. Final Consonant Digraph and Blend Word Sorts -ank, -ink, -unk

-ank tank	-ink sink	-unk trunk
tank	wink	dunk
bank	link	punk
thank	pink	clunk
blank	stink	hunk
sank	sink	sunk
yank	think	skunk
crank	rink	bunk

225. Final Consonant Digraph and Blend Word Sorts -lp, -ld, -lf, -lt, -lk

-lp scalp	-ld cold	-lf shelf	-lt belt	-lk milk
pulp	mold	elf	felt	silk
yelp	told	golf	bolt	elk
help	cold	gulf	melt	talk
gulp	bold	self	wilt	bulk

226. Final Consonant Digraph and Blend Word Sorts -ash, -ish, -ush

-ash trash	-ish fish	-ush brush
smash	dish	slush
flash	fish	flush
crash	wish	crush
rash	swish	brush
mash		blush
dash		rush
trash		hush

227. Final Consonant Digraph and Blend Word Sorts -ss, -ff, -ll

-ss glass	-ff cliff	-ll bell
kiss	stiff	small
glass	cuff	wall
miss	sniff	smell
floss	bluff	spell
grass	stuff	chill
cross	muff	drill
dress	whiff	doll

Within-Word Pattern Stage Sorts

Pictures and words from sorts 228 to 261 can be used in connection with activities in Chapter 6.

228. Picture Sort Contrasting
 Short and Long Sound of A

ă (hat)	ā (rain)
(grass)	(train)
(man)	(snake)
(bat)	(skates)
(gas)	(tape)
(plant)	(cane)
(bath)	(whale)
(mask)	(grapes)
(pants)	(chain)
(flag)	(wave)
(can)	(nail)
(graph)	(cave)

229. Picture Sort Contrasting
 Short and Long Sound of O

ŏ (clock)	ō (soap)
(sock)	(coat)
(box)	(bowl)
(mop)	(road)
(knot)	(rope)
(dog)	(globe)
(frog)	(toes)
(stop)	(nose)
(block)	(comb)
(doll)	(goat)
(golf)	(stove)
(fox)	(smoke)

230. Picture Sort Contrasting
 Short and Long Sound of U

ŭ (bus)	ū (fruit)
(plug)	(glue)
(cup)	(juice)
(thumb)	(suit)
(nut)	(tube)
(bug)	(stool)
(gum)	(shoe)
(gun)	(spoon)
(sun)	(school)
(duck)	(mule)
(truck)	(zoo)
(drum)	(moo)

231. Picture Sort Contrasting
 Short and Long Sound of I

ĭ (fish)	ī (five)
(pig)	(bike)
(chin)	(dive)
(hill)	(slide)
(ship)	(nine)
(kick)	(dime)
(sink)	(dice)
(king)	(fly)
(ring)	(tire)
(swim)	(knife)
(sick)	(ice)
(six)	(mice)

232. Picture Sort Contrasting
 Short and Long Sound of E

ĕ (pen)	ē (wheel)
(desk)	(feet)
(leg)	(leaf)
(dress)	(three)
(egg)	(key)
(bed)	(teeth)
(bell)	(leash)
(neck)	(bee)
(ten)	(peel)
(check)	(tea)
(nest)	(cheese)
(web)	(tree)

233. Community Concept Sort
(This sort is laid out with pictures and words in a full-page format on page 319 of the Appendix.)

Urban	Rural	Waterway
skyscraper	ranch	harbor
subway	farm	port
taxi	horses	dock
(metropolitan)	cattle	shipping yard
businesses	(silo)	(barge)
(museum)	(irrigation)	(cargo carrier)
factory	harvest	drawbridge

234. Matter Concept Sort
(This sort is laid out with pictures and words in a full-page format on page 320 of the Appendix.)

Solids	Liquids	Gas
ice	water	air
(statue)	rain	(helium)
steel	(puddles)	clouds
(volcano)	(lava)	(contents inside a balloon)
fruit	juice	steam
trees	(sap) sap	bubble
mountain	stream	wind

235. Ecosystem Concept Sort
(This sort is laid out with pictures and words in a full-page format on page 321 of the Appendix.)

Pond Ecosystem	Ocean Ecosystem	Desert Ecosystem
frogs	sand	cactus
(lily pads)	coral reef	sagebrush
mallard duck	starfish	snakes
dragonfly	(anemones)	(coyote)
reeds	seaweed	sand
water flea	octopus	(jackrabbit)
(algae)	(crustaceans)	bobcats

236. Word Sort Contrasting
 Short and Long Sounds
 of A (CVC and CVCe)

ă (hat)	ā (rain)
that	tape
(cat)	cane
bad	make
ran	(grapes)
tap	same
grab	sale
slam	gave
bag	came
fat	place
(man)	page

237. Word Sort Contrasting
 Short and Long Sounds
 of O (CVC and CVCe)

ŏ (clock)	ō (soap)
rock	(globe)
(frog)	more
jog	home
sob	(bone)
blob	those
not	whole
plot	close
boss	stole
song	joke
(mop)	phone

238. Word Sort Contrasting
 Short and Long Sounds
 of U (CVC and CVCe)

ŭ (bus)	ū (fruit)
nut	(tube)
(gum)	use
shut	cube
rub	(flute)
club	huge
fun	June
jump	tune
hung	rude
thump	dude
(truck)	mule

239. Word Sort Contrasting Short and Long Sounds of I (CVC and CVCe)

ĭ (fish)	ī (five)
wig	(fire)
(swim)	like
hid	write
thin	(slide)
spin	line
pill	while
fill	life
him	time
stick	mile
(sink)	fine

240. Word Sort Contrasting Spelling Patterns for Long A (CVCe and CVVC)

CVCe	CVVC
make	**rain**
same	main
came	tail
place	train
take	pail
name	sail
page	wait
face	claim
gave	gain
space	paint
state	paid
game	
take	
base	

241. Word Sort Contrasting Spelling Patterns for Long O (CVCe and CVVC)

CVCe	CVVC
home	**road**
those	boat
hole	coat
close	float
lone	goat
wrote	soap
hope	coach
cone	goal
note	loan
globe	groan
code	soak
pole	oak
stone	

242. Word Sort Contrasting Sounds and Spelling Patterns for Long A and O

	nail		goat
CVCe	CVVC	CVCe	CVVC
take	fail	rope	coast
same	maid	broke	foam
wake	waist	chose	load
brake	trail	owe	loaf
cape	braid	cope	
hate		stole	

243. CVCe/CVVC Word Sort with Long A, O and E

CVCe	CVVC
nose	**soap**
globe	boat
phone	road
cone	coax
made	brain
gate	wait
cake	sail
race	claim
tame	teach
spoke	seat
these	peel
Pete	weed
vote	

244. Word Sort Contrasting Spelling Patterns for Long I (CVCe and CV)

CVCe	CV
like	**by, tie**
write	
line	my
while	dry
side	sky
life	cry
mile	fly
five	try
price	die
fine	lie
ice	why
size	pie
wide	

245. Word Sort Contrasting Spelling Patterns for Long U (CVCe and CVVC)

CVCe	CVVC
use	**fruit, food**
cute	suit
cube	room
tube	cool
huge	bruise
dude	spoon
prune	juice
June	cruise
mute	scoop
flute	tooth
rude	gloom
tune	
mule	

246. Word Sort with a_e, ai, and ay

a_e	ai	ay
name	**rain**	**day**
make	main	may
page	paid	play
base	stain	say
plane	mail	lay
late	trail	stay
wave		way
blame		tray
fake		clay

247. Word Sort with o_e, oa, and ow

o_e	oa	ow
bone	**soap**	**low**
close	roam	grow
wrote	coal	slow
broke	toast	know
home	groan	show
pose	float	snow
slope	road	throw
joke		bowl
froze		

248. Word Sort with u_e, ew, and ue

u_e	ew	ue
tube	**new**	**blue**
rule	grew	true
flute	few	clue
cute	flew	sue
use	chew	due
June	threw	glue
mule	crew	
rude	drew	
huge	screw	

249. Word Sort with i_e, igh, and y

i_e	igh	y
line	**high**	**my**
like	might	by
write	light	dry
while	night	sky
life	fight	cry
time	sight	fly
white	thigh	try
mile	bright	shy

250. Word Sort with Long-Vowel R Words

a	e	i	o	u
care	hear	tire	more	cure
hair	year	fire	soar	pure
mare	near	wire	roar	lure
stare	steer	hire	wore	
pair	deer		tore	
dare	gear			

Words Their Way with English Learners Appendix ©2007 by Pearson Education, Inc.

251. R-Influenced Word Sort

ar	er	or	ur	ir
car	her	for	fur	bird
tar	per	or	turn	sir
bar	term	corn	curb	girl
far	clerk	fork	hurt	stir
star	germ		burn	first
shark				

252. Word Sort with Diphthongs (oi/oy, ou/ow)

oi	oy	ou	ow
oil	boy	found	plow
spoil	joy	mouth	growl
boil	toy	shout	owl
join	enjoy	count	gown
moist		south	town
coin		pound	howl
soil			
voice			

253. Word Sort with Ambiguous Vowel Sounds

o	aw	au	al	w + a	ough
strong	draw	pause	tall	wash	ought
golf	law	sauce	small	want	bought
cloth	thaw	launch	salt	watch	fought
toss	yawn	taught	calm		
	crawl		walk		

254. Word Sort with spr, str, and scr

spr	str	scr
spray	strap	scrape
spread	straight	scram
spring	strange	scrap
sprout	straw	scratch
sprain	stray	scream
	stream	screen
	street	screw
	strong	
	strict	
	string	
	stripe	
	strike	

255. Word Sort with squ, thr, and shr

squ	thr	shr
squeak	three	shrink
squash	throw	shrank
squeeze	threw	shred
squint	thrill	shriek
squirm	throne	shrimp
squish	through	shrill
squad	thread	shrub
squirt	threat	
square		

256. Word Sort with Endings dge and ge

dge	ge	r, l, n + ge
dodge	age	large
bridge	page	gorge
edge	cage	urge
smudge	stage	bulge
trudge	huge	change
wedge		hinge
judge		sponge
		strange
		twinge

257. Word Sort with Endings tch and ch

tch	ch	r, l, n + ch
catch	rich	march
clutch	each	arch
crutch	teach	church
ditch	speech	porch
patch	which	bench
scratch	such	branch
itch	pouch	French
		inch
		punch
		pinch
		mulch
		belch

258. Word Sort with Two-Syllable Words

a-	be-	other
across	before	many
any	because	people
around	between	over
away	below	even
along	begin	until
above	believe	enough
ago		money
about		upon
		really

259. Word Sort with Contractions

not	are	is	will
don't	you're	he's	I'll
didn't	we're	it's	we'll
can't	they're	that's	you'll
couldn't		there's	
won't		what's	
wasn't			
isn't			
doesn't			
wouldn't			
hadn't			
aren't			
haven't			

260. Word Sort for Plural Endings

+s	+es
makes	**inches**
eyes	beaches
times	churches
trees	classes
lines	glasses
houses	losses
ones	splashes
pants	ashes
horses	brushes
sides	wishes
friends	catches
tests	boxes
miles	

261. Word Sort for Past Tense Endings

/d/	/id/	/t/
mailed	**added**	**missed**
killed	faded	helped
leaned	flooded	knocked
showed	heated	looked
feared	lifted	marked
snowed	landed	mixed
burned	listed	reached
	needed	coached
	feasted	

Syllables and Affixes and Derivational Relations Stages Sorts

Pictures and words from sorts 262 to 287 can be used in connection with activities in Chapter 7.

262. Adding -ing to Words with *VC* and *VCC* Patterns

-VC	double	-VCC	nothing
let	**letting**	**call**	**calling**
cut	cutting	think	thinking
drip	dripping	work	working
stop	stopping	help	helping
plan	planning	tell	telling
tap	tapping	form	forming

263. Adding -ing to Words with *VCe* and *VVC* Patterns

-VCe	e-drop	-VVC	nothing
like	**liking**	**rain**	**raining**
make	making	read	reading
give	giving	look	looking
move	moving	feel	feeling
owe	owing	load	loading
rule	ruling	wait	waiting

264. Adding -ed to words with *double, e-drop,* and *no change*

-VC	-VCe	-VVC	-VCC
fanned	**hated**	**rained**	**walked**
slipped	rhymed	jailed	asked
hugged	named	cooked	picked
spotted	phoned	floated	twisted
begged	sneezed	mailed	missed
slammed	shaved	poured	
	traded		

265. Plural endings: Adding -es

add es				add -s	
-ch	-sh	-x	-s		
punches	ashes	boxes	crosses	houses
inches	bashes	mixes	classes	roses
catches	pushes	axes	misses	chases
watches	dishes		passes	freezes
	rashes		buses	changes
			gases	causes
				noises

266. Compound Words

bookmark	**daylight**	**sideways**	**playtime**	**mailbox**
bookcase	birthday	inside	playground	mailbag
bookkeeper	daytime	outside	playhouse	airmail
bookstore	someday	sidestep	playmate	
scrapbook	yesterday	sidewalk	playroom	
bookshelf				

267. Syllable Juncture in *VCV* and *VCCV* (Doublet) Patterns

VCV	VCCV
hoping	**hopping**
writer	pepper
moment	sunny
human	killer
silent	Bobby
music	foggy
taken	happen
using	runner
prevent	message
below	better
paper	traffic
closer	follow

268. More Syllable Juncture in *VCV* and *VCCV* Patterns

-VCV-	-VCCV- doublet	-VCCV- different
defend	**funny**	**carpet**
baby	common	signal
stolen	mammal	basket
robot	office	dentist
flavor	tennis	infant
pirate	sudden	enjoy
hotel	hollow	capture
final		sentence
		twenty

269. Prefixes (<u>re-, un-</u>)

re-	un-	oddball
reuse	**unbroken**	**under**
repay	unclean	reading
reorder	unclear	
recount	uncommon	
recharge	uncover	
replace	unkind	
recover	unreal	
recall	untie	
reproduce	unread	
regroup	unspoken	
react	unknown	

270. Prefixes (<u>dis-, mis-</u>)

dis-	mis-	oddball
dislike	**misspell**	**dishes**
disarm	mismatch	missed
disinfect	misplace	mishmash
disloyal	misbehave	
disobey	miscount	
disagree	misfit	
disorder	mislead	
disregard	mistake	
disrespect	mistrust	
distaste	misuse	
	misdial	

271. Less Familiar and Ambiguous Vowels in Accented Syllables

oy	oi	ow	ou	au	aw
boyish	boiling	brownie	mouthful	auto	sawdust
enjoy	jointly	cowhide	outside	exhaust	drawing
royal	pointed	crowded	groundhog	saucepan	sawhorse
soybean	loiter	downtown	rounded	daughter	
	moisture				

272. Final Unaccented Syllables *-er, -or, -ar*

-er	-or	-ar
power	**error**	**lunar**
either	elevator	cheddar
under	flavor	cedar
slipper	tutor	molar
enter	humor	pillar
eraser	armor	polar
hamster	doctor	
sister	scissor	
feather	visor	

273. Spanish and English Hard and Soft <u>G</u> and <u>C</u>

soft c	soft g	hard c	hard g
circus	**giant**	**canoe**	**goal**
celebrate	gem	calendar	guide
cemetery	general	calm	gorilla
center	generous	coconut	garage
ceremony	geography	control	gasoline
cycle	gymnasium	curve	guard

soft c	soft g	hard c	hard g
circo	**gigante**	**canoa**	**gol**
celebrar	gema	calendario	guía
cementerio	general	calma	gorila
centro	generoso	coco	garaje
ceremonia	geografía	control	gasolina
ciclo	gimnasio	curva	guardia

274. Comparatives *-er* and *-est*

-er	-est	-ier	-iest
faster	**fastest**	**happier**	**happiest**
nicer	nicest	luckier	luckiest
hotter	hottest	angrier	angriest
finer	finest	earlier	earliest
cleaner	cleanest	fancier	fanciest
bigger	biggest	funnier	funniest
longer	longest		

275. Suffixes *-y, -ly,* and *-ily*

-y (having / like)	-ly (in the manner of)	-ily (in the manner of)
dusty	**partly**	**easily**
runny	friendly	busily
fishy	kindly	angrily
funny	badly	crazily
smelly	safely	happily
leafy	highly	luckily
picky	lonely	
bumpy	tightly	
glassy	carefully	

276. Homophones

principle	principal	
merry	marry	
weather	whether	
allowed	aloud	
flour	flower	
pedal	petal	peddle
they're	there	their
presents	presence	
patience	patients	
desert	dessert	
medal	metal	
berry	bury	
wait	weight	

277. Homographs

noun	verb
present	pre**sent**
project	pro**ject**
record	re**cord**
permit	per**mit**
contest	con**test**
insult	in**sult**
refill	re**fill**
replay	re**play**
produce	pro**duce**
suspect	sus**pect**
transport	trans**port**
upset	up**set**
subject	sub**ject**

278. Adding -ion, No Spelling Change

base -t	base + -ion
prevent	**prevention**
quest	question
invent	invention
suggest	suggestion
adopt	adoption
insert	insertion
erupt	eruption
opt	option
except	exception
disrupt	disruption
exert	exertion
digest	digestion

279. Adding -ion, e-Drop and Spelling Change

base -te	e-drop + -ion
celebrate	**celebration**
concentrate	concentration
cultivate	cultivation
rate	ration
dictate	dictation
educate	education
integrate	integration
elevate	elevation
estimate	estimation
evaporate	evaporation
locate	location
migrate	migration

280. Vowel Alternation: Long to Short

long vowel	short vowel
know	**knowledge**
wise	wisdom
crime	criminal
please	pleasant
nature	natural
decide	decision
athlete	athletic
precise	precision
hide	hidden
divide	division
write	written
shade	shadow

281. Vowel Alternation: Long to Short/Schwa

base word: long vowel	derived word: short vowel	base word: long vowel	derived word: schwa
unite	**unity**	**compete**	**competition**
prefer	preference	confide	confident
invite	invitation	propose	proposition
produce	production	photograph	photography
clean	cleanse	define	definition
cycle	cyclical	compose	composition

282. Greek Roots -tele-, -graph-

-tele-		-graph-
television		**paragraph**
telecommunication	telegraph	autograph
telescope		photograph
telephoto		biography
telephone		calligraphy
telegram		choreograph
telecast		cinematography
telepathic		geography
telethon		graphic
televise		oceanography
		pictograph
		seismograph
		polygraph

283. Greek Roots *-photo-, -auto-*

-photo-	-auto-
photograph	**autofocus**
photos	autograph
photocopy	automobile
photocopier	autobiography
photographer	autoharp
telephoto	automatic
photosynthesis	automatically
photographic	automated
photography	automotive
photojournalist	autos
photomap	semiautomatic
photosensitive	automaton

284. Latin Roots *-spect-, -port-*

-spect-	-port-
inspect	**transport**
perspective	deport
retrospective	import
spectator	exporter
circumspect	report
respect	portfolio
suspect	heliport
spectacle	portable
spectacular	airport
spectrum	carport
unsuspecting	portal
prospect	transportation

285. Cognate Sort

(This sort is laid out with pictures in a full-page format on page 322 of the Appendix.)

(bank)	(music)	(park)	(train)	(computer)	(telephone)
bank	**music**	**park**	**train**	**computer**	**telephone**
banco	musique	parque	tren	computador	teléfono
banque	música	parc	treno	komputer	Telefon
	musik		trem	computator	
	muziek				
	musikk				

286. Adding Suffixes: Vowel Alternation, Accented to Unaccented

base word	derived word
combine	**combination**
similar	similarity
facile	facility
reside	resident
popular	popularity
confide	confident
agile	agility
sterile	sterility
oppose	opposition
legal	legality
brutal	brutality
adore	adoration
vacate	vacation

287. Adding Suffix *-ity:* Vowel Alternation, Schwa to Short

Schwa	Accented
normal	**normality**
dual	duality
individual	individuality
general	generality
final	finality
central	centrality
typical	typicality
personal	personality
musical	musicality
legal	legality
original	originality
technical	technicality

SAMPLE PICTURE AND WORD SORTS

Sort 1: Furniture and Household Item Picture Sort

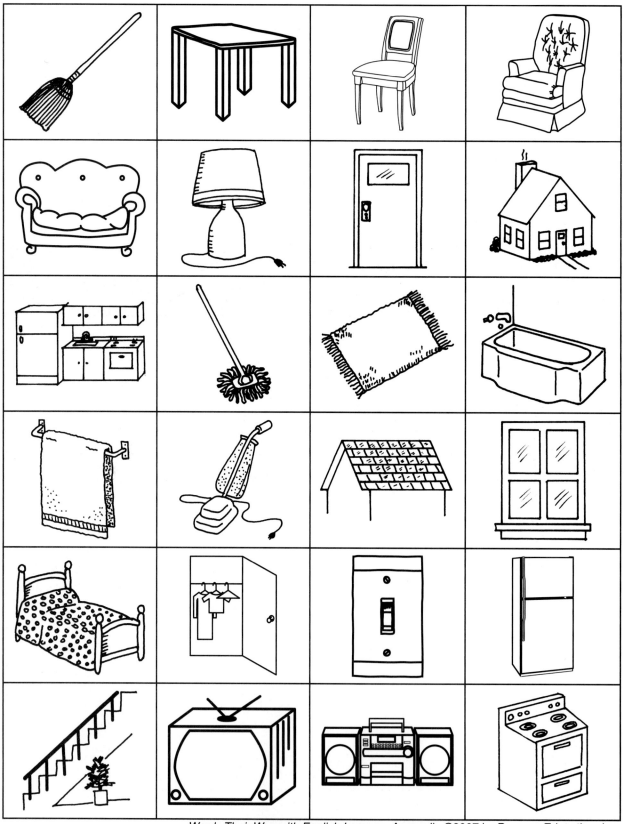